About the Author

Travel writer and journalist George Cantor worked as a sports writer and city editor for the *Detroit Free Press* before becoming the travel editor in 1973. He's now a *Detroit News* columnist. His travel books include *The Great Lakes Guidebook, Where the Old Roads Go,* and *Historic Landmarks of Black America.*

NORTH

A

AMERICAN

Traveler's

INDIAN

Guide

LANDMARKS

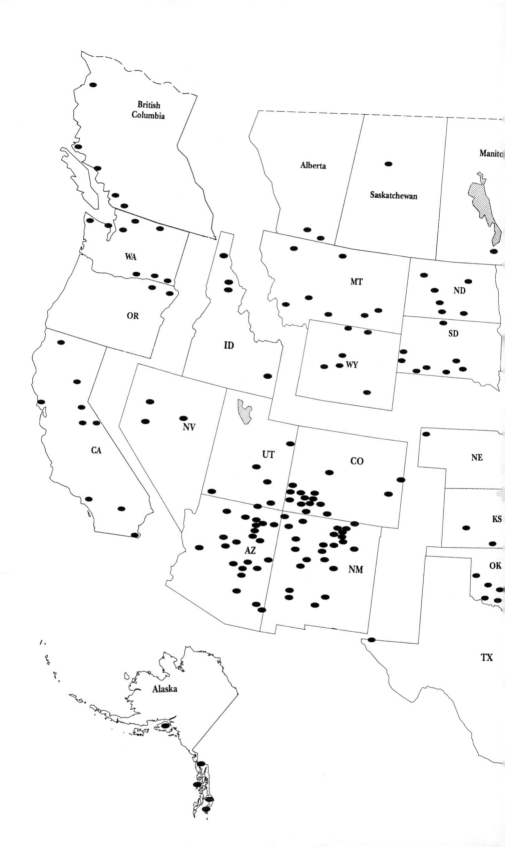

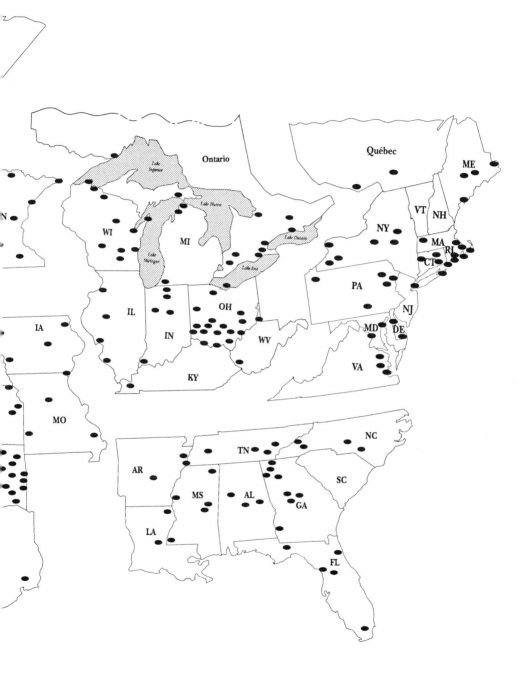

NORTH

A

AMERICAN

Traveler's

INDIAN

Guide

LANDMARKS

by GEORGE CANTOR, 1941-

foreword by
Suzan Shown Harjo
of The Morning Star Foundation

 **Gale Research Inc.** • *DETROIT* • *WASHINGTON, D.C.* • *LONDON*

Rebecca Nelson, *Developmental Editor;* with thanks to: Diane Dupuis,
Marie MacNee, Peg Bessette, Julie Winklepleck, Jane Hoehner;
Lawrence W. Baker, *Senior Developmental Editor*

Mary Beth Trimper, *Production Director;* Evi Seoud, *Assistant Production Manager;*
Mary Kelley, *Production Assistant;* Cynthia Baldwin, *Art Director;* Barbara J. Yarrow,
Graphic Services Supervisor; Kathleen A. Hourdakis, *Cover and Page Designer;*
Willie F. Mathis, *Camera Operator;* Nicholas A. Jakubiak, *Map Illustrator*

Benita L. Spight, *Data Entry Supervisor;* Gwendolyn S. Tucker, *Data Entry Group Leader;*
Civie Ann Green, Constance J. Wells, *Data Entry Associates*

For my mother, the most devoted of readers

CONTENTS

Highlights

North American Indian Landmarks is a reference source designed for students seeking information on landmarks and events in the history of native peoples, and for travelers planning visits to sites of historical interest. The guide includes:

▶ sketches on 340 sites related to North American Indian history from earliest times to the present, including:

- monuments
- plaques
- parks
- historical museums
- tribal museums
- art museums
- reservations
- birthplaces
- grave sites
- battlefields

▶ sites in 45 states and 6 provinces
▶ practical information for planning visits to sites, including:

- exhibits and facilities
- special programs
- location
- hours
- admission fees
- telephone number

▶ seven regional sections, with states and provinces listed alphabetically within each section
▶ more than 70 illustrations of people, places, and events
▶ map of the United States and Canada, showing where the sites are located
▶ map showing tribe locations on the North American continent, prior to European incursion
▶ seven regional maps, with locators identifying the sites in each region
▶ foreword outlining North American Indian history and current issues
▶ timeline noting important dates in North American Indian history
▶ an alphabetical listing of North American Indian tribes mentioned in the book, including their related sites
▶ glossary of terms used in the text
▶ bibliography of selected further reading
▶ index of people, sites, and events mentioned in the text

ACKNOWLEDGEMENTS

Photographs and illustrations appearing in *North American Indian Landmarks* were received from the following sources:

On the cover: Salinas Pueblos National Monument, courtesy of National Park Service; petroglyphs at Petrified Forest National Park, courtesy of Robert J. Huffman; Mrs. Dean, one of the few remaining Delaware Indians, died in 1984, photo courtesy of Pocono Indian Museum; 1812 baidarka engraving, housed at Beinecke Library, Yale University.

Photograph by Clay Childs (c) 1992 Painter Ridge Publishers, courtesy of The Institute of American Indian Studies: **p. 7;** Courtesy of the Iroquois Indian Museum: **p. 21;** UPI/Bettmann: **p. 32;** Courtesy of Abenaki Museum: **p. 37;** Courtesy of National Park Service, U.S. Department of the Interior: **pp. 51, 123, 124, 179, 183, 343, 347, 371;** Photograph by Ed Elvidge, courtesy of National Park Service: **p. 52;** Courtesy of Hampson State Museum: **p. 56;** Courtesy of Florida Department of State: **p. 61, 62;** Courtesy of Miccosukee Tribe of Indians of Florida: **p. 64;** Courtesy of Georgia Department of Natural Resources: **p. 67;** Reproduced by permission of Aerial Photography Service: **p. 68;** Georgia Department of Natural Resources: **p. 69;** Courtesy of Winterville Mounds Museum: **p. 77;** Courtesy of Mississippi Department of Archives and History: **p. 79;** Courtesy of Museum of the Cherokee Indian: **p. 84;** Courtesy of Oconaluftee Indian Village: **p. 86;** Courtesy of Cherokee Historical Association: **p. 87;** Courtesy of Town Creek Indian Mound State Historical Site: **p. 89;** Courtesy of Chucalissa Museum: **p. 94;** Courtesy of Sequoyah Birthplace Museum: **p. 96;** Courtesy of Dickson Mounds Museum: **p. 104;** Photograph by Marlin Roos, courtesy of Illinois State Museum: **p. 105;** Courtesy of Chicago Natural History Museum: **p. 110;** Courtesy of Marquette Mission Park and Museum of Ojibwa Culture: **p. 119;** Photograph by R. Glotzhober, courtesy of Ohio Historical Society: **p. 134;** Courtesy of First Frontier, Inc.: **p. 137;** Courtesy of London Museum of Archaeology: **p. 142;** Courtesy of Huronia Museum: **p. 144;** Drawing by Gerald R. McMaster (Plains Cree): **p. 146;** Water drum courtesy of Hubert Buck, wooden rattle courtesy of Vic Johnson, Tab a Hon courtesy of Michael Patrick: **p. 147;** Courtesy of Writing-on-Stone Provincial Park: **p. 166;** Courtesy of Grand Portage National Monument, National Park Service: **p. 172;** (c) 1992 Dick Miller, courtesy of State of Minnesota Department of Natural Resources: **p. 177;** Courtesy of Lower Sioux Agency: **p. 181;** Courtesy of the Museum of the

PREFACE

"I'm in love with American names," wrote American author Steven Vincent Benet. The map of North America is, indeed, speckled with wonderful place names. Names that come dancing off the tongue or resonate with the sound of ancient thunder. Chillicothe and Medicine Hat, Uncompahgre and Bad Axe, Wallowa and Standing Rock. Names derived from native languages or hearkening back to some long ago event, before the Europeans came to this continent.

In many regards, the problem I faced in organizing and writing this book was precisely the opposite of the one I experienced with its predecessor, *Historic Landmarks of Black America*. In the earlier book I was dealing with places that were, in large part, hidden or forgotten. It was an exercise in detection, in discovering secrets. But in this case the material was overwhelming. The Native American presence underlies everything on the map. It is the historical bedrock of the continent. Hardly a county in the United States or Canada doesn't have a museum showing some kind of Indian artifacts found on the land. The problem in writing this work became one of sorting out, deciding which places were the ones that best displayed the pageant of this rich and varied history.

On one research trip for the book, I took my 13-year-old daughter and one morning we found ourselves in the early mists of Ocmulgee National Monument. The museum wasn't even open yet. So we drove out to the largest mound, climbed to the top, and looked out over the awakening city of Macon, Georgia. We could hear the noise of traffic and see the industrial haze. But from that height and distance, we could detect no movement. It was almost as if we were watching a still picture, a painting of an imaginary town. The place where we stood was a community when Macon had been forest. People had lived, worked, and worshiped there, while Europe only surmised another world across the ocean. In that morning stillness we could feel the power of the past as a living presence. That morning crystallized for me what this book is about: the pervasive Indian presence that is part of the daily backdrop of life in America. This presence broods above our great cities and whispers in the wind. It is a past that we have obscured but can never lose. I hope that some of that morning's spell stayed with my daughter, too.

The lines I quoted at the beginning come from the same poem that ends with the words: "Bury my heart at Wounded Knee." Benet used the South Dakota place as the epitome of the vigorous, evocative names that are a part of the American heritage. But several years later, when used as the title of a book, the words conveyed an entirely different meaning. Rather than vigor, Wounded Knee and the massacre that occurred there in 1890 have come to symbolize the epitome of cruelty, the crowning injustice of the native people's confrontation with white armed force in North America.

I wanted this book to be more than a compendium of injustice, a guide to brutal places. I hope I have succeeded in also presenting the achievements and glories of Native American civilization. To be sure, there is no shortage of injustices here: the Trail of Tears; Sand Creek; land grabs and broken promises; racism and indiscriminate slaughter. But throughout American history, a sizeable number of whites have protested, demanded an accounting, and defended the interests of original peoples. I think it is important to understand that the sense of injustice among whites is not something that has emerged just now in this politically correct era.

For the last century, many North Americans have experienced a profound and mystic identification with the Native American way of life. As the environment is increasingly ravaged, there is a growing appreciation of the harmony in which original peoples lived with the land. A yearning to learn more about it. A longing for what is perceived as a better way of life. Interest in this land's indigenous cultures continues to grow in the hearts and minds of the

North American public, as the successes of many recent media releases attest, including the movie *Dances with Wolves*. These pages are offered in answer to that interest and as a means of deepening our understanding of North America and its heritage.

George Cantor
January 1993

EDITORS' NOTE

This book's title may give some readers pause in its reference to North American Indians. Why, some may wonder, did we select this phrase over Native American; and what about First Peoples, Indigenous North Americans, or other newer, but no less appropriate terms? Our advisors for this project, as well as advisors for other Native American projects forthcoming from Gale Research and Visible Ink Press, were not unanimous on what to call the population groups treated in this work. This is a question on which the community itself is not of one voice. Certainly the question will continue to be asked wherever one culture has supplanted a pre-existing one, and the answer will evolve along with the coexistence of those cultures. While Native American is now the more popular term, it is not necessarily the scholarly choice, and some consider the term to exclude Canadian native peoples, who are represented in this book as well (our perspective on this may reflect the fact that one of us is part Canadian native). Perhaps we will see the phrase Indigenous Peoples take hold on a worldwide basis, and we'll reflect the change in titling subsequent editions. However, throughout the text of this book, the terms Native American and North American Indian are both used, generally following the lead of terminology found in the information gathered about the individual sites.

In choosing the arrangement for this book, we, of course, tried to anticipate probable regional travel goals in order to facilitate trip planning. In addition, for students and history buffs, we sought an arrangement illustrative of the culture groups that are represented. Because of the present-day boundaries we weren't able to perfectly separate the book's regions into the traditional culture group regions, but we hope the choices we've made in arranging this book will prove useful for the purposes of roadside and armchair travelers alike.

A note to the traveler: When visiting reservations, observing ceremonies, or attending powwows, please inquire about special rules or regulations that may apply. You may learn there are restrictions on photography, sketching, note-taking, filming, videotaping, or audio recording, or there may be fees for those activities. Always ask a person's permission before taking his or her photograph. Also ask about restricted buildings or archaeological zones, or about wilderness areas where you may not hike or drive. Many events are spiritual in nature, and a guest's respect may be shown by a quiet demeanor, a polite and unobtrusive presence, and modest dress.

This project has won the enthusiasm of everyone involved. Virtually every time we contacted someone at a site, we came away rededicated to the endeavor and encouraged by the responses to our inquiries. The book's inspiring sweep infused the skilled contributions of Marie MacNee, Peg Bessette, Julie Winklepleck, Cheryl McDonald, Nicholas Jakubiak, Kathy Hourdakis, and the photo permissions staff. And our creative and ever-patient typesetter at Atlis Publishing Services, Mike Boyd, greeted this project with more than his typical cheerful energy as he proudly declared that he is one-sixteenth Cherokee.

For their valuable input, we wish to thank Peter Nabokov, department of anthropology at the University of Wisconsin-Madison; Frederick Hoxie, director of the McNickle Center for the History of the American Indian, Newberry Library (Chicago); Mary L. Young at the Institute of American Arts Library (Santa Fe); Dennis Moristo, program assistant at the American Indian Studies Center (UCLA); and Arthur Amiot, artist and consultant on cultures of the Northern Plains.

Diane L. Dupuis, *executive editor,* Visible Ink Press
Rebecca Nelson, *developmental editor,* Gale Research Inc.

Timeline

1300 B.C. —Establishment of one of earliest dating settlements—at Poverty Point, Louisiana.

200 B.C.—Beginning of Mound City, Ohio, complex.

A.D. 350 —Hohokam build first habitations in Canyon de Chelly, Arizona.

500 —Peak of Hopewell Culture in Ohio Valley.

600 —Pueblo Grande settlement begins on Colorado River.

900 —Mississippian culture begins work on Great Mound at Cahokia, Illinois.

950 —Growth of Ocmulgee, Georgia, mound-building culture.

1150 —Hopi settle the mesa at Oraibi, Arizona.

1160 —Acoma, New Mexico, pueblo is settled.

1200 —Mesa Verde cliff dwellings begin.

1200 —Navajo arrive in the Four Corners country.

1200 —Mandan settle on the Missouri River in North Dakota.

1300 —Drought forces abandonment of Anasazi pueblos throughout the Southwest.

1325 —Taos, New Mexico, pueblo established.

1350 —Hohokam build Casa Grande ("big house") in Arizona.

1400 —In broad section of the Midwest, an "empty quarter" develops, possibly the result of poorer climate for agriculture.

1450 —Iroquois Confederacy formed.

1539 —Estavenico slain by the Zuni in first European contact with Southwestern tribes.

1540 —The Coronado Expedition arrives in New Mexico.

1541 —The DeSoto Expedition encounters the Native people of the Southeastern states.

1609 —Henry Hudson opens fur trade with the Indian nations of present-day New York.

1614 —Pocahontas of the Powhatan Confederacy weds English planter John Rolfe, who is credited with beginning the European tobacco industry.

1615 —Algonkian-speaking nations (Ottawa, Potawatomi, Chippewa, and Cree) continue a westward migration through St. Lawrence River basin, ending up in the Lake Michigan and Lake Superior area.

1615 —Huron Indians, in alliance with other Iroquoian-speaking nations, establish a vast trade network in the eastern interior of North America. In the late 1640s, the Iroquois destroy the Huron trade empire.

1616-20 —Smallpox epidemic ravages New England Indians living along the coastline from present-day Massachusetts to Maine.

1618 —Powhatan dies. His brother, Opechancanough, assumes leadership of tribal confederation. Relations between colonists and Indians grow more hostile.

1620 —Pilgrims arrive at Plymouth, Massachusetts. In their fight to survive the first winter, they are helped by Indians, including Tisquantum (Squanto) and Massasoit, chief of the Wampanoag.

1622—Opechancanough moves against English settlers in Virginia, who lose more than one-third of their colony. The English Crown takes over, aiding settlers and invading Indian lands. Native population in Virginia begins to decline.

1626—Governor of the Dutch colony New Netherlands buys Manhattan Island from a band of Shinnecock. He later has to buy it again from Manhattan band, which claims hunting rights to the island.

1627—Aptuxcet Trading Post opens on Buzzard's Bay, Massachusetts.

1629-33—Spanish missionaries establish Catholic churches at Acoma, Hopi, and Zuni pueblos (in present-day New Mexico).

1630—Puritans arrive in Massachusetts to establish a perfect Christian society. They consider the Indians outsiders—the "accursed seed of Canaan."

1636-37—Tensions between Puritans and the native populations rise. Massachusetts colony legislature raises an army against the Pequot—the Pequot War ensues.

1638—Puritans establish a "reservation" for the Quinnipiac nation near present-day New Haven, Connecticut. Quinnipiac retain only 1,200 acres of their original land and are subject to the jurisdiction of English agent.

1644—Powhatan Confederacy stages a second war against the Virginia colony. The rebellion is crushed.

1646—Treaty prohibits English land expansion in Virginia, but Indians are left only a portion of their former territory and are subject to colonial rule. By 1649 English colonists disregard the treaty, moving onto Indian lands.

1649-1700—The Beaver Wars: The Iroquois (supported by the Dutch) sustain a series of wars with the Indian nations of the interior (including the Susquehannock, Huron, Neutral, Erie, Wyandotte, Ottawa, and Chippewa), pushing them farther into the Great Lakes region. In 1649, the Iroquois invade the Huron homeland on Georgian Bay and crush the French mission at Sainte Marie, Michigan. In 1652, the Iroquois defeat the Neutrals and Erie to gain control of southwestern Ontario.

1660—Mashpee reservation in Massachusetts becomes one of the first set up for Native Americans.

1661—Massasoit, chief of the Wampanoag Indians, dies.

1671—Father Marquette begins his mission to the Ojibwa and Ottawa at the Straits of Mackinac, Michigan.

1671-80—Apache begin southwest migration from the Southern Plains.

1675-77—Bacon's Rebellion: Nathaniel Bacon leads colonists in a rebellion to free the Virginia colony from English rule. Before the English restore order, Bacon's army kills and enslaves many Indians. Indian losses are heavy.

1676—King Philip's War: Massasoit's son, Metacom, leads an alliance of northeastern Indian nations (including the Abenaki, Nipmuck, Narragansett, and Wampanoag) in a war against the English. Fighting rages through southern New England, ending in the extermination of several tribes and the expulsion of others. Remaining tribes are placed on five reserves.

1677—Some Indian nations sign peace treaty with Virginia colonists. Indians are guaranteed at least three miles of land in each direction from their villages and the Indians are subject to Virginian rule.

1677-1731—Shawnee migrate east and south from present-day Kentucky and Ohio, ending up in present-day Georgia, Virginia, and Pennsylvania.

1680—The Lily of the Mohawks, Kateri Tekakwitha, dies in Quebec.

1680—The Iroquois use diplomacy and armed force to expand their hunting and trading south of the Great Lakes area.

1680—Pueblo Revolt, led by Popé of the San Juan pueblo, drives the Spanish from New

Mexico for a decade.

1681—LaSalle allies the French settlers with the Miami and Illinois Indians to halt Iroquois expansion to the west.

1682—Ysleta Pueblo established in Texas.

1682—The Delaware agree to a treaty with William Penn, ceding lands in Pennsylvania, and beginning a fifty-year period of mostly peaceful relations between Quakers and Indians.

1689-97—King William's War begins a series of colonial wars that lasts for more than 125 years, during which, Indian nations side with European powers for trading and weapons.

1690s—The Shawnee in present-day eastern Pennsylvania are joined by remnant bands of Delaware, Munsee, and Susquehannock. The Iroquois use these mostly landless Indian nations to create a buffer zone between themselves and English colonies.

1691—The Spanish, under the leadership of Diego de Vargas, begin the recovery of lands in New Mexico. Many Pueblos flee to the north, joining small Navajo bands.

1700—Relying on Indian labor, Spanish priests establish missions from Atlantic to Pacific. Native American population declines by as much as 45 percent during Spanish occupation of California—mostly the result of sickness.

1701—The Iroquois sign a peace treaty with the French.

1702-13—Queen Anne's War takes place in Europe, but is also fought in the American colonies. The English and Indian allies attack Indians in present-day southeast Georgia and northern Florida.

1729-30—The Natchez population is all but annihilated when the French invade Mississippi.

1737—Walking Purchase cheats the Delaware out of lands in Pennsylvania.

1740-1805—Russians explore the Alaska coastline and encounter Pacific coast tribal groups, including the Haida and Tlingit.

1742—The Nanticoke are expelled from Delaware.

1750—The Ojibwa drive the Dakota out of Minnesota and onto the Plains.

1754-63—The French and Indian War begins when the French build Fort Duquesne (in present-day western Pennsylvania) on land claimed by Virginia. The European colonies go to war over lands along the Ohio River. The French lose nearly all claims.

1763—The Treaty of Paris cedes French claims in North America (including Canada and territories east of the Mississippi) to the British; some territories in Louisiana are ceded to Spain. Spain yields Florida to Britain.

1763—The Ottawa chief Pontiac unites the western tribes (including Delaware, Wyandotte, Seneca, Potawatomi, Shawnee, and Miami) against the English, but fails to dislodge them from the Great Lakes.

1763—British government establishes a boundary (Proclamation Line of 1763) along the Appalachian Mountains; Indians are to settle lands to the west. Colonists disregard the act, moving across the Appalachians.

1768—Treaty of Fort Stanwix: Iroquois Confederacy cedes land from south of the Ohio River into present-day northern Kentucky, to the British, even though most of this land is home to Shawnee. In response, the Shawnee organize an Indian confederacy of western tribes; the Iroquois Confederacy declines.

1769—Rev. Eleazer Wheelock opens Dartmouth College as a school for Indian youth.

1769—The Spanish establish the California mission system.

1772—Schoenbrunn Mission is established in Ohio.

1773—Cornstalk's forces are defeated by militia at Point Pleasant, West Virginia, regarded by some as the opening engagement of the Revolutionary War.

1775 —The First Continental Congress assumes control of Indian affairs, establishing northern, southern, and middle departments. As commissioners of the departments, Benjamin Franklin, Patrick Henry, and James Wilson are authorized to make treaties and arrest British agents.

1777-87—Under the Articles of Confederation (the first U.S. laws of national government), Native Americans are treated as sovereign nations.

1778 —Walter Butler leads a force of Tories and Iroquois on a raid through the Wyoming Valley of Pennsylvania.

1779 —The Sullivan-Clinton expedition destroys Seneca lands in western New York.

1781—The Yuma revolt and wipe out Colorado River mission.

1782—Colonists massacre Wyandot refugees at Gnadenhutten Mission, Ohio.

1783 —Treaty of Paris is signed, incorporating the earlier agreement with Britain. United States receives claim to all land from the Atlantic to the Mississippi River, and from the Great Lakes to the Florida border.

1784 —The Northwest Company opens fur trading post at Grand Portage, Minnesota.

1785 —Joseph Brant and Mohawk followers who fought with Britain in the Revolutionary War move onto new lands on the Grand River in Ontario.

1787—Delegates arrive in Philadelphia to frame the U.S. Constitution. Article 1, Section 8 ("the Commerce Clause") empowers Congress to make all laws pertaining to Indian trade and diplomatic relations.

1787—Northwest Ordinance calls for division of lands north of the Ohio River into territories that will later become states.

1789 —War Department is created; Indian Affairs are delegated to first Secretary of War, Henry Knox.

1793 —Defeat of Little Turtle at Fallen Timbers drives Native Americans from northern Ohio and Michigan.

1797—Big Tree Treaty cedes Seneca lands of western New York.

1797—San Xavier del Bac Mission built in Arizona.

1803 —Louisiana Purchase: United States buys territories west of the Mississippi River from France. President Thomas Jefferson proposes that many of the Indian nations living east of the Mississippi River be moved west.

1804 —Lewis and Clark expedition meets Sacajawea, a Shoshone woman, in Knife River villages in North Dakota. She accompanies their expedition to the Pacific coast.

1804 —Tlingit are driven from Sitka, Alaska, by Russian gunboats.

1810 —Handsome Lake, a Seneca clan leader, preaches the Longhouse religion to an Iroquois band in New York.

1811—Tecumseh's village is destroyed by William Henry Harrison at Battle of Tippecanoe.

1812-15 —War of 1812 devastates Indian land and populations of the Old Northwest. Treaty of Ghent ends the war: British agree all territory south of the Great Lakes belongs to the United States. Indian nations living east of the Mississippi River are now within the sphere of U.S. government.

1814—When U.S. citizens are killed, the United States enters into the Red Stick War (or Creek Civil War). The Creek are defeated by Andrew Jackson at Horseshoe Bend, Alabama.

1818 —Chickasaw relinquish claims along the eastern bank of the Mississippi River.

1818 —Jackson invades Florida in First Seminole War.

1821—Sequoyah successfully demonstrates his alphabet to the Cherokee Tribal Council.

1824 —Office of Indian Affairs is created within the War Department; it is formally recognized by Congress in 1831.

1824 —Wyandot mission is built in Ohio.

1825 —Creeks are expelled from Georgia in Treaty of Indian Springs.

1825 —Shawnee arrive in Kansas Territory, which has been designated as Indian homeland.

1825—The Osage and Kansa agree to open Santa Fe Trail to American traders.

1825 —New Echota, Georgia, becomes capital of Eastern Cherokees.

1828 —Georgia strips Cherokees of rights as a sovereign nation.

1830 —Choctaw relinquish land in Mississippi under treaty of Dancing Rabbit Creek.

1830 —Congress approves the Indian Removal Act, permitting the U.S. Army to force thousands of Indians to lands west of the Mississippi. The removal period lasts until 1860.

1832 —Black Hawk War begins in present-day Illinois. U.S. troops repress remnant bands of the Sauk and Fox tribes, who oppose the cession of their lands.

1833 —Mexico breaks up the California missions and liberates Indians.

1834 —Bent's Old Fort opens in Colorado on the Santa Fe Trail.

1835 —Second Seminole War: U.S. troops battle the Seminole in Florida. In 1837, Osceola is captured under a flag of truce.

1836 —Whitman Mission opens in Walla Walla, Oregon Territory.

1837—Smallpox epidemic on the Plains decimates the once numerous Mandan and Hidatsa.

1838 —Cherokee are removed to the West on the "Trail of Tears"; a remnant stays in North Carolina on the Qualla reserve.

1839 —Eastern and Western Cherokee reunite in Oklahoma and move joint capital to Tahlequah.

1842 —Sauk and Fox expelled from Iowa.

1846-48 —United States fights Mexico; the war ends with the Treaty of Guadalupe Hidalgo. Mexico cedes to the United States all claims to California and the Southwest. U.S. government brings American Indian policy to that region and to Pacific Northwest.

1847—New Mexico tribes rebel against American rule and kill territorial governor at Taos.

1847—Whitman Mission (Washington) destroyed by Cayuse.

1848 —California Gold Rush begins; officials estimate that more than one-half of miners are natives.

1848 —First systematic excavation of the Ohio mounds.

1849 —Office of Indian Affairs is transferred from War Department to newly created Department of the Interior, which manages public as well as Indian lands.

1853-56 —More than 52 treaties are made with Indian tribes; United States gains 174 million acres of Indian land.

1855—Oklahoma Seminole withdraw from the Creek nation and create their own government.

1855—Chief Seattle signs Port Elliott Treaty, ceding lands in Washington. Natives retain the right to hunt and fish on their former lands.

1855—Nez Perce Reservation established in Idaho.

1856—Chickasaw nation adopts a constitution—modeled after the U.S constitution.

1856—Fox return to Iowa and re-establish a presence there.

1860—Cochise begins his rebellion with Chiricahua Apache.

1860—Paiute War breaks out in Nevada.

1860—Choctaw, in present-day Oklahoma, adopt a centralized constitutional government.

1862—Sioux Uprising rages across Minnesota. Led by Little Crow, the Sioux attack Minnesota settlements. Thirty-eight Sioux are hanged for their part in the uprising.

1863—"Thief Treaty": After Nez Perce leaders complain of invasion, the U.S. government reduces the reservation to one-tenth its original size. Chief Joseph and other Nez Perce leaders refuse to comply with the terms.

1864—Navajo rounded up by Kit Carson and forcibly transported to Bosque Redondo, New Mexico.

1864—Sand Creek Massacre: U.S. Army Colonel John Chivington leads an unprovoked attack, wiping out Cheyenne village in Colorado. Five hundred Indian men, women, and children are killed.

1866—Plains tribes unite briefly under Red Cloud. Fetterman Massacre takes place on Bozeman Trail, Wyoming.

1867—U.S. buys Alaska from the Russian government.

1867—Medicine Lodge Treaty brings short-lived peace to the southern Plains.

1867—The Creek living in Indian Territory (Oklahoma) adopt constitutional government. U.S. marshals and troops step in to defend the move in the face of opposition from Creek conservatives.

1868—Navajo return to ancestral lands.

1868—Standing Rock Reservation established for Sioux in Dakota Territory.

1868—Black Kettle killed by Custer's troops at Battle of Washita, Oklahoma.

1869—First Métis Revolt led by Louis Riel, opposing Canadian rule in Manitoba.

1869—President U.S. Grant appoints Seneca Indian Brigadier General Ely Parker to Commissioner of Indian Affairs.

1870—Fort Apache established in Arizona.

1871—Congress decrees it will no longer negotiate treaties with Indian nations; agreements with Indian groups are subsequently made by congressional acts and executive orders.

1871—Oklahoma Indian Nations approve confederation plan but Congress refuses to act on it.

1872—Cochise make peace with Americans.

1875—Quanah Parker's band surrenders, ending Comanche resistance in Oklahoma.

1876—Bureau of Indian Affairs for Southern Plains established at Anadarko, Oklahoma.

1876—Sioux bands protect the sacred Black Hills from miners. Three army columns converge on the Sioux and their allies. Custer's seventh cavalry is wiped out at Little Big Horn (in present-day Montana).

1877—Cheyenne surrender to U.S. troops and agree to move to Indian Territory (Oklahoma).

1877—Chief Joseph surrenders in Montana, just short of safety in Canada, ending his masterful retreat. His band of Nez Perce are allowed to settle on a reservation in Idaho.

1877—Crazy Horse slain at Fort Robinson, Nebraska; army soldiers claim the Sioux chief was attempting an escape.

1878—Hubbell Trading Post opens at Ganado, Arizona.

1878—Bannock War flares in Idaho.

1878—Wind River Reservation established in Wyoming for Shoshone and Arapahoe.

istered and controlled by a tribe, is established by the Navajo, in cooperation with the Bureau of Indian Affairs.

1967—In his January 10 State of the Union address, President Lyndon Johnson urges the nation to "embark upon a major effort to provide self-help assistance to the forgotten in our midst—the American Indians."

1967—On January 16, the Bureau of Indian Affairs announces formation of National Indian Education Advisory Committee.

1967—In March, Congress approves bill extending the life of Indian Claims Commission to 1972.

1967—In September, the NAACP announces a report describing the United States' genocide of American Indians; the report will be submitted to the United Nations.

1968—On March 6, President Lyndon Johnson delivers a "Special Message to Congress on the Problem of the American Indian: 'the Forgotten American.'" Johnson also signs an executive order establishing National Council on Indian Opportunity, which is charged with improving programs for Indians.

1968—On April 11, Congress passes the American Indian Civil Rights Act.

1968—American Indian Movement is founded by Indians to improve social services in urban neighborhoods.

1968—In October, Arizona's Yavapai agree to a $5 million settlement for the federal government's illegal seizure of 9 million acres of land in 1874.

1969—Navajo Community College opens at Many Farms, Arizona—the first modern community college completely administered and controlled by a tribe.

1969—N. Scott Momaday, a Kiowa, wins the Pulitzer Prize for his book *House Made of Dawn*. He is the first American Indian to be awarded that prize.

1969—Louis R. Bruce, a Mohawk-Oglala Sioux and a founder of the National Congress of American Indians, is appointed commissioner of Indian Affairs.

1969—National Indian Education Association is organized in Minneapolis.

1969—On November 3, the Senate Subcommittee on Indian Education reports that "our national policies for educating American Indians are a failure of major proportions."

1969-70—Sit-ins and protests are staged by Indian activists and sympathizers in San Francisco, Sacramento, Santa Fe, Washington state, Denver, Chicago, Minneapolis, and Cleveland.

1970—On December 15, Nixon signs the Taos Land Bill, returning 48 thousand acres of land to the Taos Pueblo. He also authorizes the payment of $1.1 million to the Nez Perce and Colville tribes for lands that had been illegally seized.

1971—Native American Rights Fund is established; its aim is to protect Indian lands, treaty and individual rights, and tribal law.

1971—U.S. Census Bureau reports that 1970 census counted almost 800,000 Indians— an increase of more than 50 percent since the 1960 count.

1972—Congress passes the Indian Education Act, creating an Office of Indian Education and National Advisory Council on Indian Education.

1972—In November, 500 Indians march on Washington, D.C., to protest government policy toward Indians.

1973—In late February, American Indian Movement activists occupy mission church at Wounded Knee (on Pine Ridge Reservation, South Dakota).

1973—In August, an Office of Indian Rights is created within the Civil Rights Division of the Justice Department.

1975—On January 4, Congress passes the Indian Self-Determination and Education Assistance Act, expanding tribal control over reservation programs and authorizing federal funds to build public school facilities on or near reservations.

1975 —On August 6, President Ford signs the Voting Rights Act Amendments, protecting the voting rights of non-English speaking citizens by permitting voting in more than one language.

1977—Seneca nation opens its museum in Salamanca, New York.

1977—On October 13, President Jimmy Carter appoints Forrest Gerard, a Blackfoot, as first assistant secretary of Indian affairs, elevating the Bureau of Indian Affairs to the level of other Interior Department agencies.

1978 —In August, President Carter signs the American Indian Religious Freedom Act, reversing a long history of government actions that suppressed tribal religions.

1978 —In September, the new Federal Acknowledgement Program is organized in an effort to recognize an estimated 250 previously unrecognized tribes.

1979 —Congress enacts the Archaeological Resources Protection Act, safeguarding important sites on federal public lands and Indian lands.

1980 —The Vatican beatifies Kateri Tekakwitha, a Mohawk-Algonquin who died 300 years earlier. She is the first American Indian beatified by the Catholic Church.

1980 —The Helsinki conference is provided with a federal study of the United States's compliance with the 1975 Helsinki Accords. The report concludes that the American record is "neither as deplorable as sometimes alleged nor as successful as one might hope."

1981 —One hundred and fifty tribal leaders send a letter to President Ronald Reagan demanding the immediate resignation of Secretary of Interior James Watt, for his "callous disregard" of Indian matters.

1981 —The International Olympic Committee restores to Jim Thorpe's family the two gold medals he won in the 1912 Olympic Games.

1983 —Secretary of the Interior James Watt's remarks during a television interview provoke an outcry across Indian Country, once again demanding his resignation.

1984—Presidential Commission on Indian Reservation Economies presents its report to President Reagan. It characterizes the Bureau of Indian Affair's organization and administration as "incompetent."

1985 —Wilma Mankiller becomes principal chief of the Cherokee nation of Oklahoma. She is the first woman to lead a large tribe in modern history.

1986 —Indian organizations request that all Indian remains be returned for reburial. The Smithsonian agrees to comply when a clear biological or cultural link can be established. In 1989, Stanford University also complies, repatriating the remains of 550 Ohione Indians to descendant tribes.

1986 —The Institute of American Indian and Alaska Native Culture and Arts Development is founded and charged with promoting the contributions of native arts to American society.

1986 —Amerind Vietnam Plaque is dedicated at Arlington National Cemetery, commemorating the service of 43,000 American Indians who served in Vietnam.

1987 —Pope John Paul II addresses a group of 1,600 American Indian leaders in Arizona, urging them to forget the past and focus on the church's current support of Indian rights.

1988 —President Reagan holds a meeting with sixteen Indian leaders; it is the first White House meeting of Indian leaders and the U.S. President in modern times.

1990 —Congress declares November as American Indian Heritage Month.

1990 —Congress passes the Indian Environmental Regulatory Act, reinforcing the protection of environmentally important lands in Indian Country.

1990 —Congress enacts the Native American Graves Protection and Repatriation Act, safeguarding Indian grave sites and providing for the return of remains and artifacts to tribes.

1990 —Secretary of the interior Manuel Lujan announces an advisory task force to recommend reorganization plans for the Bureau of Indian Affairs.

1991 —The new National Museum of the American Indian announces a policy to return Indian artifacts to tribes.

1991 —President Bush issues a policy statement reaffirming the federal government's commitment to the government-to-government relationship with Indian nations.

1991 —Custer Battlefield is officially renamed Little Big Horn Battlefield by the National Park Service.

1992 —On the 500th anniversary of Columbus's arrival in the New World, Indians across the U.S. protest against celebrations of his "discovery."

Tsimshian
Haida
Kwakiutl

Squamish

Lummi

Makah

Yakima

Chinook

Coos

Wallawalla

Coer d'Alene

Cayuse Nez Perce

Blackfoot

Piegan

Assiniboin

Hidasta Dakota

Mandan Dako

Arikara

Crow

Yankton Dako

Hoopa (Hupa)

Modoc Northern Paiute

Bannock

Northern Shoshone

Northern Cheyenne

Teton Dakota

Oglala

Western Shoshone

Wind River Shoshone

Arapaho

Ponca

O

Washoe

Miwok

Pawnee

Chumash

Ute

Serrano

Chemehuevi

Southern Paiute

Southern Cheyenne

Kansa

Hopi

Navajo

Jicarilla

Jemez

Taos

Mohave

Havasupai

Zuni

Tano

Tigua

Cahuilla

Yavapai

Yuma

Maricopa

Western Apache

Acoma

Isleta

Kiowa

Wi

Papago

Piro

Apache

Pima

Mescalero

Comanche

Inuit

Aleut

Tlingit

Ton

Coahuilte

TRIBES BEFORE
EUROPEAN INCURSION

TRIBES AND THEIR SITES

ABNAKI: Maine—*Damariscotta*, Shell Heaps; *Skowhegan*, Fisherman's Memorial. **Quebec**—*Odanak*, Abanakis Museum.

ACOMA: New Mexico—*Acoma*, Acoma Pueblo.

ALABAMA: Texas—*Livingston*, Alabama–Coushatta Museum.

APACHE: Arizona—*Fort Apache*, Apache Cultural Center; *Pearce*, Cochise Stronghold. **New Mexico**—*Dulce*, Jicarilla Apache Center; *Mescalero*, Apache Cultural Center.

APALACHEE: Florida—*Tallahassee*, San Luis Historic Site.

ARAPAHO: Wyoming—*Saint Stephens*, Mission Heritage Center.

ARIKARA: North Dakota—*New Town*, Three Affiliated Tribes Museum.

BANNOCK: Idaho—*Fort Hall*, Fort Hall Reservation.

BLACKFEET: Montana—*Browning*, Museum of the Plains Indian. **Alberta**—*Lethbridge*, Indian Battle Park.

CAHUILLA: California—*Banning*, Malki Museum.

CAYUSE: Washington—*Walla Walla*, Whitman Mission Historical Site.

CHEMEHUEVI: Arizona—*Parker*, Colorado River Tribes Museum.

CHEROKEE: California—*Oroville*, Cherokee Ghost Town. **Georgia**—*Calhoun*, New Echota State Historic Site; *Chatsworth*, James Vann House; *Rome*, Chieftains Museum. **Missouri**—*Cape Girardeau*, Trail of Tears State Park. **North Carolina**—*Cherokee*, Quallah Reservation Headquarters, Oconaluftee Village, "Unto These Hills" Pageant, Museum of the Cherokee Indian. **Oklahoma**—*Gore*, Cherokee National Courthouse; *Sallisaw*, Home of Sequoyah; *Tahlequah*, Cherokee National Capital, Cherokee Heritage Center, Murrell House. **Tennessee**—*Cleveland*, Red Clay State Historical Site; *Vonore*, Sequoyah's Birthplace.

CHEYENNE: Colorado—*Chivington*, Sand Creek Massacre Site. **Montana**—*Lame Deer*, Northern Cheyenne Tribal Museum. **Nebraska**—*Crawford*, Fort Robinson State Park. **Oklahoma**—*Cheyenne*, Washita Battleground.

CHICKASAW: Arkansas—*Wilson*, Hampson State Museum. **Kentucky**—*Paducah*, Chief Paduke Memorial. **Mississippi**—*Tupelo*, Chickasaw Village. **Oklahoma**—*Ada*, Chickasaw Cultural Center; *Tishomingo*, Chickasaw Council House. **Tennessee**—*Memphis*, Chucalissa Indian Museum.

CHIPPEWA (OJIBWA): Michigan—*Mackinac Island*, Indian Dormitory;

Saint Ignace, Marquette Mission and Museum of Ojibwa Culture. **Minnesota**—*Duluth,* Ni-Min-Win Ojibwa Festival; Grand Portage National Monument; *Onamia,* Mille Lacs Chippewa Museum. **Wisconsin**—*Lac du Flambeau,* Ben Guthrie Cultural Center; *Odanah,* Bad River Cultural Center; *Red Cliff,* Buffalo Arts Center.

CHOCTAW: Mississippi—*Philadelphia,* Choctaw Indian Fair and Museum of the Southern Indian; *Preston,* Nanih Waiya State Historic Site. **Oklahoma**—*Heavener,* Peter Conser Home; *Millerton,* Wheelock Mission Church; *Tuskahoma,* Choctaw National Museum.

COCHITI: New Mexico—*Cochiti,* Cochiti Pueblo.

COEUR D'ALENE: Idaho—*Kellogg,* Old Mission State Park.

COLVILLE: Washington—*Omak,* St. Mary's Mission.

COMANCHE: Oklahoma—*Cache,* Quanah Parker Starr House.

CREE: Alberta—*Lethbridge,* Indian Battle Park. **Manitoba**—*Winnipeg,* Riel House. **Saskatchewan**—*Batoche,* Batoche National Historic Park.

CREEK: Alabama—Horseshoe Bend National Military Park; *Wallsboro,* Little Tallasse Plantation. **Georgia**—*Jackson,* Indian Springs State Park; *Macon,* Ocmulgee National Monument. **Oklahoma**—*Okmulgee,* Creek Council House.

CROW: Montana—*Crow Agency,* Crow Reservation Fair; *Pryor,* Chief Plenty Coups State Monument.

DELAWARE: Ohio—*Gnadenhutten,* Historical Park; *New Philadelphia,* Schoenbrunn and "Trumpet in the Land" Pageant. **Oklahoma**—*Anadarko,* Delaware Tribal Museum. **Pennsylvania**—*Bushkill,* Pocono Indian Museum.

ERIE: Ohio—*Kelleys Island,* Inscription Rock.

FOX (AND SAC): Illinois—*Rock Island,* Black Hawk Historic Site. **Iowa**—*Keokuk,* Chief Keokuk Monument; *Tama,* Mesquakie Pow Wow. **Kansas**—*Highland,* Iowa Sac and Fox Mission. **Oklahoma**—*Yale,* Jim Thorpe Home. **Pennsylvania**—*Jim Thorpe,* Jim Thorpe Memorial.

GITSKAN: British Columbia—*New Hazleton,* Ksan Indian Village.

HAIDA: Alaska—*Ketchikan,* Totem Heritage Center.

HAVASUPAI: Arizona—*Supai,* Havasupai Reservation.

HIDATSA: North Dakota—*New Town,* Three Affiliated Tribe Museum; *Stanton,* Knife River Villages Historic Site.

HOOPA: California—*Hoopa,* Tribal Museum.

HOPI: Arizona—Canyon de Chelly National Monument; *Oraibi,* Old Oraibi; *Second Mesa,* Hopi Cultural Center; *Keams Canyon,* Walpi.

HURON (WYANDOT): Kansas—*Kansas City,* Huron Cemetery. **Michigan**—*Saint Ignace,* Marquette Mission and Museum of Ojibwa Culture. **Ohio**—*Upper Sandusky,* Wyandotte Mission. **Ontario**—*Midland,* Sainte-Marie among the Huron, Huron Village.

ILLINOIS: Illinois—*Alton*, Piasa Bird Paintings.

IOWA: Kansas—*Highland*, Iowa, Sac and Fox Mission.

IROQUOIS: New York—*Cobleskill*, Iroquois Indian Museum. Pennsylvania—*Wilkes-Barre*, Wyoming Battlefield. Ontario—*Brantford*, Woodland Indian Cultural Centre, Brant County Museum; *Ohsweken*, Six Nations Pageant; *Burlington*, Joseph Brant Home.

KANSA (KAW): Kansas—*Council Grove*, Council Oak, Kaw Mission.

KIOWA: Oklahoma—*Anadarko*, Kiowa Murals; *Carnegie*, Kiowa Tribal Museum.

KWAKIUTL: British Columbia—*Alert Bay*, U'Mista Cultural Center; *Quadra Island*, Kwakiutl Museum.

LAGUNA: New Mexico—*Laguna*, Laguna Pueblo.

LUMBEE: North Carolina—*Pembroke*, "Strike at the Wind" Pageant.

LUMMI: Washington—*Bellingham*, Lummi Stommish and Reserve.

MAKAH: Washington—*Neah Bay*, Makah Cultural and Research Center.

MANDAN: North Dakota—*Mandan*, Slant Village; *New Town*, Three Affiliated Tribes Museum.

MARICOPA: Arizona—*Sacaton*, Gila Basin Indian Center.

MASHPEE: Massachusetts—*Mashpee*, Old Indian Meeting House.

MENOMINEE: Wisconsin—*Egg Harbor*, Chief Oshkosh Museum.

MIAMI: Indiana—*Pendleton*, Falls Park Memorial; *South Bend*, Council Oak. Ohio—*Piqua*, Historic Indian Museum.

MINGO: West Virginia—*Logan*, "Aracoma" Pageant.

MIWOK: California—*Novato*, Miwok Tribal Museum; *Volcano*, Indian Grinding Rock State Historic Park.

MOHAVE: Arizona—*Parker*, Colorado River Tribes Museum.

MOHAWK: Massachusetts—*Charlemont*, Mohawk Memorial. New York—*Fonda*, Shrine of Kateri Tekakwitha. Ontario—*Brantford*, Her Majesty's Chapel of the Mohawks.

MOHEGAN: Connecticut—*Mohegan*, Fort Shantock State Park, Tantaquidgeon Lodge Museum; *Norwich*, Indian Burial Grounds.

MONO: California—*North Fork*, Sierra Mono Indian Museum.

NANTICOKE: Delaware—*Millsboro*, Nanticoke Museum.

NARRAGANSETT: Connecticut—*Mohegan*, Fort Shantock State Park. Rhode Island—*Charlestown*, Narragansett Burial Ground; *Narragansett*, Canochet Memorial.

NATCHEZ: Mississippi—*Natchez*, Emerald Mound, Grand Village.

NAVAJO: Arizona—Canyon de Chelly National Monument; *Ganado*, Hubbell Trading Post; Monument Valley Tribal Park; Navajo National

Monument; *Window Rock,* Navajo Tribal Headquarters and Museum. **New Mexico**—*Gallup,* Navajo Code Talkers Exhibit; *Santa Fe,* Wheelwright Museum of the American Indian.

NEUTRAL: Ontario—*London,* Museum of Indian Archeology.

NEZ PERCE: Idaho—*Moscow,* Appaloosa Museum; Nez Perce National Historic Park. **Montana**—Big Hole National Battlefield; *Chinook,* Bears Paw State Monument. **Oregon**—*Joseph,* Old Chief Joseph Monument. **Washington**—*Omak,* St. Mary's Mission.

OMAHA: Nebraska—*Bancroft,* Susette LaFlesche Monument; *Macy,* Omaha Powow.

ONEIDA: Wisconsin—*Green Bay,* Oneida National Museum. **Ontario**—*Delaware,* Ska-Nah-Doht Indian Village.

ONONDAGA: New York—*Nedrow,* Onondaga Reservation.

OSAGE: Missouri—*Nevada,* Osage Village Historic Site. **Oklahoma**—*Pawhuska,* Osage Museum.

OTO: Iowa—*Council Bluffs,* Council Monument.

OTTAWA: Michigan—*Harbor Springs,* Andrew Blackbird Museum.

PAIUTE: California—*Bishop,* Owens Valley Paiute-Shoshone Culture Center. **Nevada**—*Pyramid Lake,* Paiute Reservation.

PAMUNKEY: Virginia—*Lanesville,* Pamunkey Indian Museum.

PAPAGO: Arizona—*Tucson,* Mission San Xavier del Bac.

PASSAMAQUODDY: Maine—*Perry,* Passamaquoddy Reservation.

PAWNEE: Kansas—*Courtland,* Pawnee Village Museum.

PENOBSCOT: Maine—*Old Town,* Penobscot Island and Museum.

PEQUOT: Connecticut—*Mohegan,* Fort Shantock State Park.

PICURIS: Kansas—*Scott City,* El Cuartelejo Ruins. **New Mexico**—*Picuris,* Picuris Pueblo.

PIMA: Arizona—Casa Grande Ruins National Monument; *Sacaton,* Gila Basin Indian Center.

POTAWATOMI: Indiana—*Plymouth,* Chief Menominee Monument. **Kansas**—*St. Marys,* Potawatomi Pay Station.

POWHATAN: Virginia—*Hampton,* Pocahontas Window; *Jamestown,* Pocahontas Statue, Powhatan Indian Village.

SAN ILDEFONSO: New Mexico—*San Ildefonso,* San Ildefonso Pueblo.

SANTA CLARA: New Mexico—*Santa Clara,* Santa Clara Pueblo.

SEMINOLE: Florida—*Bushnell,* Dade Battlefield State Historical Site; *St. Augustine,* Osceola Historic Site; *Tamiami Station,* Miccosukee Indian Village. **Oklahoma**—*Wewoka,* Seminole National Museum.

SENECA: New York—*Portageville,* Letchworth Museum and Seneca

Council House; *Salamanca,* Seneca-Iroquois National Museum.

SERRANO: California—*Banning,* Malki Museum of the Morongo Reservation.

SHAWNEE: Indiana—*Lafayette,* Tippecanoe Battlefield. **Kansas**—*Kansas City,* Shawnee Mission. **Ohio**—*Chillicothe,* "Tecumseh" Pageant; *Piqua,* Historic Indian Museum; *Xenia,* "Blue Jacket" Pageant. **West Virginia**—*Logan,* "Aracoma" Pageant; *Point Pleasant,* Battle Monument State Park.

SHINNECOCK: New York—*Southampton,* Shinnecock Reservation.

SHOSHONE: California—*Bishop,* Owens Valley Paiute-Shoshone Indian Culture Center. **Wyoming**—*Fort Washakie,* Shoshone Reservation Headquarters and Graves of Sacajawea and Washakie; *Thermopolis,* Gift of the Waters Pageant.

SIOUX (DAKOTA): Iowa—*Sioux City,* War Eagle Monument. **Michigan**—*Niles,* Fort St. Joseph Museum. **Minnesota**—*Faribault,* Sioux Window in Cathedral of Our Merciful Saviour; *Granite Falls,* Upper Sioux Agency State Park; *Hutchinson,* Little Crow Memorial; *Pipestone,* Pipestone National Monument; *Redwood Falls,* Lower Sioux Agency. **Montana**—Little Big Horn National Battlefield. **Nebraska**—*Crawford,* Fort Robinson State Park. **North Dakota**—*Fort Totten,* State Historic Site; *Fort Yates,* Standing Rock; *Kulm,* Whitestone Battlefield. **South Dakota**—*Chamberlain,* St. Joseph's School; *Custer,* Crazy Horse Memorial; *Mitchell,* Oscar Howe Art Center; *Mobridge,* Sitting Bull Memorial, Scherr-Howe Arena Murals; *Pine Ridge,* Red Cloud Heritage Center; *Rapid City,* Sioux Indian Museum; *St. Francis,* Buechel Lakota Museum and Mission; *Wounded Knee,* Wounded Knee Battlefield. **Wyoming**—*Sheridan,* Fetterman Massacre.

STOCKBRIDGE-MUNSEE: Wisconsin—*Bowler,* Stockbridge-Munsee Tribal Council Museum.

SUQUAMISH: Washington—*Suquamish,* Museum and Grove of Chief Seattle.

TAOS: New Mexico—*Taos,* Taos Pueblo.

TESUQUE: New Mexico—*Tesuque,* Tesuque Pueblo.

TIGUA: Texas—*Ysleta,* Tigua Museum and Reservation.

TLINGIT: Alaska—*Haines,* Alaska Indian Arts and Chilkat Dances; *Ketchikan,* Totem Heritage Center; *Sitka,* Sitka National Historic Park.

TONKAWA: Oklahoma—*Tonkawa,* Tonkawa Tribal Museum.

TSIMSHIAN: Alaska—*Annette Island,* Duncan Cottage Museum.

TULALIP: Washington—*Marysville,* St. Anne's Church and Tulalip Reserve.

UMATILLA: Oregon—*Pendleton,* Pendleton Roundup.

UTE: Colorado—*Ignacio,* Sky Ute Center; Mesa Verde National Park; *Montrose,* Ute Indian Museum; *Towaoc,* Ute Mountain Tribal Park.

WAMPANOAG: Massachusetts—*Bourne,* Aptuxcet Trading Post;

Plymouth, Massasoit Memorial; *West Tisbury*, Mayhew Chapel. **Rhode Island**—*Bristol*, King Philip's War.

WASHOE: Nevada—*Carson City*, Stewart Indian Museum.

WINNEBAGO: Nebraska—*Macy*, Omaha Powwow. **Wisconsin**—*Wisconsin Dells*, Stand Rock Winnebago Ceremonials.

YAKIMA: Washington—*Toppenish*, Yakima National Cultural Center.

YAVAPAI: Arizona—*Camp Verde*, Yavapai-Apache Visitor Center.

YUMA: California—*Winterhaven*, Fort Yuma Quechan Museum.

ZIA: New Mexico—*Zia*, Zia Pueblo.

ZUNI: New Mexico—*Zuni*, Zuni Pueblo.

A Native American Guide to Indian Country

BY SUZAN SHOWN HARJO
PRESIDENT AND EXECUTIVE EDITOR,
THE MORNING STAR FOUNDATION

One media icon made a career-long effort to expand the limited coverage of American Indian news, often chiding his fellow journalists with, "America is missing the Indian story." Here, another good newsman, George Cantor, offers a way to find as many stories as there are peoples' pasts and futures converging at each landmark in his traveler's guide. This well-researched and readable book points to more places than most people have been. It also points out how much there is to know, giving teaser backgrounds about the Native origins and namesakes of familiar-sounding sites and providing glimpses of whole cultures that have escaped the notice of most travelers.

North American Indian Landmarks will take even the armchair traveler to new places where more can be learned about, and from, the Indigenous Peoples of Turtle Island, as the Haudenesaune (Iroquois) call what is now known as the United States and Canada. This is a guide to the mighty of the distant past, to the countries of unique thriving peoples, to natural and human-made monuments, to cultural centers, to the records of women and men who left their marks in stone and ink. These are some landmarks of Native North Americans, as well as those of other peoples as they relate to Natives. Readers will not make this journey without meeting new people—or themselves—along the way.

What's in a Name?

The question asked most often by non-Indians is about what term to use when referring to the collective race of people who are indigenous to the Western Hemisphere. The first thing to know about traveling in Indian Country is that words and protocol are important, but that many terms, especially those rising out of European Manifest Destiny notions and colonization, are inaccurate though not necessarily inappropriate. Other names, however, are best left to history.

The name "Indian" is the legacy of the lost European sailors in 1492 who thought this quarter of Mother Earth was another continent to the west, the one with India. "American" is derived from the first name of another European. Native Peoples here could have been called "Vespuccinders" as easily as "American Indians" or "Native Americans," the most commonly used misnomers these days. With North American-born descendants of immigrants referring to themselves as "Natives," the issue becomes further clouded.

"Indian" is the term of art that has made its way into U.S. and Canadian treaties, statutes, caselaw, governance documents, and modern English and French parlance. "Indian" replaced far less desirable names in popular North American culture, such as "Savage," "Redskin," or "L'Indian Rouge," which are still considered fighting words. Compared to these, "American Indian," "Canadian Native," "Native American," "Indian," and "Native" seem mild, and are currently viewed as inexact and silly, rather than offensive.

Most Native Peoples in North America use these imprecise and awkward terms interchangeably when referring to the race as a whole. With some 600 different Indian Nations in the United States and Canada, having nearly as many separate languages, histories, territories, religions, and cultures, more emphasis is placed on the tribal names than on the collective. The most notable exceptions to this involve 1) intertribal coalitions to stop name-calling and discrimination against the race as a whole and 2) dealings with Canadian or U.S. laws affecting Natives nationwide.

A greater Native priority now is on Indian national and personal names, and on substituting traditional tribal names for those imposed through the missionizing and colonizing processes. The Diné, for example, in the early 1990s, issued a formal call for all to use their traditional name, which means "People," rather than the name they are widely known as, Navajo. With the success of the movie *Dances with Wolves*, the general public is now more aware of the original and preferred names Lakota and Dakota over the imposed name Sioux, a French variation of an Ojibwa (Chippewa) word meaning "enemy."

Throughout world history, when one group has exerted control over another, it has first stripped that group of its basic identity by using pet names, misnomers, or pejorative terms. The dominant group has then forced others to use the foreign names. This is evident in North American history with slave-owners imposing their names on slaves, European churches placing "Christian names" on those to be converted, and assimilationists at Ellis

Island "Americanizing" the given names of refugees.

Both U.S. and Canadian church and state zealously pursued this practice, imposing French, English, and Spanish names or poor or insulting translations of Native names on Indian people, families, clans, tribes, and nations. Often, the Indians were made to use national names of places or objects, as with the British-imposed "Creek" for the Muscogee Nation, because the English saw that the Muscogees lived near running waters. As the Tohono O'Odham leaders told U.S. Bureau of Indian Affairs (BIA) officials in the early 1980s, they wanted their name changed back to the original in all the agency's subsequent records, not solely because "Papago" means "bean-eater," but because it is not their name for themselves in their own language.

This matter was addressed poetically by Pulitzer Prize-winning author N. Scott Momaday, a Kiowa, in his 1976 memoir *The Names*. Written "in devotion to those whose names I bear and to those who bear my names," its opening words are: "My name is Tsoai-talee. I am, therefore, Tsoai-talee; therefore I am. The storyteller Pohd-lohk gave me the name Tsoai-talee. He believed that a man's life proceeds from his name, in the way that a river proceeds from its source."

The reader and traveler should not be discouraged about what is or is not correct, only mindful of what is or is not respectful. The basic rule, as it applies to all human relations, is to simply ask Indians how they would like to be addressed and referred to, and to respect their responses.

Do Indians Still Live in Tipis?

This, believe it or not, is the second most commonly asked question of Native Peoples. The Indians of the Great Plains—the Lakota, Cheyenne (whose name is Tsistsistas, the "Human Beings"), Arapaho, Arikara, Mandan, Hidatsa, and others—have become the prototypical Indian in the minds of many non-Indians and even some Indians. The image of Indians on horseback in full-feathered headdresses and their finest cut-glass beadwork, battling the Cavalry or hunting buffalo is a powerful one that has led even some Indians whose traditional head wear is the turban to honor federal dignitaries with "war-bonnets" and Plains Indian songs and dances.

Native North Americans are generally thought of only in the past tense. This is perpetuated primarily by the film and television industries, which bury Indians sometime between the discovery myths and the end of the nineteenth century, and the automotive, advertising, and sports industries, which single out Indians for cartooning and stereotyping and use their names and images in ways they would not dare for any other living group of people. Were this not the case, North Americans could be driving home in "Zulu" pick-up trucks or "Tibet" sedans to catch the televised game between the "White Trash" and the "Frito Banditos." While this would not and should not happen in this enlightened era, its equivalent—and worse—is daily fare for Indians. Anti-Indian racism is commonplace, and goes virtually unnoticed.

Native People in North America are the invisible population, in part because Indians in North America are few in number—less than two million in the United States and fewer than half that in Canada—and most non-Indians are merely uninformed about Indians in the present day. The best sources of information are the Native Peoples themselves, especially those who follow their traditional tribal ways.

Travelers to landmarks on Indian lands, which are called "reservations" in the United States and "reserves" in Canada, should be aware that they are entering other countries (subject to tribal jurisdiction and laws) and other peoples' homes. These lands were specifically reserved by Indian Nations in treaties or through other federal laws. These countries vary in size from single-digit acreage of most rancherias in California to the vast total Native lands in Canada, where one-fifth of the territory within its exterior boundaries is in reserve status or is Native-owned unreserved land.

In the United States, the average size of reservations is about 300,000 acres. The Diné (Navajo) Nation is larger than West Virginia and shares borders with Arizona, Colorado, New Mexico, and Utah. The Tohono O'Odham (Papago) Nation borders Mexico and Arizona and is the size of Connecticut. One-fifth of all lands in Arizona are tribally owned. New Mexico boasts 18 of the 19 Pueblos, as well as two Apache Reservations and part of the Diné lands, and the state itself has a distinctive Indian character, as do North and South Dakota and Nebraska, where most of the Sioux Reservations are. Oklahoma was supposed to have been the first Indian State and was the end of the road for those who did not die along the infamous Trail of Tears and other federally enforced marches. That state has the largest Indian population and the greatest number of Indian Nations—nearly 40—within its borders, including the most populated one in the United States, the Cherokee Nation.

Some Native Peoples, like the Cree Nation in Canada, have vast territories, large numbers, and growing economies. Others, like the Agua Caliente Band and the Puyallup Nation, are small in number and acreage but are financially secure, with parts of Palm Springs and Tacoma, respectively, within their boundaries. One small tribe in Connecticut had been pronounced dead in history books and by famous Indian orators such as Tecumseh of the Shawnee, who began a speech 100 years ago with "Where today are the Pequots? . . . and many other once powerful tribes of our people?" In the early 1980s, the 250-citizen Mashantucket Pequot Tribe settled a land claim with the United States for a small amount of land and less than one million dollars, and bankrolled that sum in fewer than ten years into a billion-dollar annual profit from a tribal gambling casino. The Pequots today are a major employer of traditional and contemporary Indian performers, as well as of thousands of their non-Indian neighbors. In 1993, the Pequots struck a deal for exclusive statewide use of certain casino games in exchange for bailing Connecticut out of its deficit.

The Passamaquoddy Tribe and Penobscot Nation of Maine were the poorest people in the poorest state in the United States until their land claim was settled by Congress in 1980 for 300,000 acres of land and a multi-million-dollar development fund. The Passamaquoddy have gone on to make financial history with record-breaking profits from wise business decisions and to make environmental history by developing the only machine that does anything about the problem of acid rain: the Recovery Scrubber, which scrubs acidic wastes and converts them into fertilizer. The Passamaquoddy and Penobscot, who tried for 150 years before finding some measure of justice in the legal system for their valid claim to two-thirds of Maine, are now significant land owners and entrepreneurs, and Maine no longer is the poorest state in the nation.

These and other success stories give hope to the many more Native Peoples in North America who live at the bottom end of the socioeconomic scale. Indians in the United States, where more than 50 percent live in cities outside their tribal territories, are the poorest of any population. Conditions have improved dramatically for some Natives during the last third of this century, primarily through an infusion of natural resources regained in legal battles and through cash acquired in gaming and other business enterprises. However, on the national scale, Natives collectively suffer the poorest health and housing conditions, the lowest per capita incomes, the highest rate of unemployment, the lowest level of educational attainment, and the shortest lives.

But both the health and the economies of Indians have improved in recent decades as more traditional Indian sources of foods and commerce have been reincorporated. The percentage of diabetic Pimas and Maricopas dropped by some ten points with the growth of the Gila River Farms, the most successful tribal farming operation in the United States. Similar trends are being experienced by Alaska and Canadian Natives in relation to whaling, by Pacific Northwest and Great Lakes Indians in relation to salmon and walleye fishing, and by Plains Indians in relation to buffalo herding.

Many of these returns to traditional foods and economies have come about only after generations of litigation. In 1979, the U.S. Supreme Court ruled that under U.S. and Indian treaty rights, Native Peoples in the Pacific Northwest were entitled to 50 percent of the allowable harvest of salmon and another anadromous fish in their on- and off-reservation usual and accustomed fishing places. In its landmark decision in *U.S. v. Washington,* the Court chided the state for its recalcitrance in obeying treaty law and other federal rulings, saying that the case had been tried five times this century and it would not be heard again. The Court ordered a tripartite fisheries management system by tribal, federal, and state governments to revive the diminishing salmon population—specifically reaffirming the Indian treaty rights to fish for subsistence, commercial, and ceremonial purposes. The decision was the beginning of the end of a 100-year fish war between Indians and non-Indians in Washington, during which Indians were denied their treaty-guaranteed food, economy, and religious rights. The decision also began the return of the numbers and health of the salmon from its prior state of emergency.

In the 1980s similar cases were won by or settled in the Native Peoples' favor in Michigan, Wisconsin, and the Columbia River area. In Wisconsin in the mid-1980s, the non-Indian backlash against Indian fishers and their children was so violent and vituperative that federal and state law enforcement agents had to protect the Indians' rights, and Wisconsin became known as the "Mississippi of the North." Anti-Indian hate groups there, which had started over the same issue in Washington state in the 1970s, organized efforts to have Congress wipe out the Court victories and to abolish all treaties, but the efforts failed. The anti-Indian groups raised the court-rejected argument that Indian treaties made Indians "super-citizens."

Are Indians Citizens of the United States and Canada?

This, the third most commonly asked question about Native Peoples, was addressed by the United States in its 1979 report to the world community of nations on its domestic compliance with the human rights and self-determination principles of the Helsinki Accords:

American Indians have much in common with other U.S. minority groups. However, it would be extremely misleading to view the rights of American Indians solely in terms of their status as a racially distinct minority group, while neglecting their tribal rights. The Indian tribes are sovereign, domestic dependent nations that have entered into a trust relationship with the government. Their unique status as distinct political entities within the U.S. federal system is acknowledged by the U.S. Government in treaties, statutes, court decisions and executive orders, and recognized in the U.S. Constitution. This nationhood status and trust relationship has led American Indian tribes and organizations, and the U.S. Government to conclude that Indian rights issues fall under both Principle VII of the Helsinki Final Act, where the rights of national minorities are addressed, and under Principle VIII, which addresses equal rights and the self-determination of peoples . . . . The policy of the U.S. Government . . . is designed to put Indians, in the exercise of self-government, into a decision-making position with respect to their own lives. The United States has recognized that it has not always lived up to its obligations in its protection of the rights of Native Americans to a continuing political existence, to land and natural resources and to cultural distinctness. The U.S. Government, however, is improving its performance and attempting to close the gap between policy and practice.

—*Fulfilling Our Promises: The United States and the Helsinki Final Act,* U.S. Commission on Security and Cooperation in Europe, November, 1979, pp. 148-149.

Indians are, in the first instance, citizens of their nations, giving Canada and the United States vast territory over which to govern, most often through treaties of peace and friendship. In exchange, Indian peoples reserved rights in perpetuity to lands and hunting, fishing, gathering, religion, and health-care in order to combat the imported diseases that were decimating whole peoples. The Native Peoples in North America had no way of treating or curing the diseases from Europe—the common cold, influenza, tuberculosis, smallpox, the plague, syphilis, measles, and tetanus, among others—that, combined with outright murder, killed some eight million Indians in the

Caribbean region between 1492 and 1500 and reduced the North American Natives from more than 50 million to fewer than 500,000 by the year 1900.

Virtually all treaties and other legal agreements with Indian Nations have been violated by Canada and the United States. The two countries honored only those promises to keep ceded lands and to teach Indians "the arts of civilization." Under the color of the law or through outright coercion and theft, the governments took as much additional land, water, and other resources as they could and "educated" Indians by outlawing traditional tribal religions (first in the United States in 1894—a mere 16 years after the official end of U.S. treaty-making with Indian Nations), granting exclusive franchises to Christian denominations to proselytize to specified Natives, and removing Indian children from their families and placing them in far-away government boarding schools, where they were forced to speak only English or French, cut their hair, and dress and pray like "civilized" people.

The treaty-making era began when it was clear that the extermination era failed to do the job, marking the start of assimilation. The mainstreaming and deculturalization practices did not turn North American Natives into brown white folks, but did result in tragic social and economic deprivation that caused great embarrassment to the United States and Canada—internationally as well as to people of conscience in both countries. Beginning in the 1930s, the Canadian and U.S. governments embarked on social welfare and self-determination assistance programs to stem the tide of disappearing Native populations and of distressed lives at the bare survival level. Canada did a better job than did the United States in this area, with dependable sources of financing flowing to tribal governments for programs and infrastructure development. This trend reversed in the 1970s, when the United States was just beginning to turn program aid and decision-making authority over to the Indians. As one example of this contrast, by 1980, Canadian Natives had developed a broad communications network of hundreds of radio stations, newspapers, and television outlets while American Indians had only a handful of weekly newspapers, fewer than 15 radio stations, and no television stations.

Because Canada initially adopted the British system of top-down sovereignty—the divine right of kings theory, with sovereignty flowing from God to kings to some of the people some of the time and most of the people none of the time—Natives were not recognized in Canadian law as having sovereignty beyond that granted by the dominant government. Because the United States, on the other hand, adopted the Iroquois Six Nations Confederacy and other nearby tribal governance models of inherent sovereignty, it thereby recognized the national sovereignty of Indian Tribes from their inception. When tested as a matter of law, the sovereign rights of Native Peoples have fared better in the American courts than in the Canadian. Therefore, a benevolent sovereign's duty to care for its people has provided for greater tangible help to Native Peoples in Canada than in the United States.

The first right of a sovereign nation is to determine who its people are, and its citizenship criteria are an internal matter subject to the sole discretion of the nation itself. The question of who has the authority to decide who are citizens of an Indian nation rose in the 1970s in a case involving the Santa Clara Pueblo in New Mexico. The U.S. Supreme Court decided in favor of the Pueblo, definitively stating that its "membership" was its own to decide, as a matter of sovereignty. Prior to this decision, the BIA and other federal agencies had encroached upon the tribal prerogative, designating people as Indians or non-Indians as a form of punishment-and-reward, cash-and-poverty politics.

At the outset of its formation, Canada embarked on a course of action to destabilize and undercut the power of the Iroquois Nations' traditional matrilineal system of determining citizenry. The Canadian government disenfranchised the Native women and empowered non-Native women by declaring that only the children of Native *men* were Natives. The Iroquois Nations' territories are in both Canada and the United States, with the Oneida citizens on lands in New York, Wisconsin, and Ontario and with the U.S.-Canada border drawn through Mohawk lands. The United States and Canada recognize the Native Peoples' cross-border rights for certain purposes and not at all for others. While Canada, the United States, and the Native Nations are now working to resolve some of the inappropriate inclusions and unjust exclusions, the generations of confusion will not be resolved in this century.

Under its first Constitution, Canada considered Natives as citizens, whether or not the Natives wanted citizenship. The United States approved the "Indian Citizenship Act" in 1924 as a reward for Indians having volunteered and served in the U.S. armed forces in disproportionately high numbers during World War I. Under U.S. law and new recognitions of tribal sovereignty in Canada, both countries acknowledge Natives as having dual citizenship in their Native Nations and in the United States or Canada, or as having tri-citizenship rights for "border tribes." Several North American Native Peoples consider themselves citizens of only their Indian Nations, irrespective of U.S. or Canadian law, the most highly visible of which is the Onondaga Nation in

New York, whose own passports are widely accepted internationally.

Under both U.S. and Canadian policy, Indians do not pay federal taxes for income derived from their territories, nor for income derived under treaties or other applicable law. Native Peoples have tribal laws that apply to governance and law-enforcement within their territories, although a mix of federal and state or provincial laws also applies in certain situations. For the most part, Indians in off-reservation areas are subject to the laws of the jurisdiction in which they happen to be or reside. Non-Indians visiting or living in Indian Country are subject to the tribal law of the land. Only Natives can vote in their tribal processes and then only if they are recognized by their Indian governments as tribal citizens who are eligible to vote. Indians can vote in federal, provincial, or state matters if they meet the eligibility standards set for all voters in general. In most instances, U.S. and Canadian treaties with Native Peoples are interpreted in the courts in the way that the Native signatories understood they were intended, and the laws of the two countries are supposed to bend to tribal law, custom, and tradition when they vary from the law as applied to others.

These laws and broad policy guidelines are what were challenged as "supercitizenry" rights by most states, the anti-Indian organizations, state and local tax entities, and recreational and commercial interests, including those of the sports-fishing and sports-hunting groups, resorts, and organized gaming interests. The U.S. Supreme Court has long held that because of their status as Indians, the rights of Indians do *not* interfere with the constitutional rights of non-Indians, but that they are simply different in some respects, mainly because Indian Nations are inherently sovereign, gave up territory to the United States, and retained lands and rights in treaties that are still legal and contractually binding.

Am I Welcome in Indian Country?

The short answer to this next most often asked question is "Yes." Most of the landmarks detailed in this guide are either public lands or are on tribal lands that are intended for the general public to visit. The listed landmarks in these categories include all museums and cultural centers, parks and monuments, and battlefields. Other listed landmarks in Indian Country are subject to the rules, hours, and restrictions set by the Native Nations. For the landmarks described as Indian Nations, Tribes, Pueblos, Reserves, or Reservations, travelers are well advised to call or write beforehand to inquire about any upcoming events where the public is welcome; any ceremonial or other periods when people from other places would not be permitted; and any such visitor guidance as weather, terrain, recommended itinerary of activities, and special rules or protocol to follow.

Some Native Peoples have hotels, resorts, camping areas, golf course, and recreation activities on their lands. Others may have limited public areas and facilities, depending on their traditions, geographic location, land area, population, or economic condition. Most have tourism offices or visitor centers. In Canada, there is a nationwide Native Tourism board. In the United States, there is no comparable nationwide group, but the first Indian tourism organization of any state, the New Mexico Indian Tourism Association, was just formed in 1990. In both Canada and the United States, Natives work with the provincial and state tourism boards.

Native Peoples in North America have launched full-fledged visitor programs for several purposes: to inform travelers; to put to rest myths and stereotypes; to gain understanding and support for their efforts to live as culturally distinct peoples; to expose visitors to the range of fine arts, crafts, and other products that are available; to enhance their economies; and to combine efforts with tourism entities in the surrounding areas and with the visitors themselves to channel travelers to places where they are welcome and away from sacred, endangered, or delicate areas, as well as to protect the privacy of their people's homes.

The Pueblos in the Southwest, for example, have exquisite traditional and contemporary art, jewelry, clothing, and other items for sale on their lands. The Picaris Pueblo is the majority-owner of one of the finest hotels in New Mexico, the Hotel Santa Fe, which is not on their lands. There they exhibit contemporary paintings and sculpture by artists including Allan Houser (Chiricahua Apache), whose work is also displayed at the United Nations in New York City and who was awarded the National Medal of Arts in 1992, a first for a Native American artist. The Pueblos and Apaches have public feast days when it is considered good fortune to feed visitors from other places and the public is invited to the ceremonies. But they also have ceremonial times when duties are carried out in private and their lands are closed to any Indians or non-Indians who are not practitioners of the religion of that particular Pueblo.

In the twentieth century, with the domestic and international recognitions of Native sovereign, religious, and human rights—especially with the passage of the American Indian Religious Freedom Act of 1978 and the inclusion of American Indians in the protection of the Helsinki Accords in

1979—some of the previously outlawed ceremonies, virtually unchanged during the period of overt federal threat, began to be shared with non-Indians and to resume their incorporative and reflective natures. However, with the growing availability of Indian cultural information, more often inaccurate than otherwise when written about by non-Indians, there has also been an increased level of stealing Indian burial and other sacred objects, marketing religious items as non-contextual art, prostituting tribal ceremonies by non-Indians and Indians, commercializing and bastardizing tribal names and symbols, and by non-Indians masquerading as Indians for profit in the world of culture and art.

The culture vultures' appropriation of Indian religious and artistic symbology and personas have led to a recent trend toward Native Peoples once again closing ceremonies, their renewed fear of sharing their power and beauty with others, and an increased focus on conducting observances in private. These situations, coupled with a late-1980s ruling by the U.S. Supreme Court that removed First Amendment religious freedom protection from the holy places of Native Peoples, left the U.S. courts no constitutional door to defend sacred sites against desecration, increasing the risk that these places would be plundered or destroyed. As of this printing, many powerful members of Congress are working with Indian spiritual leaders to gain a new law to provide for due process in the American justice system. Until the objections of the forest products and mining industries and other special interests are overcome and a new law is enacted, travelers in Indian Country will need to be especially sensitive to the need to protect these areas in their natural state as well as be respectful of the tribal wishes.

In 1992, many North American Natives declared the year of the five-hundredth anniversary of the first of the Columbus voyages as "The Year of the Indigenous Peoples." The United Nations proclaimed 1993 as "The Year of the Indigenous People." In the December 1992 official announcement ceremony by the U.N. at its New York headquarters, Native leaders from various parts of the globe took issue with the world body for having dropped the "s" from "Peoples"; the U.N. maintained that the "s" represented a distinction without a difference. The Native leaders rightly maintained that international law recognizes only the individual human rights of people in the singular, while peoples in the plural are accorded group, collective, and national rights as well, even as a standard for inclusion in the United Nations itself. It is no wonder that the status and goals of Native Peoples are so often misperceived, when such large matters can be mightily affected by so small a thing as a single letter on a written document.

What Do the Indians Want?

This last question is best answered by Indian Peoples in relation to a specific matter and in an appropriate context. One excellent response was written as a collective effort by some 100 Native artists, writers, and wisdom-keepers at a four-day gathering at Taos, Pueblo, in October 1992. The participants, ranging in age from 21 to 91 and from more than 60 distinct Indian Nations, issued a communique, "Statement of Vision Toward the Next 500 Years," which reads, in part:

> "We envision that in five hundred years Indigenous Peoples will be here, protecting and living with Mother Earth in our own lands. We see a future of coming generations of Native Peoples who are healthy in body and spirit, who speak Native languages daily, and who are supported by traditional extended families.

> "We look forward to leadership that encourages the religious and cultural manifestations of our traditions, and the reclamation and continuing use of our traditional ceremonies, hairstyles, foods, clothes, music, personal and tribal names, and medicines. Our cultural renewal will assure the perpetuation of natural species that are dying, and perhaps even some of those thought to be extinct....

> "Native Peoples are strengthened by relations among each other at all levels of community life. Commitment, integrity, patience, the ability to build consensus and respect are essential components to the flourishing of culture, friendship, strengthening of economies, and the pursuit of a common peaceful world.

> "All life is dependent upon moral and ethical laws which protect earth, water, animals, plants, and tribal traditions and ceremonies. Humanity has the responsibility to live in accordance with natural laws, in order to perpetuate all living beings for the good of all Creation. We share a bond with all the world's Peoples who understand their relationship and responsibility to all aspects of the Creation. The first of these is to walk through life in respectful and loving ways, caring for all life. We look forward to a future of global friendship and the integrity of diverse cultures."

Welcome to *North American Indian Landmarks*. It is a good step toward making the next 500 years different from the last ones—a clear path for a personal journey.

NORTHEAST

NORTHEAST

CONNECTICUT
1 Fort Shantock State Park, *Mohegan*
2 Tantaquidgeon Lodge Museum, *Mohegan*
3 Indian Burial Grounds, *Norwich*
4 American Indian Archeological Institute, *Washington*

DELAWARE
5 Delaware State Museum, *Dover*
6 Nanticoke Museum, *Millsboro*

MAINE
7 Shell Heaps, *Damariscotta*
8 Penobscot Island and Museum, *Old Town*
9 Passamaquoddy Reservation, *Perry*
10 Fisherman Memorial, *Skowhegan*

MARYLAND AND WASHINGTON, D.C.
11 Lacrosse Hall of Fame, *Baltimore*
12 National Museum of the American Indian, *Washington, D.C.*
13 National Museum of Natural History and the Interior Museum, *Washington, D.C.*

MASSACHUSETTS
14 Aptuxcet Trading *Post, Bourne*
15 Mohawk Memorial, *Charlemont*
16 Old Indian Meeting House, *Mashpee*
17 Massasoit Memorial, *Plymouth*
18 Mayhew Chapel, *West Tisbury*

NEW YORK
19 Iroquois Indian Museum, *Cobleskill*
20 The National Shrine of Kateri Tekakwitha, *Fonda*
21 Onondaga Reservation, *Nedrow*
22 Museum of the American Indian, *New York*
23 Native American Center for the Living Arts, *Niagara Falls*
24 Letchworth Museum and Seneca Council House, *Portageville*
25 Seneca–Iroquois National Museum, *Salamanca*
26 Shinnecock Reservation, *Southampton*

PENNSYLVANIA
27 Pocono Indian Museum, *Bushkill*
28 Indian School, *Carlisle*
29 Jim Thorpe Memorial, *Jim Thorpe*
30 Battle of Wyoming, *Wilkes–Barre*

QUEBEC
31 Canadian Museum of Civilization, *Hull*
32 Abenakis Museum, *Odanak*

RHODE ISLAND
33 King Philip's War, *Bristol*
34 Narragansett Burial Ground, *Charlestown*
35 Canochet Memorial, *Narragansett*

VIRGINIA
36 St. John's Church Pocahontas Window, *Hampton*
37 Pocahontas Statue, *Jamestown*
38 Powhatan Indian Village, *Jamestown*
39 Pamunkey Indian Museum, *Lanesville*

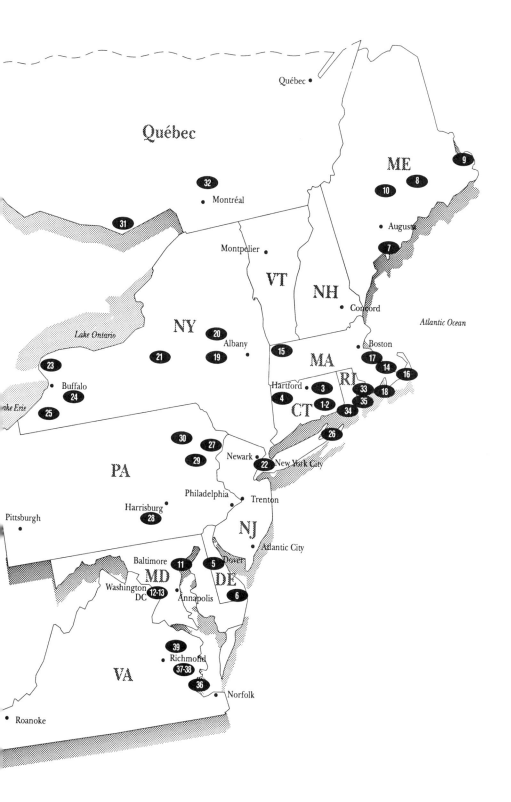

CONNECTICUT

FORT SHANTOCK STATE PARK

E arly in the seventeenth century, the Pequot came into the valley of the Thames as a powerful, united people, migrating from somewhere to the northwest. But political rivalries were taking shape. As English settlers began moving into Connecticut in the 1630s, Sassacus, the grand sachem (chief) of the Pequot, decided to oppose them. But his brother-in-law, Uncas, saw in the arrival of the colonists his main chance.

Uncas aspired to power and saw that an alliance with the colonists could give him the leverage he needed to unseat Sassacus. The Pequot War of 1637 was the first clash between Native Americans and colonists in the East. Had the Pequot, who numbered about four thousand, remained united and made an alliance with the Narragansett, as Sassacus wanted, they might have been able to drive the settlers out of their territory. But when Uncas formed a new tribe, the Mohegan, and enlisted on the English side, the Pequot cause became hopeless. In two battles that turned into slaughters, one at the main Pequot village near the mouth of the Mystic River, the other in the swamps outside of present-day Fairfield, the Pequot were destroyed. The tribe was dispersed and Sassacus forced to flee to the Mohawk, where he was killed. (A small group who identify themselves as the Mashantucket Pequot now make their home in the village of Ledyard, about five miles away on the eastern side of the Thames.)

Uncas, meanwhile, remained an ally with England, which proved useful in another eight years. The Mohegan and Narragansett went to war over the Pequot lands—lands that would be lost to the English within a generation. Uncas was besieged in his fort above the Thames but managed to get word through to his white allies. Lieutenant Thomas Leffingwell led a relief column up the river by canoe and lifted the siege. In gratitude, Uncas gave Leffingwell title to land that became the city of Norwich.

The Mohegan remained on the English side through King Philip's War, in the 1670s. But with all other Indian threats removed from the area, the Mohegan were of no further use as allies and by the eighteenth century had lost their ancestral lands. Most eventually moved to New York, into Oneida country. It was here that young James Fenimore Cooper grew up and heard bits and pieces of the story of the Mohegans and Uncas's alliance with England. In later life, he moved the event about one hundred years ahead in time and in *The Last of the Mohicans* portrayed Uncas as fighting with the Redcoats in the French and Indian War. Cooper's novel was the first popular treatment of Indians in a sympathetic manner, and the popularity of his novels in Europe gave rise to the cult of the Noble Red Man. So this rather obscure Pequot dissident carried an influence that lasted far beyond his own life. His policies could not save his own people, but they made Uncas immortal.

Fort Shantok preserves the site of Uncas's fort, above the town of Mohegan. Many of its residents are descendants of the tribe. In the cemetery near the fort are several Indian graves, among them that of Fidelia Fowler. According to the marker, Fowler, who died in 1908, was the last man who could speak both the Pequot and Mohegan languages. In that regard, he truly was the last of the Mohegans.

LOCATION: *The state park is 1 mile north of Mohegan by way of Connecticut 32.*
EXHIBITS: *The outline of the fortification is traced, and there are markers dedicated to Uncas and Leffingwell.*
HOURS: *Daily, dawn to dusk.*
ADMISSION: *Free.*

TANTAQUIDGEON LODGE MUSEUM

The Tantaquidgeon Lodge Museum, devoted to objects of the Mohegans and other New England tribes, was founded by John and Harold Tantaquidgeon. They were descendants of a famed Mohegan leader who captured the Narragansett chief Miantonomo in a battle fought five miles north of here in 1645. Traditional crafts and tools are displayed, as well as examples of typical New England Indian dwellings.

Many other buildings in this town, including the adjacent Congregational Church, built in 1831, are associated with the group of Mohegans who chose not to accompany the main body of the tribe west to New York in the eighteenth century. Also born here was Samson Occum, the first ordained minister from his tribe. His preaching caused such a sensation in England that money was raised to found the first school of higher education for Indian youths in America, an institution that developed into Dartmouth College.

LOCATION: *The museum is at 1819 Norwich-New London Turnpike (Connecticut 32).*
HOURS: *Tuesday through Sunday, 10–4, May through October.*
ADMISSION: *Donation.*
TELEPHONE: *(203) 849-9145.*

Norwich

INDIAN BURIAL GROUNDS

T he Indian Burial Grounds is traditionally believed to be the resting place of Uncas. The grounds were maintained as a burial site for sachems (chiefs) and their relatives by the Mohegan. When Europeans took over the land and built the town of Norwich around it, they respected its sanctity. The cornerstone of the monument to Uncas was laid in 1833 by President Andrew Jackson, an exercise in political hypocrisy by a man whose domestic policy was based on unremitting hostility toward Indians and their removal to the West. The monument's shaft was completed in 1842.

LOCATION: *The burial ground is just off Connecticut 32, on the corner of Washington and Sachem Streets.*
HOURS: *Daily, dawn to dusk.*
ADMISSION: *Free.*

Washington

INSTITUTE FOR AMERICAN INDIAN STUDIES

I n one of the more scenic corners of Connecticut, high in the Litchfield Hills, the Institute for American Indian Studies displays the way the earliest residents of Connecticut lived. The Museum, which also serves as an educational and research center, is dedicated to findings among ancient Algonquian settlements in the area, as well as other prehistoric artifacts. Other exhibits, such as longhouses and wigwams, are from more recent Indian epochs, and are exceptionally well displayed. This is one of the most intelligently presented Indian museums in the East.

▲ *A reconstructed Algonkian Village (circa 1600) at the Institute for American Indian Studies.*

LOCATION: *South of Washington at the junction of Connecticut Highways 199 and 47. The town is 14 miles from the Southbury exit of Interstate 84.*
HOURS: *Monday through Saturday, 10–4:30; Sunday, 12–4:30.*
ADMISSION: *$2.50.*
TELEPHONE: *(203) 868-0518.*

DELAWARE

DELAWARE STATE MUSEUM

I n the sandy strip along Delaware Bay, near the old oystering town turned cottage resort of South Bowers, the remains of an Indian culture more than twelve hundred years old were found. The area is closed now but items from the site have been incorporated into the collection at Delaware State Museum. Many of the artifacts found at South Bowers suggest that the site was an outpost of the Woodland Indian culture, with trade connections as far west as Ohio.

The museum is located on Meeting House Square, which was laid out by William Penn in 1717.

LOCATION: *The museum is just south of town, at 316 South Governors Avenue, Dover.*
EXHIBITS: *Museum with audiovisual displays and portions of the ancient cemetery.*
HOURS: *Tuesday through Saturday, 10–3:30; closed State Holidays.*
ADMISSION: *Free.*
TELEPHONE: *(302) 739-4266.*

NANTICOKE MUSEUM

T he survival of this group is a tribute to the perseverance of a small group of individuals who over the generations refused to surrender their tribal identity. The Nanticoke once occupied the middle section of the Delmarva Peninsula, building their villages on the rivers that ran inland from Delaware and Chesapeake bays. John Smith visited them from Jamestown in 1608 and noted their industrious habits with approval.

But with the settlement of the Maryland colony, successive encroach-ments were made on their lands. Reservations were set aside, redrawn, shrunk. Finally, in 1742, the Nanticoke were accused of taking part in a rebellion plot and forced to relinquish the right to choose a chief, or emperor. Finding it impossible to conduct tribal affairs under those conditions, they requested permission from the Iroquois to move into their lands, on the Susquehanna River in southern New York. Eventually, they joined them in exile to Canada after the Revolutionary War.

One tiny remnant chose to stay in southern Delaware to cling to their identity as Nanticoke. They formed a tightly knit community in the area known as Angola Neck, ridiculed by both their white and black neighbors for what was regarded as a spurious claim to Indian ancestry. The state, however, was sympathetic in a backhanded way. During the days of segregation, it set up four separate school systems in the area: white, black, "Moor" (a group who considered themselves an Indian-Negro mixture), and Nanticoke. The com-munity of Harmon School, midway between Millsboro and Angola, preserves the name of the "Moor" school. Nonetheless, the Nanticoke tried to keep alive certain rituals they had come to associate with their Indian identity. Finally, in 1922, with the help of testimony from University of Pennsylvania anthropolo-gists, they were given the legal right to incorporate as a tribe. They now operate this small museum and hold an annual gathering.

Housed in what was once a community schoolhouse, the museum contains exhibits of artifacts, implements, clothing, and other American Indi-an articles. A resource center contains information on the Nanticoke Indians and other Native American groups. Since its beginning in 1977, the tribe's annual powwow has drawn more than 10,000 people. The cultural celebration, held on the second weekend in September, includes Nanticoke dancers, sing-ers, and drummers who wear native beadwork, featherwork, quillwork, and carvings.

LOCATION: *The Nanticoke Museum is located just north of Millsboro on Delaware 24.*
HOURS: *Tuesday through Thursday, 9–4; Saturday, 12–4.*
ADMISSION: *Suggested donation: Adults $1, Children 50 cents.*
TELEPHONE: *(302) 945-7022.*

MAINE

SHELL HEAPS

I n the spring months, the Abnaki tribes would descend the inland rivers on which they lived in colder weather and begin to harvest the sea. They fished the shallow waters and dug for shellfish along the tidal inlets, subsisting on their catch and smoking what remained for food during the long winter. For centuries they gathered near the mouth of the Damariscotta River, a rich clamming center, well into the twentieth century. The piles of discarded shells that they used here were then mixed with the soil to a depth of about six feet. The shell heaps have been uncovered and give an astonishing picture of the work of perhaps one thousand summers by the Abnaki on the Maine coast.

LOCATION: *The shell heaps are north of town, on a road branching off U.S. 1 Business to the river.*
HOURS: *Daily, dawn to dusk.*
ADMISSION: *Free.*

PENOBSCOT ISLAND AND MUSEUM

T he Abnaki Confederacy dominated what is now Maine in precolonial times. It consisted of three tribes, the Penobscot, Passamaquoddy, and Malecite. They were an agricultural people who lived in fortified villages and also fished extensively in the rivers and coastal areas of Maine.

Their typical homes were dome shaped and covered with birch bark and woven mats. The Abnaki name for these habitations was wigwam. English settlers picked up the word and applied it to the homes built by all Indian peoples.

Early New Englanders were convinced the Abnaki controlled all of North America as far south as Virginia, and seventeenth-century maps reflected this belief. A chief named Bashaba was credited with ruling over this entire domain from an island stronghold on the Norumbega River. Both the river and Bashaba's tribe later became known as the Penobscot, a word that means "it flows on rocks," which is the perfect description of the rippling waters.

We know that the Penobscot were the largest tribe of the Abnaki and that their influence did not extend beyond central Maine. The Abnaki aligned themselves with France in the colonial wars. As a result, most of the confederacy, especially the western tribes, were forced to flee to Quebec by the middle of the eighteenth century. But the Penobscot stayed, retreating to the island that so fascinated the settlers, which became known as Indian Island. The settlement there was called Old Town in Abnaki, because of the countless generations they had been living there. The white community that formed a few miles farther south on the river took the same name.

The island is now part of the Penobscot Reservation, which consists of 146 islands in the river. This is the only one inhabited year-round, though. Unlike other reservations, the Penobscot come under the auspices of the state rather than the federal government, and the tribe is represented in the Maine legislature.

The island was accessible only by boat until 1951, when a bridge was opened. The Penobscot National Historical Society Museum on the island contains exhibits of the history and crafts of this tribe, which now numbers just a few hundred members. There is also an annual pageant with traditional dances and ceremonies during the last week of July. Call in advance for the exact date.

Those with a taste for sports history will want to look for the grave of Louis Sockalexis in the Protestant cemetery. An outstanding athlete at Holy Cross University, he was regarded as the finest Native American baseball player of his era. When he joined the Cleveland team in 1897, the excitement was such that its name was changed to the Indians, a title it has borne ever since, to the irritation of many Native American leaders. His career was short-lived, however, and Sockalexis died here in 1913.

LOCATION: *Indian Island is reached from U.S. 2, just north of Old Town.*
HOURS: *Monday through Friday, 10–4.*
ADMISSION: *Donation asked.*
TELEPHONE: *(207) 827-6544.*

Perry

PASSAMAQUODDY RESERVATION

The Passamaquoddy were the easternmost tribe of the Abnaki, and they still retain that distinction within the United States. The reservation overlooks Passamaquoddy Bay from its perch on a windswept Atlantic spit just a few miles from the most easterly point on the American mainland.

The Point Pleasant Reservation, just southeast of Perry, is the administrative center for all of Maine's coastal native lands. There are shops here featuring intricately handwoven baskets. In the cemetery, the Daughters of the American Revolution have erected a monument in memory of the Passamaquoddy who fought with the colonials during the War for Independence.

On August 1, there is a Ceremonial Day celebration featuring dances and traditional rituals.

LOCATION: *The reservation is located on Maine 190, south from U.S. 1 at Perry on the road to Eastport.*
TELEPHONE: *(207) 853-2551.*

Skowhegan

FISHERMAN MEMORIAL

Skowhegan was another Abnaki settlement on an island in a stream, in this case the Kennebec River. The name means "place to watch," and the pool below the falls here was a favored fishing spot for river salmon. Maine sculptor Bernard Langlais commemorated the Abnaki with a sixty-two-foot-high pine carving of one of these ancient watchers. Unveiled in 1960, it stands close to the falls in central Skowhegan.

LOCATION: *Center of town, on U.S. 201.*
HOURS: *Daily, dawn to dusk.*
ADMISSION: *Free.*

MARYLAND / WASHINGTON, D.C.

LACROSSE HALL OF FAME

L ong before anyone ever thought of baseball, the pastime of Native Americans was ball-and-stick games. All across the continent, European explorers noted the prevalence of such games and the significance they occupied in each culture. In some areas, such games were used to settle disputes between factions or neighboring tribes. The Choctaw were famous for that sort of athletic diplomacy. Other ball courts found in Mexico and Central America seemed to carry a religious significance, although precisely what it may have been is uncertain.

Among the tribes of the northern United States, lacrosse was the most commonly played game. Many woodland tribes in the Great Lakes area, especially, cleared a space that was set aside for the game near every village. It was a carefully staged game of lacrosse that lulled the British garrison at Fort Michilimackinac into letting its guard down, with fatal results for them, in the opening act of Pontiac's Rebellion of 1763.

Among the Iroquois, the game was called *baggataway* and was played on an intertribal basis. The French gave the game its current name because it resembled a European sport they were familiar with called *chouler a la crosse*. It was popular with both French and English colonists, and developed into a major college sport in the late nineteenth century. It was even included as part of the Olympic Games in 1904 and 1908. Over the years, it became established at schools in the East (especially in the Middle Atlantic states) and Canada, and many of its greatest players have been of Indian ancestry. Johns Hopkins University is noted for its medical school rather than its athletic prowess, but it excels at lacrosse, having won seven NCAA titles between 1974 and 1987. Appropriately, the game's Hall of Fame is on its campus, and many displays feature Native American athletes who starred in the past.

LOCATION: *The Johns Hopkins campus is north of downtown, on Charles at 34th Streets. The Hall of Fame is housed within the Newton H. White, Jr., Athletic Center.*
HOURS: *Monday through Friday, 10–4, and open during home lacrosse games.*
ADMISSION: *Free.*
TELEPHONE: *(301) 235-6882.*

Washington, D.C.

NATIONAL MUSEUM OF THE AMERICAN INDIAN

Until recently, there has been no museum dedicated exclusively to Native Americans in either the federal or Smithsonian complexes of the nation's capitol. In May 1989, the Heye Foundation and the Smithsonian Institution signed an agreement to transfer the collections of the Museum of the American Indian to the Smithsonian. Later that year, an act of Congress established the National Museum of the American Indian as part of the Smithsonian.

The collections, currently housed in the Audubon Building in upper Manhattan and in a research branch in the Bronx, include some one million artifacts, spanning more than 10,000 years; there are objects from the entire Western Hemisphere, from the Arctic to Tierra del Fuego. It is acknowledged to be one of the finest collections of Native American cultural material in the world.

A major new museum will be built on the last available space on the National Mall in Washington, D.C., the preliminary estimate for which is $106 million. The site is across the street from the National Air and Space Museum and near the U.S. Capitol, and is bounded by Independence Avenue, Third Street, Fourth Street, Jefferson Drive and Maryland Avenue in southwest Washington, D.C.

Scheduled to open by the end of the decade, the museum's formal mission statement reads as follows: The National Museum of the American Indian shall recognize and affirm to native communities and the non-native public the historical and contemporary culture and cultural achievements of the natives of the Western Hemisphere by advancing—in consultation, collaboration and cooperation with natives—knowledge and understanding of native cultures, including art, history and language, and by recognizing the museum's special responsibility, through innovative public programming, research and collections, to protect, support and enhance the development, maintenance and perpetuation of Native culture and community.

In addition to the Washington, D.C. site, the museum will operate a significant exhibition and education facility in lower Manhattan in the Alexander Hamilton U.S. Custom House, and will be known as the George Gustav

Heye Center of the National Museum of the American Indian. A collections research center for the museum will be located at the Smithsonian's Museum Support Center in Suitland, Maryland, and will accommodate associated activities such as research, collections conservation, exhibition support functions and community services. For more about the National Museum of the American Indian, Heye Foundation, *see* The National Museum of the American Indian, New York.

NATIONAL MUSEUM OF NATURAL HISTORY AND THE INTERIOR MUSEUM

Until the Smithsonian took over the Heye Foundation's collection (*see* the Museum of the American Indian under New York and Washington), there was no museum dedicated exclusively to Native Americans in either the federal or Smithsonian complexes of the nation's capital. Up until the Smithsonian's agreement with the Heye Foundation, the best representatives of Native American artifacts in the District of Columbia were the National Museum of Natural History and the offices of the Department of the Interior.

The first of these museums is part of the Smithsonian group, but its primary tourist high points are dinosaurs, the Hope Diamond, and a life-size model of a blue whale. The Native American exhibits, although done with the Smithsonian's customary flair, simply do not make an especially memorable impression.

The Interior Museum houses photographs, historic and contemporary artifacts that tell the story of the department's nine bureaus, including the Bureau of Indian Affairs. Holdings include two thousand American Indian artifacts, although only a small portion of those are currently on display. The museum's best collections come from California, the Southwest, and the Northwest coast. Displays include ceramics of the San Ildefonso Pueblo, intricately designed Pima baskets, Alaskan tribal crafts, and colorful bird feather baskets from the Pomo tribe. There is also a small shop on the premises selling Indian-made items.

LOCATION: *The Natural History Museum faces The Mall, on the south side of Constitution Avenue at 10th Street, NW. The Interior offices are between C and E and 18th and 19th Streets, NW.*
HOURS: *Natural History Museum is open daily, 10–5:30. Interior Museum is open Monday through Friday, 8–5.*
ADMISSION: *Both museums are free.*
TELEPHONE: *Natural History is (202) 357-2700. Interior is (202) 208-2743.*

MASSACHUSETTS

APTUXCET TRADING POST

S even years after landing at Plymouth, the basics of survival secured, the Pilgrims were ready to get down to business. Their contacts with the Native Americans to the south, between Buzzards Bay and Narragansett Bay, had been friendly thanks to the personal relationship between the leaders of the Plymouth Colony and the Wampanoag chief, Massasoit. The colonists decided to establish an outpost in their territory to establish trade between them on a regular basis, and in 1627 the Aptuxcet Trading Post was opened at the shoulder of Cape Cod. The Dutch, who had set up a colony at Manhattan Island the previous year, also came to Aptuxcet.

While the post survived just a few years, it was the prototype of the sort of business that would precede European expansion across the continent. The trading posts introduced the concept of goods that were valued not because they served any basic necessity but because they were scarce. That undercut the Native American way of life, which was based on need and availability. It drew them into the rivalries and trade wars between the colonial powers, but also secured for them weapons and tools that altered their way of viewing the world. Aptuxcet may not actually be the first such trading post in America. There is evidence that the Dutch had set up a similar operation before actually establishing their colony of New Amsterdam. But it is the oldest to have been restored, and it gives an indication of what one such post looked like at the dawn of Indian-European trade.

LOCATION: *Aptuxcet is just west of the U.S. 6 bridge over the Cape Cod Canal, on Shore Road.*

EXHIBITS: *The post is set up as it would have looked in the 1620s, with the trade goods and furnishings that would likely have been found here then.*

HOURS: *Monday through Saturday, 10–5; Sunday, 1–5, mid-April to mid-October. Closed Wednesday, except in July and August.*

ADMISSION: *$2.*

TELEPHONE: *(617) 759-7597.*

MOHAWK MEMORIAL

The Mohawk Trail was among the first scenic automobile roads built in the East, opening in 1915 and running west from Boston through some of Massachusetts's finest mountain greenery. The name is something of a misnomer, however. While the Mohawk were the easternmost tribe of the Iroquois Confederacy, their homes were situated to the west of the Hudson, in what is now New York State. There is some evidence that they carried on trade with tribes along the Atlantic seaboard, however, so maybe some Mohawk actually did walk this trail. The memorial was built shortly after the road was opened. The eight-foot statue of a Native American looking out proudly across the land is situated on a knoll above the Deerfield River, facing an inspiring vista of Hoosac Mountain. Its official name is *Hail to the Sunrise* .

LOCATION: *The memorial is 2 miles west of Charlemont on Massachusetts 2.*
HOURS: *Daily, dawn to dusk.*
ADMISSION: *Free.*

OLD INDIAN MEETING HOUSE

The Mashpee occupied the Cape Cod boglands at the time of European colonization, and are believed to have been part of the Wampanoag tribe. Richard Bourne worked among them as a missionary, and in 1660 managed to get 10,500 acres set aside for them, which may be the earliest attempt at setting up a reservation in North America. It no longer exists, however, and most of those who identify themselves as Mashpee are employed in cranberry farming in this area. The meeting house of the Christianized tribe was built in 1684. This typical New England church, with its box pews and organ gallery, is among the oldest surviving Indian houses of worship in the country. The burial grounds hold the remains of many early members of the congregation.

LOCATION: *The meeting house is just north of Massachusetts 28, 1 mile past the turnoff to the village of Mashpee.*
HOURS: *The interior is open to visits only on weekends, June to October. It is best to call in advance.*
ADMISSION: *Donation asked.*
TELEPHONE: *(617) 477-0208.*

Plymouth

MASSASOIT MEMORIAL

About three months after the landing of the Pilgrims in Plymouth, the chief of the Wampanoag received word of their arrival at his home, atop Mount Hope, near what is now Bristol, Rhode Island. Drawn by curiosity about these newcomers, he walked the sixty miles to their encampment in March 1621, accompanied by several tribesmen. Among them was Squanto, who had been kidnapped by a party of English slavers years before and managed to escape, after picking up the rudiments of the language. So in this first meeting of Indians and Europeans in Massachusetts, the Englishmen were astonished to be addressed in their own tongue.

Before returning home, Massasoit signed a treaty of alliance with King James I. He really had no choice: it was not a good time for his people. A mysterious illness, now believed to have been jaundice, had swept over the tribe and reduced their fighting capacity to about sixty men. Massasoit badly needed allies to help his people fend off any possible assaults from their neighbors. The English with their guns and armor seemed perfectly suited for this task. For his part, Massasoit had no idea how desperate the colonists were. They had lost more than half the 102 original members of the settlement during the first winter and buried them secretly in Coles Hill. So it was two emaciated groups of human beings who met here and decided to help each other.

The story about Squanto teaching the English how to plant corn is probably apocryphal, although he may have shown them the technique of using dead fish as fertilizer. A series of visits between the two groups ensued, culminating in the mythic Thanksgiving feast, probably held in December 1621, to which Massasoit contributed several deer.

Massasoit permitted the English to send missionaries among his tribe, although he himself clung to the traditional beliefs. He also agreed to land purchases, which weakened the Wampanoag hold on the best hunting and fishing grounds. The relationship deteriorated and could not survive his death in 1661. The terrible King Philip's War, which virtually eradicated the Indian presence in southern New England, followed (*see* King Philip's War, Bristol,

Rhode Island). But the memory of Massasoit's friendship and how it enabled the colony to take root is part of American legend. His statue, sculpted by Cyrus Dallin, was placed, fittingly enough, at the crest of Coles Hill, where the victims of the first Pilgrim winter in America are interred.

LOCATION: *Coles Hill is opposite Plymouth Rock, in the heart of historic Plymouth.*
HOURS: *Daily, dawn to dusk.*
ADMISSION: *Free.*

West Tisbury

MAYHEW CHAPEL

After the disastrous King Philip's War, the remnant of the Wampanoag people survived on the island of Martha's Vineyard. The rest were either dead, sold into slavery, or absorbed by the Saconnet tribe. But the island branch of the Wampanoag had refused to join the war. Most had been converted to Christianity by the Reverend Thomas Mayhew and were referred to as "praying Indians." That designation had not been enough to save most mainland converts. The colonists were fired with zeal to kill any Indians they could reach, whether allied with Philip or not. But the reservation established by Mayhew on the Vineyard in 1659 escaped the worst of the bloodshed.

Many Vineyard natives are of Wampanoag ancestry, and they maintain a tribal council in Gay Head. Examples of their traditional colored clay pottery are for sale in stores in most of the island's resorts. The little chapel in West Tisbury is a memorial to the praying Indians who kept the tribal identity alive on the island.

LOCATION: *The chapel is located on South Indian Hill Road, between West Tisbury and Vineyard Haven.*
EXHIBIT: *Besides the chapel, there is an Indian burial ground and wildflower sanctuary. West Tisbury is noted on the Vineyard for the number and variety of its wildflowers.*
HOURS: *Daily, dawn to dusk.*
ADMISSION: *Donation.*

NEW YORK

IROQUOIS INDIAN MUSEUM

About fifty years before the landing of Columbus, the fertile lands of central New York held a wide mixture of tribes. Warfare was almost constant and there was no opportunity to enjoy the abundance of the good lands around them. It was at this time that two visionary leaders appeared. One was named Dekanawida. Thought to be a Huron by birth, he began to preach the concept of a great confederacy of all the Iroquoian tribes. If they united in peaceful cooperation, he said, they could concentrate on trade and combine against any hostile rivals.

His teachings initially met with ridicule. But he won over a powerful ally, Hiawatha, a Mohawk who lived among the Onondaga and saw the logic in Dekanawida's plan. A gifted orator, he traveled among the tribes to explain how a confederation would enhance the strength of all. He finally convinced the powerful Onondaga by promising them the balance of power in the confederacy, and for the next three hundred years the Iroquois became the most powerful Native American force in the East, both economically and militarily. The original five tribes—Mohawk, Oneida, Onondaga, Cayuga, and Seneca—were joined in the eighteenth century by the Tuscarora to form the Six Nations. (When Henry Wadsworth Longfellow borrowed Hiawatha's name for his famous epic poem of the nineteenth century, he moved him several hundred miles to the northwest, in the northern Great Lakes, and set him down among the Chippewa. The Hiawatha of history, however, lived in New York.)

The Iroquois became the buffer between the colonial empires of France and England. Implacable enemies of the French, the confederates blocked them from expanding southward. Some of the confederacy later defected, but the majority of Iroquois aligned themselves with the British during the French and Indian War and during the American Revolution. In the revolution's bitter aftermath, many Iroquois were forced to resettle in Canada. But remnants of each member of the confederacy remained in New York on reservations.

Some scholars believe they also left behind a significant political heritage. The federal council of the Six Nations is regarded as one of the models

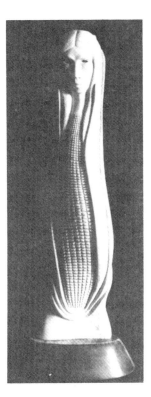

▲ *Artist Stan Hill's* Corn Spirit *(antler) is among the works on display at Iroquois Indian Museum.*

the Founding Fathers used in drawing up a system of government for the new American republic.

The stunning Iroquois Indian Museum, which opened in 1992, is built in the shape of an Iroquois longhouse. Through artifacts, artwork, crafts, and ceremonies, it tells the story of the Iroquois from the founding of the confederacy to contemporary tensions over tribal rights with the governments of New York and Quebec. A hands-on section has been set up to make the exhibits more meaningful for children. The exhibits show what everyday life was like in the traditional villages and the role each tribal member played in the group. Special displays explore the role of women, who determined clan affiliation and were also given a voice in political affairs. All members of the confederacy are represented in the museum, although the displays are particularly strong in Mohawk items, since the museum is located in "the Eastern Door," which was once their stronghold.

LOCATION: *The museum is adjacent to Howe's Cavern, on a side road running north from New York 7, just east of Cobleskill and accessible from the Central Bridge exit of Interstate 88.*
HOURS: *Daily, 10-5.*
ADMISSION: *$5.*
TELEPHONE: *(518) 296-8949.*

Fonda

THE NATIONAL SHRINE OF KATERI TEKAKWITHA

The Mohawk Valley was the battle line between French ambitions and Iroquois resistance in the mid-seventeenth century. Jesuits who attempted to establish missions in the area were suspected of being agents of the French government. In some cases, they were subject to death. Father Isaac Jogues came to work in this area and in 1642 was captured by the Mohawk. He was taken to the village of Ossernenon, tortured, and compelled to watch the execution of another priest before managing to escape. When he returned to the Mohawk Valley four years later, he was captured again and put to death. Jogues and two of his martyred companions were made the first north American saints by the Roman Catholic church in 1925.

Ten years after the death of Father Jogues, Kateri Tekakwitha was born in the village of his martyrdom. Her father was Mohawk, her mother a Christian of Algonquian descent. When a smallpox epidemic swept the village in 1660, both her parents were killed and she was left facially scarred for life. Taken to live with an uncle at the nearby village of Caughnawaga, she came under the influence of Christian teaching. She was baptized, took vows of virginity, and set about to live a life of dedicated piety. Forced by her relatives to wed, she instead fled to a Mohawk settlement near Montreal. Her religious ardor continued until she died at age 24 in 1680.

Since that time, several miraculous cures have been attributed to her. Known as The Lily of the Mohawks, she is now just one step from canonization and would be the first Native American to become a saint.

The site of her birthplace, Ossernenon, has been a place of Catholic pilgrimage for many years because of the martyrdom of the three priests. For centuries, the location of the village in which she grew up and was baptized was lost, but in 1950, archaeologists working in cooperation with the Albany Archdiocese determined that it had been located just west of Fonda, on the north bank of the Mohawk River, a few miles upstream from Ossernenon.

The outline of the village has been entirely excavated and staked out, the only such work done on a Mohawk site. A barn on the property was converted into a shrine and a small Indian museum, in which the story of Kateri is related. The site has become a place of pilgrimage for Catholic Native Americans from around the country.

> LOCATION: *The shrine is west of Fonda on New York 5. The National Kateri Tekakwitha Center is located at the National Shrine of North American Martyrs, 6 miles southeast, near the town of Auriesville, on New York 5S. There is another small museum there as well as informational material on Kateri.*
> HOURS: *The shrine is open daily, 9–4, mid-May to mid-October. The center is open daily, dawn to dusk, May through October.*
> ADMISSION: *Donations are asked.*
> TELEPHONE: *The shrine is (518) 853-3646. The Center is (518) 853-3033.*

Nedrow

ONONDAGA RESERVATION

In the days of the Iroquois Confederacy, it was the Onondaga who held the balance of power among the six affiliated tribes. They controlled fourteen of the fifty hereditary titles of sachem, more than any other tribe. The confederacy capital was always located in their main city, which also kept the Council Fire, and the chief of the council was always an Onondaga. At the height of Iroquois power, this capital was situated just east of Nedrow, near what is now the town of Pompey Center. From there, the confederacy governed a domain that stretched from Lake Michigan to the Hudson River and from Ontario's Lake Simcoe to central Pennsylvania.

The Onondaga remained loyal to Britain during the revolution, and afterward most of them were forced to relocate in Canada. Those who remained gathered on a small reservation south of the salt fields that would grow into the city of Syracuse. It was at this point, when the people's spirits were at their lowest, that a remarkable figure appeared among the Iroquois.

His name was Ganeodaio, which he translated as Handsome Lake. A heavy drinker and aimless spirit, he had accomplished nothing of note until age 64. Dissipated and apparently near death, he experienced a spiritual awakening and began to preach among the Iroquois remaining in New York. He advocated returning to traditional values and renouncing strong drink, and called his message the Longhouse Religion; with some borrowing from Christianity, it became a vital force among the Iroquois. It still has many adherents, especially among the Onondaga. On a trip to the Onondaga reservation in 1815, Handsome Lake died. His grave remains a place of pilgrimage.

Because the grounds are sacred, photography is not allowed.

LOCATION: *The reservation is located along New York 11A, south of Nedrow. The Grave of Handsome Lake, situated next to the Onondaga Council House, is 3 miles south of town.*
HOURS: *Daily, dawn to dusk.*
ADMISSION: *Free.*
TELEPHONE: *(315) 469-8507.*

New York

MUSEUM OF THE AMERICAN INDIAN

The Museum of the American Indian, Heye Foundation, has one of the finest and most comprehensive collections of Indian cultural materials in the world: it contains over one million artifacts, spanning 50,000 years, covering the cultures of native peoples from the Arctic Circle to the tip of Tierra del Fuego. The collection was assembled over a 54-year period, beginning in 1903, by George Gustav Heye (1874-1957), a New York banker who traveled throughout North and South America accumulating the collection.

The majority of the collection (70 percent) comes from North America (of which 67 percent is from the United States and 3 percent from Canada); approximately 30 percent of the collection comes from Central and South America. Artifacts include both rare and more commonplace items: Inuit (Eskimo) fur parkas; Karaja dance regalia; 2,000-year-old duck decoys; Geronimo's warrior cap and cane; Sitting Bull's war club; a feather bonnet worn by Crazy Horse; and the Van Cortlandt suit, one of the oldest extant deerskin suits made by Native Americans of New York.

The museum's collection policy takes great care to respect the cultural and spiritual values of the native peoples. The collection includes materials of not only cultural, historic, aesthetic and scientific significance, but also of profound spiritual and religious significance. For this reason, public access may be restricted if such access offends the religious or cultural practices of a tribal or cultural group. Religious and ceremonial objects are exhibited only after consultation with the appropriate culturally affiliated group, and planning of an exhibition's format is done in consultation with representatives of the tribe and/or culture involved to assure historical and cultural accuracy and to avoid desecration, insensitive treatment and inappropriate interpretation of religious or ceremonial materials.

The museum's board of trustees adopted a repatriation policy in 1991 that specifies that, upon request, human remains, funerary objects, communally owned native property, ceremonial and religious objects, and objects transferred to or acquired by the museum illegally, must be returned to their respective Indian tribes or individuals.

The museum's 1 million artifacts are currently housed in the National Museum of the American Indian on Broadway at 155th Street (in the Audubon building), and in the museum's research annex in the Bronx. In May 1989, the Heye Foundation and the Smithsonian Institution signed an agreement to transfer the collections of the Museum of the American Indian to the Smithsonian. Later that year, an act of Congress established the National Museum of the American Indian as part of the Smithsonian, making it the 15th museum of the Smithsonian Institution and the first national museum dedicated to the native peoples of this hemisphere. The new museum will be built on the last available space on the National Mall in Washington, D.C., and a collections research center for the museum will be located at the Smithsonian's Museum Support Center in Suitland, Maryland.

In addition to the Washington, D.C., site, the museum will operate a significant exhibition and education facility in lower Manhattan. The George Gustav Heye Center is scheduled to open in 1994 with an exhibit tentatively titled "Points of View," which will contain approximately 700 objects illustrating the diversity and continuity of native cultures. Three other exhibitions scheduled to open in 1994 are: an exhibit tentatively titled "Celebrations," which will be a collaboration of native painters, sculptors, writers, and dancers; an orientation exhibit; and a major exhibition from one of the premier museums of American Indian art in North America. The center will be housed in the Alexander Hamilton U.S. Custom House (formerly known as the Old U.S. Custom House), a Beaux Arts-style building that is a designated National Historic Landmark and a New York City landmark.

For more about the Smithsonian's new facility in Washington, scheduled to open by the end of the decade, *see* The National Museum of the American Indian, Washington, D.C.

LOCATION: *The museum is at Broadway and 155th Street, in upper Manhattan.*
HOURS: *Tuesday through Saturday, 10–5; Sunday, 1–5.*
ADMISSION: *$3 adults; $2 students and senior citizens.*
TELEPHONE: *(212) 283-2420.*

NATIVE AMERICAN CENTER FOR THE LIVING ARTS

The Native American Center for the Living Arts is a distinctive turtle-shaped museum (its nickname is The Turtle) that focuses on the traditions, lore, and symbols of Native Americans as expressed in art. The turtle is a powerful figure in the creation myths of many native cultures, and several tribes in the Iroquois Confederacy—the Mohawk, Cayuga, and Oneida—had a Turtle clan. Art exhibits and dance performances are held here throughout the summer months, and there is also a crafts shop. Many North American tribes are represented, although the center emphasizes Iroquois traditions.

LOCATION: *The museum is just a few blocks from the American falls, in downtown Niagara Falls, at 25 Rainbow Boulevard Mall.*
HOURS: *Daily, 9–6, May through September; 12–5, closed Mondays and weekends rest of year.*
ADMISSION: *$4.*
TELEPHONE: *(716) 284-2427.*

LETCHWORTH MUSEUM AND SENECA COUNCIL HOUSE

In October 1872, an extraordinary gathering was held in newly created Letchworth State Park, along the gorge of the Genesee River. Buffalo processor William P. Letchworth, who donated much of the land for the park, was also interested in displaying local Indian culture. He arranged for an exceptionally fine example of a Senecan longhouse to be moved here from Canada, in the heart of what had been the Seneca homeland, several miles to the south. The Seneca were the most numerous tribe of the Iroquois Confederacy, and its warriors had carried Iroquois authority as far west as the Illinois country.

When this longhouse, measuring fifty by twenty feet, was brought here, Letchworth decided to convene a historic council. The grandson of Joseph Brant was invited to represent the Mohawk. Descendants of the great Seneca leaders, Red Jacket and Cornplanter, who had remained friendly to the American cause during the War of 1812, also attended. Sitting at the same council fire was former U.S. President Millard Fillmore. The Seneca adopted Letch-worth into the tribe at the ceremony, giving him the name "man who always does the right thing." While Red Jacket was regarded as one of the greatest of all orators among the Iroquois, this gesture seemed to prove that the art of always saying the right thing lived on among his descendants. The Seneca Council House is part of the Letchworth Pioneer and Indian Museum.

LOCATION: *The museum is located 5 miles in from the park's southern boundary, on New York 19A.*
HOURS: *The museum is open Tuesday through Friday, 11–5; weekends, 10–6, May through October.*
ADMISSION: *Free with $2.50 state park fee.*
TELEPHONE: *(716) 493-2611.*

Salamanca

SENECA-IROQUOIS NATIONAL MUSEUM

T he Seneca were the Keepers of the Western Door in the Iroquois Confed-eracy. But after the American Revolution, the door of history slammed shut on them. Troops who had ravaged their villages during the punitive Sullivan-Clinton raid in 1779 spread the word in the East about the fertility and beauty of the Iroquois land. With the coming of peace, they returned by the hundreds and their neighbors by the thousands. Many of the Seneca moved to Canada, and those who stayed were forced to relinquish their claim to the lands in the Big Tree Treaty of 1797.

The Seneca made a treaty with Philadelphia financier Robert Morris, who in turn sold it to the Holland Company. The treaty allotted the tribe twelve parcels of land as reservations. Under the preemption rights reserved to the buyers, however, these parcels were reduced to four in 1810. There followed a shameful period in which corrupt Seneca chiefs accepted payoffs from speculators for the remaining land. In 1842, state courts ruled that these agreements were nonbinding, and the tribe regained title to the land. The experience convinced the Seneca to do away with the traditional tribal govern-ment to form an elective republic, a system that still exists today.

Because of all the land switches, Salamanca wound up as the only white town in America located in the middle of a reservation. The Seneca-Iroquois Museum is at the western edge of town. It gives visitors a glimpse of this rich tribal history, with examples of wampum belts and various clan animals, and a sampling of both traditional and contemporary crafts.

LOCATION: *The museum is just off New York 17, on the Broad Street Extension, at the western Salamanca exit.*
HOURS: *Monday through Saturday, 10–5; Sunday, 12–5, May through September; closed Monday, rest of year.*
ADMISSION: *Donation.*
TELEPHONE: *(716) 945-1738.*

Southampton

SHINNECOCK NATION CULTURAL CENTER COMPLEX

On four hundred acres of some of the most expensive seaside real estate in America, the Shinnecock hang on to the reservation lands set aside for them in 1703. The tribe was part of the Montauk Confederacy that ranged across eastern Long Island at the time of European settlement. In 1640, colonists from Massachusetts purchased from Nowdeonah, the Shinnecock chief, the land where the elegant resort of Southampton now lies.

Whaling was vital to the colonists' economy, and the Shinnecock made up a large part of the crews who sailed from the old port of Sag Harbor. But when that industry went into decline, most were forced to leave to seek other means of employment. The few that remain hold an annual powwow, on Labor Day weekend, with traditional dances and crafts.

LOCATION: *The center is on New York 27A, Montauk Highway.*
HOURS: *Monday through Friday, 9–5.*
ADMISSION: *Free.*
TELEPHONE: *(516) 287-4923.*

PENNSYLVANIA

POCONO INDIAN MUSEUM

T he British called them the Delaware, after the name they had given to the great river on which most of the tribe's villages were found. They called themselves Lenni Lenapee, which roughly translates as "real men." The other Algonquian tribes referred to them as "grandfather," in recognition of their ancient origins and position of preeminence in the area between the Delaware and Hudson rivers.

They first came into contact with Europeans in 1609, when they encountered Henry Hudson on his first voyage up the river that bears his name. The competition for manufactured goods that Hudson set in motion involved the area tribes in the fur trade and in the colonial ambitions of the European powers. This was ruinous to the Delaware: by the late seventeenth century, they had become dominated by the more powerful Iroquois and their lands had been reduced to eastern Pennsylvania.

Their chief village, Shackamaxon, was located within what is now Philadelphia. It was there that they signed a treaty with William Penn in 1686. Penn was a decent man who respected Indian claims, but his successors were more devious. One provision of the treaty was the Walking Purchase, which permitted white land claims over a territory that could be covered in a walk of a day and a half. Penn observed the spirit of the agreement, and his walk was done in a leisurely fashion.

In 1737, the governor asked for the clause to be reopened, and the Delaware obliged. This time the governor hired trained walkers, provided with packhorses, who covered more than sixty miles in the stipulated time. One of the walkers, Edward Marshall, made his own claim in the area; a town a few miles south, Marshalls Creek, is named for him.

The Delaware were defrauded of their homeland and in a few more years were totally displaced by the Iroquois in negotiations with whites. The Walking Purchase began the slow western migration of the Delaware, with tragic interludes in Ohio (*see* Gnadenhutten and New Philadelphia, Ohio) and Kansas. Today the remnants of the tribe are scattered across portions of Oklahoma, Wisconsin, and Ontario, while many more have been absorbed by the Cherokee.

The Pocono Indian Museum, near the Delaware Water Gap, lies amid the lands taken from the tribe in the notorious purchase. The museum contains displays of Delaware housing and tools, most of which were uncovered in nearby excavations.

LOCATION: *The museum is south of town, on U.S. 209.*
HOURS: *Daily, 9:30–6.*
ADMISSION: *$2.50.*
TELEPHONE: *(717) 588-9338.*

Carlisle

INDIAN SCHOOL

On October 6, 1879, in the rolling hills of central Pennsylvania, the people of Carlisle turned out to watch the most extraordinary parade in anyone's memory. A group of eighty-four children from the Sioux tribe, from the faraway Dakota Territory, marched from the railroad depot to the old army barracks. Most were still dressed in blankets and leggings, just as they had been when taken from their families on the Rosebud and Pine Ridge agencies.

Carlisle had been through a lot in its history. It was the last settlement before the Appalachian peaks on the overland trail west from Philadelphia. There had been a military post there since 1750, and troops marching to the French and Indian War and Pontiac's Rebellion were bivouacked in Carlisle. The oldest part of the barracks had been built in 1777 to house Hessian prisoners captured at the Battle of Trenton. General J. E. B. Stuart raided the town in 1863, mistakenly believing that it was here—rather than Gettysburg, twenty-seven miles to the south—where he would link up with the army of General Robert E. Lee.

The arrival of these Indian children, members of the tribe that had defeated Custer only three years earlier, sent a shiver of apprehension through Carlisle. This sentiment was shared by both sides: most of the children had no idea why they were there. Many of them had been virtually kidnapped when Indian agents "volunteered" them for the school.

This first all-Indian school of higher education was the dream of Lieutenant Richard H. Pratt, a Civil War veteran who had been dispatched to Oklahoma for frontier duty. Pratt wanted to help the native people and was convinced that the best way to do so was to educate their children to be assimilated into the white world. Historian Oliver LaFarge wrote: "The idea was to break (the children) down completely away from their families and their tribes, forbid any speaking of their native language or any manifestation of their native culture, and put them through a course of sprouts that would make them over into white men." All items of native dress were discarded, students were given English names, and, since Pratt believed in discipline, they were put through military drills. Pratt has been severely criticized in this century for his Victorian benevolence; nonetheless, he believed sincerely in what he was doing and was a revered figure among many of his former students.

Pratt first sent the Indians in his program to Hampton Institute, a Virginia college for black students founded right after the Civil War. Having decided that the ethnic gap was too great and that the Indians needed a school of their own, he petitioned the government and soon won permission to adapt the Carlisle barracks for his school.

In its thirty-nine-year existence, Carlisle educated about five thousand students from every major tribe in the country, although only one in seven actually received a degree. While it identified itself as a college, the courses were more of a vocational nature, on the level of a high school. A good percentage of its students managed to use their training to live well in the white world. But many others returned to their reservations and found themselves alienated from both the Indian and white cultures.

Ironically, Carlisle's greatest fame came during its last years, when Jim Thorpe (*see* the following entry) helped to turn its teams into leaders in college football and track. Pratt, who was gone by then, had hired Glenn "Pop" Warner as coach in his determination to have the school compete at the highest level of athletics.

In 1918, with reservation schools being established across the country, the Carlisle barracks were returned to military use to serve the effort for World War I. They now house the Army War College, and markers on the premises explain the role the barracks played in Native American history. There is also a small cemetery on the grounds. In it rests those children who succumbed sooner to disease than to the white man's culture.

LOCATION: *The barracks are located north of the center of town on U.S. 11, just off the Pennsylvania Turnpike.*
HOURS: *The grounds are open daily, except on federal holidays, dawn to dusk.*
ADMISSION: *Free.*
TELEPHONE: *(717) 245-3611.*

▲ *Jim Thorpe, a member of the Sauk and Fox tribe, won both the pentathlon and decathlon at the 1912 Olympics. Here he is shown competing in the shot put.*

Jim Thorpe

JIM THORPE MEMORIAL

In 1950, Jim Thorpe was voted the best American athlete of the first half of the twentieth century. Not much has changed since then to alter the standings. He won both the pentathlon and decathlon at the 1912 Olympics, led the Carlisle Indian School to victories over the greatest powers in college football, played in a World Series for the New York Giants, and helped to establish and then starred in the organization that grew into the National Football League. Jim Thorpe remains the stuff of legend.

This town in the eastern Pennsylvania hills still has mixed emotions about that legend. In 1954, the year after Thorpe's death, the towns of Mauch Chunk and East Mauch Chunk merged, changed their names, and built a memorial to him. In return, they were promised a tourist bonanza, an Olympic stadium, a hospital, even a cut of NFL gate receipts. Little or none of this came to pass. The townspeople even considered changing the berg's name back to the original, but the proposal lost by 150 votes in 1966.

Nonetheless, visitors come to pay their respects, and there is a certain element of pride among younger residents, who do not remember any other name for their town, in bearing the name of a legend.

Thorpe was born in Oklahoma, a member of the Sauk and Fox tribe. Orphaned at an early age, he became a federal ward and was sent to the Haskell Indian Institute in Kansas to learn a trade. While he was there, his athletic skills attracted the attention of school officials, who notified Glenn "Pop" Warner, coach of the Carlisle Indian School (*see* the preceding entry). Warner persuaded the 19-year-old to enroll at Carlisle in 1907. Thorpe kicked three field goals to beat Penn State, and his sixty-yard run tied a heavily favored Pennsylvania team. He did not care for the rigors of academia, and he dropped out of school for three years, but Warner persuaded him to return in 1911. It was then that Thorpe's story really begins.

He was named to the All-American football teams in 1911 and 1912, beating Harvard with a forty-eight-yard drop kick with his injured leg encased in bandages, and beating Army on a one hundred-yard kickoff return right after a ninety-five-yard return was nullified by a penalty. When the Carlisle track team showed up for a meet with Lafayette, only Thorpe and four other men got off the train: Thorpe alone took five first-place finishes and a second. At the Olympics in Stockholm, his unprecedented sweep of the grueling fifteen events in the decathlon and pentathlon still stands as a mark of strength and endurance. Many shared the sentiment of King Gustav V, who had said to the Olympian, "Sir, you are the greatest athlete in the world."

Within a few months, however, Thorpe was forced to return his medals. Officials had learned that for a few months in 1910, after he had dropped out of Carlisle, Thorpe had played minor league baseball. This nullified his amateur status. Although it was fairly common in those days for college athletes to pick up some extra money by playing professionally under an assumed name, Thorpe had not bothered with such subterfuge. It was not until 1983, long after his death, that Thorpe's medals were finally reinstated by the International Olympics Committee.

Giants manager John McGraw, always looking for a gate attraction, signed Thorpe to play big-league baseball. But this was not his best game: his inability to hit the curveball kept him from stardom, although he did hit over .300 in his final season with the Boston Braves.

While still playing for the Giants, Thorpe went to Canton, Ohio, and organized a team of professional football players. The Bulldogs are now recognized as the first pro team in history, which is why Canton was chosen as the site for the Professional Football Hall of Fame. Other teams soon joined them, and Thorpe was named president of the new league, the predecessor of the NFL. He went on to star with the football Giants in New York, and along with Red Grange, he became the premier gate attraction of the new sport. Those who saw him play say that he had no equal in that era in combining speed, power, and an instinctive ability to find the hole; it was impossible for a single tackler to bring him down. In a 1950 Associated Press poll, he was named the greatest football player of the first half-century.

After retiring from sports, however, Thorpe could not find a niche. He drifted from job to job, working as a security guard at the Ford Motor Company Rouge plant for a time, and as a greeter in a Hollywood restaurant. When he was admitted to a hospital in 1952 for surgery, his wife stated that he was destitute. He died a few months later of a heart attack.

Originally, Thorpe was to be buried in Oklahoma near his birthplace. A campaign to erect a memorial there failed to raise the necessary funds, and his wife had his body exhumed and reburied at the site of the current memorial in an emotional ceremony in 1954. The town's name was changed a few months later. Ironically, the place that at one time claimed that more millionaires per capita resided there than in any town in America, was named in memory of a man who died with hardly a penny to his name.

LOCATION: *The 20-ton Thorpe mausoleum is just east of town, on Pennsylvania 903.*
HOURS: *Daily, dawn to dusk.*
ADMISSION: *Free.*

Wilkes-Barre

BATTLE OF WYOMING

P art of the British strategy during the American Revolution was to attack the colonists at their most vulnerable point, the lightly defended settlements on the western frontier. They made alliances with several tribes who were angered at the incursion of white settlers into lands reserved for them. The British thought this would be a powerful demoralizing factor, and they encouraged their allies to act with the utmost ferocity, while claiming later that they were powerless to control them.

The most far-reaching of these campaigns, in terms of consequences for the native people involved, came in northeastern Pennsylvania. Early in the summer of 1778, as George Washington was driving the British army back across New Jersey to Manhattan, a force of Tories and Iroquois, led by Walter Butler, made its way south from New York into the Wyoming Valley. Earlier that year, preliminary raids had led settlers to urge Congress, meeting in York, to send back to Wilkes-Barre troops that had been sent to the national army. But with the situation grave on the main front, the request could not be met. On July 2, however, with the British occupation ended, Congress finally was able to return to Philadelphia to consider the Wyoming issue.

But time had run out. With Butler's force of one thousand advancing on them, the settlers at Forty Fort, on the Susquehanna River, decided on July 3 to confront them head on. The Iroquois surprised the settlers by attacking by way of swampy terrain. The battle became a rout, and the settlers retreated to Forty Fort, where they surrendered. With the Wyoming Valley defenseless, Butler's men were able to wage a campaign of terror for several days.

The move backfired, however. Public opinion demanded reprisal. The following spring an expedition under General John Sullivan was sent into the heart of the Iroquois country to carry out a war of extermination. The heartland of the Iroquois Confederacy was destroyed, its villages and crops burned, and in many cases its population massacred (*see* Iroquois Indian Museum, Cobleskill, New York). Moreover, Sullivan's report of what he had seen in the Iroquois lands fueled a postwar rush by white settlers into western New York. The Iroquois, as well as most of the Tories, were forced to flee to Canada, and their ancestral homeland was lost.

LOCATION: *The Wyoming Battle monument is located 5 miles from Wilkes-Barre, on the west bank of the Susquehanna, by way of U.S. 11.*
HOURS: *Daily, dawn to dusk.*
ADMISSION: *Free.*

QUEBEC

CANADIAN MUSEUM OF CIVILIZATION

The Canadian Museum of Civilization is a major new facility directly across the river from the national capital in Ottawa. It traces the cultural development of Canada from prehistory to present times. There is a special emphasis on native cultures, and many of the displays, especially those featuring the Inuit, of the far north, and the tribes of the Pacific Northwest, are outstanding. Because the places in which these people live are difficult to reach, the museum, which will not be completed until 1995, fills a worthwhile role of bringing a sampling of their cultures to the major centers of population. It is a striking complex, with a children's museum and two wraparound-screen theaters showing Canadian-theme films.

LOCATION: *The museum is at the foot of the Alexandra Bridge, on Laurier Street at St.-Laurent Boulevard.*
HOURS: *Tuesday through Sunday, 9–5.*
ADMISSION: *$4.50.*
TELEPHONE: *(819) 776-7000.*

ABENAKI MUSEUM

The Abenaki Confederacy was the dominant power in northern New England at the time of the European arrival (*see* Penobscot Island and Museum, Old Town, Maine). They quickly became involved in the colonial competition between France and England, with most of them becoming allied with France. As Britain slowly extended its rule northward toward the end of the seventeenth century, most of the Abenaki fled into Quebec for protection.

▲ *Traditional masks are among the historical objects on view at the Abenaki Museum.*

By the end of the American Revolution, only the Penobscot remained in their traditional homeland. The Odanak reserve, near the junction of the Saint François and Saint Lawrence rivers, was set aside for those who left.

A museum now exhibits historical material relating to the Abenaki and their lives in Quebec. Inaugurated in 1965, the museum contains permanent, temporary, and annual exhibits. Displays include costumes and clothing from the turn of the century and now, basket-work, vintage photographs of families and events, drums, spiritual items, and books that belonged to missionaries. Videotapes give a glimpse into native artisanry and the Abenaki language, and an illustration depicts tribal life. There are also reconstructions of a fort from around 1700, and of the salon of Chanoine Joseph de Gonzague, a missionary who had a great impact on the Abenaki people.

LOCATION: *On Quebec 226 just west of the Saint François bridge at Pierreville. It is about 25 miles northwest of the Drummondville exit of Highway 20 by way of Highways 255 and 226.*

HOURS: *Monday through Friday, 10-5; weekends, 1-5; mid-May to end of October.*

ADMISSION: *$3; children under 12, $1.50; students, $2; seniors, $2.50.*

TELEPHONE: *(514) 568-2600.*

RHODE ISLAND

Bristol

KING PHILIP'S WAR

Half a century after the Plymouth Colony gave Europeans their first tenuous foothold in New England, a leader emerged among the people who had aided the struggling settlement in its most desperate days. Metacom was the younger son of Massasoit, leader of the Wampanoags (*see* Massasoit Memorial, Plymouth, Massachusetts), who had decided to befriend the English as possible allies against stronger neighboring tribes. But in the time since, the Europeans had steadily expanded their territory while the Wampanoag were forced to surrender their best lands through inequitable treaties. Metacom saw that the only possible outcome of this process was the end of his people. In 1675, he took action, touching off a war in which the issue was survival.

Massasoit had petitioned the English to give his two sons names in their language. The colonists refused to give them Christian names but reached back, instead, into pagan history, to the rulers of ancient Macedonia. The elder son, Wamsutta, they renamed Alexander. Metacom became Philip.

Massasoit died in 1661 and his successor, Alexander, was summoned to Plymouth. He was treated there as a subject and demands made of his loyalty. Alexander was outraged. He developed a fever during his stay in Plymouth, and on the voyage home he died. The suspicion was that he had been poisoned. Philip became the chief of the Wampanoag at age 24.

The demands of the British became steadily harsher and more expansive. Philip lived in the ancestral home of the tribe, Montaup, anglicized to Mount Hope. By 1671, English expansion had reached the edge of these lands, in the very heartland of the Wampanoag. There were now about forty thousand whites in New England, far too many for Philip to fight alone. But if it were possible to unite all the native people of the region, then the Europeans might be pushed back to the coastal settlements, or, if the best happened, driven away altogether. In June 1675, he was ready. He attacked the village of Swansea, now in Massachusetts, and the furious colonists responded with a massive assault aimed at Mount Hope. But Philip anticipated this and evacuated his home base.

For two years, the war raged across all of New England, with Philip constantly on the move to direct campaigns. By one estimate, fifty-two of the ninety European settlements in the region were attacked, and thirteen were destroyed. Even Plymouth itself was attacked and sixteen houses burned. More than six hundred colonists are believed to have been killed, and they responded, in turn, by eradicating Indian villages wherever they found them, allied with Philip or not.

In 1676, with the war implacably turning against him, Philip returned to Mount Hope, pursued by a large British force. Finally, on August 12 he was cornered in the swamp near the base of the hill that had been his home and gunned down by an Indian ally of the colonists. When the famed minister Cotton Mather heard the news, he exclaimed, "God hath sent us the head of Leviathan for a feast." Philip's corpse was, indeed, decapitated (as well as quartered) and his head and other remains exhibited in Plymouth on public poles for the next twenty-five years.

Indian survivors of the war, including Philip's son, were sold into slavery. Others escaped to the west and were absorbed by the Iroquois. But for fourteen months, Philip came closer to driving off the colonists than any other Native American leader in history. The war was also the first time in which the various New England colonies felt compelled to act in a unified way. To some historians, this was the first spark of an impulse to combine that exactly one century later would ignite a revolution.

LOCATION: *The site of Philip's death is south of Bristol by way of Rhode Island 136 (Metacom Avenue), on the slopes of Mount Hope. It is marked by a stone cairn. Nearby is another stone pile, known as King Philip's Chair, which is assumed to have been the place from which he addressed his tribe. This is now part of the grounds of the Haffenreffer Museum of Anthropology, which contains more exhibits on King Philip and an outstanding display of Native American items.*

HOURS: *The site itself is open daily, dawn to dusk. The museum is open Tuesday through Sunday, 1–5, June through August; weekends only, March through May and September through December.*

ADMISSION: *The site is free. The museum is $1.50.*

PHONE: *(401) 253-8388.*

Charlestown

NARRAGANSETT BURIAL GROUND

The remnant of what was once the most powerful tribe in southern New England lives around the village of Charlestown. It was the growing strength of the Narragansett, in fact, that concerned the Wampanoag deeply enough to make an alliance with the English colony at Plymouth (*see* Massasoit Memorial, Plymouth, Massachusetts). But they were drawn into both of the early wars with the colonists with fatal results. The Pequot War of 1635 severely reduced their strength, and King Philip's War nearly destroyed them as a people.

The Narragansett were reluctant participants in King Philip's War. They had resisted his entreaties to join the native alliance against the colonists, but agreed to shelter refugees from the English. That was enough to lead the colonists to suspect that they would enter the war on Philip's side. In December 1675, they made a preemptive strike on the main Narragansett winter village, near the present town of West Kingston. The surrounding swamps, which usually protected the place from surprise attack, were frozen over. The engagement is referred to as The Great Swamp Fight, but it was more like a slaughter of the Narragansett.

Those that escaped the retribution that followed the war were absorbed by the Niantic. Eventually, the two people adopted the Narragansett name, and reservation lands were set aside for them. The land was reacquired by the state in 1880. But the Indian Reorganization Act of 1934 established the Narragansett as a distinct people. Charlestown, where their offices are located, is rich in tribal associations. The Royal Burial Grounds, where sachems were laid to rest, and the Old Indian Church are just north of town. In addition, an annual tribal meeting is held in August at which traditional ceremonies are performed. The dates vary, so it is best to check by phone in advance.

LOCATION: *The burial ground is north from town on Rhode Island 2, then west on Narrow Lane. The church is about 1 mile north of U.S. 1 on Rhode Island 2.*
EXHIBITS: *A longhouse adjoining the church is the site of performances during the annual gathering.*
HOURS: *Daily, dawn to dusk. Services are held at the church each Sunday.*
ADMISSION: *Donation asked at the church.*
TELEPHONE: *(401) 364-1100.*

CANOCHET MEMORIAL

After The Great Swamp Fight brought the reluctant Narragansett into King Philip's War, it was their sachem, Canochet, who actually led the campaign in this part of New England. He had tried to follow a policy of neutrality. But when the English demanded that he turn over Wampanoag fugitives, he replied, "Not a paring of a Wampanoag nail." That defiance brought on the colonists' attack.

While Philip was on the run in northern New England, Canochet led effective assaults on Providence and North Kingstown. He was captured in April 1676 and taken to Stonington, Connecticut, for execution. "I like it well that I should die before my heart is softened and I say things unworthy of myself," he told his captors. They obliged him.

The resort town that grew up here on Rhode Island Sound was built on the site of Canochet's favorite summer camping ground. A statue of him stands on Exchange Place.

LOCATION: *Just west of Rhode Island 1A in the center of town.*
HOURS: *Daily, dawn to dusk.*
ADMISSION: *Free.*

VIRGINIA

St. John's Church Pocahontas Window

The story of the Indian princess who saved the life of John Smith, leader of the first English colony in America, and then married John Rolfe to make an alliance between the two peoples is one that is ingrained deeply in American history. It has been taught to schoolchildren for centuries and is still a charming tale. It is a myth of origins, of the first contact between whites and Indians. Carried within it is the implicit message that history could have developed differently if only these amicable relations were built on. But even this alliance was short-lived and ended in blood, as the sheer weight of English numbers placed intolerable pressure on the Indian way of life.

The Smith part probably is not true, either. Smith was known for his tendency to embellish the facts, much as contemporary political leaders do. The image of the young Indian girl throwing herself across his body just as he was about to be executed in her father's village is just right as melodrama, but not many historians believe it. Too many of Smith's hair-raising accounts of the colony's early years have been proven false to trust this one. The site of Werowocomoco, the village in which Pocahontas's selfless act was supposed to have occurred, has been identified in Gloucester County, on the east bank of the York River. For years, a tumble-down chimney, called Powhatan's Chimney, stood there. According to local legend, it belonged to the European-style house built for Pocahontas's father in 1608 as part of the alliance. His name, however, was actually Wahunsonacock. Powhatan was the term for the tribal confederacy he headed when the Jamestown colony was founded. The chimney's name is just as spurious. His daughter's marriage to Rolfe, however, is documented fact (*see* Pocahantas Statue, Jamestown, Virginia).

Pocahontas remains the earliest figure in the European history of Indians whose name survives heroically. When St. John's Church was restored in 1869, following its partial destruction in the Civil War, Indian students from nearby Hampton Institute donated a window dedicated to her. The church building itself dates to 1728, and the parish, established in 1610, is regarded as the oldest in the nation.

LOCATION: *St. John's Church is located at 100 West Queensway, just west of Interstate 64 at the County Street exit.*
EXHIBITS: *Besides the Pocahontas window, the church displays communion silver dating to 1618 and items that were used in the earliest services.*
HOURS: *Monday through Friday, 9–3; Saturday, 9–12.*
ADMISSION: *Free.*
TELEPHONE: *(804) 722-2567.*

Jamestown

POCAHONTAS STATUE

I t was at the Jamestown settlement that Pocahontas married John Rolfe in 1614. He described the match as not being made for "carnal affection, but for the good of this plantation, for the honor of our country." The marriage did secure a much-needed peace for the colony, which was hanging on by a shred. The pair moved to Rolfe's estate near the present town of Varina, on the east bank of the James River, below Richmond. Rolfe successfully cultivated large-scale tobacco growth there and established America's first export industry. It was also there that their son, Thomas, founder of a great Virginia dynasty that proudly traced its roots to Pocahontas, was born in 1616.

Pocahontas went to England with Rolfe in 1617 and was treated with great curiosity and ceremony by the court of King James I. She died there that year, never returning to her homeland. This bronze of her as a young girl, sculpted by William Ordway Partridge, overlooks the James. Along with the statue of John Smith, it is the oldest such memorial on the site.

LOCATION: *Jamestown is part of Colonial National Historical Park, at the western end of the Colonial Parkway.*
EXHIBITS: *Several structures that figured in the history of the first permanent English settlement in America have been reconstructed at Jamestown.*
HOURS: *Daily, 9–5.*
ADMISSION: *$5 per car.*
TELEPHONE: *(804) 898-3400.*

POWHATAN INDIAN VILLAGE

This reconstructed village is part of Jamestown Festival Park, a museum complex adjoining Jamestown that was established during the colony's 350th anniversary, in 1957. In a living history framework, it tries to show what daily life was like for both the English and Indian occupants of this area at the time of the first colony.

The Powhatan actually were made up of a confederacy of about thirty tribes stretching along the eastern shore of Chesapeake Bay and the great tidal rivers of Virginia. They numbered about nine thousand in two hundred separate villages in 1607. Within a century, the villages had been reduced to a dozen, and today no more than a few hundred members of these tribes survive in Virginia.

The Powhatan built long log houses behind palisades as tall as twelve feet. They grew corn, as well as beans, pumpkins, and some fruit, and were also skilled in basketry.

The marriage of Pocahontas to John Rolfe resulted in about a decade of peace between the Europeans and Indians. But she died in England in 1617, and her father, Wahunsonacock, passed away the following year. His brother, Opechancanough, fearing the growing strength of the colony, tried to drive the Europeans off with a surprise assault in 1622. He came very close to succeeding. About 350 whites were killed, but Jamestown, the largest settlement, received advance warning and survived. The resulting counterattack was so severe that most of the Powhatan were driven back to the falls of the James. Twenty-two years later, Opechancanough decided to try again. But this time the cause was hopeless, and while the Powhatan managed to inflict some damage on the most far-flung frontier settlements, they were easily defeated. Opechancanough was brought back to Jamestown for trial but was murdered by a colonist before it began. That ended all hostilities between the Indians and the Tidewater settlements.

LOCATION: *Jamestown Festival Park.*
EXHIBITS: *Besides the Powhatan Village, there are reproductions of the three ships that brought the colonists to Virginia and the first fort erected at Jamestown, in 1607.*
HOURS: *Daily, 9–5.*
ADMISSION: *$6.50.*
TELEPHONE: *(804) 229-1607.*

PAMUNKEY INDIAN MUSEUM

The Pamunkey were the largest group of the Powhatan Confederacy, with a population estimated at about one thousand. The largest settlement was near the present town of West Point, where the Pamunkey and Mattaponi rivers join to form the York. It was from this town that Opechancanough (*see* previous entry) led his final, futile attempt in 1644 to dislodge the English settlers. His descendants later helped English authorities subdue Bacon's Rebellion, the frontier upheaval partially provoked by inhumane treatment of the Indians. In 1781, a reservation was set aside for the remaining members of the tribe, and it still exists on the Pamunkey River near Lanesville in King William County.

The museum focuses on the Pamunkey way of life from the ice age to the present. Tools and artifacts are displayed with information on how they were made and used.

The Pamunkeys are one of the tribes east of the Mississippi to practice the art of pottery continuously since aboriginal times. The museum's craft shop offers pots made by Pamunkey women from clay dug from the Pamunkey River; the pots, made in the coil method, retain traditional design elements.

LOCATION: *The museum is just north of Lanesville, in King William, near the junction of Virginia 30 and Virginia 633.*

HOURS: *Monday through Saturday, 10–4; Sunday, 1–5.*

ADMISSION: *Adults (13 and up), $1; School Groups and Seniors, 50 cents.*

TELEPHONE: *(804) 843-4792.*

SOUTHEAST

SOUTHEAST

ALABAMA
1 Battlefield and Museum, *Horseshoe Bend National Military Park*
2 Mound State Monument, *Moundville*
3 Little Tallasse Plantation, *Wallsboro*

ARKANSAS
4 Toltec Mounds State Park, *England*
5 Hampson State Museum, *Wilson*

FLORIDA
6 Dade Battlefield State Historic Site, *Bushnell*
7 Crystal River State Archeological Site, *Crystal River*
8 Osceola Historic Site, *Saint Augustine*
9 San Luis Historic Site, *Tallahassee*
10 Miccosukee Indian Village, *Tamiami Station*

GEORGIA
11 Kolomoki Mounds State Park, *Blakely*
12 New Echota State Historic Site, *Calhoun*
13 Etowah Mounds State Historic Site, *Cartersville*
14 James Vann House, *Chatsworth*
15 Rock Eagle Mound, *Eatonton*
16 Indian Springs State Park, *Jackson*
17 Ocmulgee National Monument, *Macon*
18 Chieftains Museum, *Rome*

LOUISIANA
19 Poverty Point State Commemmorative Area, *Epps*
20 State Commemmorative Area, *Marksville*

MISSISSIPPI
21 Winterville Mounds State Park, *Greenville*
22 Emerald Mound, *Natchez*
23 Grand Village of the Natchez, *Natchez*
24 Choctaw Indian Fair and Museum of the Southern Indian, *Philadelphia*
25 Nanih Waiya State Historic Site, *Preston*
26 Chickasaw Indian Village, *Tupelo*

NORTH CAROLINA
27 Museum of the Cherokee Indian, *Cherokee*
28 Oconaluftee Indian Village, *Cherokee*
29 Unto These Hills, *Cherokee*
30 Judaculla Rock, *Cullowhee*
31 Town Creek Indian Mound State Historic Site, *Mount Gilead*
32 Strike at the Wind, *Pembroke*

TENNESSEE
33 Red Clay State Historical Area, *Cleveland*
34 Old Stone Fort State Park, *Manchester*
35 Chucalissa Indian Museum, *Memphis*
36 Pinson Mounds, *Pinson*
37 Sequoyah's Birthplace, *Vonore*

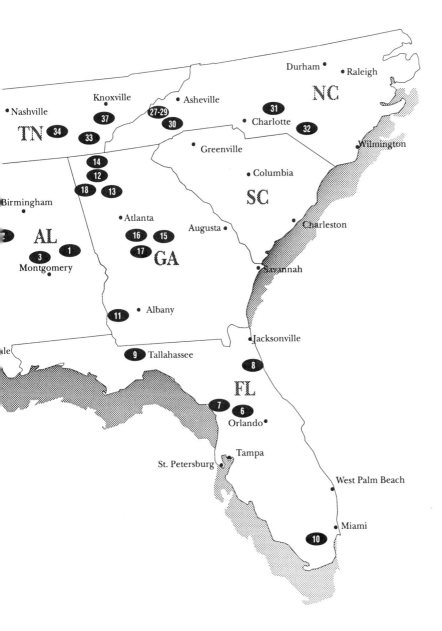

ALABAMA

BATTLEFIELD AND MUSEUM

A fter his alliance of northern tribes collapsed following the 1811 Battle of Tippecanoe (*see* Tippecanoe Battlefield, Lafayette, Indiana), the great Shawnee leader Tecumseh continued to urge the Creek to oppose the American advance onto their lands by joining their fortunes with the British.

Tecumseh was related to the Creek through his mother, and while his plans were not universally accepted, he was given a respectful hearing. A sizable contingent, mostly bands related to the pro-British leader Alexander McGillivray, agreed with the Shawnee spokesman. They began receiving British arms through the sympathetic Spanish government in Florida.

As the War of 1812 began in the north, McGillivray's nephew, William Weatherford, who was called Red Eagle, led his band against the white settlements of Alabama. They overwhelmed the stockade at Fort Mims, thanks to the incompetence of the commander, who refused to take precautionary measures and had several black slaves whipped for reporting that the Creek had arrived in the vicinity. Despite Weatherford's attempts to protect noncombatants, many women and children were killed in the assault.

The news sent a ripple of horror through the state of Tennessee, and settlers demanded revenge. A militia unit of twenty-five hundred men, including Cherokee and northern Creek allies, was sent after Weatherford under the command of Andrew Jackson. This was the turning point of Jackson's life. Detested in Washington, his left arm in a sling as the result of one of his many duels, Jackson had been removed from an earlier military commission. But his friend, Tennessee Governor William Blount, had simply filled in Jackson's name on a blank federal form and put him in charge of the Creek expedition.

Advancing south, burning and pillaging indiscriminately, Jackson's force finally encountered the main body of Creek near the looping bend of the Tallapoosa River. On March 27, 1814, he attacked and through sheer force of numbers managed to breach the Creek defenses.

The battle was a disaster for the Creek. Jackson enforced a brutal treaty that dispossessed most of the southern Creek from their lands and fully opened Alabama to the waiting flood of white settlement. The northern Creek could

▲ *Horseshoe Bend is named for a looping bend in the Tallapoosa River, site of a disastrous battle for the Creek Indians.*

not withstand this tide, and within a matter of years they, too, were forced to leave. Jackson's victory, coming at a time when American morale was low, turned him into a national hero and led to his command at the Battle of New Orleans in 1815. Having surmised that hostility toward Indians ensured political popularity in the West, Jackson maintained that stance throughout his career. His election to the presidency in 1828 sentenced all the southern tribes to displacement to the West.

LOCATION: *The National Battlefield is located 12 miles north of the town of Dadeville, on Alabama 49.*

EXHIBITS: *A 3-mile road circles the battlefield and explains the course of the military action. There is also an interpretive center and displays of artifacts from the site in a museum.*

HOURS: *Both the road and museum are open daily, 8–4:30.*

ADMISSION: *Free.*

TELEPHONE: *(205) 234-7111.*

▲ *The Creek Indian Chief Menawa.*

Moundville

MOUND STATE MONUMENT

The grouping of mounds at Mound State Monument, on a bluff above the Black Warrior River, so dominates the landscape that there was no question what to name the town built adjacent to it. The pioneers were awed by this evidence of an unknown people who had inhabited the land long before them.

This was a metropolis by twelfth-century standards, built by an accomplished agrarian people. They left behind a vast array of pottery, tools, and ornaments, all done with a high degree of artistic skill. The twenty mounds here were the cultural and religious center for a large group of surrounding villages, much as a core city is surrounded by its suburbs today. The mounds range from 3 feet to 58 feet in height and once were surmounted by temples and dwellings of religious leaders. One of the temples has been reconstructed, and in other places figures have been placed depicting inhabitants engaging in typical activities.

The museum shows off artifacts that demonstrate the level of achievement these people had attained in working with copper and stone; most anthropologists say this skill level is unmatched at any prehistoric site north of Mexico. Two wings of the museum, once devoted to burial remains and artifacts, have been closed at the request of Native American groups.

LOCATION: *Moundville is located 20 miles south of Tuscaloosa, and the Mound State Monument is on its northern edge, along Alabama 69.*
HOURS: *Daily, 9–5.*
ADMISSION: *$2.*
TELEPHONE: *(205) 371-2572.*

Wallsboro

LITTLE TALLASSE PLANTATION

L ittle Tallasse Plantation, standing on the banks of the Coosa River, was the home and probably the birthplace of one of the great diplomatic strategists in American history. In an era when three colonial powers fought for advantage in Alabama Territory, Alexander McGillivray played one against the other in an effort to build lasting security for his own people, the Creek.

His father, Lachlan McGillivray, was a Scottish trader who went into the wilderness from Charleston early in the eighteenth century and made a fortune trading with the Creek. He married Sehoy, a member of the Wind clan, and through her Alexander occupied a position of authority with the Creek; never a chief, he was something like a counselor.

The elder McGillivray sent his son to Charleston for a formal education, after which he was apprenticed to a firm in Savannah. Young McGillivray felt compelled to return to his mother's people, and by the eve of the American Revolution, he had attained a significant position with the Creek. Meanwhile, although Little Tallasse was confiscated by the Americans, and his father fled to Scotland, Alexander stayed and accepted the rank of colonel with the British. He sheltered Tory refugees and led several raids on Georgia settlements.

But McGillivray had chosen the losing side in the war, and he was left without property or funds. While retaining his British rank, he agreed to become a colonel with the Spanish forces in Florida, in return for channeling Creek trade through their ports. In 1790, he visited the detested Americans in New York and accepted a third commission, as a brigadier general, from

President Washington, agreeing to another secret treaty that would shift trade to U.S. ports.

In exchange, McGillivray asked for educational opportunities for Creek youth and for permanent title to their lands. He lived at a time when such concessions were possible. The Creek were valued as allies by the three contending powers, and a skilled statesman such as McGillivray could wrest an advantage for his militarily weaker people.

When McGillivray died in 1793, his successors could not continue the balancing act he had perfected. In twenty years, the Americans became the sole power in Alabama. With a Creek alliance no longer useful, the tribe was quickly expelled from the lands to which they had been given permanent title.

LOCATION: *Wallsboro is located on U.S. 231 about 30 miles north of Montgomery. A historic marker points the way to the site of Little Tallasse.*

EXHIBIT: *A boulder marks the location of the plantation, and a nearby marker tells the story of the McGillivrays.*

ARKANSAS

TOLTEC MOUNDS STATE PARK

While many Native American remains throughout the West were linked with the Aztecs by imaginative white settlers (*see* Montezuma Castle National Monument, Arizona; and Aztec Ruins National Monument, New Mexico) the people of Arkansas were more subtle. When they found these mounds, they named them for the Toltec, a Mexican people who preceded the Aztecs. The Toltec actually were prolific mound builders and many of their monuments may be found around Mexico City.

John Baldwin, a nineteenth century historian who wrote extensively on the origins of mounds in the United States, was convinced that the Toltec had migrated north, taking their mound culture with them. Although many anthropologists now believe that some Mississippi Valley groups were influenced by trade contact with the Toltec, there is no evidence linking them to Arkansas. The religious and governmental complex at Toltec Mounds State Park was probably associated with the Temple Mound Culture, which flourished in many areas of the American South. This community peaked between 700 and 950 A.D. There are guided tours of the site, a small museum, and the chance to watch archaeologists at work during the summer months.

LOCATION: *The park is off U.S. 165, about 9 miles north of England and about 20 miles southeast of Little Rock.*
HOURS: *Tuesday through Saturday, 8–5; Sunday, 12–5.*
ADMISSION: *Free. Tours are $2.*
TELEPHONE: *(501) 961-9442.*

▲ *On exhibit at the Hampson State Museum are many items of personal adornment, such as those shown in this rendering of a decorative motif, which are thought to have been worn in great quantities by the Nodena people.*

Wilson

HAMPSON STATE MUSEUM

Amid the cotton fields of the delta, the remains of a Temple Mound people were found along the Mississippi River. Researchers uncovered Nodena, a fifteen-acre palisaded farming village. It was occupied from about 1350 to 1700 by ancestors of the Chickasaw, who lived in this region when the first Europeans came. In the 1930s and 1940s, James K. Hampson headed the excavations on land owned by one of the largest cotton plantations in the world, the R. E. Lee Wilson Company. After Hampson's death, his collection of archaeological material was donated to the state of Arkansas; in 1961, the collection was moved from the plantation museum to its current location.

The museum houses an impressive selection of artifacts from a number of different culture periods. Collections include rare head pots which have a unique design and specialized technology, and are believed to have been made only during the Mississippi time period; the function of these pots is still a mystery to anthropologists. There are ceramic vessels with symbols that indicate they had ceremonial significance. And the many items of personal adornment—such as imported shell, copper, animal claws, teeth, and bones, fashioned into beads, pendants, and ear spools—were, according to the evidence, worn in great quantities by the Nodena people. Archaeological materials are accompanied by graphics and written material that describe the farming-based civilization that inhabited the area. Exhibits aim to place objects within their cultural context: the pottery exhibit, which includes the distinctive Nodena red and white pottery, describes the process of creating a pottery vessel, and the tool exhibit attempts to explain the function of the implements, relating them to their modern counterparts.

LOCATION: *The museum is on U.S. 61 in Wilson, which is about 40 miles north of Memphis, Tennessee, by way of Interstate 55.*
HOURS: *Tuesday through Saturday, 8–5; Sunday, 1–5.*
ADMISSION: *Adults, $1.50; Children, 75 cents (plus tax).*
TELEPHONE: *(501) 655-8622.*

FLORIDA

DADE BATTLEFIELD STATE HISTORIC SITE

The Seminole of Florida were actually made up of many tribes, exiles from their own lands in American territory to the north. Oconee Indians were known to be living in the area early in the eighteenth century, and within a few years they were joined by Yamasee from South Carolina. A constant stream of black slaves, offered freedom by the Spanish government as a disruptive influence on the British colonies, also came into the Seminole lands. After the revolution, Britain encouraged Spain to continue this effective policy. Finally, the Creek arrived after their disastrous defeat in 1813, swelling the number of those identified as Seminole to about five thousand. The name itself first appeared in 1775 and is thought to be a corruption of the Spanish *cimarron*, meaning wild and untamed.

Andrew Jackson invaded the area in 1818 on the pretext of recovering escaped slaves and subduing the refugee Creek. This First Seminole War was actually a pretext to grab Florida for the United States. The States gained Florida and the Seminole were pushed further south. In the next generation, the influx of white settlers brought the groups into conflict again. American policy toward the Indians in other parts of the south was expulsion to the West, and the same course was pursued in Florida. In 1832, the Seminole signed a treaty by which the tribe agreed to removal. However, in 1835, several younger leaders denounced the treaty, and the Second Seminole War began.

Although Osceola (*see* Osceola Historic Site, Saint Augustine, Florida) was the most effective of the Seminole leaders, the most brilliant piece of generalship came three days after Christmas in 1835 when the forces of Micanope and Jumper caught a detachment of 108 men, making their way overland from Tampa to Ocala under Major Francis Dade. Caught near here in an open pine barren and cut to pieces, only one man of Dade's forces survived.

Oddly enough, the Seminole resistance and the ability of their leaders fueled the imagination of the American press. For the first time, public sympathy swung to the side of the Indians in their fight for independence, and Americans avidly followed the seven-year war. While some observers genuinely sympathized with the Seminole, most others saw it as a way for Northern opinion leaders to embarrass the South at a time of growing sectional tension.

LOCATION: *The site is on a country road, 1 mile west of Bushnell.*
EXHIBITS: *There is a museum, reproductions of the breastworks used in the battle, and memorials marking the battlefield site.*
HOURS: *The grounds are open daily, 8 to dusk; the museum 9–5.*
ADMISSION: *$3.25 per car.*
TELEPHONE: *(904) 793-4781.*

Crystal River

CRYSTAL RIVER STATE ARCHEOLOGICAL SITE

The Crystal River Mounds, a complex of six burial and temple mounds, are considered to be one of the longest continually occupied sites in Florida. They are believed to have been started by the Indians of the Deptford culture (500 B.C. to about A.D. 300), who lived at a simple social level, with no apparent chiefdoms or social classes. The construction of the early burial mound and a portion of the temple mound suggest that the Indians of this culture were beginning to form some interest in social complexities. The Weedon Island culture (A.D. 300–A.D. 900)—who are noted for their increased ceremonialism and who displayed a growing interest in social awareness— continued the burial mound placements and temple mound construction, as did the Safety Harbor culture (A.D. 900 to historic contact)—who had orga- nized chiefdoms and who became increasingly involved in ceremonialism.

The Crystal River complex of mounds was occupied until about 1400 A.D. What has most intrigued archaeologists is the strong similarity among artifacts uncovered here and those from Mexico and the Hopewell mounds, which were built at roughly the same time in the Ohio Valley (*see* Mound City National Monument, Chillicothe, Ohio). Excavations done here early in the twentieth century seem to confirm the hypothesis that there was extended trade contact between Ohio and Mexico, over an area that included Florida. Among the artifacts discovered, the stelae, two types of ceremonial limestone found at the mounds, have puzzled archaeologists as to their role in the ceremonial life of the Indians.

LOCATION: *2 1/2 miles west off US 19, north of Crystal River.*
EXHIBITS: *Visitor center with artifacts and interpretive displays, as well as a midden mound, made up of seafood shells.*
HOURS: *Grounds are open daily, 8 to dusk; museum, 9–5.*
ADMISSION: *$2 per vehicle.*
TELEPHONE: *(904) 795-3817.*

Saint Augustine

OSCEOLA HISTORIC SITE

O sceola's message to General Duncan Clinch at the start of the Second Seminole War in 1835 has come down the years as a symbol of unconquerable defiance. "You have guns," he wrote, "so do we. You have powder and lead, so do we. Your men will fight, so will ours."

Osceola was a member of the Red Stick band of Creek and was brought into Florida as an infant in 1808. While he was never a chief among the Seminole, his leadership, and his animosity toward whites, was so intense that higher-ranking men, such as Micanope, came under his influence. Having been present at the execution of Charley Emathla, a chief who had signed the 1832 expulsion treaty, Osceola later met with an Indian agent at Fort King. When the agent waved the treaty in his face and threatened to cut off payments, Osceola pinned the paper to the agent's desk with a knife and shouted, "This is the only treaty I will make with the whites."

Although his grandfather was a Scot (which contemporary observers claimed could be discerned by the lightness of his eyes), Osceola remained implacably hostile toward whites after his wife was carried off by fugitive-slave hunters on the grounds that she was an escaped slave. On the same day that Major Dade's force was annihilated near Bushnell (*see* Dade Battlefield State Historic Site, Bushnell, Florida), Osceola and his band appeared at Fort King and killed the agent who had threatened him.

For two years, he waged a successful campaign. But in 1837, while attending a meeting he believed to be held under a flag of truce, he was seized by American forces. The incident was described as "perfidious" by the Eastern press, and public opinion rallied behind the Seminole. After a brief imprisonment at Castillo de San Marcos in Saint Augustine, Osceola was taken to Fort Moultrie, South Carolina, where he died of illness.

LOCATION: *A historic marker is situated where Osceola was seized. It is 6 miles south of Saint Augustine, then west off U.S.*

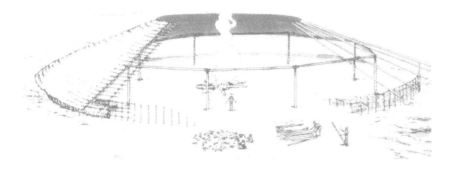

▲ *The San Luis council house is one of the largest known native buildings in the Southeast, and was used for native ceremonies, rituals, civic meetings, and as a lodge for visitors.*

Tallahassee

SAN LUIS HISTORIC SITE

W hen the first Spanish explorers made their way across the Florida panhandle, they described the fields of the Apalachee, which stretched for miles between prosperous villages. At the time, the Apalachee numbered more than six thousand and were acknowledged to be the wealthiest tribe in what is now Florida. The De Soto expedition arrived in 1539 looking for plunder after having been told by other tribes that the Apalachee owned great stores of gold. "Pass through, robbers and traitors," they were told; the conquistador dared not challenge the Apalachee show of strength.

In 1703–04, an alliance of South Carolina militia and southern Creek invaded the Apalachee country and shattered them. In a disastrous campaign, half of their towns were destroyed and fourteen hundred members of the tribe were carried off as prisoners. The rest escaped west, eventually scattering and losing their tribal identity. By the end of the eighteenth century, the Apalachee no longer existed as a people.

San Luis, one of the eight major Apalachee towns, was situated just outside what is now the state capital. Archaeologists have uncovered evidence of a seventeenth-century village and a Catholic mission, where work is still in

▲ *At the annual San Luis Heritage Festival visitors can celebrate history and learn from stories told by a Native American in 17th-century costume.*

progress. An interpretive center describes the project and gives a historical overview of the site.

LOCATION: *San Luis is on Mission Road just west of the city and north of U.S. 90.*
EXHIBITS: *Besides looking at museum displays, you can watch archaeologists at work here, Sunday through Thursday, February through June.*
HOURS: *Monday through Friday, 9–4:30; Saturday, 10–4:30; and Sunday, 12–4:30.*
ADMISSION: *Free.*
TELEPHONE: *(904) 487-3711.*

Tamiami Station

MICCOSUKEE INDIAN VILLAGE

The Miccosukees, who had wandered into central Florida even before the migrations of the 1700s, subsisted primarily by hunting and fishing. By the turn of the eighteenth century, they had begun to push further and further south into Florida, partly as a response to the establishment of Spanish missions and forts across northern Florida during the seventeenth century. Within less than a hundred years, the Timucua and Apalachee Indians living in the Spanish mission settlements were wiped out, largely by sickness.

By the early 1700s, much of the north of Florida was uninhabited. Sometime between 1715 and 1730, the main ancestors of the Miccosukees were back in the area of the Florida Panhandle, some of whom settled in the Apalachee Bay region, others along the Chattahoochee and Apalachicola Rivers.

In 1821, Spain sold Florida to the United States. The Americans, who recognized the rights of the Indians over much of the peninsula at that time, negotiated for land in the "Treaty of Moultrie Creek" in 1823. Tantamount to a land grab, the treaty forced the Miccosukees to pull back to a reservation in central Florida, where they were allowed to live in peace for twenty years.

In 1829–30, agitation by new American settlers led the government to dictate that all the Indians in the southeast had to move west. The Second Seminole War, which lasted from 1835–1842, left many of the Miccosukee dead or deported, and the Third Seminole War, which lasted from 1855–1858, further decimated the tribe. After the wars, about three hundred Seminole retreated deep into the Everglades, and the federal government abandoned hope of ever finding them. Since the war had already cost more than one thousand soldiers and millions of dollars, the government left the remaining Seminole alone, and eventually established these reservations. The remainder of the Miccosukees who escaped removal to Oklahoma reside on four Seminole reservations. By 1860, there were only about 150 to 200 Mikasuki speakers still living in Florida; sixty years earlier, there had been more than 6,000 Indians in the area.

Although Miccosukee is the smallest reservation—a strip of 333 acres along the Tamiami Trail—most public activities are held here, including the annual green corn ceremonies. (Call in advance for dates.) A museum displays the traditional chickees, open-sided cypress houses built on stilts and thatched with palmetto fronds. Traditional crafts shops showcase colorful Seminole clothing, and a restaurant serves traditional Native American dishes. The adjacent Everglades National Park offers airboat rides.

LOCATION: *The village is about 25 miles west of Miami, on U.S. 41, the Tamiami Trail.*
HOURS: *Daily, 9–6.*
ADMISSION: *Grounds are free. Museum is $2.50.*
TELEPHONE: *(305) 223-8380.*

▲ *The Miccosukee Indian Village showcases traditional crafts such as the textile artistry of colorful Seminole clothing.*

GEORGIA

KOLOMOKI MOUNDS STATE PARK

K olomoki is the most southern of the state's significant mound groupings. There are seven mounds on the site, two of which were built to a height of more than twenty-five feet. A museum details the historic period during which the mounds were built, which lasted from 5000 B.C. into the thirteenth century. One of the mounds has been left open; you can see how the archaeologists made their cuts when most of the work was done, in the 1930s and 1940s.

LOCATION: *The mounds are 6 miles north of Blakely by way of U.S. 27 and a county road, on what was once the Mercier Plantation. Notice that the adjacent creek is called the Little Colomokee, an example of how pioneer spellings of native names often wound up with vastly different renderings.*
HOURS: *The park is open daily, 7 A.M. –10 P.M. The museum is open Tuesday through Saturday, 9–5; Sunday, 2–5:30.*
ADMISSION: *$1.50.*
TELEPHONE: *(912) 723-5296.*

NEW ECHOTA STATE HISTORIC SITE

T here is no other place in the Southeast in which the tragedy of the Cherokee Nation is more intensely felt than in the reconstructed village of New Echota, a few miles from the busiest Interstate highway in Georgia. The path of this road once ran north through the Cherokee heartland from the Standing Peachtree, in what is now Atlanta, a landmark that once marked the separation between the territories of the Creek and the Cherokee. According to legend, the Cherokee lost the lands to the south in a series of ball games.

New Echota was the capital of the Cherokee from 1825 to 1838, the seat of a nation within a nation. Its legislature resided here, making laws and electing leaders in a form of government modeled after that of the United States. The settlers had always promised that if the Indians would give up their tribal ways and adapt to the white system of government, the two peoples would be able to live together in amity.

The Cherokee were the one native people who emphatically took the settlers at their word. Their territory extended across the north Georgia highlands and into adjacent areas of Tennessee, North Carolina, and Alabama. Many of the Cherokee had fought with white settlers against the Creek during the War of 1812: even though the Creek were being expelled from southern Georgia in the 1820s, the Cherokee leaders felt secure in their lands. President John Quincy Adams supported them, despite Georgia's Governor's insistence that the federal government adhere to an 1802 agreement that called for the removal of all Indians from the state. Washington received the Cherokee as a sovereign nation, and it respected the concept of Cherokee self-government. The government they shaped at New Echota was a democratic republic, with a bicameral legislature and a principal chief elected by the upper house.

It was apparent by 1828, however, that Andrew Jackson would be elected president in that year's election. The Georgia legislature, under the goading of Governor Troup, passed a law extending its jurisdiction over the Cherokee lands and revoking the Indian government. When Jackson took over, he immediately turned on his former comrades-in-arms and embraced the Georgia law.

Even worse for the Cherokee, gold was discovered on their lands almost simultaneously with Jackson's election. No diplomatic niceties would stop the prospectors who poured into the Cherokee nation and often settled land claims by murdering the Indian occupants. Any hope for Cherokee resistance ended in 1832. The state simply subdivided and sold their lands out from under them, and passed a law forbidding them to hold public assemblies. The prospect of Indians living under a democratic government, publishing a newspaper in their own language seemed to enflame white suspicion and hatred: the more the Cherokee tried to adapt, the more they were feared as an impediment to unrestricted white settlement.

Recognizing the futility of further resistance, some tribal leaders accepted an offer of five million dollars and new lands in the West in 1835. These treaty signers were a minority, but when the federal government approved the treaty, the entire Indian population was given two years to leave the state. Jackson ignored a U.S. Supreme Court decision that favored the Cherokee and ordered the expulsion to proceed. By 1838, the last of them were gone from New Echota, taken westward along the Trail of Tears. The buildings were torn down and the land plowed for crops. Only a home built by the Reverend Samuel A. Worcester, a missionary from Boston who had come to New Echota in 1827 and followed the Cherokee west on their exile, remained standing to mark the site.

About 120 years later, some residents of Calhoun, the town that had

▲ *Some exhibits at New Echota highlight the landmark development of a written form of the Cherokee language.*

grown up nearby, purchased two hundred acres on what was determined to have been the site of New Echota. In 1955, a tavern once owned by Cherokee leader James Vann was moved there to save it from inundation by a dam-made lake. The project was galvanized. The Worcester House was restored in 1959 and offices of the Cherokee national newspaper, *The Phoenix,* were rebuilt. New Echota was made a state historic site in 1962, and the Cherokee Nation Supreme Court Building and a typical homesite in the village were reconstructed. That same year, the Georgia legislature also repealed the laws that had taken these lands away from their rightful occupants.

    Other significant sites in New Echota have been marked out and a museum has opened. A monument to the Trail of Tears was erected on its sesquicentennial, in 1988.

LOCATION: *One mile east of Interstate 75, exit 131, by way of Georgia 225.*
EXHIBITS: *In addition to the reconstructed village of New Echota, a museum displays artifacts found on the site and shows a film, several times daily, on the history of the Cherokee.*
HOURS: *Tuesday through Saturday, 9–5; Sunday, 2–5:30.*
ADMISSION: *$1.50.*
TELEPHONE: *(404) 629-8151.*

▲ *An aerial view of the Etowah Mounds demonstrates the scope of the ceremonial center that was home to several thousand individuals more than 400 years ago.*

Cartersville

ETOWAH MOUNDS STATE HISTORIC SITE

The Cherokee who migrated into the lands of the Temple Builders were as puzzled by the meaning of the mounds they found there as the whites who succeeded them. The first record of the Etowah Mounds dates back to 1819, when the local Cherokee led Reverend Elias Cornelias to them. White owners subsequently turned the sixty-foot-high table atop the tallest mound into a cotton patch.

Systematic excavations began in 1871. Archaeologists determined that the mounds dated from about 1000 to 1500 and had been used as temples, burial places, and residences for the priest-chiefs. Several smaller mounds were rich in artifacts, including stone effigies of human beings lavish with ornamentation. Trade items from Michigan's Upper Peninsula and Mexico were also found on this site. The whole complex, surrounded by a moat, could be fortified.

▲ *Ceremonial objects made of stone, wood, shell, and copper provide clues to the culture that built the Etowah Mounds.*

LOCATION: *The mounds are south from the Cartersville exit of Interstate 75, by way of Georgia 61.*

EXHIBITS: *In addition to the mounds themselves, a museum displays a sampling of the rich trove of carved items that were found inside them.*

HOURS: *Tuesday through Saturday, 9–5; Sunday, 2–5:30.*

ADMISSION: *$1.50.*

TELEPHONE: *(404) 387-3747.*

Chatsworth

JAMES VANN HOUSE

J ames Vann is one of those shadowy figures who turn up repeatedly on the southern frontier in the late eighteenth century. Although Georgia was one of the original thirteen states, its northern area, the Cherokee lands, was still an unsettled place. Frequently, men on the run from the seaboard cities or the neighboring Carolinas would turn up there to begin a new life.

Vann was one such man. He turned up in the Cherokee lands in the years after the revolution and married an Indian woman. He made a fortune as a trader and eventually became a chief. There was something dangerous in his makeup, contemporaries observed, that inspired respect, but not love.

Almost as if in penance for the actions of his past, he dedicated himself to bringing Christianity to his tribe. He imported Moravian missionaries from North Carolina in 1802 and sent his own children to their school. Two years later, he built this home across the road from the mission. The two-story red brick mansion stands on a slight elevation and was obviously built to inspire awe and a sense of stability. A hanging staircase and native carvings are its finest interior features.

Although Vann urged his tribe to take up Christianity, he was a polygamist with three wives, and in 1809, he was killed in retaliation for having shot one of his brothers-in-law in a duel. His son, Joseph, inherited the house and the family fortune. Soon, however, having violated a newly passed state law when he hired a white man to work for him, Vann's property was seized and he was sent west with his expelled people.

While on a visit to this house in 1835, John Howard Payne, the author of "Home Sweet Home," was arrested by Georgia guardsmen and charged with sedition. Payne insisted that he was simply writing a history of the Cherokee and was released after twelve days.

LOCATION: *The Vann Home is just west of Chatsworth, on Georgia 225.*
HOURS: *Tuesday through Saturday. 9–5; Sunday, 2–5:30.*
ADMISSION: *$1.50.*
TELEPHONE: *(404) 695-2598.*

Eatonton

ROCK EAGLE MOUND

R ock Eagle is the best-preserved animal effigy mound in the state, measuring 120 feet across its outspread wings. Built of quartz stones, the bird is painstakingly proportioned, right up to the relative size of the feathers in its wings. The shape becomes apparent only when viewed from above; visitors may gain that perspective from an adjacent tower.

LOCATION: *The mound, now part of a 4-H Club center, is 7 miles north of Eatonton by way of U.S. 441.*
HOURS: *Daily, dawn to dusk.*
ADMISSION: *Free.*
TELEPHONE: *(404) 485-2831.*

INDIAN SPRINGS STATE PARK

T he eighteenth century Creek favored Indian Springs as a campground because of its sulfurous waters and reputed restorative powers. It later became associated with the final disaster to befall the Creek nation. After the British withdrew from the region after the War of 1812, the Creek were subjected to the fury of the U.S. government. Many of the southern Creek had allied themselves with England, and Georgia demanded that they be expelled from the state, under the terms of an 1802 agreement with the federal government. Early in 1821, in a treaty signed at this spring, the Creek ceded most of their lands. They retained only a few tracts, including one surrounding the spring.

That was not enough for Georgia's Governor George Troup. Demanding the total expulsion of all Indians from the state, he bullied the government into obtaining the rest of the land. Creek leader William McIntosh, who had fought with the Americans in the war and was Troup's cousin, was happy to comply. In a second treaty signed in 1825 at Indian Springs, he agreed to the cession of the remaining Creek lands and expulsion to the west. The tribal leaders were outraged, and ordered McIntosh executed a few months later. Nevertheless, the agreement was upheld by the U.S. government, and the Creek were displaced across the Mississippi. The spring was turned into a state park immediately after the signing of the second treaty and has remained one ever since.

LOCATION: *The park is south of Jackson by way of U.S. 23 and Georgia 42.*
EXHIBITS: *A small historical museum recounts the events that occurred around this spring.*
HOURS: *The park is open daily, dawn to dusk. The museum is open daily, 8–5, June through August.*
ADMISSION: *Free.*
TELEPHONE: *(404) 775-7241.*

OCMULGEE NATIONAL MONUMENT

There are higher and more numerous mound groupings in the Southeast, but none contain such a clear record of continuous habitation, or are so impressively situated, as those at Ocmulgee. Ocmulgee is located on the Macon Plateau, just to the east of the central Georgia city of Macon. The view over modern Macon from the ancient mounds adds to their sense of majesty.

Spear points of nomadic hunters provide evidence of human occupancy on this site along the Ocmulgee River from as early as 9000 B.C. The fertile bottomlands, rich game, and elevated position attracted one group after another to the place for ten millennia. But the residents who left the most lasting impression were there for only two hundred years. The Early Mississippians, given their name because the culture arose in the Mississippi River valley, arrived here around 900 A.D. They were farmers who planted crops systematically, developed elaborate religious traditions, and built villages of one thousand people or more.

The community was abandoned for no clear reason in about 1100, and a new settlement was built nearby by a people who adapted many elements of the Mississippian culture. Finally, a Creek village was established in the late seventeenth century, and a British trading post operated here until 1715.

The visitor center at the park entrance supplies a historic overview of the site and discusses the significance of many of the artifacts found here. A short walk away, there is an earth lodge, a reconstructed version of a ceremonial building that was actually found in the village. It is capable of holding about fifty people and probably housed village leaders during important religious or political meetings. The clay floor is original, estimated to be about one thousand years old.

Right behind the lodge is the small Cornfield Mound, and the clear evidence of an ancient field, one of the oldest examples of cultivation in the Southeast, is intriguing.

In cool or dry weather it is an easy walk to the temple and funeral mounds, which you can see across the land once occupied by the Mississippian village. Otherwise, it is just a short drive on a park road.

The Great Temple Mound, which rises forty-five feet from a base of about three hundred feet, has a staircase to its summit. Archaeologists believe the mound had important religious significance and that a rectangular wooden structure once stood at its top. Beyond that they can only guess. There is no clear indication of what the relationship of this mound was to the Lesser Temple Mound, across the road.

The Funeral Mound, which lies at the end of the park road, was built up over seven successive stages, and more than one hundred burials have been uncovered there. More than half the mound was destroyed when a railroad was cut through the area in the 1870s, more than half a century before the first scientific examination of the site began.

Visitors can also stop at the site of the trading post, which stood slightly behind the Lesser Temple Mound and has yielded many important colonial era artifacts.

LOCATION: *Ocmulgee National Monument is within the city limits of Macon, and access is clearly marked from eastbound Interstate 16.*
HOURS: *Daily, 9–5.*
ADMISSION: *Free.*
TELEPHONE: *(912) 752-8257.*

Rome

CHIEFTAINS MUSEUM

Major Ridge, a leading tribal statesman, played a tragic role in the final years before the Cherokee expulsion to the west. He built this log cabin in 1794; it now lies at the core of the mansion that grew up around it, in what was the village of Chiaha, one of the most populous Cherokee settlements in northern Georgia. Operating a ferry service in the late nineteenth century, he turned his riverside home into a gathering place.

Ridge allied himself with the American forces in the war against the Creek, and his name probably reflects the rank he held in that conflict. As pressure grew for a state takeover of Indian lands, he joined John Ross, the leading advocate of resistance to the white incursion. Late in 1835, however, Ridge reversed his position and signed the treaty of New Echota, relinquishing all Cherokee land claims east of the Mississippi. He accompanied his people on the Trail of Tears, but was executed in 1839 in accordance with a tribal mandate that sentenced to death all who had signed the treaty.

Ridge's home is now a museum of the area's Indian heritage.

LOCATION: *The Chieftains Museum is just off the center of town, at 501 Riverside Parkway.*
EXHIBITS: *Besides a tour of the home, there are also displays and dioramas dealing with the Indian history of northern Georgia.*
HOURS: *Tuesday through Friday, 11–4; Sunday, 2–5.*
ADMISSION: *$1.*
TELEPHONE: *(404) 291-9494.*

LOUISIANA

POVERTY POINT STATE COMMEMORATIVE AREA

P overty Point had to wait until the airplane came along before its importance could be understood. These mounds along the bayous of northeastern Louisiana were first studied in 1872, but they were regarded as insignifi-
cant. But eighty-one years later, aerial photos taken by the U.S. Army Corps of
Engineers, which was mapping the flood plain of the Mississippi River, were
sent to the American Museum of Natural History. The staff discovered that
when viewed from the air, the group resolved itself into a shape that could not
be grasped from the ground.

The complex of six mounds, one set down inside the other, took the
shape of octagonal figures when viewed from above. One side had been washed
away by a shift in the river channel, making the shape impossible to discern at
ground level. Moreover, from the outlines visible in the pictures, the researches
estimated, in 1956, that the original structure may have been eleven miles
long, six feet high, and eighty feet thick. The largest of the mounds is
birdshaped and rises to a height of seventy feet. To move the amount of earth
required to build all this would have taken twenty million basketloads of soil,
each weighing fifty pounds. What is more astonishing is that there was no
evidence of a settled, agricultural community here. Poverty Point was put
together by people gathered for what was probably a religious motive and who
were capable of highly structured activity. Archaeologists have debated for
decades the possible relationship of these people to similar mound builders in
Mexico and Ohio. But carbon dating indicates that Poverty Point may be older
than either one of those cultures. The complex was built between 1300 and
700 B.C.

There is a museum on the site and visitors may climb an observation
tower to get some idea of what it looks like from the air. Archaeologists also
work here during the summer months.

LOCATION: *Poverty Point, named for the area's untillable soil, is 5 miles east of Epps by way of Louisiana Highways 134 and 577. From Interstate 20, take Louisiana 577 north at the Waverly exit.*
HOURS: *Wednesday through Sunday, 9–5.*
ADMISSION: *The site is free; museum is $2.50.*
TELEPHONE: *(318) 926-5492.*

Marksville

STATE COMMEMORATIVE AREA

T his is one of the oldest mound sites in the mid-South, dating from about 100 to 400 A.D. Of greater importance is the clear evidence found here of extensive contact with the Hopewell culture (*see* Mound City National Monument, Chillicothe, Ohio) far to the north. The practice of building enclosures for mounds and creating a central plaza are definitely Hopewell attributes, and Marksville is the earliest known site at which it was copied in the South. The mounds here were built in a conical shape, rather than the flat-topped variety favored by the Temple Mound people who later came to dominate this part of the country. There is a museum on the site explaining its archeological significance.

LOCATION: *The area is just east of Marksville, on Louisiana 5, overlooking the Old River.*
HOURS: *Wednesday through Sunday, 9–5.*
ADMISSION: *$2.50.*
TELEPHONE: *(318) 253-9546.*

MISSISSIPPI

WINTERVILLE MOUNDS STATE PARK

The Mississippi delta is among the flattest places in America, and the view from the top of the central mound seems almost alpine amid the surrounding flatness. The mounds are worth a visit if or no other reason than to see the dramatic appearance they make in the otherwise level landscape.

Winterville represents a major community of the Temple Mound people, a religious center that flourished around 1000 A.D. There are fifteen mounds in the group, the highest being fifty-five feet. The mounds were built by women carrying basket loads of dirt, and individual loads are visible within the mounds. When the mounds were completed, a temple or a chief's house was constructed on top of it. Eventually, these buildings were ceremonially destroyed by fire, they were covered over with more earth, and another building was erected on top of the mound. In this way, the mounds grew in successive layers over as many as 800 years. A museum displays articles recovered from the area, in addition to some donated by private collectors. Artifacts include rare pipes, weapons, beads, and tiny effigy owl and game stones.

LOCATION: *The mounds are 3 miles north of Greenville by way of Mississippi Highway One.*
HOURS: *Wednesday through Saturday, 8–5; Sunday, 1–5.*
ADMISSION: *$1 adults; 50 cents, children.*
TELEPHONE: *(601) 334-4684.*

▲ *Drawing of a carved stone pipe that is on view at Winterville Mounds Museum.*

Natchez

EMERALD MOUND

The Natchez Trace was one of the most important roads in early America, running northeast from Natchez through the lands of the Chickasaw and Choctaw. It was ancient when the Europeans found it, used for generations as a trade route between tribes of the Mississippi Valley and the Tennessee Valley. In 1801, the tribes gave the U.S. government the rights to run a wagon road through their lands along the old trail. It became one of the most important links between the lower Mississippi and the rest of the country. Flatboat crews would transport goods down the big river, but could not return by water because the bulky crafts were useless against the strong current. So they went back overland along the trace, and it became a legendary trail (*see* Chickasaw Indian Village, Tupelo, Mississippi).

Just a few miles from its start was the Emerald Mound, the great ceremonial center of the Natchez tribe. This thirty-five-foot high mound covers eight acres and is one of the largest in area in the country. It was built around 1300 A.D.

LOCATION: *North of Natchez, off the Natchez Trace Parkway on a county road.*
HOURS: *Daily, dawn to dusk.*
ADMISSION: *Free.*

GRAND VILLAGE OF THE NATCHEZ

Natchez is where legend met history in America. The Natchez were the last tribe of Mound Builders to survive until the coming of the Europeans, an arrival that proved devastating to them. In the late seventeenth century, when the French reached their home in the lower Mississippi Valley, the Natchez were still practicing a religion built around the construction of temple mounds. It was a religion that worshiped the sun, and the king was an absolute ruler known as The Great Sun. Each Natchez village had a temple mound and a residential mound for its ruler. What was unique about the Natchez, setting it apart from all other known absolutist societies, was that members of the nobility were required to marry commoners, or stinkards. These stinkards had absolutely no rights and were locked into their class. But every member of the tribe had both a noble and commoner background, which seemed to make for a stable society.

By this time, most of the tribes who inhabited former Mound Builder land had forgotten the origin of these earth hillocks. But around 1700, French missionaries started living among the Natchez and left detailed accounts of the Mound Builder culture. (Curiously enough, the writings, which explained the significance of the mounds, were themselves forgotten in the next century. Many white scientists who later studied the mounds refused to believe that Indians were capable of building them.)

The impact with France was fatal to the Natchez. Within six years, almost one-third of the tribe had fallen victim to smallpox or measles. One French observer professed to see a design in this. "So true is it," he wrote, "that it seems God wishes to make them give place to others." To speed the process, France established Fort Rosalie in the area of the great Natchez village in 1716 and began the systematic exploitation of the native people. Finally, in 1729 the Natchez rebelled, took the garrison, and wiped it out. The French response was quick and ruthless. A military expedition was sent into the Natchez country the following year on a campaign of extermination and enslavement. Only a few families escaped death or transport to the Caribbean; they joined the Chickasaw and Creek and, apparently, were welcomed into the tribes as possessors of special powers. The Natchez influence among the Chickasaw was especially strong. It was one reason for that tribe's ongoing hostility toward France, blocking the way to the French dream of unifying their colonies in the southern and midwestern portions of the Mississippi.

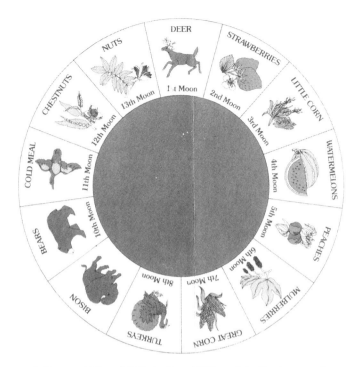

▲ *Between 1682 and 1729 the Grand Village of the Natchez was the center of activities for the Natchez people, who based their calendar on the sustaining elements of their culture.*

Grand Village was eradicated during the 1730 campaign. This reconstruction is on its site. Mounds have been renovated and many of the buildings erected according to the descriptions left by European observers. A museum tells the story of the Natchez and displays items recovered in digs on the site.

LOCATION: *The village is south of downtown on U.S. 61 at 400 Jefferson Davis Boulevard.*
HOURS: *Monday through Saturday, 9–5; Sunday, 1:30–5.*
ADMISSION: *Free.*
TELEPHONE: *(601) 446-6502.*

CHOCTAW INDIAN FAIR AND MUSEUM OF THE SOUTHERN INDIAN

One of the most prosperous of the southern tribes, the Choctaw had agricultural villages spread throughout central Mississippi. They were regarded as a practical people, unencumbered by the more complex religious and social structures of their neighbors. Chiefs had limited power and government was handled on the local level. The people were industrious, growing enough food to export staples to their neighbors. They preferred settling conflicts through stickball games, but their frontier towns were fortified and they were known as formidable warriors.

They aligned themselves with the U.S. government almost from its inception. Their leading chief, Pushmataha, understood the futility of opposing American force and rejected the pleas of Tecumseh to take up arms with the British in the War of 1812. He visited Washington in 1824 to remind the government of the Choctaw's ongoing friendliness.

None of it did any good. In 1830, the Treaty of Dancing Rabbit Creek, signed by a small minority of the tribe when most leaders walked out of the negotiations in disgust, committed the Choctaw to giving up their lands and removal to the West. Unlike the case in neighboring states, however, Mississippi did not require all Indians to leave. About three thousand Choctaw decided to stay behind, although losing title to their lands and giving up their tribal government. The result was economically ruinous. Promises of aid for land acquisition were not kept, and the Choctaw were reduced to sharecropping or squatting on their former lands. They also were victimized by Mississippi's rigorous Jim Crow laws.

Finally, in 1918 the Choctaw Agency was established here by the federal government and twenty-one thousand acres acquired for a reservation, centered around this town. It has governed itself through a tribal council since 1945, and in 1949 put on the first Choctaw Fair, now a major Indian event in the South. The Choctaw also have become the major employers in Neshoba County, operating several tribal manufacturing enterprises.

LOCATION: *The museum is located in the Pearl River community, which is immediately east of Philadelphia. This is also the location for the annual fair.*
EXHIBITS: *The museum gives a historical overview of the development of the tribe. A crafts shop is adjacent. During the Choctaw Fair, there is traditional dancing and pageantry, including hotly contested stickball games.*
HOURS: *The museum is open Monday through Friday, 8–4:30. The four-day Choctaw Fair begins on the Wednesday following the Fourth of July.*
ADMISSION: *Free.*
TELEPHONE: *(601) 656-5251.*

Preston

NANIH WAIYA STATE HISTORIC SITE

N anih Waiya is the sacred mound of the Choctaw, origin of many of the tribe's most enduring legends. It is said that from a cave within this Mother Mound emerged the Choctaw, Creek, Chickasaw, and Cherokee, to go in separate directions and live on earth. Before establishment of the Choctaw reservation, a substantial number of the tribe lived in the immediate vicinity. The mound could not be acquired for reservation land, but the state turned it into a protected historic site.

LOCATION: *Nanih Waiya is part of Noxapater State Park, 8 miles west of Preston by way of Mississippi 21 and 393.*
EXHIBITS: *There is a trail to the legendary cave and picnic grounds on the site.*
HOURS: *Daily, dawn to dusk.*
ADMISSION: *$1.*
TELEPHONE: *(601) 773-7988.*

Tupelo

CHICKASAW INDIAN VILLAGE

T he Chickasaw were some of the most formidable warriors in pre-European America. From their base in the northeastern corner of Mississippi, near the headwaters of the Tombigbee River, they ranged all across western Kentucky and Tennessee, winning hunting rights from numerically superior neighbors because of their skill at war. Although their language came from the same stock as that of the Choctaw, and tribal legends gave them a similar origin, the tribes were pulled into the competing colonial ambitions of England and France and warred against each other.

The Choctaw were allies of the French. But the Chickasaw saw that their interests lay in keeping the French out of the Mississippi Valley, and so they cast their lot with Britain. It was France's peculiar misfortune in both the northeastern and southwestern corners of its colonial empire to arouse the enmity of some of the most effective fighters among Native Americans—the Iroquois and the Chickasaw.

When the United States took title to the land, though, past alliances made no difference. The Chickasaw were also forced to relinquish their vast holdings through a series of treaties, between 1801 and 1832, and then expelled to the west along the Trail of Tears.

The northern portion of the Natchez Trace ran through their heartland, and just outside of Tupelo the site of one of their fortified villages has been set aside as a memorial. Interpretive displays explain how the village was designed and audio stations relate the history of the tribe. A nature walk also has been laid out to identify some of the native plants the Chickasaw used for food and medicine.

LOCATION: *The village is just northwest of Tupelo on the Natchez Trace Parkway, between U.S. 78 and Mississippi 6.*
HOURS: *Daily, dawn to dusk.*
ADMISSION: *Free.*

NORTH CAROLINA

QUALLA RESERVATION

C herokee is the administrative center of the Qualla Reservation, home of
the eastern band of Cherokee. With a population of eighty-five hundred,
it has the greatest concentration of Native Americans in the East. Since it
adjoins the most popular facility in the National Park system, Great Smoky
Mountains, the reservation also has become one of the top Indian attractions in
the country.

It exists, primarily, by accident. In the 1830s, the land of the Cherokee
spread across four states—Alabama, Georgia, Tennessee, and North Carolina.
At the inception of the Trail of Tears, the forced expulsion of the Cherokee to
Oklahoma, it was a fairly easy matter for federal troops to round up the settled
tribes. But as word began trickling back of the cruelty and deprivation that
awaited them on the forced march, groups of Indians began to elude the army
and make their way into the mountains. By 1838, as the last of the Cherokee
left their homeland, about fourteen hundred members of the tribe remained
hidden in these ancestral hills.

General Winfield Scott, who was charged with completing the expulsion, knew it was hopeless to try to find them. So he struck a deal with
Yonaguska, the chief of this remnant, through his agent, Colonel William
Thomas, a white man who was sympathetic to their situation. A man named
Tsali and some of his relatives had been charged with murder for killing a
soldier during their escape. Tsali testified that the soldier had prodded his wife
with a bayonet, and he had acted to protect her. Nonetheless, in the best
interests of the tribe, he agreed to surrender himself to Scott if the other
fugitives could remain unmolested. Through this heroic act, the Cherokee
remained here, and eventually purchased the reservation lands through a
congressional grant.

▲ *Videotape presentations help illuminate displays at the Museum of the Cherokee Indian,*
where the most outstanding examples of ancient craftsmanship are exhibited within the
framework of their historical and cultural contexts.

LOCATION: *Cherokee is located at the junction of U.S. Highways 19 and 441, 3 miles*
south of the border of Great Smoky Mountains National Park.
EXHIBITS: *The Cherokee Visitor Center, on Main Street, carries information on activities*
and attractions in the area.
HOURS: *The visitor center is open daily, 8–9, June though August; 8–5, rest of year.*
ADMISSION: *Free.*
TELEPHONE: *(800) 438-1601.*

MUSEUM OF THE CHEROKEE INDIAN

In place of the living history approach, the museum (a non-profit corporation
owned by the Eastern Band of the Cherokee Indians), takes a decidedly
modern approach. Extensive collections of tribal artifacts, clothing, and crafts
are presented within the framework of their historical and cultural contexts,
supplemented by an impressive range of audio and video tapes. Six mini-
theaters offer presentations about prehistoric thorough modern times. "Hear-
phones" allow visitors to listen to ancient legends in the Cherokee language; a
display illuminates each written character of the Sequoyan syllabary (which has
preserved the language in written form since 1821) as it is pronounced, so that

visitors may learn about the language while hearing it spoken. A presentation in the museum's auditorium provides an inside glimpse into the present-day Cherokee community.

LOCATION: *North on U.S. 441.*
HOURS: *September to mid-June: Daily, 9–5. Mid-June to late August: Monday through Saturday, 9–8, and Sunday, 9–5:30.*
ADMISSION: *$3.50. Children (ages 6–12) $1.75.*
TELEPHONE: *(704) 497-3481.*

OCONALUFTEE INDIAN VILLAGE

A re-created Cherokee village of the eighteenth century, Oconaluftee is one of the best living history museums on Native Americans. Authentically costumed members of the tribe demonstrate traditional crafts in a setting that is meant to reflect an actual Indian community. The eastern Cherokee are noted for their skills in basketry, and examples of this art are given frequently each day.

There is also a reconstructed seven-sided council chamber and several typical dwellings filled with items that would have been used during the daily work routine. An authentic herb garden also is on the site.

LOCATION: *Oconaluftee is about 2 miles north of Cherokee, on the road to the national park, U.S. 441.*
HOURS: *Daily, 9–5:30, mid-May to the last weekend in October.*
ADMISSION: *$7.*
TELEPHONE: *(704) 497-2315.*

UNTO THESE HILLS

T his annual summer pageant re-creates the history of the Cherokee, with special emphasis on the story of the group that broke away from the Trail of Tears to make their home here. The outdoor drama has been presented each year since 1950 from a script written by Kermit Hunter and first produced with the assistance of the University of North Carolina.

The focus of the drama is the story of Tsali (*see* Cherokee, North Carolina), who surrendered himself to an uncertain white justice so that his tribe could live in peace in their new home. The actors are residents of the Cherokee reservation, many of them direct descendants of characters being portrayed.

▲ *The Cherokee practice the art of basket-weaving at Oconaluftee Indian Village.*

LOCATION: *The pageant takes place in the Mountainside Theater, north of the town of Cherokee and adjacent to Oconaluftee Village.*
HOURS: *Monday through Saturday at 8:30, mid-June to late August.*
ADMISSION: *$9.50 for reserved seats, $7.50 for general admission.*
TELEPHONE: *(704) 497-2111.*

Cullowhee

JUDACULLA ROCK

Judaculla Rock, a sandstone boulder covered with pictures and messages that never have been deciphered, was a mystery even to the Cherokee, who found it on their land. They built a legend about a giant named Tsul'kula who landed on it while leaping from his home on a nearby mountaintop to the creek

▲ *The Eagle Dance is featured in the tragic and triumphant outdoor drama "Unto These Hills."*

below. The markings are supposed to be his footprints. The pictographs are prehistoric in origin but have never been attributed to a specific people or time.

LOCATION: *Cullowhee is about 25 miles south of Cherokee by way of U.S. 441 and North Carolina 107. The rock is 6 miles past the town on the state highway and Caney Fork Road.*
HOURS: *Daily, dawn to dusk.*
ADMISSION: *Free.*

Mount Gilead

TOWN CREEK INDIAN MOUND STATE HISTORIC SITE

Town Creek is the only significant mound grouping in the state and is thought to be the work of a tribe related to the Creek. The main activity here came in the fifteenth century, when the site functioned as a religious and ceremonial center for surrounding agricultural villages.

Many of the Indian villages that fringed the ceremonial ground have been located by archaeologists, and much of the area at Town Creek has been excavated, including the mound itself, which has been rebuilt. The major temple on top of the mound, and the minor temple, or priest's dwelling, have also been reconstructed, and many burials have been located, some of which have been excavated. One of the thatch-roofed burial huts has been rebuilt, and the stockade wall replaces one that originally surrounded the area.

The exhibit area has special displays that interpret the way of life of the Indians of Town Creek, with audio-visual shows that complement the artifacts. There are examples of pottery made by Pee Dee women with the coil method, which makes the clay bowls look as though they're made of wood. The archaeological section gives an idea of the work that has been done at the site since it was first excavated in the thirties, and includes photographs of early excavations and explanations of techniques, such as dating artifacts. A five-panel depiction of life during the Town Creek period—illustrating the crops they grew, the games they played, and other aspects of their daily life—places artifacts within their social and cultural context.

LOCATION: *Mount Gilead is located near the Yadkin River power project, in the south-central part of the state, 20 miles north of Wadesboro and U.S. 74 by way of North Carolina 109. The mound is east of town on North Carolina 73.*
HOURS: *Monday through Saturday, 9–5, and Sunday, 1–5, April through October; Closed Monday and at 4 P.M. on other days, rest of year.*
ADMISSION: *Free.*
TELEPHONE: *(919) 439-6802.*

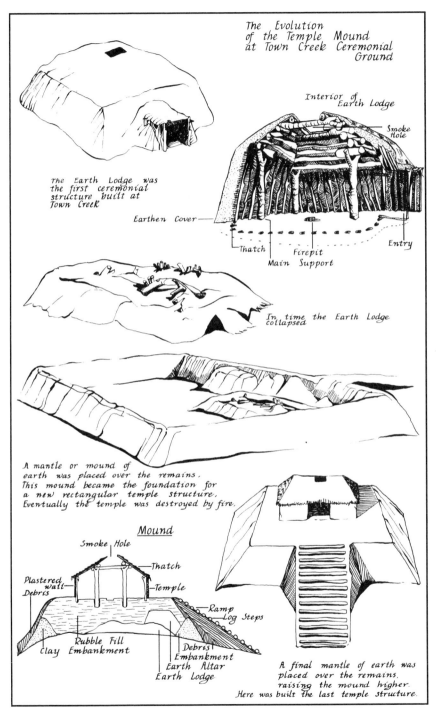

The Evolution
of the Temple Mound
at Town Creek Ceremonial
Ground

Interior of Earth Lodge

Smoke Hole

The Earth Lodge was the first ceremonial structure built at Town Creek

Earthen Cover

Thatch

Main Support

Firepit

Entry

In time the Earth Lodge collapsed

A mantle or mound of earth was placed over the remains. This mound became the foundation for a new rectangular temple structure. Eventually the temple was destroyed by fire.

Mound

Smoke Hole

Thatch

Plastered wall Debris

Temple

Ramp

Log Steps

Rubble Fill

Clay Embankment

Debris Embankment Earth Altar Earth Lodge

A final mantle of earth was placed over the remains, raising the mound higher. Here was built the last temple structure.

▲ Town Creek is the only significant mound grouping in North Carolina and is thought to be the work of a tribe related to the Creek.

Pembroke

STRIKE AT THE WIND

E arly in 1958, the Lumbee Indians suddenly burst from generations of obscurity and mystery into the headlines of the nation's newspapers. On the evening of January 13, the Ku Klux Klan decided to burn a cross in the nearby town of Maxton. The era of civil rights demonstrations had begun throughout the South. While black people were the targets of most of their racial intimidation, the local Klan decided it was time to send a message to the large Indian population of Robeson County, just in case they got any funny ideas about equal rights. But the Klan got more than it bargained for. As it prepared its white-sheeted parade, the group was suddenly attacked by a war-whooping, rifle-brandishing crowd of Lumbee Indians. The Klansmen bolted and ran, and delighted newspapers ran front-page pictures of their flight across the country.

It was the first time the Lumbee had attracted much attention beyond North Carolina. But they had formed a major presence in this southeastern county for years. They did not live on a reservation, did not practice traditional crafts, nor did they dress in anything recognized as Indian garb. Neighboring tribes did not regard them as Indians. The Cherokee, Cheraw, and Catawba insisted they were not members of their groups. Early white settlers, who found them here in the 1770s, noted their features differed from other Indians and that their complexions were somewhat darker. They put two and two together and decided these must be the Croatans, the Indians who were encountered by the Lost Colony of North Carolina before its disappearance in 1587. They theorized that their distinct features were the result of intermarriage with members of that colony.

The Lumbee indignantly denied this, although admitting they had no idea what their origins were. They were treated as a separate entity in Robeson County. They were classified as "free persons of color" during the era of slavery, but were made to use segregated facilities, separate from both white and black, in the Jim Crow days.

During the early years of Reconstruction, early predecessors of the Klan murdered James Lowrie, an unarmed Indian. His son, Henry, went underground for the next ten years and with a band of raiders struck back at the whites he thought were responsible for his father's death. His story is dramatized at the annual outdoor pageant Strike at the Wind. The incident was first dramatized in 1922, and the pageant is adapted from that play.

For almost a century after the Civil War, these Indians fought for some sort of legal recognition. Finally, in 1953 they were recognized as the "Lumbee Indians of Robeson County" by an act of the North Carolina legislature. The name stems from the river that runs through the county. About twenty-six thousand people who identify themselves as Lumbee continue to live in the area.

LOCATION: *Pembroke is located just west of Interstate 95 by way of North Carolina 711 at the Lumberton exit.*
HOURS: *The pageant is put on Thursday through Sunday at 8:30 P.M. in July and August.*
ADMISSION: *$7.*
TELEPHONE: *(919) 521-3112.*

TENNESSEE

RED CLAY STATE HISTORICAL AREA

I n the fall of 1838, the Cherokee tribal council assembled at Red Clay for the last time. Georgia had outlawed any public gathering by Indians three years earlier. Tribal leaders were forced to abandon the capital at New Echota to continue the fight against expulsion. A three-year delaying action was led from Red Clay by principal chief John Ross. But time had run out on the Cherokee Nation. Mass removals to the west began that summer. The hardships in the heat were so great that federal authorities decided to wait until October before removing the bulk of the tribe. Still, one in four would die on the march.

Gathering in despair, representatives of the dissolved nation met to resolve last matters in their ancestral land. Then they were divided into thirteen groups and herded away on the Trail of Tears. The place has been turned into a State Historical Area, with a museum and interpretive center and a reconstruction of the last council house.

LOCATION: *The historical area is south of town by way of Tennessee 60, just north of the Georgia state line.*
HOURS: *Daily, 8:30–4.*
ADMISSION: *Free.*
TELEPHONE: *(615) 472-2627.*

OLD STONE FORT STATE PARK

O ld Stone Fort, measuring more than a mile around, on the bluffs above the Duck River, illustrates the incredulity with which white settlers viewed ancient remains. The work on these earth walls is so skillful and intricate that the pioneer mentality could not grasp that Indians were capable of such an achievement. Instead, they attributed the fort to the expedition of Hernando De Soto in 1541, although there is no evidence that he ever made it to this part of Tennessee.

When the technique of tree-ring dating became known, a local historian sampled trees growing on the ruins of the fortification. He found that they would have been almost one hundred years old when De Soto landed. The story typifies, however, the condescending attitude of most European settlers. Well into the twentieth century, they attributed such ancient monuments to some "vanished race," rather than the Indians (*see* Seip Mound State Memorial, Bainbridge, Ohio). The walls, which enclosed a religious center, are thought to have been built between 100 and 300 A.D.

LOCATION: *North of the Manchester exit of Interstate 24 by way of U.S. 41.*
EXHIBITS: *There is a trail around the walls, as well as an interpretive center, a museum, and recreational facilities.*
HOURS: *The museum is open daily, 8–4:30. The park closes at dusk.*
ADMISSION: *Free.*
TELEPHONE: *(615) 723-5073.*

Memphis

CHUCALISSA INDIAN MUSEUM

W hen Hernando De Soto became the first European in recorded history to view the Mississippi River, he saw it from bluffs occupied by Chickasaw villages. The site would become Tennessee's largest city. A veteran looter in Peru and Mexico, De Soto passed on to Arkansas in search of gold, leaving the Spanish flag behind. The Chickasaw ignored the claim and went about their business, until disturbed by the next European incursion, more than a century later.

When De Soto arrived, the Chickasaw were the dominant tribe of the Mississippi Valley. Their extensive hunting rights, which extended across most of western Tennessee and Kentucky, had been won through their skill as warriors.

Even before the Chickasaw reached the Mississippi bluffs, however, the site of Memphis had been occupied by an older people. Chucalissa Village had been inhabited for half a millennium before De Soto's appearance, and only in the early years of the sixteenth century were its residents displaced by the Chickasaw. Chucalissa is now an archeological site of Memphis State University. Several typical huts and a chief's home have been reconstructed, and an

▲ *Chucalissa Village was inhabited for half a millennium before its residents were displaced in the early years of the sixteenth century by the Chickasaw.*

interpretive center explains the historic significance of the place. In addition, the National Native Arts and Crafts Fair is held here annually in May.

LOCATION: *The village is located in the southwestern corner of Memphis, west on Mitchell Road from U.S. 61, within T. O. Fuller State Park.*

HOURS: *Tuesday through Saturday, 9–5; Sunday, 1–5. The park is closed the last two weeks of December.*

ADMISSION: *$3.*

TELEPHONE: *(901) 785-3160.*

Pinson

PINSON MOUNDS

This is the most significant mound grouping in Tennessee. There are twelve mounds clustered here along the Forked Deer River, the highest of which measures 73 feet. Like many other southern mounds, they served primarily as a ceremonial center for surrounding agricultural villages. While the largest mounds were used for various ceremonies, the smaller ones, as well as Twin Mounds, held burials. A number of cremation and activity areas have been found nearby, and mound sites contain related earthworks.

Managed by the Tennessee Department of conservation, Division of Parks and Recreation, Pinson Mounds is listed on the National Register of Historic Places and is protected by the Tennessee State Antiquities Act. It consists of 1,162 acres of field and forest, wild flowers, creeks, and a nursery of the Division of Forestry. There are hiking trails through the area.

The museum is designed to replicate an Indian mound; it houses the park offices, an archaeological library, an 80-seat theater, 4,500 square feet of exhibit areas, and the West Tennessee Regional Archaeology Office.

LOCATION: *The mounds are at 460 Ozier Road, off U.S. 45 in Pinson, which is 12 miles south of Jackson.*
HOURS: *Monday through Saturday, 8:30–4:30, and Sunday, 1–5, April–September. Monday through Friday, 8–4:30, rest of year.*
ADMISSION: *Free.*
TELEPHONE: *(901) 988-5614.*

Vonore

SEQUOYAH'S BIRTHPLACE

There was little doubt the man was obsessed. He would spend hours scribbling strange little marks that no one could decipher on pieces of bark, grunting in sounds that no one could recognize. His wife, disgusted by what she regarded as his worthless eccentricity, burned down the hut in which he was working and destroyed months of labor. But Sequoyah persevered, and in 1821 he gave his people, the Cherokee, a priceless gift, a written language.

He was born George Gist, or possibly Guess, in a cabin along the Little Tennessee River on land that was claimed by North Carolina, sometime around the start of the American Revolution. There were stories later that his father was Nathaniel Gist, the agent sent by General George Washington to negotiate with the Cherokee. But these were never proved. What is known about him is that he was lame from a childhood injury or illness, that he was an accomplished silversmith, that he preferred to be known by his Indian name, and that sometime after the War of 1812 he became convinced that the salvation of his people was a written language.

Leaving his unsympathetic spouse, he joined an early Cherokee emigration to the Arkansas Territory and worked for three years in solitary concentration. Using symbols he had found in an old spelling book, he tried to match them to the basic sounds of the Cherokee language. He felt that

▲ *Cherokee scholar Sequoyah was born in a cabin along the Little Tennessee River, on land that was claimed by North Carolina, sometime around the start of the American Revolution.*

teaching the tribe to write in English would make them subservient to the white man's way of thinking. He wanted to preserve the Cherokee way of expression, and the only way to do that was to write in the Indian language.

In 1821, he was ready to return home. He gathered his daughter and went to call on the Tribal Council, led by John Ross. While he waited outside the meeting, his daughter transcribed with his written symbols what was said. She then showed the writing to her father, who repeated the words perfectly. Still not convinced, the council called for several young men to be taught the language; then were given separate messages, which were shuffled at random, and then made to repeat what had been written. When they succeeded, Sequoyah's alphabet was officially adopted. It spread across the Cherokee Nation within months, taught one-to-one by travelers to every village and farm, and was mastered in a day or two. Within a year, virtually all the Cherokee people were literate. Messages were exchanged, the Bible translated, and a written constitution adopted. Language was knowledge and knowledge was power. A national newspaper, the *Cherokee Phoenix*, was started in New Echota. Ironically, the literacy of the Cherokee only made them seem more threatening to the white settlers who were hungry for their lands. Knowledge was power, but the forces aligned against them were more powerful still, and literacy could not save their nation.

Sequoyah returned to his new home in the West in 1822, after receiving the lifetime bequest of a salt bed by a grateful nation. He went on to new projects (*see* Home of Sequoyah, Sallisaw, Oklahoma and Cherokee Ghost

Town, Oroville, California) and eventually was honored by having a forest of giant coastal redwoods, the tallest living things on earth, bear his name.

LOCATION: *The birthplace is 1 mile east of town on Tennessee 360, about 35 miles south of Knoxville.*

EXHIBITS: *There are displays on Sequoyah's life and the alphabet he invented. Visitors can put on headphones and hear the language being spoken. Other exhibits relate to Cherokee history and legends, and adjacent to the museum is a memorial to the tribe.*

HOURS: *Monday through Saturday, 10–6; Sunday, 12–6, March through December.*

ADMISSION: *$2.50.*

TELEPHONE: *(615) 884-6246.*

GREAT LAKES AND OHIO VALLEY

GREAT LAKES AND OHIO VALLEY

ILLINOIS
1 Piasa Bird Paintings, *Alton*
2 Cahokia Mounds State Historic Site, *East Saint Louis*
3 Dickson Mounds State Museum, *Lewistown*
4 Black Hawk Historic Site, *Rock Island*

INDIANA
5 Angel Mounds State Historic Site, *Evansville*
6 Tippecanoe Battlefield, *Lafayette*
7 Falls Park Memorial, *Pendleton*
8 Chief Menominee Monument, *Plymouth*
9 Council Oak, *South Bend*

KENTUCKY
10 Chief Paduke Statue, *Paducah*

MICHIGAN
11 Andrew Blackbird Museum, *Harbor Springs*
12 Indian Dormitory, *Mackinac Island*
13 Fort St. Joseph Museum, *Niles*
14 Marquette Mission and Museum of Ojibwa Culture, *Saint Ignace*

OHIO
15 Seip Mound State Memorial, *Bainbridge*
16 Flint Ridge State Memorial, *Brownsville*
17 Mound City National Monument, *Chillicothe*
18 Tecumseh Pageant, *Chillicothe*
19 Ohio Historical Center, *Columbus*
20 Sun Watch Archeological Park, *Dayton*
21 Gnadenhutten Historical Park, *Gnadenhutten*
22 Inscription Rock State Memorial, *Kelleys Island*
23 Fort Ancient State Memorial, *Lebanon*
24 Serpent Mound State Memorial, *Locust Grove*
25 Mound Cemetery, *Marietta*
26 Miamisburg Mound State Memorial, *Miamisburg*
27 Moundbuilders State Memorial, *Newark*
28 Schoenbrunn and Trumpet in the Land Pageant, *New Philadelphia*
29 Historic Indian Museum, *Piqua*
30 Fort Hill State Memorial, *Sinking Spring*
31 Wyandotte Mission, *Upper Sandusky*
32 Blue Jacket Pageant, *Xenia*

ONTARIO
33 Brant County Museum, *Brantford*
34 Her Majesty's Chapel of the Mohawks, *Brantford*
35 Woodland Indian Cultural Education Centre, *Brantford*
36 Joseph Brant Home, *Burlington*
37 Ska-Nah-Doht Indian Village, *Delaware*
38 Serpent Mounds Provincial Park, *Keene*
39 Museum of Indian Archeology, *London*
40 Sainte–Marie Among the Huron, *Midland*
41 Huron Village, *Midland*
42 Six Nations Pageant, *Ohsweken*
43 Thunder Bay Art Gallery, *Thunder Bay*
44 Petroglyphs Provincial Park, *Woodview*

WEST VIRGINIA
45 Aracoma Pageant, *Logan*
46 Grave Creek Mound, *Moundsville*
47 Battle Monument State Park, *Point Pleasant*

WISCONSIN
48 Stockbridge–Munsee Tribal Council Museum, *Bowler*
49 Chief Oshkosh Museum, *Egg Harbor*
50 Panther Intaglio Mound, *Fort Atkinson*
51 Oneida Nation Museum, *Green Bay*
52 Ben Guthrie Cultural Center, *Lac du Flambeau*
53 Aztalan State Park, *Lake Mills*
54 Bad River Cultural Center, *Odanah*
55 Buffalo Arts Center, *Red Cliff*
56 Lizard Mound State Park, *West Bend*
57 Stand Rock Winnebago Ceremonials, *Wisconsin Dells*

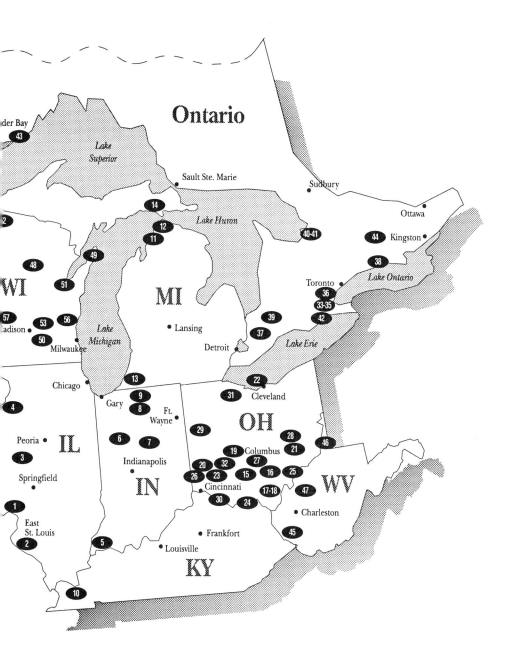

ILLINOIS

PIASA BIRD PAINTINGS

The Piasa paintings on the bluffs above the Mississippi River are not authentic, but their interest lies in their contribution to legend. Only the first set of paintings in this area were actually painted by native people; these, the second set to replace the original paintings, demonstrate how Indian legends can permeate the history of an American community long after those who created them have gone.

These rock paintings of a monstrous bird on the Illinois side of the river were first observed by Father Jacques Marquette on his voyage of 1673. They became a familiar landmark for the next two hundred years, and were believed to be the work of the Illinois tribe, who occupied these lands in the seventeenth century. The most common version of the story of the paintings is that they represent the Piasa, a hideous bird that lived along the river and captured everyone it encountered. When a chief named Quatoga allowed the bird to spot him, twenty of his warriors rose from concealment and shot it down when it swooped to capture him.

The original paintings were destroyed by quarrying in the 1870s. Redone from old drawings in 1934, these, too, were destroyed when the Great River Road was widened. By now regarded as an integral part of Alton's history, the paintings were again recreated, on a site slightly upstream from the original.

LOCATION: *The paintings are northwest of Alton and are best viewed from the river or from the opposite bank, on Missouri 94.*

CAHOKIA MOUNDS STATE HISTORIC SITE

The massive Cahokia Mounds earthwork is frequently referred to as the largest mound in America north of Mexico. Standing slightly more than 100 feet tall, the mounds are 1,080 feet long and 710 feet wide. In his book *The First American,* C. W. Ceram compares these mounds to Egypt's largest pyramid, the Pyramid of Cheops, at Gizeh. While that pharaoh's tomb is 480 feet high, its ground area covers approximately 200,000 square feet less than Monk's Mound, the main structure at Cahokia. The sixteen-acre mound was at one time surrounded by one hundred smaller mounds, and within a seven-mile radius there were yet another three hundred mounds.

Built by people of the Temple Mound culture of the lower Mississippi Valley (*see* Grand Village of the Natchez, Natchez, Mississippi), the mounds are believed to have been part of an enormous religious and political community that housed thousands of inhabitants in a six-square-mile city. Evidence indicates that the earthwork was also a solar observatory, with sighting posts aligning the sun with certain landmarks to indicate the change of the agricultural seasons. The main mound itself was assembled over a 350-year period, and was left incomplete sometime around 1250 A.D. Several of the smaller mounds surrounding it were built later; we do not know why these mound builders switched their priorities.

The site was already completely abandoned by the time the first Europeans arrived, and pioneer farmers were put off by the bones that turned up in plowing. In the early nineteenth century, Trappist monks attempted to establish a community at the base of the largest mound. They grew vegetables along its four terraces, but gave up and returned to France in 1813. The mounds were not systematically excavated until 1922. Today, a resident archeologist explains the historic significance of what has been found at the mounds.

LOCATION: *The mounds are just east of East Saint Louis, by way of the Kings Highway exit of Interstate 55, 70.*
HOURS: *Daily, 9–5.*
ADMISSION: *Free.*
TELEPHONE: *(618) 344-5268.*

▲ *Dickson Mounds Museum offers workshops and demonstrations
relating to the daily life of the Mississippian culture.*

Lewistown

DICKSON MOUNDS STATE MUSEUM

D ickson Mounds, an excavation exhibit of some 234 open graves from the
Late Woodland and Mississippian periods, was opened to the public in
1927. The mounds, located on a riverside bluff, are thought to be the work of a
people who blended the Temple Mound culture, which is found elsewhere in
Illinois, with that of the Hopewell People, who were most active in Ohio.
Standing at the margins of several major culture areas, the Dickson Mounds—
comprised of single burials, mass graves and a wealth of funerary items—
provided archaeologists with insight into the changes that were taking place in
lifestyles over a large area of North America from A.D. 900 to 1300.

For years, Native American groups protested the open-burial exhibit,
and, in 1989, a World Archaeological Congress meeting held in South Dakota
declared the exhibit unacceptable. A movement away from open burials had
already prompted the closing of similar exhibits in response to Native Ameri-

▲ *The Dickson Mounds Museum focuses on the archaeological record left by native people who lived along the Illinois River Valley over a period of 12,000 years.*

can pressure to repatriate native burial sites. In April of 1992, the Dickson Mounds burial sites were closed to the public.

The decision to entomb the skeletal remains beneath limestone vaults pleased neither faction in the debate. Locals are skeptical about ever receiving the $4 million promised to the museum by the state in order to expand other exhibits (in recompense for closing the centerpiece exhibit), and Native American groups are concerned that the burial method leaves open the possibility of reopening the sites at a later date. And the concrete burial does nothing to address the Native American belief that a life span is complete only when the earth reclaims a person's bones.

Despite the closure of the grave sites (the skeletal remains were actually locked up in April of 1992, awaiting the museum's financial reward for their final interment), the museum is well worth visiting. The exhibits examine the archaeological record left by the people who lived along the Illinois River Valley over a period of 12,000 years. Displays focus on the daily life of the Mississippian culture (A.D. 900-1300), illustrating the ways in which people used their environment to obtain food, clothing and shelter; they illustrate the ways settlements were organized, the kinds of buildings and artifacts used in ceremonies, and the ways in which the dead were buried. The museum also offers a range of special exhibits and public programs on archaeology, Native American culture, and other topics.

LOCATION: *Dickson Mounds is southeast of Lewisburg by way of Illinois 100 and County Road 9.*
HOURS: *Daily, 8:30–5.*
ADMISSION: *Free.*
TELEPHONE: *(309) 547-3721.*

Rock Island

BLACK HAWK HISTORIC SITE

In 1804, five chiefs of the Sauk and Fox traveled to Saint Louis to meet with federal officials in an effort to win the release of a young Indian who was charged with murder. During these discussions, the chiefs were given plentiful amounts of liquor; while intoxicated, they signed an agreement that ceded the rights to their lands in Illinois for an annual payment of one thousand dollars. They were to retain hunting and residential privileges as long as the federal government controlled the land.

When the treaty was renewed in 1816, one of the younger Sauk chiefs, Black Hawk, was horrified to learn what his predecessors had signed. The tribe's two great villages were a few miles apart, near the confluence of the Rock and Mississippi rivers. Black Hawk had seen the influx of miners pouring into the Galena area, in the northern part of the tribal lands, when lead deposits there were opened for private development. He sensed that settlers would not be far behind and that they would be particularly interested in the fertile tribal heartland.

Leaders of the Sauk and Fox had debated what to do for years. Keokuk (*see* Chief Keokuk Memorial, Keokuk, Iowa) counseled peace and moved his followers to the western bank of the Mississippi. Black Hawk, however, decided that the only immediate confrontation would secure Indian rights to the land. In 1831, he began to challenge white farmers, whom he accused of digging up Indian burial grounds to plant their corn. The farmers appealed in terror to the governor, who declared that Illinois was "in a state of actual invasion," an ironic phrase to use regarding people who inhabited the land when the settlers arrived.

The Black Hawk War is now recalled as an almost comic affair, with self-important white commanders shuffling troops to fight a hopelessly outnumbered enemy. At the time, though, this war was deadly serious, with both sides convinced that the future of the upper Midwest was hanging in the balance. There were reports that the British, who sought to protect their interests in the Northwest by stopping American expansion, were among those who encouraged Black Hawk. A volunteer army attacked the Indian village in late June at Rock Island, but Black Hawk had already moved his followers to safety on the far bank of the Mississippi. Things were calm for a while.

Black Hawk had no inkling of the furor he had instigated. The following spring, he crossed back into Illinois with the intent of innocently joining the Winnebago in Wisconsin to plant crops. Their movements were reported to the state militia, which overtook them along the Rock River, near the present town of Byron. The soldiers fired shots during an attempted parley, and a Sauk who was holding a flag of truce was shot down. Both sides attacked, and the white troops were routed at the Battle of Stillman's Run. Black Hawk's force of about four hundred men seemed like a greater menace than ever.

When federal troops were sent into the campaign, Black Hawk tried to retreat to the Mississippi. The troops ignored his appeals for a truce, and he was forced into a guerrilla action. As he reached the river, however, near the present-day city of La Crosse, Wisconsin, Black Hawk was attacked in force, and the Indians were overrun. A federal gunboat fired on those who tried to cross the river, and the few who reached the opposite shore were attacked by their traditional enemies, the Sioux, who had been watching the battle develop.

As a result of the war, all Indians were expelled from Illinois; it would only have been a matter of time before the onrush of white settlers forced the Indians off the land. Black Hawk was captured and taken on a tour of the East. For the first time, he realized the numbers that opposed him. He dictated an autobiography, and dedicated it to the general who had defeated him: "That you may never experience the humility that the power of the American government has reduced me to, is the wish of him, who in his native forests was once as proud and bold as yourself." The U.S. Army, which had great difficulty in coping with Black Hawk's tactics, formed six permanent companies of cavalry after the war, the first peacetime mounted units it had ever authorized.

The Black Hawk Historic Site is located at the Sauk village that was the chief's home. The promontory commands a gorgeous view of the Rock River Valley. The Hauberg Museum contains historical displays on the Black Hawk War and the daily life of the Sauk and Fox when this was their home. A statue of an Indian, usually identified as Black Hawk, stands near the town of Oregon, the work of the famed sculptor Lorado Taft. It is a popular attraction in the picturesque Rock River Valley.

LOCATION: *The Black Hawk site is at the southern edge of Rock Island, by way of U.S. 67 and Illinois 5.*
HOURS: *The museum is open Wednesday through Sunday, 9–12 and 1–5.*
ADMISSION: *Free.*
TELEPHONE: *(309) 788-0177.*

INDIANA

ANGEL MOUNDS STATE MEMORIAL

The Angel Mounds community, located on the banks of the Ohio River, was settled by Mississippian people known the as Mound Builders. Raised between 1200 and 1400 A.D. , the site is the largest grouping of mounds in the state. Excavation, which did not begin until 1939, revealed that the area was a substantial farming community with a few thousand inhabitants: part of an advanced culture, the site was occupied for nearly 250 years. The Mississippians probably chose this site because of the nearby river, the abundant food supply, and the great number of plants and animals available to them.

The town originally covered 103 acres and served as an important religious, political and trade center for people living within a fifty mile radius. This society built 11 earthen mounds for elevated buildings; there are no burial mounds. The community was abandoned over a period of years before white explorers came to America; archaeologists can offer no explanation for the community's abandonment, since there is no evidence of warfare or disease. Several typical buildings from this settlement have been reconstructed from archeological evidence, including winter houses, a round house, summer houses, a temple, as well as a portion of a stockade wall similar to the one that surrounded the village. The interpretive center exhibits artifacts recovered from the mounds, and a nature walk traverses the 103-acre site.

LOCATION: *The Angel Mounds are 7 miles east of downtown Evansville on Pollack Road. Take the Covert Avenue/Hwy. 662 exit off I-64, and follow signs to Angel Mounds.*
HOURS: *Tuesday through Saturday, 9–5; Sunday, 1–5. Closed Monday. Open Memorial Day, July 4th, Labor Day and Good Friday. Closed January 1 to March 15.*
ADMISSION: *Free.*
TELEPHONE: *(812) 853-3956.*

TIPPECANOE BATTLEFIELD

For more than a century, the Shawnee were steadily pushed back from their ancestral lands along the Cumberland River of Kentucky. Other tribes, driven from the Atlantic seaboard by pressure from white colonists, forced them north and west into the Ohio Valley. There, they formed a wall of resistance against the onrush of settlement.

These were the Indians who fought Daniel Boone and his followers at the end of the Wilderness Road. The Shawnee also fought settlers who defied British law by moving into the rich lands west of Fort Pitt, a clash that helped precipitate the American Revolution. Joined by another branch of the tribe that had moved to Pennsylvania, and by other native people in Ohio, they fought a thirty-year delaying action. Finally, in 1793, the American forces of Anthony Wayne defeated them at Fallen Timbers and drove them to northern Indiana.

Remarkable Native American leaders began to emerge. Tecumseh, twenty-five years old at the time of the bitter defeat at Fallen Timbers, was enraged by the treaty that ensued, ceding tribal lands in Ohio. He scorned the counsel of his elders to accept the inevitable and realized that the various tribes could avoid persecution only by unifying politically and by allying with the British. Tecumseh realized there was no other way to halt the westward-moving flood.

Tenskwatawa, his brother, was a stirring orator who preached a return to traditional ways and avoidance of the corrupting influence of the whites. He became known as The Prophet. The brothers built a settlement on Tippecanoe Creek, near its mouth at the Wabash River. It was called Prophet's Town and became a rallying point for those who wished to resist.

Tecumseh urged other leaders to halt land cessions. In defiance, older leaders of other tribes signed the Fort Wayne Treaty in 1809, giving up more land rights in Indiana. They ridiculed Tecumseh and the Shawnee as interlopers who had no right to tell them what to do with their lands. The Wyandot and Potawatomi were infuriated by this, and they, together with restless young men who had left the Miami and Delaware tribes, flocked to Prophet's Town to join Tecumseh.

The British, quick to size up what was happening, agreed to supply Tecumseh with arms as long as he kept the northwestern frontier in ferment. Tecumseh also traveled south to Alabama to spread his message to his mother's people, the Creek nation, who occupied a similarly strategic position on the edge of white settlement.

In 1810, the governor of Indiana territory, William Henry Harrison, requested a parley with Tecumseh. Each was deeply suspicious of the other's designs, however, and they could not agree on a formula for peace. In the

▲ *The tribal unity Tecumseh had stitched together unraveled at the battle at Tippecanoe.*

following year, the governor received orders from President James Madison, under pressure from alarmed westerners, to strike at Prophet's Town.

Harrison set out from the territorial capital of Vincennes early in the fall of 1811 with a force of about one thousand men. He arrived at the Tippecanoe on November 6 and, after meeting under a flag of truce, made his camp about a mile from the village. Harrison's timing could not have been better. Tecumseh was absent, having left to visit the Creek, and no effective war leader replaced him at home. Nonetheless, Tenskwatawa spent the night rallying the men, and they attacked at the first light of morning. Harrison had prepared his defenses well, and in a bitter hand-to-hand struggle fought in an icy drizzle, the American lines held. The Indian alliance retreated, and although Harrison took heavy losses, he had managed to destroy Prophet's Town.

Although not a decisive defeat in terms of manpower, the battle undermined the prestige Tecumseh had garnered with such difficulty. His brother's message, undergirded by the promise of magical protection, was discredited. The Miami and Delaware returned to their own tribes, and, although Tecumseh became an effective British ally in the War of 1812, the tribal unity he had stitched together had unraveled at Tippecanoe. Tecumseh was killed in the war. In its aftermath, the white flood gathered momentum, and the Shawnee were forced into Kansas. Harrison rode his victory to the White House in the election of 1840, in a campaign that featured the slogan "Tippecanoe and Tyler, too."

LOCATION: *Tippecanoe Battlefield is north of Lafayette, at the Indiana 43 exit of Interstate 65.*
EXHIBITS: *An 85-foot monument marks the site of Harrison's encampment and is surrounded by interpretive markers that explain the course of the battle. A nearby museum has historical exhibits that discuss the battle from both the white and Indian viewpoints. There are also nature trails and a picnic area on the site.*
HOURS: *The park is open daily, dawn to dusk. The museum is open February through December, Monday through Saturday, 10–5; Sunday, 1–5.*
ADMISSION: *$1.50.*
TELEPHONE: *(317) 567-2147.*

Pendleton

FALLS PARK MEMORIAL

E arly in 1824, a small group of witnesses gathered quietly at dawn to watch an execution. Three white men, found guilty of murdering a party of nine Indians the previous year, had been sentenced to hang. Among the observers were several Miami tribesmen from the surrounding area.

Indiana had been a state for just eight years, and its central portion, the New Purchase territory, had only been open to settlement since 1820. Most white and Indian residents remembered the bitter warfare that had swept across this frontier during the previous decade.

The execution really settled nothing. Agitation for removal of remaining Indians continued, and by 1838, most Miami and Potawatomi had been expelled from Indiana to the west. Nonetheless, in the first such decision in American jurisprudence, white men had been sentenced to death for a capital crime against Indians. Indiana-born novelist Jessamyn West dramatized the incident in her book *Massacre at Falls Creek*.

LOCATION: *Falls Park is just outside downtown, on Pendleton Avenue. The monument is not far from the waterfall that gives both the park and the creek their name.*
HOURS: *Dawn to dusk.*
ADMISSION: *Free.*

Plymouth

CHIEF MENOMINEE MONUMENT

T he final expulsion of the Potawatomi from northern Indiana took place in
1838. They had moved into Indiana from the north, where they had been
close allies of the Ottawa and fought with Pontiac in his 1763 rebellion against
British rule. They had also joined Little Turtle, the Miami leader whose
campaign to dislodge the Americans ended in defeat at Fallen Timbers in
1793 (*see* Tippecanoe Battlefield, Lafayette, Indiana). The Potawatomi were
enthusiastic supporters of Tecumseh when the Shawnee became their neighbors. By the following generation, however, resistance had run its course: the
Potawatomi were the last tribe to be transported to Kansas.

One Potawatomi leader, Menominee, chose to make a final stand. He
refused to acknowledge evacuation orders and prepared to defy units of the
state militia. Finally, surrounded and hopelessly outnumbered, Menominee
and his band of 859 men, women, and children surrendered, and after a final
visit to the graves of their forebears, were removed to the west.

The monument, a life-size statue of Menominee looking out across his
lands, was erected in 1909. It stands at the site of the Potawatomi village and
the adjoining Roman Catholic mission.

LOCATION: *The monument is 7 miles southwest of Plymouth, on the road to Twin
Lakes.*
HOURS: *Daily, dawn to dusk.*
ADMISSION: *Free.*

South Bend

COUNCIL OAK

T he enormous Council Oak, situated in Highland Cemetery, was once
located in the heart of a Miami village. The south bend of the Saint
Joseph River lay on the main portage route between the eastern Great Lakes
and the Mississippi River, and was one of the most strategic locations in the
region.

In the last quarter of the seventeenth century, the Iroquois arrived here
from the East. They had been expanding steadily westward for thirty years
from their base in New York. A powerful confederacy, they overwhelmed

individual tribes who tried to oppose them. Robert Cavalier, Sieur de LaSalle, who made his first voyage of exploration through the area in 1679, also arrived from the East. LaSalle knew that the Iroquois, implacable enemies of the French, had already attacked Illinois villages in the area. He hoped that an alliance of the Miami and Illinois tribes might stop the Iroquois; by no coincidence, this would protect the fur trade he was trying to establish between the Mississippi and New France.

The historic meeting beneath the Council Oak in 1681 accomplished LaSalle's aims. Under its terms, the entire Mississippi Valley was delivered to the French as the Louisiana Territory.

LOCATION: *The Council Oak and Highland Cemetery are northwest of downtown, by way of Portage Avenue.*
HOURS: *Daily, dawn to dusk.*
ADMISSION: *Free.*
TELEPHONE: *(219) 234-0036.*

KENTUCKY

CHIEF PADUKE STATUE

M any American cities bear Indian names, but this is one of the few that actually honors its namesake with a memorial. Paduke was a Chickasaw chief, a friend of the town's founder, who was a member of one of the country's most famous pioneer families.

The site of Paducah was originally granted to George Rogers Clark, in recognition of the service he rendered the United States in the western campaign of the Revolutionary War. He was awarded seventy-three thousand acres along the south bank of the Ohio River in 1795 by the state of Virginia. However, the land was not Virginia's to give. Under the colonial charter, the land west of the Tennessee River was retained by the Chickasaw. Clark never benefitted from it and died encumbered by debt in 1818.

That same year, however, the Jackson Purchase was concluded, part of a series of treaties by which the Chickasaw relinquished their claims and were removed to Oklahoma. Clark's claim passed to his younger brother, William, who was the co-leader of the Lewis and Clark expedition to the Pacific Northwest. At this time, he was Superintendent of Indian Affairs for Missouri and had struck up a friendship with Paduke, the last tribal leader in this district. When he finally was able to start laying out a city on this site, thirty-two years after his brother's emolument, he decided to pay tribute to a man who had won his respect for his dignity in the face of adversity.

The statue of Paduke, on a main city thoroughfare, was unveiled in 1909. It is the work of Lorado Taft, one of the country's outstanding sculptors. Paduke is depicted staring off in the distance, as if surveying once more the lost lands of his people.

LOCATION: *The Paduke Memorial is on the median strip of Jefferson Street, between 18th and 19th Streets, just south of downtown.*

MICHIGAN

ANDREW BLACKBIRD MUSEUM

F rench explorers called the Lake Michigan coast in this area L'Arbre
Croche (Crooked Tree), after a huge, gnarled landmark that stood atop a
bluff and was visible from the water. This was the heartland of the Ottawa, a
tribe that once ranged all across Michigan's Lower Peninsula. The tribe
functioned as middlemen between the Hurons to their east and the Plains
tribes on the west: Ottawa means "traders" in the Algonquian language.

This delicate balance was upset in the middle of the seventeenth century. The Iroquois, with access to European arms, set in motion a chain of events
that uprooted tribes from their traditional lands and modes of production. The
Huron were shattered and the Ottawa were pushed by relentless Iroquois
pressure from their home on the north side of Georgian Bay. They moved west,
as far as Minnesota, until they encountered the Sioux and were driven back
east. About a century after they were originally displaced, they came to rest at
the Straits of Mackinac, and slowly filtered south through the Michigan
mitten.

Pontiac, who led the great unified Native American rebellion against
the British in 1763, was an Ottawa chief. Coordinating attacks on outposts
across the whole Great Lakes region, he came within a hair of wiping out the
British military presence in the West. But Detroit and a few other places held
out, and Britain was able to bring in enough troops to turn the tide.

It was nearly fifty years before settlers began arriving in Michigan in
large numbers, slowly forcing the Ottawa into the northern forests. They
established villages along L'Arbre Croche and Little Traverse Bay, on land that
was to become some of the most expensive resort property in the Midwest.

Although born into the Sioux tribe, Andrew J. Blackbird lived among
the Ottawa. He was educated at the Holy Childhood of Jesus Mission, which
was set up in Harbor Springs in 1827. While not a chief, he served the Ottawa
as an interpreter and used his knowledge of law and of the English language to
negotiate on their behalf. He led a delegation to Washington in 1836, when
Michigan became a state, to ensure that lands would be set aside for the Ottawa
and that they would retain their hunting and fishing rights. The reservation
was broken up in 1875, however, and the land was opened to white settlement.

The estimated forty-five hundred Ottawa descendants in the area live among the general population.

The Andrew Blackbird Museum displays articles relating to Ottawa culture and to the history of the tribe in this area. It is housed in what was once Blackbird's home, which later became the post office in this resort village.

LOCATION: *The museum is at 368 East Main Street (Michigan 119), just east of the business district. At the eastern end of Main Street is the Holy Childhood church and school, both of which now serve the general population. A historical marker, however, describes their Native American associations.*
HOURS: *The museum is open Monday through Saturday, 10–5, Sunday 12–4, Memorial Day through Labor Day. Weekends only through October.*
ADMISSION: *Donation.*
TELEPHONE: *(616) 526-7731.*

Mackinac Island

INDIAN DORMITORY

The treaties by which Native Americans relinquished their land rights in Michigan's north stipulated that they annually visit the office of the Indian agent on Mackinac Island to receive payment and supplies for the necessities of life. In 1838, the state erected a dormitory to house the tribal leaders on these visits.

After the agency was closed, it became the island's school. In recent years, the building has been restored to how it appeared in about 1840, when Henry Schoolcraft worked here. The young Detroiter had been sent to Sault Sainte Marie in 1822 to be their Indian agent. He married the part-Indian granddaughter of John Johnson, the Soo's first white settler, and was sympathetic toward the Chippewa people and their problems. Curious to know more about the Chippewa, he talked with them endlessly about their traditions, beliefs, and legends. After several years at Mackinac, he published *History and Statistical Information of the Indian Tribes of the United States*. It was the first book to attempt a systematic study of Native Americans. An invaluable reference work, it became something of a best-seller.

The book also excited the imagination of a writer in New England. Henry Wadsworth Longfellow took many of the Chippewa legends recorded by Schoolcraft and composed his epic poem, "Hiawatha," around them. While the poem has very little to do with the historic Hiawatha, who was a Mohawk from New York, the lines "By the shores of Gitche-Gumee, By the shining Big-Sea-Water" are familiar to generations of Americans. For many, it was their first taste of Indian legend. Appropriately, one room of the Indian Dormitory is decorated with depictions of scenes from Longfellow's poem. There is also a restored, working kitchen from that era, with a cook preparing dishes typical of the time.

LOCATION: *Indian Dormitory is at the eastern end of Marquette Park, at the foot of Fort Mackinac, on Huron Street.*
HOURS: *Daily, 11–5, mid-June through Labor Day.*
ADMISSION: *The dormitory is part of the Historic Mackinac Island package, which includes admission to several noteworthy buildings for $3.50.*
TELEPHONE: *(906) 847-3328.*

Niles

FORT ST. JOSEPH MUSEUM

When Sitting Bull returned from his Canadian exile in 1881, five years after he led the Indian alliance that had annihilated General George Custer's forces at the Little Big Horn (*see* Little Big Horn National Battlefield, Montana), he found himself with time on his hands. Although he had heard that a pardon would be forthcoming after he surrendered to U.S. troops, he was imprisoned for two years at Fort Randall, South Dakota. To get through the long months of confinement, Sitting Bull began to paint. A German newspaper illustrator, Rudolph Cronau, who was visiting the West on assignment, stopped in to see the Hunkpapa chief, and gave him lessons in the rudiments of drawing.

Sitting Bull set out to illustrate the story of his life in a series of vividly colored and energetic pictographs. The drawings primarily depicted the achievements of Sitting Bull and his tribe at war, as they defeated both their traditional Indian enemies and cavalry officers. Alice Quimby, the daughter of the fort commandant, befriended Sitting Bull, and when he was released from confinement, he gave her the pictures as a gift. She kept them for the rest of her life, and left them to the Fort St. Joseph Museum in her hometown when she died in 1947. Sitting Bull's saddle and gun were also part of her bequest, and they now form a remarkable exhibit in this small museum, dedicated mainly to local history.

LOCATION: *The museum is right in the heart of town, at Fifth and Main Streets, near the intersection of U.S. 12 and Michigan 51.*
HOURS: *Tuesday through Saturday, 10–12 and 1–4; Sunday, 1–4.*
ADMISSION: *Free.*
TELEPHONE: *(616) 683-4702.*

Saint Ignace

MARQUETTE MISSION AND MUSEUM OF OJIBWA CULTURE

Sooner or later, all travelers through the Great Lakes region must pass through the narrow Straits of Mackinac that divide the two peninsulas of Michigan and separate Lake Huron from Lake Michigan. It was no different three hundred years ago.

When Father Jacques Marquette built a mission here in 1671, the site at the northern edge of the straits was occupied by Huron and Ottawa villages. These people had been displaced by the militarily advanced Iroquois and were living among the Ojibwa, their predecessors in this area. The Ojibwa were also in the process of expanding westward, a movement that would end only when they reached the plains of North Dakota. For several years the three tribes lived amicably along the straits, joined by the French.

Saint Ignace was at that time a major center of the fur trade, and was protected by a military garrison, Fort de Buade. Historians estimate that the town was about twice its current size. Marquette's mission was situated right next to a major Huron village. Although he did not remain here long since his work involved arduous trips across the upper Great Lakes and Mississippi Valley, in areas almost unknown to Europeans, he nevertheless retained a special fondness for this mission. Before his death in 1675, returning from one of his journeys, Marquette asked to be buried at Saint Ignace. He died near Ludington, further south on Lake Michigan, and was interred there, but Indians from the mission carried out his request: they retrieved his remains and took them where he had asked to rest.

When the mission burned in 1706 and was abandoned, the location of Marquette's gravesite was lost. In 1877, it was accidentally rediscovered, and a park was established around it.

This is considered to be one of the richest archeological sites in Michigan: many artifacts of both Native American and French cultures have been recovered here. The Huron village that adjoined the mission has been partially reconstructed: longhouses have been placed in the village, and there is a garden with the sorts of crops that were grown by the Huron.

▲ *The Marquette Mission and Museum of Ojibwa Culture is dedicated to a native people who inhabited the beautiful but harsh lands around the Straits of Mackinac.*

The Ojibwa are now the most heavily represented group in this part of the Upper Peninsula, and a former church next to Marquette Park has been turned into a museum of the Ojibwa culture. Exhibits illustrate the history of these people, the structure of their families, and their relationship to their natural surroundings. Ojibwa from the Bay Mills Reservation, which is located about fifty-five miles north of Saint Ignace, just west of Sault Sainte Marie, put on traditional dances at the museum on Labor Day weekend.

LOCATION: *The museum is located at 500 North State Street, in the middle of town, on the main road from Interstate 75.*
HOURS: *Daily, 10–8, Memorial Day through Labor Day. Tuesday through Saturday, 1–5, early May and through September.*
ADMISSION: *$2.*
TELEPHONE: *(906) 643-9161.*

OHIO

Bainbridge

SEIP MOUND STATE MEMORIAL

When the first European settlers began moving up the Ohio River and its
tributaries, they were awestruck by the huge, silent earth mounds that
stood at many places along the banks. They had no idea who had built them.
Although Hernando de Soto had encountered many active mound-building
cultures in his sixteenth-century exploration of the South, and French missionaries had actually lived amid the mounds of the Natchez tribe (*see* Grand
Village of the Natchez, Natchez, Mississippi), that part of the historical record
had been forgotten by the time the new American republic came into being.

Using imagination rather than scientific inquiry, nineteenth-century
writers spun elaborate fantasies about a vanished mound-building race, believed to be somehow related to the ancient cultures of Central America. These
writers also attributed the mounds to the Egyptians and to the lost continent of
Atlantis, but never to the Native Americans who had actually built them. The
early writings about the Mound Builders tell more about racist attitudes of the
time than anything else.

It was not until well into the twentieth century that scientists came to
agree on the origin of the mounds and their approximate dates. Robert Silverberg's publication of "Mound Builders of Ancient America" in 1968 put
together a concise history of the mounds by correlating all the available data.

The confusion multiplied when archaeologists discovered that in southern Ohio, where most of the mounds were found, there had actually been two
such cultures, one overlapping the other. The first was called the Adena
culture, after the estate on which its most distinctive mound was uncovered.
The second, which left the most impressive monuments, was named the
Hopewell culture, after the farmer on whose land a large grouping was situated.

The people of the Hopewell culture began moving into Ohio from the
Woodland tribes area of the Northeast in about 400 B.C., and reached their
peak of influence about one thousand years later. Seip Mound, named for the
brothers on whose farm it was discovered, is one of the largest of the Hopewell
mounds, measuring 30 feet high and 250 by 150 feet wide. The mound was
excavated between 1926 and 1928, and was a job so complicated that a cave-in

almost killed the chief archeologist. But the findings—thousands of pearls (river pearls, to be sure, but pearls, nonetheless), along with a twenty-eight-pound ceremonial ax, richly ornamented breastplates, and items made of silver, copper, and mica—created a sensation, prompting the press to name the mound "the great pearl burial." Archaeologists determined that the mound had been a burial place for royalty.

The mound has been restored, although what you see today represents only a partial recomposition of the original material. Even so, Seip Mound fared better than the original Hopewell Mound, located about twelve miles east. Although artifacts found at Hopewell Mound were exhibited at the Columbian Exposition of 1893, and drew wide media attention to the Ohio mounds, Hopewell Mound has never been restored.

LOCATION: *Seip Mound is located 3 miles east of Bainbridge on U.S. 50, about 17 miles west of Chillicothe.*
EXHIBITS: *In addition to the mound itself, there are other surrounding earthworks and a display pavilion.*
HOURS: *Daily, dawn to dusk.*
ADMISSION: *Free.*
TELEPHONE: *(614) 297-2300.*

Brownsville

FLINT RIDGE STATE MEMORIAL

F lint Ridge preserves an area where Ohio's native people quarried flint. The stone was universally used for weapons and utensils, and the ridge, five miles long and half a mile wide, was a vital gathering place. It was so important that the ridge was maintained as neutral ground by all peoples. A system of footpaths lead to the main part of the quarry, and an exceptionally good museum explains the importance of flint in these ancient Indian cultures.

LOCATION: *Flint Ridge is 3 miles north of U.S. 40 on Ohio 668, about 16 miles west of Zanesville.*
HOURS: *The site is open daily, dawn to dusk. Museum hours are Wednesday through Saturday, 9:30-5; Sunday, 12-5, Memorial Day through Labor Day. Saturday, 9:30-5, and Sunday, 12-5, through October.*
ADMISSION: *$2 to the museum.*
TELEPHONE: *(614) 787-2476.*

Chillicothe

MOUND CITY NATIONAL MONUMENT

S o little appreciated were these mounds along the Scioto River that during
World War I they were almost obliterated to create an army training base.
Many of them were leveled to make room for Camp Sherman. Only after the
war did systematic excavation begin, and the site was not protected as a
national treasure until 1923.

Mound City was assembled by the Hopewell culture between 200 B.C.
and 500 A.D. During that period the inhabitants erected twenty-three burial
mounds within a thirteen-acre enclosure. Although the site was examined—
and raided for artifacts—as early as 1846, another seventy-five years passed
before serious study began. Among the findings were a mound with a mica-
covered grave, another that contained more than two hundred effigy pipes, and
yet another containing copper figurines and a death mask. The walking tour of
the area highlights these mounds.

Since this is a National Park Service operation, the visitor center
displays are outstanding: Mound City is the best place to begin a historic
overview of Ohio's ancient cultures. There are walking paths, trailside exhibits,
and an observation deck overlooking the area.

LOCATION: *Mound City is 3 miles north of Chillicothe by way of Ohio 104.*
HOURS: *Daily, dawn to dusk. Visitor center is open daily, 8-5.*
ADMISSION: *$1, or $3 per vehicle.*
TELEPHONE: *(614) 774-1125.*

TECUMSEH PAGEANT

T he life of this extraordinary Shawnee leader is more appropriately a part of
Indiana history (*see* Tippecanoe Battlefield, Lafayette, Indiana). Nonetheless, during the years of the white settlement of Ohio, the Shawnee were the
strongest among the native peoples, and Shawnee leaders led the fight against
European expansion. Their capital, named Chillicothe, was occupied until
1795, and it is likely that Tecumseh was born there. The contemporary city of
Chillicothe—in Greene County, several miles to the southeast of the original
city—stages an annual outdoor pageant that dramatizes the Shawnee struggle
to retain their lands.

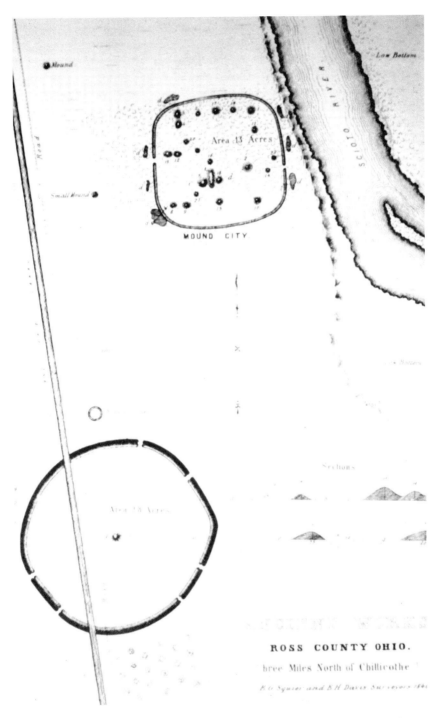

▲ *Ross County's Mound City National Monument is a good place to begin a tour of Ohio's ancient cultures.*

▲ *An Indian charm, one of the artifacts recovered during excavations at Mound City in Chillicothe.*

LOCATION: *The pageant is produced at Sugarloaf Mountain Amphitheater, northeast of the city on Ohio 159.*
HOURS: *Monday–Saturday, 8 P.M., mid-June through Labor Day.*
ADMISSION: *$10-$12.*
TELEPHONE: *(614) 775-0700; pageant is seasonal and the telephone number may change.*

Columbus

OHIO HISTORICAL CENTER

M any of the art objects recovered from Ohio mounds were scattered among various museums over the years. Some of them even wound up in the British Museum. One of the best collections, however, is in Columbus, in Ohio's state museum. While its exhibits are not strictly limited to Native American culture, the museum offers an outstanding glimpse into the wealth and skills of these ancient cultures.

LOCATION: *The museum is north of downtown, at the 17th Street exit of Interstate 71.*
HOURS: *Monday through Saturday, 9-5; Sunday, 10-5.*
ADMISSION: *$3 per vehicle.*
TELEPHONE: *(614) 297-2300.*

Dayton

SUN WATCH ARCHEOLOGICAL PARK

At most archeological sites in Ohio, the visitor has to rely on his or her imagination to visualize what the community might have looked like at its peak. Sun Watch, however, attempts to reconstruct the past to show how a functioning twelfth-century farming village might have appeared. These people have been named the Fort Ancient Culture because many of their villages were clustered around the earthworks of that name (*see* Fort Ancient State Memorial, Lebanon, Ohio). However, the earthworks were in fact built by the Hopewell people, and the "Fort Ancient" farmers occupied the land much later. Although the Fort Ancient Culture might have descended from the Hopewell people, they neither built mounds nor acknowledged any such kinship.

That there is anything here at all is surprising. In the 1960s, two amateur archaeologists discovered the first indication that this spot along the terraces of the Great Miami River contained the remnants of an eight hundred-year-old community. To their horror, they learned that the site was scheduled to be turned into a sewage treatment plant. The Dayton Museum of Natural History conducted emergency excavations, and by 1971, the site was considered to be so significant that the sewage plans were revised. Sun Watch became a National Historic Landmark and a center for ongoing research into the lives of the people who lived here just prior to the first European contact.

The name Sun Watch is derived from findings in the central plaza of the village. Archaeologists believe that a red cedar pole was set into the ground here, raised to a height of about forty feet, and aligned with the hearth of the Big House, a structure of religious significance on the western edge of the village. Twice each year, in late April and in mid-August, the pole's shadow fell squarely across the hearth, indicating to the sun watchers when to plant and harvest corn.

The park has reconstructed gardens, and there are demonstrations in house building, toolmaking, and planting and harvesting. The museum displays many of the artifacts found here, and an audiovisual show puts Sun Watch in historical perspective. Visitors may also view archaeologists at work.

LOCATION: *Sunwatch can be reached by taking the westbound Edwin C. Moses Boulevard exit of Interstate 75, and then turning left on West River Road.*
HOURS: *Monday through Saturday, 9–5; Sunday, 12–5.*
ADMISSION: *$2.50.*
TELEPHONE: *(513) 268-8199.*

Gnadenhutten

GNADENHUTTEN HISTORICAL PARK

After the Delaware Indians had been swindled out of their ancestral lands (*see* Pocono Indian Museum, Bushkill, Pennsylvania) by the infamous Walking Purchase, the tribe split into several fragments. Some went to live among the Iroquois along the Susquehanna, others continued farther west. The Huron invited them to settle in their lands along Ohio's Muskingum River, and in 1751 the Delaware began moving into the area. The land was rich and the new arrivals prospered as farmers.

About twenty years later, the Delaware in turn welcomed Moravian missionaries into the area. These Christians from the Pennsylvania Dutch country found many converts among the local tribes (*see* Schoenbrunn, New Philadelphia, Ohio), and in 1772 a group of them founded the settlement of Gnadenhutten, the name of which means "tents of grace" in German.

The Ohio frontier was a volatile battleground in the era of the American Revolution, with the Shawnee waging ongoing warfare against the settlers. In 1781, the natives of Gnadenhutten decided that it would be safest for the community to move west to the Sandusky Valley.

The crops failed, however, and a large group returned to Gnadenhutten to salvage what they could from their old fields. As they prepared to head back to the Sandusky in March 1782, a detachment of colonial militia on a punitive raid against the Shawnee overtook them at the old mission. Seizing these Indians instead of the Shawnee, the militia imprisoned them overnight and on the morning of March 8 began to slaughter them. In all, ninety defenseless people were murdered. The Gnadenhutten massacre turned all the Ohio tribes against the Americans for the next generation, and sped the Delaware on their way to new lands in the West.

LOCATION: *Gnadenhutten is located on U.S. 36, about 10 miles east of Interstate 77.*
EXHIBITS: *A memorial to the murdered Indians has been erected here. There is a museum that relates the history of the settlement, with artifacts that were used by the inhabitants of Gnadenhutten. There is also a reconstructed log church.*
HOURS: *Monday through Saturday, 10–5; Sunday, 12–5, June–Labor Day. Weekends only, 12–5, through October.*
ADMISSION: *Donation.*
TELEPHONE: *(614) 254-4143.*

Kelleys Island

INSCRIPTION ROCK STATE MEMORIAL

N ow a resort getaway in Lake Erie, this island was once inhabited by the tribe that gave their name to the lake. Having been wiped out in wars with the Iroquois in the middle of the seventeenth century, the Erie left little but that name behind. At one time, however, the Erie inhabited the entire sweep of the lake's southern shore, from the present-day New York border to what is now Toledo.

The Erie were related to the Huron, who lived in what is now Ontario. This kinship drew them into conflict with the Iroquois when members of the shattered Huron nation fled to the Erie for refuge. Known as formidable fighters, the Erie sent four thousand men into the field in 1652. The Iroquois, however, had access to English firearms, and the balance of power among Native Americans in this region was altered forever. The Erie were obliterated in a major battle, and the few who remained were dispersed among the Iroquois and the Huron.

The petroglyphs on Inscription Rock are attributed to the Erie, and are believed to depict the history of these people. Rising eleven feet above the water and measuring thirty-two by twenty-one feet, the rock drawings are among the finest of their kind in the East.

LOCATION: *The island is reached by frequent ferry service from Marblehead, on the Catawba Peninsula. Inscription Rock is just east of the ferry dock on the south shore.*
HOURS: *Daily, dawn to dusk.*
ADMISSION: *Free.*
TELEPHONE: *None.*

FORT ANCIENT STATE MEMORIAL

Near the end of their thousand-year occupancy of the southern Ohio riverlands, the Hopewell people found it necessary to build elaborate hilltop fortifications. Historians theorize that they were erected about 600 A.D. to defend against invaders who eventually drove out or absorbed the Hopewell. In any case, the earthworks at Fort Ancient are among the most impressive military works of prehistoric North America.

The earthworks occupy a 270-foot-high plateau above the Little Miami River, extending three and a half miles; in some places, the walls are more than 20 feet high. Taking advantage of the rugged terrain to make the position nearly impregnable, the walls link two cleared areas on adjacent hilltops which were intended as defensive concentrations. On the unwalled side of each hill is a sheer drop to the river.

The evidence of habitation sites in addition to several burial mounds within the walls suggests that the defenses were built for long-term occupancy in a time of ongoing trouble.

LOCATION: *Fort Ancient is on Ohio 350, immediately east of the exit from Interstate 71.*
EXHIBITS: *In addition to the impressive earthworks themselves, there is a museum that does a fine job of explaining the significance of this site and the history of the Hopewell culture.*
HOURS: *The park is open Wednesday through Sunday, 10–8, Memorial Day through Labor Day. Saturday, 10–5, and Sunday, 12–5, in April, May, September, and October. The museum closes at 5 all year.*
ADMISSION: *$3 per vehicle.*
TELEPHONE: *(513) 932-4421.*

SERPENT MOUND STATE MEMORIAL

For one-quarter of a mile Serpent Mound twists and coils across a ridge above Brushy Creek. This enormous snake effigy is the most famous and the most awe-inspiring mound of its kind in America. What it represents and exactly when it was built are questions that still puzzle archaeologists. Most effigy mounds were more recently constructed and were concentrated far to the north, in the upper Mississippi Valley (*see* Effigy Mounds National Monument, Marquette, Iowa, and Panther Intaglio Mound, Fort Atkinson, Wisconsin).

This mound is thought to have been built by the Adena culture, who predated the Hopewell in Ohio by a few hundred years and were gradually absorbed by them. No burials have been found within the mound, but a few items with clear Adena characteristics were discovered nearby. About twenty feet wide at the base, the mound stands five feet high in some places. The figure writhes seven times in gigantic loops and ends with an open mouth, about to swallow a smaller, oval mound. Some interpret this smaller mound as an egg, others as a frog.

The mound builders traced out the shape of this monster in stone and clay and then filled in the pattern with earth. It apparently had some sort of religious significance, the nature of which was lost long ago.

Early settlers, while impressed by the figure, did not fully appreciate the mound since they were not able to view it from an elevated position. Unprotected, the mound was damaged in places by souvenir hunters, and cattle were allowed to graze on its grassy slopes. The property was put up for sale in 1886, and the prospective buyer planned to level the mound to plant corn on the site.

F. W. Putnam, an archeologist with the Peabody Museum of Harvard University, began a fund-raising campaign to save the site. He wrote in a Boston newspaper: "To me it seems a greater loss than would be the destruction of our own Bunker Hill, and yet what indignation would be aroused if some dynamite fiend should topple that to the ground" (cited in *The Mound Builders* by Robert Silverberg). The drive raised almost $6,000, and for the next fourteen years Harvard kept the site in trust, turning it over to the Ohio Historical Society in 1900.

A sixty-one-acre park surrounds the mound, and an observation tower enables visitors to grasp the enormous size of the serpent. There is a small museum in addition to picnic facilities.

LOCATION: *Serpent Mound is on Ohio 73, four miles west of its junction with Ohio 41 in the town of Locust Grove. Locust Grove is 21 miles south of U.S. 50.*
HOURS: *Wednesday through Sunday, 9:30–8, Memorial Day through Labor Day; weekends only, 10–7, April, May, September, and October.*
ADMISSION: *$3 per vehicle.*
TELEPHONE: *(513) 587-2796.*

Marietta

MOUND CEMETERY

W ith the end of the American Revolution, the great land hunger of the seaboard colonies could be sated. Prior to that time, British law had prohibited settlement west of Pittsburgh, in territory reserved for Indians. The new government, however, was eager to promote western expansion. The Shawnee, who had backed Britain in the war, could no longer could retain their lands in southeastern Ohio. The Ohio Company was one of the first organized groups to take advantage of the new lands; in the spring of 1788 its first party of settlers arrived at the junction of the Ohio and Muskingum rivers. They established Marietta—named in honor of Queen Marie Antoinette—which became the capital of the newly organized Northwest Territory.

The first permanent settlement in Ohio, Marietta was the first to deal with the mounds characteristic of this area. General Rufus Putnam, the leader of this group of settlers, was a member of George Washington's military staff and a trained surveyor. Although he had no idea who built the mounds or what they represented, he suspected that they were associated with burials. Many of the mounds occupied a central position on the land where the settlers intended to build their town; Putnam took the novel approach of incorporating the mounds in his town plan, whereas many early Ohio cities leveled the mounds they encountered.

Putnam also discerned that wide avenues had been laid out by the mound builders. These he retained in his town plan: Sacra Via, especially, was laid along the route of a street that ran from the ancient town's central square to the Muskingum, and many other streets were superimposed on the outline of the ancient native settlement.

Mound Cemetery preserves the largest of these mounds, which stands about thirty feet high. The settlers referred to the mound as Conus, and, with rare reverence, left the mound undisturbed. The surrounding area was turned into a burial ground for the citizens of the town: this cemetery is reputed to contain more graves of Revolutionary War officers than any other in the country.

LOCATION: *Mound Cemetery is located at 5th and Scammel Streets, near downtown.*
HOURS: *Daily, dawn to dusk.*
ADMISSION: *Free.*

MIAMISBURG MOUND STATE MEMORIAL

This is the largest conical mound in Ohio, and it baffled the early mound-builder theorists to no end. Because most other mounds in the area are rounded or flat-topped, many nineteenth century pseudohistorians were convinced that these sixty-eight-foot-high mounds were linked to an ancient race originating in Egypt, Maya or Central America. Later investigation established, however, that these mounds—related to the Grave Creek Mound in Moundsville, West Virginia—were the work of the Adena culture.

LOCATION: *The mound is off Ohio 725, immediately west of the Interstate 75 exit.*
HOURS: *Daily, dawn to dusk.*
ADMISSION: *Free.*
TELEPHONE: *(614) 297-2300.*

MOUNDBUILDERS STATE MEMORIAL

Here, covered with the gigantic trees of a primitive forest, the work presents a truly grand and impressive appearance; and in entering the ancient avenue for the first time, the visitor does not fail to experience a sensation of awe, such as he might feel in passing the portals of an Egyptian temple, or of gazing upon the silent ruins of Petra in the desert." So wrote E. H. Squier, one of the first explorers of the Ohio mounds, in 1848. The avenue of parallel mounds that he saw, however, which enclosed an area of almost four square miles, was obliterated long ago by the growing city of Newark. This wall of mounds once connected massive earthwork constructions shaped in circles and octagons. Some of the distinctive works are still in place, and one, called the Octagon, is now part of a public golf course. Today, however, the connecting avenue has disappeared, and in only a few places is it still possible to sense the awe that Squier felt.

The Newark earthworks were built by the Hopewell people over a period of a few hundred years. Moundbuilders State Memorial preserves the Great Circle, an earthwork about twelve hundred feet in diameter that encircles an effigy mound in the shape of an eagle. This was the starting point of one of the mound avenues and is the best preserved of any of the Newark structures.

About one-quarter mile away is the Wright Earthworks, the intersection of two of the mound thoroughfares. The walls here form a large square and cover about an acre. From this point, the avenue continued to the Octagon. This eight-sided construction enclosed several smaller mounds, all of which are now part of the golf course. A small museum adjacent to the Great Circle displays artifacts recovered from several of the state's prehistoric sites.

LOCATION: *These sites occupy much of the southwestern corner of Newark. Moundbuilders State Memorial is reached by way of Ohio 79, at South 21st and Cooper Streets. Signs from that point direct you to the Wright Earthworks, at James and Waldo Streets. The Octagon is north of this site, at North 30th Street at Parkview.*

HOURS: *Moundbuilders State Memorial is open daily, dawn to dusk, April through October. The Ohio Indian Museum is open Wednesday through Saturday, 9:30-5; Sunday, 12-5, Memorial Day through Labor Day. Weekends only, through October. The other sites are open daily, dawn to dusk.*

ADMISSION: *The museum is $2. Other sites are free.*

TELEPHONE: *The museum is (614) 344-1920.*

New Philadelphia

SCHOENBRUNN AND TRUMPET IN THE LAND PAGEANT

The tragedy that ended in the massacre at Gnadenhutten (*see* Gnadenhutten Historical Park, Gnadenhutten, Ohio) was set in motion in Schoenbrunn. David Zeisberger, a Moravian missionary from Pennsylvania, was invited here in 1772 by a group of native people interested in hearing more about Christianity. Zeisberger received an enthusiastic reception, and the community he established here is regarded as the first European settlement in Ohio. Situated beside a natural spring, it bore a German name meaning "beautiful fountain."

Later in that same year, a band of Delaware moved to set up another Christianized settlement at Gnadenhutten.

This was dangerous territory, and the settlements were surrounded by tribes who opposed their very existence. The Shawnee, encouraged by the British, were against any white presence in Ohio. The settlers, on the other hand, wanted all Indians out of the way, whether they were Christian or not. With the start of the American Revolution, the frontier became uninhabitable, and the Moravians returned to the east with their converted Indians in 1776. In time, the location of the village was forgotten.

In 1923, archaeologists discovered the outline of Zeisberger's house, around which the state has reconstructed much of the Moravian-Native American village. The church and schoolhouse, the first such structures west of Pittsburgh, have been rebuilt, as have many of the residential log cabins. Every summer in a nearby amphitheater, an outdoor pageant, Trumpet in the Land, retells the sad history of Schoenbrunn and Gnadenhutten.

LOCATION: *Schoenbrunn is located southeast of New Philadelphia on Ohio 259, just off U.S. 250 Business. The amphitheater is off Exit 81 of Interstate 77.*
HOURS: *Schoenbrunn is open Monday through Saturday, 9:30–5; Sunday, 12–5, Memorial Day through Labor Day. Weekends only through October. Trumpet in the Land is presented Tuesday through Sunday, at 8:30, mid-June through the last weekend in August.*
ADMISSION: *Schoenbrunn is $3. The pageant reserved seats are $8.50.*
TELEPHONE: *Schoenbrunn is (216) 339-3636. Ticket information for Trumpet in the Land is (216) 339-1132.*

Piqua

Piqua Historic Indian Museum

This fertile, well-watered area was the homeland of several native groups in the eighteenth century. The Miami moved in from the north early in the century and established their main community, Pickawillany, which became a crossroads where several neighboring tribes visited for trade. While historically allied with the French, the Miami decided to open trade connections with the British. In the years of colonial rivalry, this was a dangerous practice. A French punitive expedition was sent to Pickawillany from Detroit in 1752. Waiting until most of the men were away from the village, the French laid siege. The leading Miami chief and British traders inside the community were killed, and Pickawillany fell. The Miami abandoned the site and retreated west into Indiana.

The Shawnee, who were slowly being driven back from eastern Ohio by white settlement, replaced the Miami. When the Revolutionary War reached this remote area, an expedition under George Rogers Clark destroyed the Shawnee settlement in 1780.

A historic re-creation of the trading post at Pickawillany—which gave its name, in shortened form, to the present-day town of Piqua—now stands near the site of the former Miami and Shawnee villages. Among the restorations is a museum that gives a good historic overview of the native people who occupied this land at the time of European settlement. The museum displays clothing, tools, and crafts from that time.

▲ *The Piqua Historic Indian Museum displays artifacts of Plains and Woodland Indian tribes, such as these canoes and snowshoes.*

LOCATION: *The Piqua historic area is northwest of the town on Ohio 66, which is reached from the westbound U.S. 36 exit of Interstate 75.*
HOURS: *Wednesday through Saturday, 9:30–5; Sunday, 12–5, Memorial Day through Labor Day. Weekends only through October.*
ADMISSION: *$4.*

Sinking Spring

FORT HILL STATE MEMORIAL

This Hopewell fortification was probably built at about the same time as Fort Ancient (see the entry on Fort Ancient State Memorial, Lebanon, Ohio). Like Fort Ancient, it was built in about 600 A.D. to deter invasion from the north. This area has been turned into a state nature preserve, and little historic restoration has been done. It is possible to see these battlements just as they appeared a century ago when Europeans first found them. In that regard, Fort Hill is one of the best places in Ohio to recapture the sense of awe that the first visitors felt when they came upon these vast, inexplicable monuments of a lost world.

The walls—about a mile and a half long and as much as twenty feet high—enclose an area of about fifty acres. There are nature trails and picnic facilities on the site.

LOCATION: *Fort Hill is just off Ohio 41, about 12 miles south of U.S. 50. It is located midway between Seip Mound and Serpent Mound; (see the entries on Seip Mound State Memorial, Bainbridge, Ohio, and Serpent Mound State Memorial, Locust, Ohio).*
HOURS: *Daily, dawn to dusk.*
ADMISSION: *Free.*

Upper Sandusky

WYANDOTTE MISSION

J ohn Stewart was a recovered alcoholic who found solace in the Methodist church. A black man who claimed to have Native American forebears, he was living in Marietta when he fell seriously ill in 1814. He vowed that if he recovered he would dedicate his life to church service, and later, while walking in the fields outside town, he heard a voice that told him, "You must declare my counsel faithfully." The voice seemed to come from the northwest, and Stewart, taking this as a sign, headed in that direction to carry the word to the Indians.

He first came to land occupied by members of the Delaware tribe, who were already Christianized. They told him of the Wyandotte, an unconverted tribe who lived further on, and Stewart concluded that this was where he was meant to go.

Stewart arrived at the main settlement, at what is now Upper Sandusky, in 1816. The Wyandotte were an offshoot of the Huron tribe, which had been shattered in the Iroquois wars of the 1640s. They had wandered around Michigan and Wisconsin before drifting south to establish themselves in northern Ohio in the mid-1700s. During the War of 1812, the Wyandotte had sided with the British, and by the time of Stewart's arrival in 1816, their holdings had been reduced to a small reservation near present-day Upper Sandusky.

Stewart's work was successful, and in 1824, the year after his death, a stone chapel was built here. When the Wyandotte were finally forced to relinquish their lands and were transported west in 1843, part of the treaty stipulated that the chapel remain under the auspices of the Methodist church.

The chapel that stands today was built in 1889 from the stones of the original mission, and the Methodists now recognize it as a shrine. Surrounding the chapel is a Wyandotte graveyard, in addition to monuments to Stewart and nine members of the tribe who chose to stay here after the removal to the west.

LOCATION: *The mission is several blocks north of downtown on Church Street and is accessible from U.S. 30 by way of the Ohio 53 exit.*
HOURS: *Vary. Call in advance.*
ADMISSION: *Donation.*
TELEPHONE: *(419) 294-4841.*

Xenia

BLUE JACKET PAGEANT

T he Blue Jacket Pageant dramatizes the Shawnee effort to hold on to their Ohio lands in the face of relentless white expansion during the Revolutionary War era. It is also something of a multiracial sermon. Blue Jacket was the name given to Marmaduke Swearingen, a young white man captured by the Shawnee and raised by the tribe. Having risen to a position of leadership, he became an adamant opponent to the white settlement campaign of the 1790s, and was joined in his fight by a semilegendary figure, an escaped black slave named Caesar.

The pageant, based loosely on fact, tells the story with great sympathy for the Shawnee cause. It is an exciting evocation of the era, containing a wealth of special effects.

LOCATION: *The pageant is staged at the amphitheater at Caesar's Ford Park, on Jasper Road, southeast of central Xenia.*
HOURS: *Tuesday through Sunday, early June through Labor Day, at 8:30 P.M.*
ADMISSION: *$10.*
TELEPHONE: *(513) 376-4318.*

▲ *The Blue Jacket Pageant tells the moving story of the fall of the Shawnee Nation.*

ONTARIO

BRANT COUNTY MUSEUM

T he Brant County Museum has a fine Six Nations Indian collection, many items of which belonged to Joseph Brant and the poetess Pauline John-son. Born a few miles from Brantford on the Six Nations reserve, Johnson was the daughter of a Mohawk chief, and was related to the writer William Dean Howells on her English mother's side. One of the first native literary voices in Canada, she caused a sensation in Toronto in 1893 when she recited from her works while dressed in Mohawk costume. Her most famous work, *The Song My Paddle Sings*, led to a national tour and further readings in Great Britain, where she was greatly admired. Her volumes quickly sold out in Canada in the early twentieth century, and she became recognized as an authority on folklore. Johnson died in 1913, and forty-eight years later became the first native Canadian to be depicted on a commemorative postage stamp. The Brant County Museum is devoted to Johnson's life and work.

LOCATION: *The museum is opposite City Hall, at 57 Charlotte St.*
HOURS: *Tuesday through Friday, 9–5; weekends, 1–4, May through August; closed Sunday, rest of year.*
ADMISSION: *$2.*
TELEPHONE: *(519) 752-2483.*

HER MAJESTY'S CHAPEL OF THE MOHAWKS

J oseph Brant was among the most contradictory and compelling personali-ties to figure in the American Revolution. He was a scholarly man, deeply committed to the task of translating the Bible into the Mohawk language. An adept political leader, he attempted to address the needs of his people amidst the revolutionary storm that was sweeping across North America. In combat he was a fierce warrior, and was involved in some of the bloodiest encounters in the war.

Brant was bound by family ties to the British interests in New York. His sister married Sir William Johnson, the Superintendent for Indian Affairs in the Mohawk Valley. He fought with the British as a teenager in the French and Indian War, and again allied himself with them in the war against Pontiac, the Ottawa chief who led the Great Lakes tribes in rebellion in 1763. By his mid-twenties Brant was recognized as a prominent leader of the Iroquois Confederacy (*see* Iroquois Indian Museum, Cobleskill, New York), and when the American Revolution began, there was no question as to where his loyalties lay. Brant split the confederacy, so that the Mohawk, Seneca, Cayuga, and Onondaga fought on the British side. Commissioned as a colonel, he led many raids on the New York and Pennsylvania frontier, including Cherry Valley and Wyoming Valley.

When peace came, Brant could not remain on the American side of the frontier because of the bitterness the settlers felt over his wartime activities. The American settlers seized Iroquois lands, and Brant and his followers were forced to relocate on claims set aside for them by the British along the Grand River of Ontario.

A new town, named after Brant, was established at the ford of the Grand River. In 1785, Brant built the Mohawk chapel, and Her Majesty's Chapel of the Mohawks is now the oldest Protestant church in Ontario; it is the only religious edifice in the world designated as a Royal Indian Chapel. Brant's tomb is adjacent to the chapel, which is a jewel of colonial architecture.

LOCATION: *The chapel is southwest of central Brantford, on Mohawk Street.*
HOURS: *Daily, 10–5, July through Labor Day; Wednesday through Sunday, 10–6, mid-May through June; weekends only, 1–5, to mid-October.*
ADMISSION: *Donation.*

WOODLAND INDIAN CULTURAL EDUCATION CENTRE

Woodland Indian Cultural Education Centre displays the culture of Ontario's native peoples, concentrating on the heritage of the Iroquois— including those who lived in this area prior to Joseph Brant's arrival in Canada as well as those who accompanied Brant to Canada.

The Cultural Centre features an Indian Hall of Fame, an art show that runs from mid-May to early June, and a winter sports festival that is held in February. A special exhibits gallery hosts original exhibitions throughout the year. Public programming includes gallery talks, live performances, artist lectures, films, and demonstrations. A handicraft bazaar takes place on the first Saturday in November.

LOCATION: *The museum is at 184 Mohawk Street.*
HOURS: *Monday–Friday, 9–4; Saturday and Sunday, 10–5. Closed Easter weekend, June 21, Labour Day & Thanksgiving, and during Christmas.*
ADMISSION: *$3.50.*
TELEPHONE: *(519) 759-2650.*

Burlington

JOSEPH BRANT HOME

T he Joseph Brant Home is a reconstruction of Wellington Square, the home Joseph Brant built in 1800 at the head of Lake Ontario (*see* Her Majesty's Chapel of the Mohawks, Brantford, Ontario). The Mohawk leader lived his final seven years here, assisuously translating the Bible into the Mohawk language. Brant's landholdings ultimately became the city of Burlington, and his house was rebuilt at its original location in 1939. In addition to displays of Brant's personal memorabilia—including the medal presented to him by King George III—the museum contains displays on native culture in this area.

LOCATION: *Immediately off the Queen Elizabeth Way, at the North Shore Boulevard exit.*
HOURS: *Monday through Saturday, 10–5; Sunday, 1–5.*
ADMISSION: *$2.*
TELEPHONE: *(416) 634-3556.*

Delaware

SKA-NAH-DOHT INDIAN VILLAGE

S ka-Nah-Doht means "a village stands again" in the Oneida language. This village is a reconstruction of a typical walled farming settlement of Iroquoian people of southwestern Ontario in about 1000 A.D.: the longhouse and fifteen other structures are consistent with a native community of that time. An audiovisual presentation in the visitor center—part of Longwoods Road Conservation Area—gives an historical overview of the village. While most of the Oneida fought with the Americans during the Revolutionary War, some chose to join the other members of the Iroquois Confederacy who fought with the British. Moving to Canada after the war, these Oneida settled nearby along the Thames River.

LOCATION: *West of Delaware on Ontario 2, about 15 miles west of London.*
HOURS: *Daily, 9–4:30, mid-May through Labor Day and January through February; closed weekends, at other times.*
ADMISSION: *$3.50 per car.*
TELEPHONE: *(519) 264-2420.*

Keene

SERPENT MOUNDS PROVINCIAL PARK

M any burial mounds appear across the eastern United States, but they do not occur as frequently in the more northern native cultures. The coil-shaped Serpent Mounds complex is one exception. On the shores of Rice Lake, where native peoples once harvested wild rice, there are nine earth mounds, the largest of which is about two hundred feet long. Burials at the site are believed to date back approximately two thousand years.

LOCATION: *The park is on the northern shore of Rice Lake, just south of Keene and about 15 miles southeast of Peterborough.*
HOURS: *Daily, mid-May to mid-October.*
ADMISSION: *Free.*

London

LONDON MUSEUM OF INDIAN ARCHEOLOGY

T he Neutral Indians were so named by the French because the tribe did its best to remain uninvolved in the escalating warfare between the Iroquois Confederacy and the Huron in seventeenth-century Ontario. An agricultural people, they were proficient at growing tobacco, which they used as a trade good. They lived along the northern shore of Lake Erie and were closely related to the Iroquois, who called them "those who speak a language slightly different from ours."

When the Iroquois defeated the Huron, they turned their attention to

▲ *The London Museum of Archaeology's Lawson Prehistoric Indian Village reconstructs the Neutral Indians' community of elm longhouses and cedar palisades.*

the Neutrals. By 1651, even though most of their villages were palisaded for protection, most of the Neutrals had been driven off their lands. The tribe disappeared, some of whom were absorbed by the Hurons, others by the Iroquois.

The site of one of the fifteenth-century Neutral villages now houses an excellent museum of native archeology of southwestern Ontario. The exhibits depict over ten thousand years of Indian history in the region with artifacts from all over the province being brought here for display. Ongoing work also goes on at the Neutral village, and archaeologists can be viewed going about work.

LOCATION: *Just off Ontario 22 and North Wonderland Road, in the northern part of London, at 1600 Attawandaron Road.*
HOURS: *Daily, 10–5, April through November; Wednesday through Sunday, 1–4, rest of year.*
ADMISSION: *$3.*
TELEPHONE: *(519) 473-1360.*

SAINTE-MARIE AMONG THE HURON

W hile the English colonies still clung to a few isolated settlements along the Atlantic seaboard, French Jesuits had reached the Canadian shore of Lake Huron and were living among the people for whom that Great Lake was named. The Huron mission was part of France's overall colonial policy, since these native people controlled the most direct access to the fur trade. With the Iroquois unremittingly hostile to their ambitions, the French recognized the importance of allying with the Hurons. As early as 1626, missionaries arrived at Nottawasaga Bay in the heart of the Huron homeland and rallied on behalf of Christianity and New France. They built the mission settlement of Sainte-Marie in 1639.

The French strategy, however, doomed the Huron Nation. The Iroquois were determined to quash their European enemies and saw that they were most vulnerable at this exposed point in the west. By 1642, they had begun to infiltrate the perimeter of the Huron country, attacking fur shipments that passed their way. With every year, the Iroquois continued to move closer to the settlements around Sainte-Marie.

In 1647 the Iroquois moved in for the kill, and one village after another fell to the invaders. In March 1649, they took the village of Saint Louis, within six miles of this site. They captured the two Jesuits who directed the mission, Fathers Jean Brebeuf and Gabriel Lalemant, and put them to death. A few weeks later, knowing the situation to be hopeless, the Huron survivors burned down Sainte-Marie and retreated to nearby islands for safety. The following year, they completely abandoned their former homeland, and dispersed in Quebec and the western Lakes area.

The location of Sainte-Marie was lost for centuries.

LOCATION: *Sainte-Marie is 3 miles southeast of Midland on Ontario 12, about 8 miles west of the Highway 12 exit of Ontario 400.*
HOURS: *Daily, 10-5, mid-May to mid-October.*
ADMISSION: *$5.*
TELEPHONE: *(705) 526-7838.*

▲ *Masks greet visitors at the entrance to Huron Village.*

HURON VILLAGE

This is a full-scale reconstruction of a Huron village, the way it would have appeared before the first contact with Europeans in the early seventeenth century. Its dimensions and features are based on archeological evidence, and it is on a site that probably was used by the Huron as a settlement.

LOCATION: *The village, on King Street, is in Midland's Little Lake Park and is part of the adjacent Huronia Museum.*
HOURS: *Daily, 10–5, mid-May to mid-September.*
ADMISSION: *$4.75, includes entry to museum.*
TELEPHONE: *(705) 526-2844.*

Ohsweken

SIX NATIONS PAGEANT

Six Nations Pageant is an outdoor drama held the first three weekends of August in the Forest Theatre on the Six Nations Reserve, in the town of Ohsweken. It depicts the history of the Iroquois and the establishment of the Grand River settlement in the 1780s. An Indian Fall Fair is held at the fairgrounds in mid-September, a crafts bazaar in is held in early November, and there are year-round historical displays in the council house in town. Call the tribal offices for exact dates on the annual observances.

LOCATION: *Ohsweken, where the reserve tribal offices are situated, is east of Brantford by way of Brant County roads 4 and 6.*
TELEPHONE: *(519) 445-2201.*

Thunder Bay

THUNDER BAY ART GALLERY

The Thunder Bay Art Gallery is one of the few public art galleries in Canada committed to the collection, preservation, and exhibition of contemporary Native Indian art, and it exhibits them under the same roof as works of Picasso, van Gogh, Rodin, and Hockney. Since 1982, the gallery's Centre for Indian Art has provided a venue for exhibiting historical and contemporary native art. The gallery's mandate has earned Thunder Bay both national and international recognition as a leader in the art world: Thunder Bay is applauded for bringing native art into the mainstream, and for helping to break the "ethnography barrier" that often relegates native art to ethnographic and anthropological collections.

The gallery's permanent collection includes more than 900 works of contemporary native art and fine craft, in addition to works on long-term loan from the Canadian Museum of Civilization, in Quebec, among other museums. There are displays of artwork, pottery, quilts, photography, and sculpture from bands all across North America, in addition to changing special exhibits, and exhibits of scientific interest, such as the Wonders of Wood, and Birds of Prey. A Regional Art Series was established to provide local and regional artists with a venue to display their work, and a museum shop sells such items as hand-crafted jewelry and baskets.

▲ *Gerald McMaster's Riel Remembered (1985, graphite on paper) is among the works of contemporary native art on display at Thunder Bay Art Gallery.*

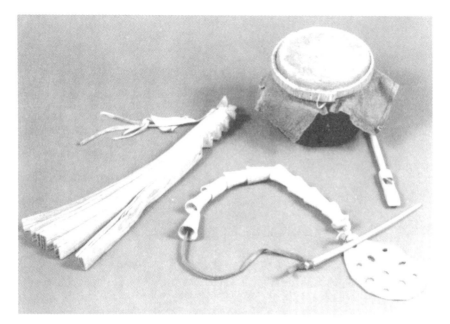

▲ *Thunder Bay Art Gallery exhibits traditional items. Clockwise: Water drum and wooden stick (c. 1980, Hubert Buck), wooden rattle (c. 1980, Vic Johnson), and Tab a Hon (c. 1980, Michael Patrick).*

LOCATION: *On the Confederation College campus, west of the city center, on Keewatin Street at Red Lake Road.*
HOURS: *Tuesday through Thursday, 12–8; Friday through Sunday 12–5.*
ADMISSION: *Voluntary donation.*
TELEPHONE: *(807) 577-6427.*

Woodview

PETROGLYPHS PROVINCIAL PARK

S ome of the rock carvings found in the secluded Petroglyphs Provincial Park were made one thousand years ago by Algonquian people in this area. The petroglyphs were not found, however, until 1954. A seventy by forty-foot protective structure has been built around them to protect them from further weather erosion.

LOCATION: *North of town by way of Ontario 28 to Northey's Bay Road. The park is about 30 miles northeast of Peterborough.*
HOURS: *Daily, 10–5, mid-May to mid-October.*
ADMISSION: *Free.*
TELEPHONE: *(705) 877-2552.*

WEST VIRGINIA

ARACOMA PAGEANT

The men who poured into the valleys of western Virginia in the 1770s were a hard-eyed lot. Many of them had lived on the edge of the law in the settled communities farther east. Their very presence in this area was in defiance of British law, which had mandated that the land west of the Ohio headwaters be reserved for the Indians. So it was little wonder that some of the bloodiest chapters in Indian relations with the European settlers were written here. As one settler wrote of the area, "Those varmints, the sheriffs and constables, are worse than the Indians; because you can kill Indians and you dare not kill the sheriffs."

Logan was the anglicized name of a Mingo chief, whose tribe had been generally friendly toward the Americans. In 1774, while Logan was away from home, an innkeeper invited his family to a party that turned into a drunken rout. In the course of the festivities, a party of whites suddenly attacked Logan's family and murdered them. The grief-stricken Mingo leader and his Shawnee allies retaliated on several white settlements. In a matter of weeks, the entire frontier was at war, and the governor of Virginia, John Murray (Lord Dunmore) called out the state militia.

Lord Dunmore's War, which West Virginians choose to call the opening engagement of the American Revolution (*see* Battle Monument State Park, Point Pleasant, West Virginia), seemingly was a contradiction in policy. The governor pressed it to divert attention from the coming conflict with Britain, but the result strengthened the position of those who were most eager to see Britain defeated, the western settlers. Murray was also a heavy investor in western land schemes, however, and was playing both ends against the middle in the conflict.

Logan refused to attend the postwar peace conference, sending instead a message explaining his actions. "There runs not a drop of my blood within any creature," it said in part. "This called on me for revenge. I have fully glutted my vengeance. For my country, I rejoice at peace. Yet who is there left to mourn for Logan? Not one."

But the killing went on. Aracoma was the daughter of the Shawnee leader Cornstalk. She married a settler in 1765 and with several members of her tribe came to live near present-day Logan, on an island in the Guyandotte River. In 1780, as the confused frontier portion of the revolution raged on, she was killed in a battle with settlers. (It was in this area a century later that the celebrated Hatfield-McCoy family feud was centered, almost as if vendettas were part of the land's legacy.) The town that grew up here was first called Lawnsville. But in the 1850s, Thomas Dunn English, a man with a poetic frame of mind—he wrote the ballad "Alice Ben Bolt"—led a movement to change the name to Aracoma. But in 1907 it was renamed again, this time to honor Logan.

Chief Logan State Park, north of town, produces a pageant, The Aracoma Story, about the Indian legends and history of the area. The pageant takes place in the outdoor amphitheater each summer.

LOCATION: *The park is 3 miles north of town on West Virginia 10.*
HOURS: *Aracoma is produced each July and August, but the dates vary from year to year. Call in advance for current information.*
ADMISSION: *$6.*
TELEPHONE: *(304) 792-7125.*

Moundsville

GRAVE CREEK MOUND

In the mid-nineteenth century, Grave Creek Mound became the most controversial mound in America as scientists, both authentic and spurious, waged a furious debate over what was found here. The 79-foot-high mound, with a circumference at the base of more than 300 yards, is one of the largest in North America. For generations, it was a familiar landmark to Native Americans of the Ohio Valley and westward-moving settlers.

In 1838, to resolve curiosity about it, the owner of the land decided to sponsor an excavation. It was the first systematic examination of one of these mounds. A shaft was sunk from its summit, and at a depth of 77 feet a chamber containing a richly ornamented skeleton was uncovered. At 111 feet, more log-walled chambers were found, and horizontal shafts at that depth turned up several more chambers, with dozens of human remains. But what really astonished the investigators was a sandstone tablet that seemed to bear writing in an unknown alphabet.

It was at about this time that Joseph Smith was spreading the teachings of the Book of Mormon, which held that the Indians were descended from the Ten Lost Tribes of Israel. The Grave Creek tablet caused a sensation, and investigators rushed to take a crack at translating it. One of them professed to discern Sumerian characters, and another said they were definitely Phoenician. In 1873, a French anthropologist presented a paper that declared the writing was unquestionably Canaanite and said, "What thou sayest, thou dost impose it, thou shinest in thy impetuous clan and rapid chamois." His audience was aghast.

Of all the experts, only Henry Schoolcraft wrote that both the mound and the tablet were probably of Indian origin. He was ignored. Only in the following century was it determined that the "writings" were merely decorative markings.

The Grave Creek mound, however, was an important milestone in the effort to sort out the prehistoric Indian cultures of America. It was determined that it belonged to the late Adena culture, centered in mid-Ohio, and that this was one of its easternmost outposts. The burials and artifacts have been dated at about the fifth and sixth centuries A.D. The mound has been protected by the state since 1907 and was landscaped for many years by inmates from the adjacent state prison.

LOCATION: *The mound is in the heart of Moundsville, at 801 Jefferson Street.*
EXHIBITS: *An outstanding museum is on the grounds and does an excellent job of relating the artifacts found here to the rest of the Adena culture.*
HOURS: *Monday–Saturday, 10–4:30; Sunday, 1–5.*
ADMISSION: *$1.*
TELEPHONE: *(304) 843-1410.*

Point Pleasant

BATTLE MONUMENT STATE PARK

P oint Pleasant, a little neck of land where the Kanawha River empties into the Ohio, was a cockpit of the American Revolution, a place where American ambitions, Indian fears, and British policy all came into collision. While not exactly the first engagement of that war, as the memorial shaft on the site of the battlefield claims, it was still a significant encounter on the path.

Chief Logan (*see* Aracoma Pageant, Logan, West Virginia) had led the Mingo and Shawnee on a war of revenge against the settlers after his family had been slaughtered by drunken whites. The tribes, concerned about the steady encroachments of Americans on grounds that had been reserved for them by Britain, had been ready to retaliate.

In the early autumn of 1774, as Governor Dunmore advanced from Pittsburgh, Brigadier General Andrew Lewis followed the Kanawha from the south, in a pincers movement aimed at the main Shawnee force under Cornstalk. The Indians, however, had slipped behind the two armies, as Cornstalk intended to attack before they had a chance to unite. On October 10, while Lewis was camped at Point Pleasant, Cornstalk struck. In a struggle that lasted several hours, Lewis managed to fight off the Shawnee. That was the only chance that Cornstalk had, since the numbers arrayed against him were now far too great. He had no alternative but to make peace. The significance of the battle, fought six months before Lexington and Concord, was that it secured the northwest frontier for the Americans in the opening years of the war and frustrated the British strategy of disrupting the exposed settlements.

Three years later, while visiting the American fort that was built here after the battle, Cornstalk was seized and murdered by settlers in retaliation for an incident in Lord Dunmore's War. He is buried in town on the lawn of the Mason County Courthouse.

LOCATION: *Point Pleasant Battlefield is on the eastern bank of the Kanawha, on West Virginia 2, within the town. An 84-foot-high shaft commemorates the engagement.*
HOURS: *Daily, dawn to dusk.*
ADMISSION: *Free.*
TELEPHONE: *(304) 675-3330.*

WISCONSIN

STOCKBRIDGE-MUNSEE TRIBAL COUNCIL MUSEUM

The Stockbridge and Munsee are two small tribes that are remnants of the Mahican and Delaware nations, who once were neighbors along the headwaters of the Susquehanna River of New York. They backed the American cause in the Revolutionary War but, like the Oneida (*see* Oneida Nation Museum, Green Bay, Wisconsin), pressure from land speculators forced them out of their ancestral lands.

They moved to Wisconsin in the 1820s, purchasing land from the Menominee. The deal went sour, however, and their holdings on Lake Winnebago were fraudulently sold to a private corporation that stripped it of all timber resources. The Stockbridge-Munsee received in exchange a small corner of the Menominee reservation, established in 1854. A few hundred members of those tribes continue to live there. The tribal museum displays examples of basketry and other crafts.

LOCATION: *The museum is located on Mohheconnuck Road, through Bowler by way of County Road J. The town is about 25 miles northwest of Shawano.*
HOURS: *Vary, best to call ahead.*
ADMISSION: *Donation.*
TELEPHONE: *(715) 793-4111.*

CHIEF OSHKOSH MUSEUM

Roy Oshkosh was regarded as the last chief of the Menominee when their reservation was broken up in 1961. The lands were returned to tribal control in 1973. The possessions and family heirlooms of Oshkosh were gathered as this small museum, in a tiny Door County village.

An Algonquin word, *Oshkosh* means "claw" and the name was carried by several chiefs of the Menominee. The first Oshkosh, born in 1795, was reputed to have fought alongside Tecumseh during the Shawnee leader's campaigns in the War of 1812. Afterward, however, he followed a policy of amity toward white people. He agreed to the sale of Menominee lands in the Fox Valley to tribes who were moved there from New York. When federal policy later mandated removal of Native Americans west of the Mississippi, the Menominee were permitted to retain reservation lands on the Wolf River.

LOCATION: *The museum is located on Wisconsin 42, the main road through town. The memorial to the original Chief Oshkosh is in his namesake city's Menominee Park, on Lake Winnebago. His remains were moved from the reservation and reinterred there in 1927.*
HOURS: *Daily, 9-5, Memorial Day through September.*
ADMISSION: *Free.*
TELEPHONE: *(414) 868-3240.*

Fort Atkinson

PANTHER INTAGLIO MOUND

T he mounds of Wisconsin, with the exception of the Aztalan complex (*see* Aztalan State Park, Lake Mills, Wisconsin), are of much more recent origin than the great mounds of the Ohio Valley. Their builders are believed to have been ancestors of the Winnebago, whose clan structures are represented by many of the animals in the mounds. These effigies, replicas of the various sacred clan symbols, were directly connected to religious rites.

Most mounds were earthwork constructions. Along the Rock River here, though, is an intaglio, an effigy shape that has actually been excavated out of the ground. The panther effigy is among the best defined anywhere in the state.

LOCATION: *The intaglio is west of town, on Wisconsin 106, at 1236 Riverside Drive.*
HOURS: *Daily, dawn to dusk.*
ADMISSION: *Free.*

Green Bay

ONEIDA NATION MUSEUM

B y the middle of the eighteenth century, the Oneida, original members of
New York's Iroquois confederacy, found themselves in an increasingly
uncomfortable position. Epidemics had depleted their numbers, and as the
clouds of war gathered, their fondest wish was to remain neutral. But their
powerful neighbors in the confederacy, the Mohawk and Onondaga, were
strong supporters of the British. Eventually, the Oneida chose to join the
colonial side, some of them even serving in the regular army. As a result, they
were raided by their former Iroquois allies, and the tribe was almost destitute
when the war ended.

The new federal government awarded them land grants in New York.
But this proved to be a mixed blessing. Much of their territory lay along the
route of the new Erie Canal, and land speculators bought out their holdings
piecemeal. To retain their tribal identity, the Oneida were persuaded in 1821
to move to Wisconsin on land purchased from the Menominee.

Misfortune followed them west. The Menominee believed they had
been coerced into the deal and cut a secret bargain with the federal government, severely restricting the Oneida lands. The tribal structures fell apart and
not until 1934 were they able to unify themselves again under the Indian
Reorganization Act. Moreover, the leading advocate of the move to Wisconsin, Eleazer Williams, suddenly decided to declare himself the Lost Dauphin,
the missing son of Louis XVI of France. Evidence indicates that the dauphin
died in prison as a child during the Reign of Terror, but claiming the French
throne was a popular pastime on the western frontier in those years, as readers
of *Huckleberry Finn* will recall. Williams got some good mileage out of his
story until someone thought of checking it out with his Oneida relatives.

The Oneida have become very active in the Green Bay area and own
several tribal enterprises, including a casino and resort hotel near the airport.
Their museum relates the tribal history with an impressive collection of artifacts and exhibits that detail its movements across the years.

LOCATION: *The museum is 7 miles southwest of Green Bay by way of Wisconsin 54
and County Roads E and EE.*
HOURS: *Monday through Saturday, 9–5, April through November. Closed weekends,
rest of year.*
ADMISSION: *$2.*
TELEPHONE: *(414) 869-2768.*

Lac du Flambeau

BEN GUTHRIE CULTURAL CENTER

Lac du Flambeau is one of three Ojibwa (or Chippewa, as the Wisconsin bands of the tribe prefer to be called) reservations in the state. This tract, surrounded by Chequamegon National Forest, is situated in the inland lake country. The name itself derives from a Chippewa practice, also observed by French explorers, of fishing at night with the aid of birch torches. The light was believed to attract fish.

Almost one thousand tribal members still live in the area. Their economic progress was held back for years by the federal practice of allotting land to individuals rather than to the tribe. The family divisions made on the small plots over the years made each one almost worthless. In recent years, however, the tribe has been able to enter the tourist business in this popular summer vacation area. The museum displays artifacts of the local Chippewa, and during the summer months ritual dances are performed at the lakefront in town.

LOCATION: *The museum is on Main Street (Wisconsin 47) in town. Dances are held in the nearby Indian Bowl.*
HOURS: *The museum is open Monday through Friday, 10–5. The ritual dances are held Tuesday at 8:30 in July and August.*
ADMISSION: *Free.*
TELEPHONE: *(715) 588-7001.*

Lake Mills

AZTALAN STATE PARK

When Judge Nathaniel F. Hyer explored the mounds near this southern Wisconsin community in 1837, he was convinced that he had come upon an outpost of the Aztecs, so he gave it a name that sounded Aztec to him.

Pioneers were familiar with the history of the conquest of Mexico, and they were quick to ascribe any evidence of an ancient culture they happened to come upon to the Aztecs. One such amateur historian even concocted a story of the Aztec ruler Montezuma escaping his Spanish captors and fleeing north, only to be recaptured in Utah. Two creeks in that state still carry the names Montezuma and Recapture as a result of that fantastic tale. But Judge Hyer was not so far off the mark. Research does indicate that the twelfth century settlement at Aztalan was related to the Temple Mound culture of the lower

Mississippi Valley, this being its most northern location. There is evidence that these people were, indeed, influenced by Mexican contacts.

There is nothing at Aztalan that resembles the culture of the native peoples who populated Wisconsin in historic times. There is, however, a strong parallel with those who built the great Cahokia mounds (*see* Cahokia Mounds State Historic Site, East Saint Louis, Illinois), suggesting that Aztalan may have been a colony of that settlement. The two mounds here are shaped like pyramids with flat tops and are surrounded by earthworks enclosing ten thousand square yards. The condition of human bones found here strongly suggests that its residents practiced cannibalism.

The entire area along the Crawfish River is now a state park. A nearby museum displays artifacts removed from the site.

LOCATION: *Aztalan is located 3 miles east of the Lake Mills exit of Interstate 94 by way of County Road B.*
HOURS: *The park is open daily, dawn to dusk. The museum is open Monday through Saturday, 10–4; Sunday, 12–4, mid-May through September.*
ADMISSION: *Park is free, museum is $2.*
TELEPHONE: *(414) 648-5116.*

Odanah

BAD RIVER CULTURAL CENTER

The Bad River Cultural Center is another of the Chippewa reservations and is located on Lake Superior, extending south into the marshlands of Ashland County. Like many such tracts, the lands were leased out by the government to white timber interests, and, after having been stripped of their resources, were returned to the tribe. The Chippewa here have been able to sustain an economy based on the cultivation of wild rice in sloughs off Lake Superior. A festival celebrating the crop is held the weekend before Labor Day. The cultural center has exhibits with native crafts and displays explaining how wild rice is grown and harvested.

LOCATION: *The center is on U.S. 2 in Odanah, about 10 miles east of Ashland.*
HOURS: *Vary; check in advance.*
ADMISSION: *Free.*
TELEPHONE: *(715) 682-4212.*

Red Cliff

BUFFALO ARTS CENTER

T he Buffalo Arts Center is an exceptionally well-designed museum facility that concentrates on contemporary arts and crafts of this Chippewa group. The reservation occupies a very scenic portion of the Bayfield Peninsula. From the town of Red Cliff there are fine views across Chequamegon Bay to the Apostle Islands National Lakeshore.

LOCATION: *Red Cliff is on Wisconsin 13, about 3 miles north of the resort town of Bayfield, starting point of boat trips to the Apostle Islands.*
HOURS: *Daily, 10–4, May through September.*
ADMISSION: *$3.*
TELEPHONE: *(715) 779-5805.*

West Bend

LIZARD MOUND STATE PARK

O ne of Wisconsin's best-preserved and most extensive groupings of effigy mounds is contained in Lizard Mound State Park. There are more than thirty effigies, some in the shapes of animals, others in geometric patterns. The most striking mound is the one that gives its name to the park. The park also houses a nature trail and picnic facilities.

LOCATION: *The park is north of town on Wisconsin 144, about 45 miles north of Milwaukee by way of U.S. 45.*
HOURS: *Daily, dawn to dusk.*
ADMISSION: *Free.*
TELEPHONE: *(414) 338-4445.*

Stand Rock Winnebago Ceremonials

The Winnebago occupied central Wisconsin when the first French explorers arrived. While the tribe shared many cultural attributes with their neighbors, the Menominee, they were more closely related to the Siouan peoples who already had migrated farther west. Why the Winnebago remained behind and how they managed to live peacefully with the Algonquian newcomers, something the main body of Sioux could not manage, is not known. But in 1634 they were reported leaving Lake Winnebago, and during the next century they gradually moved south and west through the state and into Illinois.

After the Black Hawk War in 1837, they were finally forced to cede their lands in Wisconsin and began a long, disheartening trek west. It ended with the main body of the tribe moving onto the Omaha reservation lands near Bancroft, Nebraska. But in 1874, many individuals began returning to their ancestral lands. No reservation was set aside for them, but forty-acre homesteads were allotted to families instead.

In 1963, the tribe voted to reorganize. While there is no central Winnebago settlement, the majority live close to the tourist area at Wisconsin Dells. This community changed its name from Kilbourn in 1931 to capitalize on the fantastic rock formations in the nearby Wisconsin River. The Dells were merchandised with a heavy dollop of Indian legend, some based on actual tribal tales and some just made up on the spot. The story of a giant serpent creating the Dells as he thrashed down the river was attributed to the Winnebago, who did not seem to mind much. In fact, some of the tribal group have chosen to join in the tourist bonanza. The Stand Rock Amphitheater, situated along the river amid the Dells, is now the site of some of the finest ceremonial dances held in the Midwest. An adjacent museum contains a large collection of tribal items.

LOCATION: *The amphitheater is 5 miles north of the town of Wisconsin Dells on Wisconsin 13. It can also be reached by boat.*

HOURS: *The dances are held daily, at 8:45, mid-June through August. The museum is open daily, 10–4, Memorial Day to Christmas.*

ADMISSION: *Tickets to the dances are $7.50; to the museum, $2.*

TELEPHONE: *(608) 254-2268.*

GREAT PLAINS—NORTH

Alberta
Manitoba
Minnesota
Montana
North Dakota
Saskatchewan
South Dakota
Wyoming

GREAT PLAINS
— NORTH

ALBERTA
1 Indian Battle Park, *Lethbridge*
2 Writing-on-Stone Provincial Park, *Milk River*

MANITOBA
3 Riel House National Historic Site, *Winnipeg*

MINNESOTA
4 Ni-Min-Win Ojibwa Festival, *Duluth*
5 Sioux Window in Cathedral of Our Merciful
  Saviour, *Faribault*
6 Ojibwa Settlement, *Grand Portage National
  Monument*
7 Upper Sioux Agency State Park, *Granite Falls*
8 Little Crow Memorial, *Hutchinson*
9 Grand Mound Interpretive Center,
  International Falls
10 Petroglyphs, *Jeffers*
11 Mille Lacs Chippewa Museum and Kathio
   State Park, *Onamia*
12 Pipestone National Monument, *Pipestone*
13 Lower Sioux Agency, *Redwood Falls*

MONTANA
14 Battlefield and Visitors Center, *Big Hole
   National Battlefield*
15 Museum of the Plains Indians, *Browning*
16 Bears Paw State Monument, *Chinook*
17 Crow Reservation Fair and Rodeo, *Crow Agency*
18 Northern Cheyenne Tribal Museum, *Lame Deer*
19 Battlefield, National Cemetery, and Museum,
   Little Big Horn National Battlefield
20 Chief Plenty Coups State Monument, *Pryor*
21 Madison Buffalo Jump State Monument,
   Three Forks

NORTH DAKOTA
22 Fort Totten State Historic Site and
   St. Michael's Mission, *Fort Totten*
23 Standing Rock, *Fort Yates*
24 Whitestone Battlefield, *Kulm*
25 Slant Village at Fort Abraham Lincoln State Park,
   Mandan
26 Three Affiliated Tribes Museum, *New Town*
27 *Knife River Villages National Historic Site, Stanton*

SASKATCHEWAN
28 Batoche National Historic Park, *Batoche*

SOUTH DAKOTA
29 St. Joseph's School, *Chamberlain*
30 Crazy Horse Memorial, *Custer*
31 Prehistoric Indian Village, *Mitchell*
32 Oscar Howe Art Center, *Mitchell*
33 Sitting Bull Memorial, *Mobridge*
34 Scherr–Howe Arena Murals, *Mobridge*
35 Red Cloud Heritage Center, *Pine Ridge*
36 Sioux Indian Museum, *Rapid City*

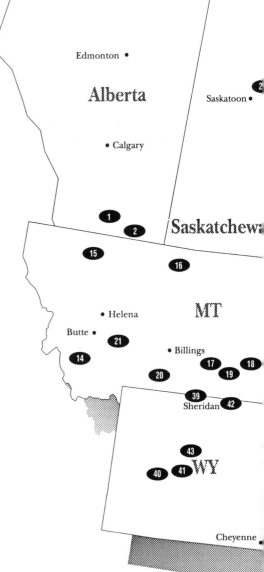

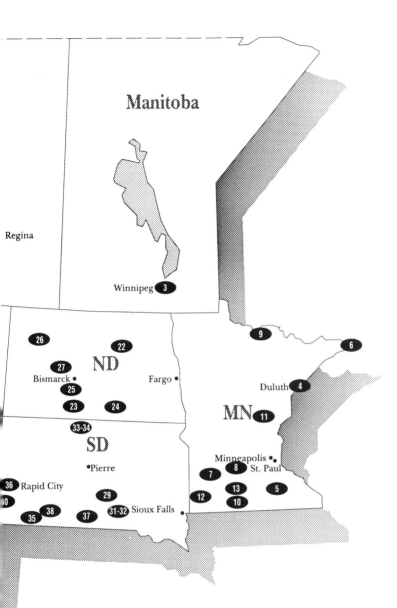

Regina

Manitoba

Winnipeg **3**

26

22

27 ND

Bismarck •

25

Fargo •

9

6

Duluth **4**

23

24

MN **11**

33-34

SD

Minneapolis •

36 Rapid City

0

35

38

•Pierre

7

8 • St. Paul

13

5

29

12

37

31-32 Sioux Falls •

10

37 Buechel Lakota Museum and Mission,
Saint Francis
38 Wounded Knee Battlefield, *Wounded Knee*

WYOMING
39 Medicine Wheel, *Bighorn National Forest*
40 Shoshone Reservation Headquarters and
Graves of Washakie and Sacajaweae,
Fort Washakie
41 Mission Heritage Center, *Saint Stephens*
42 Fetterman Massacre, *Sheridan*
43 Gift of the Waters Pageant, *Thermopolis*

ALBERTA

Lethbridge

INDIAN BATTLE PARK

E arly recorded history has the Cree ranging over a vast region of northern woodlands between the shores of Hudson Bay and Lake Superior. There were actually several bands of Cree, all of whom spoke a mutually intelligible Algonquian language. Contact with French traders set in motion a series of culture shocks, resulting in the Cree's two-hundred-year migration to the southwest. By the beginning of the nineteenth century, the lead groups in the movement had acquired horses and reached the northern bank of the Missouri River, in Montana. There they bumped against the powerful Blackfoot Confederacy, whose lands extended from the High Plains to the Rockies. A series of wars between the two peoples lasted for most of the first half of the century, culminating in the 1850s in a series of costly battles for both sides. With both the Cree and Blackfoot nearing exhaustion through war, disease, and steady diminution of the buffalo herds on which they both depended, the final battle between them was fought near what is now the southern Alberta community of Lethbridge.

The main attraction of Indian Battle Park is Fort Whoop-Up, a reconstruction of an illegal whisky fort of the 1870s. It was built by American traders who crossed the border to sell prohibited liquor to the Indians.

The park is situated in a beautiful area along the Oldman River. While many of its attractions are rather commercialized, there is still an opportunity to trace the sites of the battle, believed to be the last major engagement between Native American people on the continent.

LOCATION: *Along the Oldman River by way of Whoop-Up Drive.*
HOURS: *Daily, 10–8, mid-May through Labor Day; 12–4, at other times.*
ADMISSION: *Free.*
TELEPHONE: *(403) 329-0444.*

Milk River

WRITING-ON-STONE PROVINCIAL PARK

W riting-on-Stone Provincial Park contains the greatest concentration of rock art on the Great Plains: there are more than 50 rock art sites with thousands of figures. Archaeologists have discovered evidence that native people used this valley for at least 3,000 years, and nomadic bands of Blackfoot and Shoshone camped here for long periods of time over the centuries. Using the rock as a sort of primitive billboard, the bands communicated with one another through the messages and artwork they left on the towering sandstone in this canyon along the Milk River.

These native people left extensive evidence of their cultures. Many archaeological sites dating from the Late Historic Period (which began around 1800 years ago) have been found in the park, and much of the rock art dates from this time, leaving a pictorial record of the lives of a society that followed bison herds on foot. Later rock art, dating from the Historic Period (which began approximately A.D.1730), gives a clear picture of how the introduction of horses, guns, and metal to the northern plains had an impact on the native culture. Travel and hunting became easier, and warfare became more common throughout this period.

Some of the pictographs (rock paintings) were painted with red ochre (crushed iron ore mixed with water) while others were drawn with a lump of limestone. Most of the petroglyphs (rock carvings) were scratched on the rock with antlers and bones, and later, with metal tools. The art depicts animal figures, human figures engaged in daily activities and in warfare, and many items of material culture. Much of the rock art remains a mystery to archaeologists, and probably represented a ceremonial aspect of rituals. Whatever the meaning and function of this rock art, it leaves a fascinating legacy of the native people who inhabited the area.

LOCATION: *The park is about 25 miles southeast of the town of Milk River, by way of Alberta 501 and an unpaved road marked to the site. It is just a few miles north of the Montana border. From the end of Interstate 15 at the Alberta line, it is about 12 miles northeast on Alberta 500.*

HOURS: *Daily, dawn to dusk. Entry to the archeological site shifts from season to season. It is best to check in advance. Usually, however, there is a 2 P.M. tour every day but Saturday all year.*

ADMISSION: *Free.*

TELEPHONE: *(403) 647-2364.*

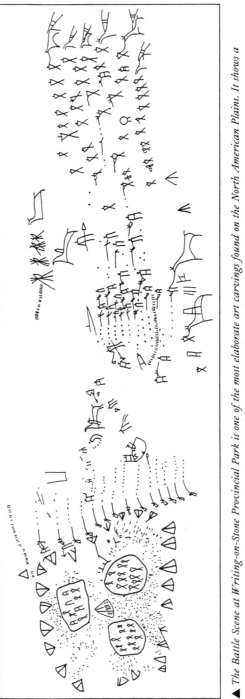

▲ *The Battle Scene at Writing-on-Stone Provincial Park is one of the most elaborate art carvings found on the North American Plains. It shows a large force of warriors attacking a tepee encampment, defended by a line of guns.*

MANITOBA

RIEL HOUSE NATIONAL HISTORIC SITE

The story of the Métis entwines all the cultural strands that continue to shape the history of Canada. As French traders entered Manitoba, they intermarried with the Cree people who lived on this land. After several generations, the families they formed established their own identities as Métis. Some of them continued to live a traditional nomadic existence well into the nineteenth century, following the buffalo herds on their seasonal migrations across the prairies. Others established an urban way of life in Saint Boniface, a French-speaking community that now has been absorbed by the city of Winnipeg.

The Red River area was then known as Assiniboia and was governed by the Hudson's Bay Company. But in 1869 dreams of confederation were gaining power, and the area was turned over as a territory to the new Canadian government. Until then, there had been an understanding between the Métis and the English-speaking settlers from the East: The traditional ways were respected, and the two peoples lived in a stern sort of friendship. When the government sent surveying teams into the area and started laying out sections that cut across the French-style ribbon farms of the Métis, the Métis began fearing their rights would be swept away. These fears were justified by what had happened when white settlers poured onto the prairies of the United States, displacing the native peoples who had lived there. That was the setting for Louis Riel's rise to power.

Riel was descended from an old Métis family, and his mother, Julie Lagimodiere, identified strongly with her Cree heritage. Riel, a fiery and inspirational speaker, had been educated in Quebec and returned to Assiniboia at age 25. He quickly rose to a position of influence among the Métis and was named to head a provisional government that opposed confederation with Canada. But the Canadian government moved quickly, dispatching troops to the area and approving legislation that would make Manitoba a province.

Later, Riel was elected to Parliament from Manitoba but was expelled in 1875 for his militant insistence on Métis rights. Twice in the next few years he entered Quebec mental hospitals because of the growing strain on him. Riel moved to Montana where he taught school.

In 1885 the final act in this drama was played out. The Canadian Pacific Railroad was making its way across the country, touching off a boom in Saskatchewan. Native peoples saw their own land sold out from under them, and the Métis in the area were on the edge of rebellion. Seeing the chance to unify the interests of both French and Cree, Riel returned to Canada. Appealing to both sides for support, he took control of the revolt. For three months, the Métis defied the Canadian government. But when troops finally reached the scene, the rebellion collapsed. Riel surrendered, was tried for treason, and hanged at Regina in November. His body lay in state at this house, which was built in 1881. After his death, he became a martyr to both the French and native causes, issues that still figure prominently in Canadian society.

An ironic result of Riel's Rebellion was that it won public support for the completion of the railroad. Work on the railroad had stalled in the tough Canadian Shield country north of Lake Superior, and it became evident that more money was needed to close the final link. When the public saw how the rails were used to quickly transport troops to the scene of the rebellion, opposition to the project faded and the railroad was completed.

The Riel house in the Saint Boniface district is now a memorial to the leader and his failed rebellion. There are displays on the history of the Métis and their struggle and many personal items belonging to the Riel family.

LOCATION: *The house is at 330 River Road, on the east bank of the Red River. Take Manitoba 42 (Pembina Highway) south from downtown Winnipeg, then east on Manitoba 165, across the bridge.*
HOURS: *Daily, 9:30–6, May through Labor Day; weekends only through September.*
ADMISSION: *Free.*
TELEPHONE: *(204) 257-1783.*

MINNESOTA

NI-MIN-WIN OJIBWA FESTIVAL

More Native Americans claim affiliation with the Ojibwa, or Chippewa, than any other tribal group. An estimated 160,000 persons in the northern United States and Canada identify themselves with the tribe. The Ojibwa once ranged over a vast territory, from the Georgian Bay country of Ontario to the plains of Montana. They were a tremendously adaptable people and seemed to thrive on whatever circumstances dictated. They were deeply involved in the fur trade when the French were the European power that controlled the North. When migration took them into Minnesota, they became experts at cultivating wild rice. The westernmost branch of the tribe moved onto the Great Plains, acquired horses, and became skilled buffalo hunters.

The Ojibwa contended with some of the most powerful Native American nations, including the Iroquois and the Lakota, and held their own. Because their northern lands were far from the expanding frontier, they managed to stay clear of the European colonial rivalries that destroyed many other tribes. Still, from the middle of the nineteenth century on, they were steadily forced to cede their lands and either move onto reserves or function in the white culture. Even those cut off from tribal life, however, seem to have retained a stronger cultural identification than most other groups.

There are seven Ojibwa reservations in Minnesota. The largest of them, the Leech Lake and White Earth Reservations, take in big chunks of prime inland lake country. Both bands have built a thriving tourist business, and also engage in wild rice cultivation and other enterprises. On the third weekend of August the various bands assemble in Duluth, near the Fond du Lac Reservation, for one of the biggest tribal gatherings in the Midwest. The Ni-Mi-Win Festival features traditional dancing and is also a good opportunity to shop for Ojibwa crafts and artwork, especially black ash baskets.

LOCATION: *The Ni-Mi-Win celebration is held in various locations around Duluth, usually along the Lake Superior shore.*
TELEPHONE: *(800) 438-5884 or (218) 722-4011.*

Faribault

SIOUX WINDOW IN
CATHEDRAL OF OUR MERCIFUL SAVIOUR

T he Sioux Uprising of 1862 panicked Minnesota, depopulating the south-western part of the state for a few months as frightened white settlers retreated to safety. The uprising lasted only a few weeks, but the memory of it was so horrific that for years afterward the army was compelled to man military posts in the state to protect settlers from the handful of Sioux who had avoided expulsion to the Dakota Territory.

Prior to the uprising, a few white observers had warned the government about what was coming. Among them was Episcopal Bishop Henry Whipple, who had established a school and mission at Faribault and had become sympathetic to the plight of the Sioux. When reserve clauses that had been cynically attached to treaties were suddenly enforced, the Sioux were made to give up half their reservation lands. There were crop failures. When the government debated on whether to pay treaty annuities in gold or paper money, the agent refused to give out any food until some form of money arrived. According to Chief Little Crow, he was told that his people "would eat grass or their own dung."

In August, the situation erupted. Four young men of the Mdewakanton band of the tribe, on the Lower Sioux Agency (*see* Redwood Falls, Minnesota), suddenly fired into a party of whites during a shooting contest, killing five of them. Authorities demanded that the tribe surrender the men for justice. But the Sioux refused, and under the leadership of Little Crow, began to raid the settlements of the Minnesota River valley. A small military column sent out against them was annihilated. Finally, the state organized a 1,400-man force and on September 23 defeated Little Crow at the Battle of Wood Lake. The final death toll was 490 white civilians and soldiers and 33 Indians.

Most of those who had taken up arms retreated to the Dakotas. But the government began rounding up all native men suspected of participating in the campaign, even members of the Wahpeton and Sisseton bands, who had remained friendly and many of whom were turned in on the dubious testimony of informers. In drumhead courts that tried up to 40 defendants a day, 303 of the men were sentenced to death. Bishop Whipple interceded on behalf of the Sioux, making a personal plea to President Lincoln. As a result, 265 of these men had their sentences reduced to prison terms. But the remaining 38, accused of either murder or rape, were hung at a public ceremony on December 26, 1862. The reservation lands then were broken up and the remaining Sioux dispersed.

"Bishop," wrote a missionary who witnessed the brutal way this policy was carried out, "if I were an Indian I would never lay down the war club while

I lived." Construction on Whipple's cathedral had begun in the same year as the Sioux Uprising. A few years later, a stained glass window showing a peace pipe and a broken war club was dedicated as a token of gratitude from the Sioux for Whipple's efforts on their behalf.

LOCATION: *The cathedral is in the middle of town, at 2nd Avenue North and 6th Street West. Faribault is about 60 miles south of Minneapolis by way of Interstate 35.*
HOURS: *Monday through Friday, 9–12.*
ADMISSION: *Donation.*
TELEPHONE: *(507) 334-7732.*

Grand Portage National Monument

OJIBWA SETTLEMENT

D uring the great era of the fur trade, the area around the present-day Grand Portage National Monument site was one of the most important places on the Great Lakes. At *Grand Portage* ("great carrying place") voyagers from French Canada transferred their canoes from Lake Superior around the rapids of the Pigeon River, gateway to the bountiful trapping country to the northwest. The area was known to European explorers by 1722, and sixty-two years after that it became the headquarters of the North West Company.

Every spring, as the ice melted from the rivers and lakes, trappers and their Native American guides and companions would come here with the year's supply of pelts for Rendezvous. They met with company representatives from Montreal. Deals were struck, trade goods from the East purchased, and celebrations held. For the Ojibwa who lived in the area, Rendezvous was a time to stock up on the manufactured goods that were playing an increasingly important part in their lives.

The Grand Portage Rendezvous was held for nineteen years, from 1784 to 1803, until the company opened a new base at Fort William, across the Canadian border. Within a few years, the buildings here had crumbled into disuse, and in time the very site was almost forgotten. But in 1958, the Ojibwa, who had been given the surrounding lands as a reservation, donated the Grand Portage location to the federal government for use as a historic park. The major buildings were reconstructed according to the records of archaeologists and historians who went over old journals. Now this first permanent settlement in Minnesota stands again, with exhibits that pay particular attention to the roles of Native Americans in the fur-trading era.

The Ojibwa own the adjacent hotel and conference center. Examples of

▲ *Each spring, Indians, trappers, and dealers from Montreal would meet for trading at Grand Portage.*

their beadwork and other crafts are sold at gift shops within the national monument.

LOCATION: *Grand Portage is located off U.S. 61, in the northeastern corner of the state, 5 miles south of the Canadian border.*
HOURS: *Daily, 8–5, mid-May to mid-October.*
ADMISSION: *Free.*
TELEPHONE: *(218) 387-2788.*

Granite Falls

UPPER SIOUX AGENCY STATE PARK

I n 1850, as settlers poured into Minnesota, the territorial government came under mounting pressure to resolve the "Indian question." In response, in 1851 the government began drawing up treaties, opening up the Sioux lands in the fertile western half of the territory and restricting the tribe to reservations.

The Sioux of Minnesota belonged to the Santee, or eastern, division of the tribe, which is more properly known as the Lakota. There were four bands within the Santee—the Sisseton, Wahpeton, Mdewakanton, and Wahpekute. The government, knowing there would be strong discontent when the terms of the Sioux Treaty (1851) were understood, refused to deal with all four bands at once. This prevented the Santee from assembling in full force for the negotiations. The government split the procedure in half, meeting first with the Sisseton and Wahpeton, and then separately with the others. Only after signing did the Santee learn that among the treaty provisions was the tribe's repayment of debts allegedly owed by individual Santee to white traders. Those debts came right off the top of funds paid for the lands that they were giving up, and the lingering grievances caused by this was one of the underlying reasons for the Sioux War, eleven years later.

White traders fought against expulsion of the tribe to the Dakota Territory because they wanted to make sure that commerce with the Santee would remain in Minnesota's boundaries. Thus when it came time to draw up the reservations lands, the government stuck to its divisive policies, laying out two separate tracts—the Upper and Lower Sioux Agencies—ten miles deep along the Minnesota River. The Sisseton and Wahpeton occupied the upper agency. Both were long, narrow strips of land that were regarded as the least likely for cultivation in the area.

By 1858, the government even regarded these lands as too expansive, and opened the area north of the river to white settlement. The upper agency tribes did not participate in the Sioux War, but they were expelled to the Dakotas. Not until the 1930s did the federal government, aware of the fact that many Santee had returned to the Minnesota lands, set aside a small reservation tract. The Upper Sioux Agency now has a population of under two hundred. A state park adjacent to the existing reservation contains historical displays as well as exhibits on local geology and wildlife.

LOCATION: *The state park is 9 miles southeast of Granite Falls, by way of Minnesota 67. One drives through the reservation to reach it. Wood Lake Historic site, marking the location of the last battle of the Sioux War, is 10 miles farther south, off Minnesota 67.*
HOURS: *Daily, 8–8.*
ADMISSION: *$4 state park pass.*
TELEPHONE: *(612) 564-4777.*

Hutchinson

LITTLE CROW MEMORIAL

L ittle Crow was among the Santee who could not bear to stay away from their ancestral homes after the Sioux War. During the uprising, he had reluctantly led the Indian forces. He seemed to recognize that the resistance was futile, but his stature among the Santee was such that he could not refuse the demands of leadership placed upon him. It is unclear whether it was his plan to attack the isolated farms along the Minnesota River in an attempt to drive white settlers out. Some of his companions claimed later that he thought it was the only chance he had of winning the conflict.

The attacks on the farms stirred up outrage in Saint Paul, as well as throughout the East, where lurid newspaper stories on the uprising caused enormous excitement. When the state managed to assemble an army against Little Crow, his demand for amnesty was refused. The public thirst for revenge was too great to allow it.

After his defeat at Wood Lake, Little Crow escaped to the Dakota Territory. But the following year he returned to his homeland. Hutchinson was not the safest place to be, because it was in this vicinity that the first shots of the war had been fired. A farmer, learning that Little Crow was in the area and out to avenge the death of relatives in the war, ambushed him while he was picking berries.

When Little Crow died on July 3, 1863, his sixteen-year-old son was his only companion. In later years, when firsthand memories had faded and new perspectives were gained on the grievances of the Sioux, the town decided to erect a monument to the native leader who was gunned down here.

LOCATION: *The statue of Little Crow is on Main Street, just off the center of Hutchinson, not far from where he was shot. Hutchinson is about 60 miles west of Minneapolis, by way of Minnesota 7.*

International Falls

GRAND MOUND INTERPRETIVE CENTER

O f all the prehistoric mounds found in the United States, this is certainly the most northern. The Grand Mound, the largest of five in the area, is the Upper Midwest's largest prehistoric structure. Probably a burial mound, this earthwork has never been opened, unlike many of the better known sites in the Ohio Valley, which are actually reconstructions of mounds that had been thoroughly excavated.

An introductory video program describes where Indian mounds are found in North America, how they've been interpreted, and which cultures used the mounds at this site. Display cases are set in an "outdoor environment" through the use of dioramas, and include ancient artifacts found at nearby mounds. There are also explanations of the Indian cultures that existed before the coming of the Ojibwa, who are now the dominant tribe in northern Minnesota. A film produced by the center demonstrates the pottery manufacturing process that was used by the culture that built these mounds. The video covers the digging and processing of the clay, and building, decorating, and firing the pots. There are also demonstrations of the *atlatl*, a prehistoric hunting implement.

The history center is accessible to physically disabled persons and offers an audio-visual program on the trails and mounds. "Hands-on" programs for groups may be scheduled in advance.

LOCATION: *Grand Mound is 15 miles west of International Falls, on Minnesota 11.*
HOURS: *Open daily, 10–5, May through Labor Day. Open the rest of the year, Saturdays, 10–4; Sundays, noon–4.*
ADMISSION: *Free.*
TELEPHONE: *(218) 285-3332.*

Jeffers

PETROGLYPHS

T he Jeffers site lies at the top of Red Rock Ridge, a rock formation extending from south-central Minnesota to southeastern South Dakota. The red quartzite rocks situated along the Little Cottonwood River are covered with about two thousand Indian carvings that tell a pictorial story of the lives and culture of these ancient people. The carvings, created by striking a chisel made of stone or antler with a hammerstone, form one of the largest groups of petroglyphs found in the Midwest. The word *petroglyph* comes from the Greek words *petros* (rock) and *glyphe* (carving).

Historians estimate that these petroglyphs were carved during the Late Archaic-Early-Woodland (3,000 B.C. to A.D. 500) and the Late Woodland (A.D. 900 to 1750) periods. The carvings served a number of functions, from recording important events and pastimes to depicting sacred ceremonies. There are carvings of Thunderbirds, turtles, shaman (holy men), *atlatls* , and arrows. Little is known of the people who carved these rocks, but the pictures they left give a detailed impression of aspects of the hunt and of their social and religious lives.

The Minnesota Historical Society has a shelter house at the site, with information explaining the petroglyphs. A numbered rope trail guides visitors through the one-hour walking tour.

LOCATION: *The petroglyphs are east from U.S. 71 on County Road 10, about 75 miles west of Mankato.*
HOURS: *Tuesday through Saturday, 10–5, May through Labor Day; Weekends only through October.*
ADMISSION: *Free.*
TELEPHONE: *(507) 877-3647 or (507) 697-6321.*

Onamia

MILLE LACS CHIPPEWA MUSEUM AND KATHIO STATE PARK

The Chippewa people began migrating into Minnesota late in the seventeenth century. Encountering scattered resistance from the Lakota, who had occupied these northern woodlands for centuries, they finally reached the main body of that tribe at its principal village, Kathio, on the southwestern shore of Mille Lacs Lake. It was here that the French explorer Daniel Greysolon, Sieur Duluth, visited the Lakota in 1679 and while the Native Americans looked on with interest, claimed the entire territory for France. The major battle fought here around 1750 between Ojibwa and Lakota was one of the most decisive in Native American history. It resulted in the Lakota being driven westward onto the Great Plains and becoming the leading political power among the Indian nations during the wars with the U.S. Army a century later. Kathio State Park is a memorial to those who fought in this battle.

Just north of the park is the small Mille Lacs Reservation. The museum here will reopen in 1995, and will house displays on the history, customs, and

▲ *An artist's conception of the Dakota village at Cooper Site (Kathio State Park) as it may have looked in the 1500s.*

crafts of the tribe. Of particular interest will be the canoe-making exhibit and items of everyday life, such as toys and musical instruments.

LOCATION: *Both the state park and the museum are located along U.S. 169 on the western shore of Mille Lacs Lake.*
HOURS: *The museum is temporarily closed but will reopen in 1995. The park is open daily, dawn to dusk.*
ADMISSION: *A $4 pass is good for entry at all Minnesota state parks.*
TELEPHONE: *Park offices are (612) 532-3523.*

Pipestone

PIPESTONE NATIONAL MONUMENT

A mong the Plains tribes, the pipe acquired a significance that ordered the meaning and rituals of life. Among the Lakota, the Arapahoe, the Omaha, the Iowa—virtually every group of Native Americans in the northern plains—the red stone pipe became a sacred item. Certain pipes carried religious significance, were stored in special animal skin bundles, and were associated with myths that sought to explain the origin of the tribes. Many pipes were buried with their owners. Pipe smoking was a ritual that accompanied almost every important event, from going to war to making peace, from trading goods to making medicine. The T-shaped pipe, known as the calumet, was smoked at ceremonial events, such as the signing of treaties, and became known to white settlers as "the peace pipe."

The most highly prized source for these pipes was a soft-red-stone quarry in southwestern Minnesota. There is evidence that digging here began in the seventeenth century. The territory was always controlled by some division of the Sioux. While the Sioux managed the distribution of the pipe-stone, the land around the quarry was regarded as a stewardship, held for the use of all tribes. The Yankton Sioux occupied the land when Minnesota became a state, and by a treaty in 1858, they retained unrestricted access to the quarry.

Inevitably, however, as white settlers moved onto the land, they began to encroach on the stone. Many of the public buildings in the nearby town of Pipestone were built with stone quarried from Indian lands. The Yankton, now situated on a reservation in South Dakota, were powerless to stop this process. In 1928, in an effort to conserve the priceless stone, the Yankton ceded their claim to the federal government. Nine years later, the Pipestone National Monument was formed and it was stipulated that only Indians would be given rights to quarry here.

Trails lead to vantage points around the quarry area. In the visitor center, Native Americans give demonstrations of the traditional art of pipe-making, which has changed little since Western artist George Catlin first described the process in the 1840s. Actual digging may be observed in the late summer and fall, when the absence of water makes the pipestone bed most accessible. The Upper Midwest Indian Cultural Center also operates crafts displays here.

LOCATION: *Pipestone National Monument is on U.S. 75, just north of the town of Pipestone, about 55 miles northeast of Sioux Falls, South Dakota.*
HOURS: *Daily, 8–5.*
ADMISSION: *Free.*
TELEPHONE: *(507) 825-5463.*

▲ *Pipestone National Monument is the quarry site for the prized red stone used to make sacred pipes—known to the settlers as "peace pipes."*

Redwood Falls

LOWER SIOUX AGENCY

W hen the government divided the Lakota tribes in Minnesota and placed them on two separate reservations, the Mdewakanton and Wahpekute were placed on the Lower Sioux Agency. (The names Upper and Lower Sioux referred to their relative positions on the Minnesota River.) It was these bands who were the leaders of the Sioux Uprising of 1862 (*see* Sioux Window in Cathedral of Our Merciful Saviour, Faribault, Minnesota). They wiped out a forty-man column sent out from Fort Ridgely, which had been established fifteen miles to the east to assure settlers that just such an event would never happen. But the Lower Sioux failed to capture the fort and the town of New Ulm, dooming the uprising. A 1,400-man force from Saint Paul defeated the Indians under Little Crow, virtually ending the Sioux presence in the state.

The Lower Sioux Reservation was reconstituted near the site of the original reserve when tribal members petitioned the government under the Indian Reorganization Act of 1934. An interpretive center here relates the history of the Lakota in the state and also recapitulates the events leading up to the Sioux War.

LOCATION: *The Lower Sioux Agency is on U.S. 71, 6 miles east of Redwood Falls.*
HOURS: *Daily, 10–5, May through October; 1–5, rest of year.*
ADMISSION: *Free.*
TELEPHONE: *(507) 697-6321.*

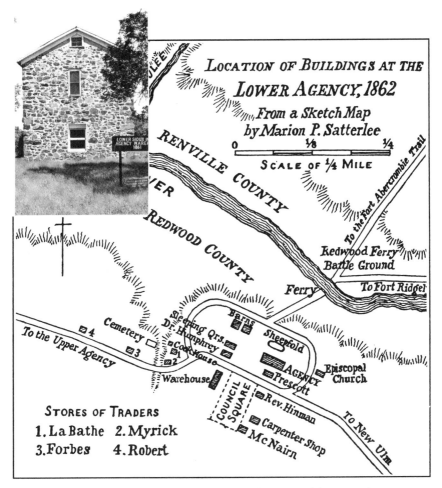

LOCATION OF BUILDINGS AT THE
LOWER AGENCY, 1862

*From a Sketch Map
by Marion P. Satterlee*

0   ⅛   ¼

SCALE OF ¼ MILE

RENVILLE COUNTY

REDWOOD COUNTY

To the Fort Abercrombie Trail

Redwood Ferry
Battle Ground

To Fort Ridgely

Ferry

To the Upper Agency

Cemetery

Dr. Humphrey

Sleeping Qrs.

Barns

Sheepfold

Court House

Warehouse

AGENCY

Prescott

Episcopal Church

COUNCIL SQUARE

Rev. Hinman

Carpenter Shop

McNairn

To New Ulm

STORES OF TRADERS

1. La Bathe   2. Myrick
3. Forbes   4. Robert

▲ *The original Agency building (built in 1861); and a sketch map of the Lower Sioux Agency in 1862.*

MONTANA

BATTLEFIELD AND VISITORS CENTER

I n the entire epic of American warfare, there have been few campaigns as heroic and as strange as the 1,500-mile running battle waged by Chief Joseph and his band of Nez Perce. Rarely numbering more than two hundred men of fighting age, they eluded or fought off thousands of U.S. cavalrymen sent against them in Idaho and Montana through the summer of 1877. Many of the commanders sent to fight them sympathized with the plight of the Nez Perce. White settlers sold them food and refused to take up arms against them. The campaign even involved tourists who were kidnapped by the Nez Perce in the newly established Yellowstone National Park. The campaign ended just forty miles from the safety of Canada, when Chief Joseph finally was compelled to surrender.

Nez Perce was a name applied by the French to several northwestern tribes who pierced their noses to wear ornaments. But this was a case of mistaken identity, because the group that became identified as the Nez Perce never followed the practice. When they encountered Lewis and Clark in 1805, the tribe was living along the lower Snake River and its tributaries in western Idaho, Oregon, and Washington. They were adept horsemen, raising Appaloosas, and were frequently raided by more eastern peoples for their stock. In 1855, they concluded a treaty with the federal government, confirming as their own the lands on which they then lived. These included the Wallowa Valley of Oregon, which was the home of Chief Joseph's band. His father had been one of the first Christian converts made by the Whitman Mission (*see* Walla Walla, Washington.)

The treaty held for only eight years, until a gold strike was made in the Wallowa Valley. The government then drew up a new agreement, reducing the Nez Perce lands by three-quarters and restricting them to the Lapwai Reservation of Idaho. Those who were already living at Lapwai ratified the agreement. The government declared that this was a majority of the Nez Perce chiefs and that the treaty was valid. But Chief Joseph protested, the Senate delayed ratifying the treaty, and in 1873 land was set aside for the tribe in the Wallowa. However, two years later the concession was canceled. It was pointed out that

▲ *Big Hole, one of the sites where U.S. cavalrymen battled Chief Joseph and his band of Nez Perce.*

the tribe was migratory and did not occupy these lands year-round, and on this technicality the Wallowa was taken from them. The Nez Perce were ordered to Lapwai.

Chief Joseph resigned himself to the move, but angry young men of the tribe began raiding white settlements on the route to Idaho. An army detachment was sent out to capture the warriors. Instead, this force was shredded at White Bird Canyon, on June 17, 1877. Joseph knew his only hope was flight; there was no compromise possible with the whites. Meanwhile, he was joined by another band under Looking Glass, who had been rousted from their encampment by federal troops. The Nez Perce now numbered seven hundred persons, of whom five hundred were women, children, and the elderly. But with their excellent horsemen serving as scouts, they were able to anticipate every move made by the pursuing troops, and crossed the Lolo Trail into Montana. They easily skirted an army barricade set up to intercept them and entered the Bitterroot Valley. Settlers there had no quarrel with the Nez Perce and recalled amicable relations with them from earlier years. So they sold the Indians supplies and sent them on their way.

Moving south, the Nez Perce stopped to make camp on the eastern slope of the Continental Divide, at a valley known as the Big Hole. General John Gibbon, sent out from Helena to stop Chief Joseph's band, caught up with them there on August 8. The Nez Perce had posted no guards, and Gibbon's dawn attack caught them by surprise. Part of the camp was captured immediately, but Joseph's war chiefs managed to rally their men and counterattacked. They captured a howitzer on the second full day of battle and wounded Gibbon before reinforcements arrived, necessitating a retreat. The army suffered sixty-nine casualties, including twenty deaths. The Nez Perce also suffered about the same number of losses, most of them women and children.

With the cavalry close behind him, Joseph moved east into Yellowstone Park. He stampeded the pack mules of his pursuers in a daring night raid, then briefly captured two bewildered tourists in the park and turned north in a desperate race for Canada. Exhausted and surrounded, he fell just short of the international border (*see* Bears Paw State Monument, Chinook, Montana).

The site of Big Hole Battlefield is now administered by the National Park Service. The visitor center is on the heights, commanding a bird's-eye view of the actual battleground. It contains an audiovisual display and artifacts of the battle. A self-guiding auto tour leads to the most important places on the battlefield.

LOCATION: *Big Hole is in the southwestern part of the state, 20 miles east of U.S. 93 on Montana 43, and about 100 miles southwest of Butte.*
HOURS: *Daily, 8–5.*
ADMISSION: *Free.*
TELEPHONE: *(406) 689-3155.*

Browning

MUSEUM OF THE PLAINS INDIANS

The town of Browning is the administrative headquarters of the Blackfeet Reservation, a 950,000-acre reserve that takes in high plains country, running to the base of the Rocky Mountains. When originally set up in 1855, it stretched from the Continental Divide to the confluence of the Missouri and Yellowstone rivers, at the border of the Dakota Territory. But it was sliced up on the east by successive government cessions, and in 1919 the tribe sold the western edge of their lands for $1.5 million to help form Glacier National Park. The tradeoff was not a bad deal. The thousands of tourists attracted by the park must pass through Browning to reach its eastern gateway and the famous Going-to-the-Sun Highway.

The Blackfeet were an Algonquian people who migrated from the east centuries ago and adapted with great success to the Plains way of life. They roamed across Montana and Alberta, as far north as the Saskatchewan River. The band that settled in this area was known as the *Piegan* ("blackfoot"). There are several versions of the origin of the tribal name. One authoritative

▲ *Both traditional and contemporary arts are presented at the Museum of the Plains Indian.*

source traces it to a creation myth, which called for warriors to dye their moccasins black in order to capture a herd of magical buffalo. Others claim the name stemmed from the tribe's crossing a prairie that was blackened by fires, which gave their footwear a distinctive coloration.

The Blackfeet were among the most adept of buffalo hunters and claimed to have more than sixty uses for the animal. But the decimation of the great herds in the 1880s virtually destroyed the economy of the tribe. In 1884, nearly six hundred Blackfeet died of starvation before relief efforts could be organized. The tribe eventually switched to raising livestock. Since the Indian Reorganization Act of 1934, the Blackfeet tribal government has been among the most efficient and economically successful in the country.

Among their efforts in the tourist business is the Museum and Crafts Center here. It is administered by the Department of the Interior's Indian Arts and Crafts Board, and the displays and sale items are indisputably authentic. Both traditional and contemporary arts are presented. The North American Indian Days observance takes place next to the museum. This four-day program is always scheduled for the second weekend of July and is the largest of its kind in the Northwest. Besides traditional dancing, a nineteenth-century encampment is put up, complete with the sorts of athletic events, meals, and games that the tribe engaged in at that time.

LOCATION: *The museum is at the junction of U.S. 2 and 89, at the western edge of town.*
HOURS: *Daily, 9–5, June through September; Monday through Friday only, 10–4:30, rest of year.*
ADMISSION: *Free.*
TELEPHONE: *(406) 338-2230.*

Chinook

BEAR'S PAW STATE MONUMENT

The end of the Chief Joseph saga (*see* Big Hole National Battlefield, Montana) was played out here, in the northern part of the state, forty miles from the Canadian border. After leaving Yellowstone country, the Nez Perce had broken off contact with their pursuers and headed due north, trying to join Sitting Bull's band of Sioux in Saskatchewan. Ironically, the main force pursuing them was the reconstituted seventh Cavalry (the original squad had been annihilated by Sitting Bull the previous summer at the Battle of Little Big Horn; *see* Little Big Horn National Battlefield, Montana). But Chief Joseph managed to elude the seventh Cavalry, as he had all the other forces set out to catch him, and he crossed the Missouri River near Fort Benton.

General Nelson Miles, along with Cheyenne scouts, a Gatling gun, and a twelve-pound mortar, set out in pursuit of Joseph. Just two days behind him, Miles reached the Missouri River and swiftly moved on. The Nez Perce had made camp north of the Bear's Paw Mountains. There is some confusion about why Joseph hesitated here. Some commentators believe that he thought crossing the Missouri had put him in Canada. Others think that the number of wounded and elderly that he was carrying did not allow him to proceed any faster. On September 30, 1877, Miles caught up to the Nez Perce and attacked. The fight went on for four days, but finally the arrival of General Oliver Howard, who had pursued Joseph all the way from Oregon, put the Nez Perce at a hopeless disadvantage.

With one of the most moving and often-quoted speeches in American history, Chief Joseph at last surrendered. "I am tired," he said. "Our chiefs are killed . . . . The little children are freezing to death . . . . My people . . . . have no blankets, no food . . . . My heart is sick and sad. From where the sun now stands I will fight no more forever."

Joseph and his band were sent to live in Oklahoma, but the toll from disease and heat in the unfamiliar climate was so great that in 1885 they were allowed to return to the Colville Reservation in Washington. Today, what is left of Chief Joseph's band lives there.

LOCATION: *Bear's Paw is 16 miles south of U.S. 2 at Chinook by way of County Road 240.*
EXHIBITS: *Markers trace the course of the four-day battle at this location and the spot of Chief Joseph's surrender.*
HOUR: *Daily, dawn to dusk.*
ADMISSION: *Free.*

Crow Agency

CROW RESERVATION FAIR AND RODEO

In the complicated tribal rivalries of the nineteenth century, the Crow were forced to choose between two evils. They could either fight against the whites, who would want their lands later, or they could join the whites and fight against the Lakota (or Sioux, as the Lakota were called by rival tribes), who wanted their lands right away. Since the threat from the Lakota was imminent, many Crow served as scouts with the U.S. Cavalry during the 1860s and 1870s. It was on land that became part of their reservation that the Battle of the Little Big Horn was fought in 1876 (*see* Little Big Horn National Battlefield, Montana).

The Crow are a Siouan people whose name in their own language is Absaroke. They originally lived with the Hidatsa in the Lake Winnipeg area of Manitoba and migrated southwest to the Missouri River. Around 1776, a dispute arose between the two tribes and they separated, the Hidatsa remaining along the big river, the Crow moving on to the Yellowstone country. Extremely skilled horsemen and buffalo hunters, the Crow ranged across southern Montana. They called it "the good country," because it contained everything they needed to sustain life. However, in the 1880s, shortly after the Crow were settled here, the buffalo disappeared. The Crow made the adaptation to raising stock and, more recently, tourism to keep the tribal economy healthy.

The Crow Fair, held on the third weekend of August, features the largest all-Indian rodeo in the country. There are also crafts booths, dancing, and displays of the tribe's intricately beaded horse decorations.

LOCATION: *The Crow Agency is along Interstate 90, about 60 miles east of Billings.*
TELEPHONE: *(406) 638-2303.*

Lame Deer

NORTHERN CHEYENNE INDIAN RESERVATION

The Cheyenne were one of the tribes uprooted from their northern woodlands existence in the seventeenth century. Peoples to the east of them
obtained rifles from white traders and with this military advantage began
pushing settled tribes steadily west. The Cheyenne were an agricultural people,
living in Minnesota, but migrated steadily onto the Plains, where they became
hunters. A tribal memory of their former way of life persisted for generations in
folktales about how they "lost the corn."

The Cheyenne migration, which involved battles with tribes the Cheyenne displaced and with those who were pressuring them, toughened them and
made them among the most formidable of fighters. It has been estimated that
they suffered the highest casualty rate per capita of any tribe in the wars with
the U.S. Army. Of course, this figure also includes the massacres of southern
Cheyenne villages in Colorado and Oklahoma by state militia and army units.
The Dog Soldiers of the Cheyenne were the most feared opponents on the
Plains.

In the 1830s when a large group of Cheyenne decided to take advantage of the trade opportunities arising from the opening of Bent's Fort (on the
Santa Fe Trail in Colorado), the Cheyenne split into northern and southern
divisions. The split was formally recognized by federal treaty twenty years later.
But both divisions were active in the Indian Wars, allying with other tribes in
their area.

In 1877, the government decided to lump both groups of Cheyenne
together, for administrative ease, and placed them in Oklahoma. But the
northern group could not adjust to this bureaucratic decision. When deaths
from hunger and disease mounted in 1878, the bands of Little Wolf and Dull
Knife decided to break out and return home. Racing ahead of pursuing
soldiers, fighting their way through Kansas and Nebraska, the bands finally
reached the North Platte. Dull Knife was killed in this campaign. But the
Cheyenne's defiant stand convinced the government to allot them land along
the Rosebud and Tongue rivers of southeastern Montana. They have lived on
this reservation since 1884.

While it is easy to emphasize the Cheyenne military achievements, they
are also a people with a strong political tradition. Each band elected representatives to the Council of 44, the governing body of the tribe. Of that group,
four were chosen to constitute a ruling body, with one of their number
becoming the head chief.

The tourist center at Lame Deer offers a selection of local crafts,
especially beadwork. The tribe holds an annual Sun Dance (call for dates/
information).

LOCATION: *Lame Deer is located on U.S. 212, about 45 miles east of Interstate 90.*
HOURS: *Daily, 8–4.*
ADMISSION: *Free.*
TELEPHONE: *(406) 477-8283.*

Little Big Horn National Battlefield

BATTLEFIELD, NATIONAL CEMETERY, AND MUSEUM

I s there any other single event in American history that has been as widely depicted, discussed, analyzed, and debated as this battle on the Montana high plains? The subject of uncounted movies, novels, histories, songs, and sermons, it is now woven into the fabric of the national experience. Its details are intimately familiar to almost anyone with even a passing interest in the West. The personalities of its leading actors, their motivations, their heroism or lack of it, resonate through time. It is as if the issues that led to this battle have still not been satisfactorily resolved and are yet to be worked out for all concerned parties.

Even in 1991, well over a century after the battle was fought, the official name of the battlefield was a matter of heated debate. Some wanted to retain the older designation of Custer National Battlefield, while others insisted that what happened here must not be viewed merely from a white perspective and that attention must be paid to Native American sensibilities to fully understand an encounter that shaped the way both groups looked at each other forever afterward.

It is hard to understand now the shock that went through the country when news of General George A. Custer's defeat was heard. To an America preparing to celebrate the one hundredth anniversary of the Declaration of Independence, it was a stunning reversal of the national mood. A nation that seemed to be the most technically advanced — the most invulnerable of any on earth — had suddenly been humbled by a people it believed had been buried in the dust of history a century before. To some Native Americans the defeat of Custer was, and still is, a galvanizing force, a reminder that when brave men fight for a cause they believe is just they may prevail. To other Native Americans the news was terrifying because they knew that a terrible revenge would be exacted for it.

Little Big Horn was part of a series of campaigns that is now known collectively as the Sioux War. Its immediate cause was 8 attacks by nontreaty Sioux (who refused to accept white-dictated limits on their territory) upon the Crow living on reservation land. The Sioux were also outraged over repeated violations of their lands by the onrush of miners to new gold strikes in the

▲ *During the Sioux Wars, Sitting Bull led the Indian forces in their defeat of Custer and the Seventh Cavalry at the battle of Little Big Horn.*

Black Hills of South Dakota. Sitting Bull, leader of the nontreaty Hunkpapa band, refused demands to return to a reservation, as the army knew he would refuse. But the planners in Washington severely underestimated the number of fighters he could bring into the field and the degree of skill with which they could be coordinated. By the spring of 1876, small groups from many of the northern Plains tribes had rallied to Sitting Bull. The most critical addition was that of Crazy Horse and the northern Cheyenne, who had severely bloodied a force under General George Crook at the Battle of the Rosebud on June 17.

The undermanned U.S. Cavalry units did not have an overall plan to converge on the Indian positions. Crook began to withdraw from the area just as the commands of Generals Alfred Terry and John Gibbon arrived. Custer's units were under Terry's command, who planned to use the Seventh Cavalry as his main striking force. Custer was ordered to sweep around the known Indian positions, assay their force, and prevent their escape. But the number of warriors in the area exceeded anything reported to the American generals. When Custer came upon the main encampment on June 25, he disregarded Terry's orders. Instead of sweeping around to enclose the encampment, Custer attacked. Moreover, he split his regiment into three parts. Custer's defenders say that Terry's orders emphasized containing the Indians and not letting them escape. His detractors say that he was trying to grab the glory. But defenders and detractors agree that Custer had no idea how large the force opposing him was. At most, Custer was expecting about 800 men. But huge herds of buffalo and antelope that summer allowed a far greater number of Indians to sustain themselves and remain in close proximity. As a result, Custer rode with 225 men into a force of about 4,000.

The cost of this battle was severe. Goaded by public demands for revenge, the army's pursuit of Sitting Bull and his allies was relentless. Village after village was destroyed throughout the rest of the year and into 1877. Sitting Bull led his band of Hunkpapa into Canada but returned to surrender in 1881. He became something of a national celebrity, even traveling for one season with Buffalo Bill's Wild West Show. But white authorities in North Dakota were convinced that Sitting Bull was involved in the Ghost Dance disturbances (*see* Sitting Bull Memorial, Mobridge, South Dakota), and he was gunned down by reservation police in 1890. Crazy Horse had met a similar end in 1877, murdered at the army post of Fort Robinson, Nebraska. Other Indian leaders were also hunted down. Neither the Sioux nor the Cheyenne were able to put a fighting force of more than 500 men into the field again. As the title of Vine Deloria's best-seller claims, "Custer died for your sins," implying that the battle sacrifice of Custer's troops was exacted on the white population. But a lot of Native Americans paid the price, too.

The battlefield itself is one of the most haunting places in the West — the bare, brown ridges dotted with headstones where the soldiers fell evoking the lonely terror of this fight. An excellent museum on the site showcases maps and dioramas of the battle and provides a perspective that attends to the motives of both sides. Walking and driving tours of the battlefield are laid out.

The area also includes a national cemetery where the remains of the dead cavalrymen rest, and the Reno-Benteen Battlefield, where the other two segments of Custer's command managed to fight a defensive action until relief arrived.

LOCATION: *The battlefield is off U.S. 212, just east of the Interstate 90 exit, about 3 miles southeast of the Crow Agency.*
HOURS: *Daily, 8–5. Extended hours in summer.*
ADMISSION: *Free.*
TELEPHONE: *(406) 638-2621.*

Pryor

CHIEF PLENTY COUPS STATE MONUMENT

The Crow were generally allied with the U.S. army during the wars of the 1860s and 1870s, because the greater threat to them came from the Lakota, who coveted lands along the Bighorn River. Among the young Crow chiefs of the time was Plenty Coups. He lived for many years and at age 72 was chosen to represent Native Americans at the dedication of the Tomb of the Unknown Soldier at Arlington Cemetery. He died in 1933; his home here is preserved as a museum of his long life and accomplishments.

LOCATION: *The monument is just southwest of town on an unnumbered reservation road. Watch for signs. Pryor is about 35 miles south of Billings.*
HOURS: *Daily, 8–5, Memorial Day through Labor Day.*
ADMISSION: *Free.*

MADISON BUFFALO JUMP STATE MONUMENT

T he buffalo was always a staple of Plains Indians life, but before these tribes acquired the horse, other hunting techniques had to be perfected. One of these involved driving herds of the animals over a cliff and then harvesting the carcasses at leisure. One such "buffalo jump" site is preserved here, with demonstrations of how the ancient hunters accomplished this dangerous job.

LOCATION: *Three Forks is just a few miles from the headwaters of the Missouri River and gets its name from the confluence of the Madison, Jefferson, and Gallatin rivers. This is also the place where Sacajawea (see Grave of Sacajawea, Fort Washakie, Wyoming) rejoined her people, the Shoshone, while guiding the Lewis and Clark Expedition in 1804. The buffalo jump site is southeast of town, by way of Interstate 90 and an unnumbered county road.*

HOURS: *Daily, dawn to dusk.*

ADMISSION: *Free.*

NORTH DAKOTA

FORT TOTTEN STATE HISTORIC SITE AND
ST. MICHAEL'S MISSION

The various branches of the Sioux who lived in Minnesota in the 1860s regarded the Dakota Territory as a refuge. But after the uprising of 1862, there was to be no refuge. The demand for revenge was so strong that even the hanging of thirty-eight Native Americans in Saint Paul could not satisfy it. The following year, two military expeditions were sent out with orders to pursue and "punish" those who had participated in the uprising. The policy led to the battle of Whitestone Hill (*see* Whitestone Battlefield, Kulm, North Dakota) and to the restriction of the Sioux bands to reservations in the Dakota Territory.

One of the first reservations set up was the Fort Totten Reservation, named for the military outpost built in 1867. Treaties were signed with the Sisseton and Wahpeton to relocate them here. These were tribes who had lived on the Upper Sioux Agency in Minnesota and generally did not participate in the 1862 uprising. But in its aftermath the tribes either fled out of fear of retribution or were expelled from that agency.

The brick buildings of the existing fort were constructed on the reservation in 1868. After the garrison was withdrawn in 1890, the buildings housed the reservation's industrial school and the agency offices.

The fort is regarded as one of the best preserved of its era, with a spacious central square and clean brick facades. Now a state historic site, it is situated on reservation land, as is the adjacent Sully's Hill National Game Preserve, a refuge for the deer, elk, and bison that once ranged freely throughout this area. Traditional tribal dances are held at the fort on the last weekend of July during the Fort Totten Days observance.

The 137,000-acre reservation occupies a beautiful site along the southern shore of Devils Lake. Its administrative center, St. Michael's, lies at the foot of Mission Hill. From its summit, there is a fine view of the lake and surrounding country. In 1874, the mission for which the hill is named was established here to educate Indian children. This was the original reservation school, which later was moved to the fort. There is also an Indian Art Galley in the town.

On nearby North Dakota 57, look for the Bell Isle Store, an emporium offering the sort of foods and goods that would have been stocked by such a country store a century ago.

LOCATION: *Fort Totten is about 10 miles south of the town of Devils Lake by way of North Dakota 20 and 57. St. Michael's is on a reservation road branching south from Highway 57, about 4 miles east of Fort Totten.*
HOURS: *The fort is open daily, 8–6, June through October. It is best to check in advance for hours at the mission and store in St. Michael's.*
ADMISSION: *Free.*
TELEPHONE: *The fort is (701) 766-4441. Reservation office is (701) 766-4221.*

Standing Rock

FORT YATES

F ort Yates is one of the legendary outposts of the West, a place where myth mixes with history to create a scene of unforgettable drama. An army post for eighteen years, in 1895 the new Northern Pacific Railroad made the fort along the Missouri River unnecessary. Fort Yates became the administrative center of the vast Standing Rock Sioux Reservation.

Sitting Bull was buried here for sixty-three years, until his remains were spirited away to a part of the reservation across the state line (*see* Sitting Bull Memorial, Mobridge, South Dakota). Standing Rock, the legendary Sioux stone for which the 875,000-acre reservation is named, is also located in Fort Yates. Though the Missouri River has been dammed to form Lake Oahe, you can still get a feel for what a lifeline this waterway was, for the tribes who used it as a migratory path to new homes in Dakota as well as for the white trappers and explorers who used it as their avenue to the Northwest.

The original reservation, organized in 1868, sprawled over 4 million acres. But treaty provisions, not fully understood by Indian signers, allowed for portions to be lopped off and opened for white homesteads. The reservation's landholdings were slowly whittled away until it reached its present size in 1910. It was this steady erosion of Indian land that drove Sitting Bull to join the Ghost Dance of 1890 and led directly to his death at the hands of the reservation's Indian police. He was brought here for burial, along with the police who were shot down in the battle over his attempted arrest. (This episode is described more fully in the entry on Sitting Bull Memorial, Mobridge, South Dakota.) An elaborate monument was erected for the police in the Fort Yates Catholic cemetery. Sitting Bull was quickly interred in the fort's military cemetery. Five years later, the army post was shut down and the remains of the white dead were removed. Only Sitting Bull was left, lying in an untended grave. When it was reported in 1953 that the formation of Lake Oahe might flood the site, Indian activists dug up Sitting Bull's remains and took them to a new burial place, near Mobridge, South Dakota. Sitting Bull's original burial spot is still marked here.

The Standing Rock itself is positioned overlooking the Missouri, across from the reservation's administrative offices. According to legend, a woman became jealous when her husband took a second wife. The first wife refused to accompany the village when it moved to a new site, and she remained behind, with her baby strapped to her back. When men were sent back to look for them, they found both mother and child turned to stone. This band of Sioux carried the rock from village to village, always putting it in a place of honor. It became the centerpiece of the reservation.

LOCATION: *Fort Yates is just west of North Dakota 24 on the west bank of the Missouri, about 60 miles south of Mandan.*
HOURS: *All sites are open daily, dawn to dusk.*
ADMISSION: *Free.*
TELEPHONE: *(701) 854-7299.*

Kulm

WHITESTONE BATTLEFIELD

The summer after the Sioux Uprising of 1862, two expeditions were sent into Dakota Territory to pursue and "punish" the participants. General Henry H. Sibley took the northern route, reached the Devils Lake area, and chased several bands of Sioux to the Missouri River without ever getting close enough for the decisive battle he wanted. Meanwhile, General Alfred H. Sully was working his way up from the south. The original plan was to have the two forces unite on the Missouri, but they never made contact.

Sibley started back for Minnesota before Sully could reach him. When Sully arrived in the area, one of the Sioux bands Sibley had been chasing had recrossed the Missouri and had started heading east. Sully decided to go after them.

He overtook the Indians in three days and stationed his forces, which included an artillery unit, on higher ground above the Indians' encampment. The Sioux lost 150 lives in the ensuing battle, which is regarded as the most violent ever fought in North Dakota.

Unfortunately, there was no proof whatsoever that any of the Sioux killed in this engagement had actually taken part in the events they were supposedly being "punished" for. The likelihood was that they had not. Nonetheless, as one historian wrote, "It was natural for the soldiers to regard any Indians they met as enemies."

LOCATION: *The battlefield is 11 miles south of Kulm by way of North Dakota 56 and a county road. It is about 65 miles south of Interstate 94, from the Jamestown exit.*
EXHIBITS: *Monuments to the slain on both sides are on the site. There is also a small museum.*
HOURS: *Daily, 8-6, mid-May to mid-September.*
ADMISSION: *Free.*

Mandan

Slant Village at Fort Abraham Lincoln State Park

Sometime in the thirteenth century, the Mandan entered the Dakotas from the southeast, following the Missouri River and building villages at easily defensible sites along its bluffs. When the first Europeans came through the area, about five hundred years later, the Mandan were the dominant tribe here. The chief Mandan settlements were near the confluence of the Missouri and Heart rivers, at the town that bears the tribe's name. But at one time, nine such villages were situated along the Missouri in this region.

By the time Lewis and Clark reached the area seventy-five years later, the nine villages had been reduced to two. A smallpox epidemic and almost constant warfare with the more numerous Lakota had reduced the Mandan numbers. And worse was still to come. The smallpox outbreak of 1837, the deadliest recorded on the northern Plains, killed all but 150 members of the tribe. In 1845, in an effort to retain some identity, the Mandan united with the neighboring Hidatsa, who were also decimated by the epidemic. The two tribes now share the Fort Berthold Reservation (northwest of Mandan) with a third tribe, the Arikara.

In 1872, the planners of Fort Abraham Lincoln selected the Mandan site for the same reasons the Indians had: easy access to the river and natural protection. The fort's primary mission was to protect surveyors for the Northern Pacific Railroad. But much greater fame came to it as the home base for General George A. Custer and the Seventh Cavalry. It was from here that they rode to their rendezvous on the Little Big Horn.

The Mandan village that preceded the fort on this site has been preserved just inside the state park entrance. Slant Village is built on a narrow point of land above the river, with bluffs guarding the water approach and moats protecting the other sides. Several Mandan structures have been restored to the condition they would have been in before the arrival of the Europeans. Among these buildings is the ceremonial lodge.

The Mandan practiced an especially rigorous version of the Sun Dance ritual, including suspension by a rope that was skewered through the chest muscles. Through recent movies, this has become the best-known version of the rite, which also involved fasting, prayer, and recitations of tribal history.

LOCATION: *Slant Village and Fort Abraham Lincoln are immediately south of the town of Mandan on North Dakota 1806, along the west bank of the Missouri.*
HOURS: *Daily, 8–dusk.*
ADMISSION: *$2.50 per vehicle.*
TELEPHONE: *(701) 663-9571.*

New Town

THREE AFFILIATED TRIBES MUSEUM

The name of this community, the administrative center of the Fort Berthold Reservation, tells its story. In 1954, when Lake Sakakawea was formed by the opening of Garrison Dam on the Missouri River, about 25 percent of the territory on this reservation was flooded. Much of the land that was then under cultivation is now under water, as are many of the towns that had been established on the reservation. The Army Corps of Engineers stepped in and built New Town as a planned community, and other settlements have formed since.

The tribes have developed a tourist industry to take advantage of the water recreation offered by the lake, and the area has become noted for its outstanding walleye fishing. Still, the flooding was an enormous upheaval in the way of life that was familiar here. Only one bridge crosses the river within the reservation, so onetime neighbors found themselves separated by hours of driving.

Upheaval is nothing new to these tribes. The Mandan and Hidatsa, both longtime inhabitants of North Dakota, unified in 1845 after smallpox and war had nearly wiped them out. They were joined by the Arikara in 1862. This tribe came from the riverlands of South Dakota and was most closely related to the Pawnee, while the other two belonged to the Siouan family. They were all predominantly agricultural people and lived in earth lodge villages. The tribes established a community on a bend of the Missouri, called Fishhook. Then in

1870 they moved onto the Fort Berthold lands, which were diminished over the decades by congressional acts, executive orders, and finally, flooding.

Four Bears Bridge is the main connecting link within the reservation. From the Crow-Flies-High observation point, just west of New Town, there is a wonderful view of the bridge and surrounding lake. The bridge itself is named for a Mandan chief, but to honor all three affiliated tribes, plaques paying tribute to eighteen other chiefs have been affixed to the bridge's eastern and western ends. Four Bears Memorial Park is on the western side of the bridge, and within it is the museum. This is an exceptional educational facility that explains the origins and relationships of the three tribes who live here.

LOCATION: *The museum is on North Dakota 23, about 5 miles west of New Town, and about 80 miles southwest of Minot.*
HOURS: *Daily, 9–5, June through Labor Day; closed weekends, rest of year.*
ADMISSION: *$2.50.*
TELEPHONE: *(701) 627-4477.*

Stanton

KNIFE RIVER VILLAGES NATIONAL HISTORIC SITE

During the first winter of Lewis and Clark's voyage up the Missouri, they stopped for the season near a group of Hidatsa villages, at the mouth of the Knife River. These villages already had been occupied for hundreds of years by the Hidatsa, who were talented farmers and traders. Long before the arrival of white trade goods, a network of Indian trade arrangements carried implements from this area all through the continent. Sea shell ornaments have been found here, while flint goods made at Knife River have been uncovered as far away as Georgia.

The Hidatsa are related to the Crow, and it is believed both tribes migrated here before separating in the seventeenth century. The Crow went farther on, to what is now Montana; the Hidatsa stayed on the Missouri. Their villages were the major population centers in North Dakota in those years, but by 1804 the Hidatsa had been severely reduced by smallpox, an epidemic that had followed the Europeans up the river. It was at the Knife River that the explorers met Sakakawea, the Shoshone woman who would guide them into the homeland of her people, far to the west. There is a discrepancy in the spelling of her name. In North Dakota, it is *Sakakawea*, according to state researchers, because that is the Hidatsa rendering. In their language it means Bird Woman. But in Shoshone it usually is spelled *Sacajawea*, meaning Boat Launcher, and that is how it is spelled in other sections of this guide.

The National Park Service has greatly expanded this site in recent years. In 1992, a new Native American Interpretive Center opened. Imaginative displays recreate what daily life was like in these villages and the impact that the Lewis and Clark expedition had on the tribes of the region. Walking tours are laid out around the three villages located here. Markers clearly indicate the sites of homes, cache pits, and fortification ditches, some of which may be thirty-five hundred years old. In the summer months, there are several events connected with the fur trade, Indian life, and the Lewis and Clark visit. The visitor center sells locally made Indian crafts.

LOCATION: *The Knife River site is 3 miles north of Stanton by county road and about 65 miles northwest of Bismarck by way of U.S. 83 and North Dakota 200A.*
HOURS: *Daily, 9–6, June through Labor Day; it closes at 4:30, rest of year.*
ADMISSION: *Free.*
TELEPHONE: *(701) 745-3309.*

SASKATCHEWAN

BATOCHE NATIONAL HISTORIC PARK

B atoche was a village on the Saskatchewan River where the Riel Rebellion of 1885 (*see* Riel House National Historic Site, Winnipeg, Manitoba) finally ran its course. This area of Saskatchewan had become a center of Métis settlement after they were driven from Manitoba by white expansion. After a fifteen-year interval, the conflict between the Métis and the settlers was merely repeated at this site.

Louis Riel returned to Canada from Montana to lead an uprising of the Métis, French-speaking westerners and Cree. But after three months, over-whelming numbers were brought to bear against Riel's troops. In early May, eight thousand soldiers confronted the rebels and in a decisive battle forced their surrender.

Visitors may tour the various sections of the battlefield, as well as the ruins of the Métis settlement. Displays and an audiovisual presentation in the park museum explain the history of the Métis and their rebellions. Costumed guides talk about the Métis and the events that occurred here.

On the last weekend of July, descendants of the Métis gather here. Back to Batoche Days celebrates their culture with music, dances, and games reflecting this unique French-Native American mixture.

LOCATION: *The park is about 45 miles northeast of Saskatoon by way of Highways 11 and 312.*

HOURS: *Daily, 8:30–5, mid-May through September; weekends only, first two weeks of October.*

ADMISSION: *Free.*

PHONE: *(306) 423-6227.*

SOUTH DAKOTA

ST. JOSEPH'S SCHOOL

Two of South Dakota's Sioux reservations—Crow Creek and Lower Brule—lie just a few miles north of Chamberlain, which was the main ferrying point across the Missouri River in frontier times. The reservations occupy both sides of the river and are home to a number of Lakota groups. There are some Yanktonai, who were the central branch of this Native American family, and a larger number of lower Brule. The Brule were a division of the Teton, or western branch of the Lakota. The second most numerous division among the Teton, the Brule split into upper and lower subdivisions, with the upper Brule occupying the Rosebud Reservation, southwest of here.

In 1927, St. Joseph's School was established in Chamberlain in buildings that had been used by a nearby college. Over the years the school has developed as an alternative for Sioux children who want a Catholic education firmly grounded in the elements of Lakota culture. About two hundred children in grades one through eight attend classes here. There is a museum of Lakota life, the Akta Lakota, on the campus and a chapel dedicated to Our Lady of the Sioux.

LOCATION: *St. Joseph's is at the northeastern edge of town. Take the main Chamberlain exit, 263, from Interstate 90.*
HOURS: *Monday through Saturday, 8–6; Sunday, 1–5, May through September. Weekdays only, rest of year.*
ADMISSION: *Free.*
TELEPHONE: *(605) 734-3455.*

Custer

CRAZY HORSE MEMORIAL

In 1940, as work was being completed on the carved presidential faces on Mount Rushmore, a visitor called on one of the assistants in that massive project. The visitor, Henry Standing Bear, was a nephew of Crazy Horse, of the Oglala Sioux, regarded as the greatest Native American military strategist who ever confronted the U.S. Army. As sculptor Korczak Ziolkowski later recalled the meeting, Standing Bear asked him to create a stone-carved memorial for the long-dead Indian leader Crazy Horse "so that the white man will know we had heroes, too."

Since the day in 1948 when work began on the Crazy Horse Memorial, it has become an epic in itself, as expansive and controversial as the man to whom it pays tribute. Ziolkowski died in 1982, leaving his sons to carry on the work. Even after all this time, however, the form of the mounted Crazy Horse is still barely discernible on the edge of the mountain. Critics claim that it has turned into a massive boondoggle, a tourist attraction dedicated merely to the glorification of Ziolkowski. Its defenders insist that Native American causes have benefitted from the work, although most of the funds raised here are plowed right back into the mountain.

The memorial has developed an influence of its own. In 1982, when the U.S. Post Office issued a commemorative stamp honoring Crazy Horse, it was based on sketches by Ziolkowski. The sculptor had interviewed men who had seen Crazy Horse when they were children. The face on the monument and the stamp was drawn from these recollections.

Crazy Horse blazed across the consciousness of white America for two years in the 1870s. The Oglala were the most numerous branch of the Teton, or western Lakota. They had come from northern Minnesota, driven off by the better-armed Ojibwa, and by 1700 made the adaptation to life on the Plains. At the end of the century, the Oglala had joined the Cheyenne and controlled South Dakota's Black Hills and eastern Wyoming, dominating the fur trade in this rich area. But relations with whites changed in the 1840s, when wagon trains began moving along the Oregon Trail, across tribal hunting lands. Because the wagon trains disturbed the buffalo herds and grasslands, the Oglala began attacking the white settlers. Despite temporary lulls, the hostilities continued into the 1860s under the leadership of Red Cloud (*see* Fetterman Massacre Site, Sheridan, Wyoming).

A treaty signed in 1868 recognized Lakota claims to the Black Hills, and that brought an interval of peace. But white incursions there touched off an even greater rebellion under the inspirational leadership of the Hunkpapa chief Sitting Bull. It was during this campaign that Crazy Horse rose to prominence. He is best known as the leader who first breached Custer's line at the Little Big Horn. The previous week, Crazy Horse had blocked a force of thirteen hundred troops under General George Crook at the Battle of the Rosebud, in Montana. In a daring succession of hit-and-run charges, Crazy Horse had kept his opponent's force so widely spread that Crook was never able to use his numbers to muster an assault. Crook was assumed to be heading for the area of the Little Big Horn, but Crazy Horse prevented him from linking up with the badly outnumbered troops there. Several weeks after Custer's death, Crazy Horse struck again, slashing at Crook in the battle of Slim Buttes, in the northwestern corner of South Dakota.

During the winter, the federal troops kept increasing the pressure, giving the Oglala, Hunkpapa, and Cheyenne no respite to gather strength and feed their families in the harsh weather. By December, Sitting Bull was in retreat toward Canada, and the following spring Crazy Horse decided to turn himself in at Fort Robinson (*see* Fort Robinson State Park, Crawford, Nebraska), where he was probably murdered.

Since then, the reputation of Crazy Horse has attained mythic proportions, especially among the Oglala in the Pine Ridge Reservation, about seventy-five miles southeast of here. In one of history's ironies, the nearest town to the place chosen for his memorial is named for Custer, the adversary he defeated and with whom he is forever linked.

When it is completed, the sculpture will depict Crazy Horse, arms extended across the land, sitting astride a war pony. Ziolkowski's inscription for the memorial was "Where My Dead Lie Buried."

Visitors can watch work in progress, view plans for its final appearance, and see an exhibit on the history of the memorial and displays of Lakota tribal materials.

LOCATION: *The memorial is north of Custer, on U.S. 16, 385.*
HOURS: *Daily, dawn to dusk.*
ADMISSION: *$7.50 per car.*
TELEPHONE: *(605) 673-4681.*

Mitchell

PREHISTORIC INDIAN VILLAGE

Mitchell is the home of the Corn Palace, the Moorish fantasy built in 1892 to celebrate the bounty of the fertile South Dakota soil. More than one thousand years ago, Native Americans had chosen the site as an agricultural community. Located along Firesteel Creek, now the shores of Lake Mitchell, the village held some one thousand individuals, who dwelled in about 70 lodges in safety behind fortifications. Archaeologists believe that the inhabitants of the village preceded the Mandan in this area by a century or two, but evidence suggests that the Mandan, too, may have lived here when the tribe moved into South Dakota in the thirteenth century.

The site is rich in clues about these prehistoric villagers and their environment. The early inhabitants were characterized by a hunting, fishing, food-gathering culture accompanied by some gardening. The Patton Gallery exhibits the artifacts found at this site, and a full-scale walk-through lodge reproduction presents the day to day life of the villagers. A garden plot is based on plant remains found at the site: the villagers probably had a plot of 5 to 10 acres where they raised corn, beans, squash, sunflowers, and tobacco. The Mitchell Village has been designated a National Historic Landmark, and is the only National Archaeological Landmark in South Dakota open to the public.

LOCATION: *The village is in the northwestern corner of Mitchell, by way of South Dakota 37 and 23rd Ave.*
HOURS: *Daily, 8–8.*
ADMISSION: *$3; children under 12 free.*
TELEPHONE: *(605) 996-5473.*

OSCAR HOWE ART CENTER

Once Mitchell's Carnegie Library, the Oscar Howe Art Center now displays the work of the Sioux artist who worked here and taught at Dakota Wesleyan University. A Yanktonai Sioux, Oscar Howe studied at The Studio of the Santa Fe Indian School in the 1930s. He began to develop a highly personalized style that blended traditional representational art with elements of cubism. His handling of native symbolism in a contemporary vernacular has become a signature of his work in many public buildings in South Dakota. Howe was hired in 1940 to decorate the dome of this building with Sioux imagery. The entire library now is turned over to displays of his paintings and those of other contemporary Native American artists.

LOCATION: *The Oscar Howe Center is at 119 West 3rd Avenue.*
HOURS: *Tuesday through Saturday, 9–6; Sunday, 1–5, Memorial Day through Labor Day. Tuesday through Saturday, 10–5, rest of year.*
ADMISSION: *Free.*
TELEPHONE: *(605) 966-4111.*

Mobridge

SITTING BULL MEMORIAL

T he death of Sitting Bull can be seen as a retelling of the entire Indian/ white tragedy in America in capsulized form. The events leading up to his death mirrored the struggle between those who believed that the progress of Indians was defined by eradicating their culture and imitating that of the whites, and those who believed the only possible way to survive was to hold fast to and build on traditions.

As the Hunkpapa Lakota chief and leader of the native alliance that destroyed George Custer's command, Sitting Bull found himself a fugitive in Canada six months after the Little Big Horn. Pursued relentlessly by federal forces, he had crossed the international border with the remnants of his band in December 1876. But he could not hold the group together. Game was scarce, and many discontented young men returned to the United States. In 1881, upon hearing that a pardon would be forthcoming, Sitting Bull turned himself in at Fort Buford, North Dakota. Instead of being pardoned, he was imprisoned for two years while the rest of his band was settled on the Standing Rock Reservation, a tract along the Missouri River and extending across both Dakotas.

Sitting Bull's story then took a peculiar twist—some would say a peculiarly American twist. Sitting Bull went into show business. He embarked on a lecture and autograph tour of the East, where his remarks were deliberately mistranslated by the promoters to make it appear that he was seething with defiance. Crowds jammed into theaters to boo the killer of Custer. Sitting Bull then signed up with "Buffalo Bill's Wild West Show" and toured with this famous extravaganza for a season. He struck up a friendship with the showman, William Cody, who was struck by the quiet rectitude of his former enemy. Both were middle-aged and had seen the West they knew as young men disappear. When Sitting Bull left the show to return to Standing Rock, Cody gave him a trained show pony as a gift.

Sitting Bull decided against making his home at the reservation's administrative center at Fort Yates, North Dakota. Instead, he settled in a remote corner along the Grand River in South Dakota. During the 1880s, the government was determined to buy back great chunks of the reservation, and offered eight cents an acre for it. The proposal, which even Congress regarded as ridiculous, was turned down by the Indians, with Sitting Bull leading the opposition. But to Major James McLaughlin, the director of the Standing Rock Sioux Agency, Sitting Bull's stand marked the chief as a dangerous man who opposed progress. McLaughlin once described his mission as "putting the raw and bleeding material which made the hostile strength of the Plains Indians through the mills of the white man . . . transmitting it into a manufactured product that might be absorbed by the nation." He set out to break Sitting Bull.

McLaughlin cut separate deals with other chiefs to accept a new treaty, bought off many younger men to get the required three-quarters majority of the tribal vote, and refused to permit Sitting Bull into meetings. Finally, McLaughlin used his hammer. A drought descended, and McLaughlin controlled the food allotments. Defying government regulations, McLaughlin let it be known that he would not dispense equal portions to those who supported Sitting Bull.

At this point, in the winter of 1890, the Ghost Dance arrived on the Plains from Nevada. A blend of Christianity and tribal religion, the Ghost Dance taught that a new messiah was coming and that this time he would be delivered to the Indians. Believers were encouraged to dance themselves into a trance, during which they would have visions. They were also told that if a shirt bearing certain magic symbols was worn, it could not be penetrated by bullets. To the frustrated Plains tribes, the Ghost Dance was a message of hope, a way of regaining their lost freedom. With growing interest, Sitting Bull watched the Ghost Dance passion build, unwilling to commit himself to it. But McLaughlin was convinced that the chief meant to take control of the Ghost Dance movement and use it to defeat the agent's policy.

McLaughlin urged General Nelson Miles, the top military official in the northern Plains, to take Sitting Bull into custody. Miles, however, came up with the idea of sending Buffalo Bill Cody to visit his old friend and persuade him to surrender. An infuriated McLaughlin intercepted Cody and turned him back.

Sitting Bull, still abiding by the law, wrote McLaughlin for permission to visit the Pine Ridge Reservation, the focal point of the Ghost Dance observances. McLaughlin decided Sitting Bull had to be arrested immediately, and dispatched forty-three Indian police to his camp. On the morning of December 15, the police burst into Sitting Bull's house and took him at gunpoint. The noise awoke the rest of the settlement. There is confusion at to what happened next. By some accounts, the leader of the police was shot and immediately turned and gunned down Sitting Bull. Others say the police were instructed to shoot the chief at the first sign of resistance. Whatever the intent, McLaughlin regarded the killing as a success. As legend has it, in the final macabre event of the day, the pony given to Sitting Bull by Buffalo Bill heard the noise and reverted to his days in the "Wild West Show." While his master lay dying and gunfire ripped through the camp, the horse reportedly went through his entire repertoire of show tricks.

Sitting Bull's body was taken to Fort Yates, and a fast, unattended burial ensued (*see* Standing Rock, Fort Yates, North Dakota). In 1953, when word spread that the damming of the Missouri River might inundate the gravesite, native activists reclaimed the remains and reinterred them here, on a bluff opposite the town of Mobridge. The site is just a few yards from a memorial to

Sacajawea, the Shoshone woman who guided Lewis and Clark. A granite bust of Sitting Bull, sculpted by Korczak Ziolkowski, marks the grave.

LOCATION: *The Sitting Bull Memorial is across the Missouri bridge from Mobridge on U.S. 12, then south on South Dakota 1806. The site of his death, which is now a park, is in the settlement of Little Eagle, about 40 miles west of Mobridge by way of U.S. 12 and South Dakota 20 and 63.*

SCHERR-HOWE ARENA MURALS

The Scherr-Howe Arena paintings by Sioux artist Oscar Howe are regarded as his finest works. They depict the history and rites of the Lakota. The ten pieces measure about sixteen by twenty feet in size and are filled with the vibrant colors and traditional symbols recast in modern forms that characterize his work.

LOCATION: *The arena is located on Main Street in the center of Mobridge.*
HOURS: *Monday through Friday, 9–12 and 1–5; Saturday, 9–12.*
ADMISSION: *Free.*
TELEPHONE: *(605) 845-2387.*

Pine Ridge

RED CLOUD HERITAGE CENTER

Through the entire history of the wars on the northern Plains, a period of thirty-five years, the figure of Red Cloud casts its shadow. In Wyoming during the 1860s, he was at the forefront of the campaigns against the miners' and settlers' incursions along the Bozeman Trail, in lands reserved for Native Americans. He was the chief strategist in the raids that led to the victory against the Fetterman party (*see* Fetterman Massacre Site, Sheridan, Wyoming). When war came again in the next decade, the preeminent roles were played by younger men, but this Oglala Sioux chief was a valued counselor. And at the very end, in the days following the massacre at Wounded Knee and the bloody conclusion of the Ghost Dance, it was the aged Red Cloud who led the final band of holdouts to the reservation. Sick of blood, weary of war, he asked only for surrender without further death.

Fearing further slaughter might follow Wounded Knee, Red Cloud and a small band had escaped into the Badlands. He thought further resistance was futile but was unable to control the younger men, who insisted on carrying on the fight. He sent word to his old adversary, General Nathan Miles, that he wished to surrender and bring in the other chiefs but would have to slip away from his people without being detected. On a wet, cold January morning in 1891, Red Cloud, accompanied only by a woman and a young girl, came limping through the newly fallen snow to surrender and end the long war.

The Indian School at Pine Ridge, headquarters of the Pine Ridge Reservation, is named for Red Cloud. There are ongoing exhibits of Indian art here, predominantly from Oglala Sioux, who are the primary occupants of Pine Ridge, the most populous reservation in South Dakota and the second largest in the country (the first is the Navaho Reservation). A permanent art collection is displayed along with the school's splendid Star Quilts. The museum shop sells quillwork and beadwork. The Oglala Nation Fair, held here on the first weekend of each August, is famous for its scrupulously traditional dancing and drumming.

LOCATION: *The Red Cloud Heritage Center is just west of the town of Pine Ridge, on U.S. 18.*
HOURS: *Monday through Friday, 9–5.*
ADMISSION: *Free.*
TELEPHONE: *(605) 867-5771.*

Rapid City

SIOUX INDIAN MUSEUM

The Sioux Indian Museum houses the finest, most extensive collection of historical items and artwork relating to the Sioux Nation. The personal belongings of many of the best-known leaders, religious items that were objects of veneration for centuries, crafts, contemporary paintings—all are presented in this exceptional facility, which is administered by the Indians Arts and Crafts Board of the U.S. Department of the Interior. Collections include nineteenth-century medicine bundles, pipe and tobacco pouches, as well as items such as a turn-of-the-century vest embroidered with porcupine-quill applique on buckskin, and a twentieth-century war bonnet. There are items of personal and religious significance, such as Sitting Bull's medicine bundle—made up of ceremonial items, some of which were gathered during dreams; Fool Bull's war shield; Crow Dog's Ceremonial pipes; and the "Big Missouri Winter Count," a symbolic illustration drawn on an elk hide.

Changing exhibitions feature art and craft displays of contemporary

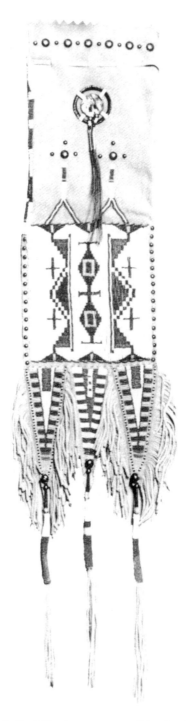

▲ *Pipe Bag (1985, beaded buckskin) is among the traditional crafts on view at the Sioux Indian Museum.*

Sioux artists and crafts people. Traditional artistry continues to play an important role in the cultural traditions of the Sioux society, and old skills are applied to the production of musical instruments, traditional dress, and ceremonial items. The Sioux are among the few tribes to maintain an unbroken tradition of porcupine quilling, a craft unique to the North American Indian, and the museum includes both historic and contemporary examples of this craft. Displays of artworks include native art concepts that have been adapted to a range of non-native art forms, as well as contemporary works that document various aspects of Sioux life. The museum also exhibits works from other tribes.

LOCATION: *The museum is just west of the business district, on West Boulevard near Main Street, just off the entrance to Interstate 190.*
HOURS: *Monday through Saturday, 9–5; Sunday, 1–5, June through September. Closed Monday, rest of year.*
ADMISSION: *Free.*
TELEPHONE: *(605) 348-0557.*

Saint Francis

BUECHEL LAKOTA MUSEUM AND MISSION

Saint Francis lies in the middle of another of South Dakota's large Sioux reservations, the Rosebud. It is populated by the upper Brule band of the Teton, or western Sioux. The museum of Sioux culture here is noted for its exhibits of traditional quillwork. It is adjacent to the Saint Francis Mission, built as a boarding school in 1885 and named in honor of Francis A. Drexel of Philadelphia, a philanthropist who gave widely to minority religious causes. Saint Charles Catholic Church, which replaced the original structure in 1920, was built from native fieldstone by reservation residents.

LOCATION: *Saint Francis is south from U.S. 18 through the town of Rosebud by way of reservation roads.*
HOURS: *Daily, 9–6, Memorial Day through Labor Day.*
ADMISSION: *Donation.*
TELEPHONE: *(605) 747-2361.*

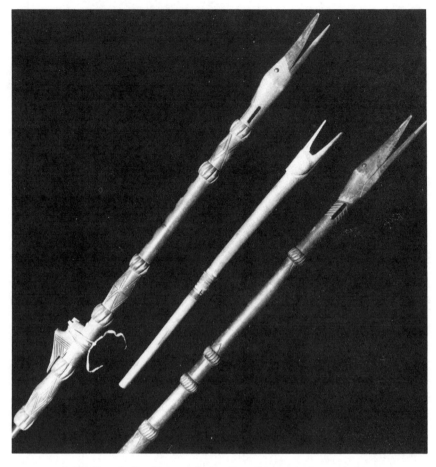

▲ *The Sioux Indian Museum displays Sioux flutes and other musical instruments.*

Wounded Knee

WOUNDED KNEE BATTLEFIELD

W ounded Knee is still referred to as a battlefield, but even the most ardent defender of the U.S. Army should admit that it was no battle. Inexperienced troops, some members of the Seventh Cavalry who were still out for revenge fourteen years after the Little Big Horn, and the fear of the mysterious passions raised by the Ghost Dance—resulted in the slaughter of more than three hundred native people. Most were unarmed; many were women and children.

The events of December 29, 1890, have themselves passed into symbol. When the poet Steven Vincent Benet wrote the lines, "Bury my heart at Wounded Knee," he meant to convey the vital, colorful nature of many of the names on the American map. But to the Native American activists and writers of the late twentieth century, the name was an open wound, the culminating, unforgivable murder of a people. More than eighty years after the massacre, the site was still the center of conflict. In 1973, it was occupied by members of the American Indian Movement. Two FBI agents and one Indian were killed in a clash here two years later. The Holy Rosary Mission, a symbol of Indian resistance that had stood since 1883, was burned to the ground by unknown arsonists.

Wounded Knee came two weeks after the death of Sitting Bull at the Standing Rock Reservation (*see* Fort Yates, North Dakota). He had sought permission to visit Pine Ridge, the center of the Ghost Dance observances, to see for himself what was going on there. But McLaughlin, the agent at Standing Rock, feared Sitting Bull planned to organize an uprising and ordered his arrest—his execution if there was resistance. The brutality with which this highly respected Sioux leader was killed enraged and shocked the tribe. Younger men left Standing Rock to come to Pine Ridge, and they were joined by families fearful of what might come next. They linked up with a group from the Wind River Reservation led by a Miniconjou Sioux, Big Foot. The group made its way into the badlands, toward Pine Ridge.

The army had responded to the Ghost Dance excitement with a show of force unequaled since the end of the Civil War. By November 1890, troops had been gathered from across the Plains and sent onto the Rosebud and Pine Ridge reservations. One of these units, commanded by Colonel James W. Forsyth of the Seventh Cavalry, overtook Big Foot at Wounded Knee Creek. Along with eight mounted units, Forsyth also had an artillery battery armed with Hotchkiss rapid-fire guns.

Convinced the Indians possessed better rifles than their own, on the morning of the twenty-ninth, Forsyth ordered the Sioux to give up their arms. Troopers went into the Sioux encampment to take the weapons. The search became rough, and one of the Sioux reminded his tribesmen that they were wearing Ghost Dance shirts, which rendered them immune to bullets. Someone opened fire on the soldiers. The shots were returned at close quarters, and the encounter became a hand-to-hand struggle. The soldiers managed to get out of the camp so that they could open fire with the Hotchkiss guns. These weapons took a horrendous toll of life, repeatedly raking across the camp and cutting down everything in their scope. Still not satisfied, the troopers charged down the slope and continued killing any survivors they could run down. Days later, burial details came upon women and babies lying dead where they had been slaughtered.

A few survivors managed to escape and tell what they had seen. Within two weeks, however, the resistance ended. The final surrender, on January 16, 1891, is the date usually given for the formal end of the wars between Native Americans and federal armed forces in the United States.

There is one ironic postscript. A few days after Wounded Knee, a young Sioux, Plenty Horses, shot down a popular cavalry officer, Lieutenant Edward Casey, during a peace talk. The army demanded that Plenty Horses be given up to stand trial for murder. But his defense attorneys argued that a state of war existed between the Sioux and the U.S. government and that the entire area was a battlefield. A representative of the top army commander, General Nathan Miles, testified to that in court. The army, even then, feared repercussions from what had happened at Wounded Knee. Miles knew that if Plenty Horses were convicted, there would be sentiment in the East for trying soldiers who were implicated in the massacre. But if their behavior was defined as an act of war, they could not be charged. So it happened that Plenty Horses was acquitted, the lone Native American beneficiary of what occurred at Wounded Knee.

A small monument marks the mass grave of the victims here. Legislation for making Wounded Knee a National Historic Landmark, with a more formal memorial, was introduced in Congress but voted down.

LOCATION: *Wounded Knee is north of U.S. 18 on Reservation Road from a point 8 miles east of Pine Ridge.*
HOURS: *Daily, dawn to dusk.*
ADMISSION: *Free.*

WYOMING

MEDICINE WHEEL

The Medicine Wheel, a huge stone circle 245 feet around and 75 feet across, predates the memory of any tribes in the area. The Crow knew of it, however, and understood that it carried religious significance. There is evidence, from marks left in the surrounding earth by countless *travois* (the carrying sledges of the Plains tribes), that it was a place of pilgrimage and was visited often.

There are twenty-eight spokes, which seem to symbolize the lunar month, radiating from a central stone pile. Other cairns, which may have served as shelters, are positioned at the ends of six spokes that extend beyond the edge of the wheel itself. While it is apparent that the wheel was somehow connected with celestial observations, its exact meaning, like that of England's Stonehenge, has been lost with time.

LOCATION: *The wheel is just off U.S. 14A, at the ten thousand-foot level of Medicine Mountain, within the western boundary of the national forest.*

HOURS: *The road usually is free of snow from late June through September. There is dawn-to-dusk access to the wheel.*

ADMISSION: *Free.*

TELEPHONE: *National forest offices are (307) 672-0751.*

Fort Washakie

Shoshone Reservation Headquarters and Graves of Sacajawea and Washakie

In the 1860s, the federal government was trying to conduct the Civil War and simultaneously deal with suddenly restive western tribes. As a result, the government was willing to promise anything to Native Americans in order to gain temporary peace. As a result, Washakie, head of the eastern Shoshone, was given the Wind River country, a magnificent slice of central Wyoming that included the rich Popo Agie Valley. However, the boundaries were drawn up in such haste and were so imprecise that they were disputed by other tribes as well as by white settlers.

Washakie was a shrewd leader who realized early on that the most realistic course of action was to make the best deal possible and accommodate himself to white expansion. He allied the Shoshone with the U.S. army in campaigns against tribes who chose resistance: the Cheyenne, Arapaho, and Sioux. So in 1872 when the reduction of his massive land grant came about, Washakie still had the political influence to wrest a good chunk of the Popo Agie for his people. Today, it remains the centerpiece of the sprawling 1.9-million-acre Wind River Reservation.

In historic times, the Shoshone tribe divided into three main groups. The northern Shoshone, who were also called the Bannock, lived in the Snake River country of Idaho. The western Shoshone migrated into the deserts of the Great Basin, where they eked out a perilous, impoverished existence. The eastern, or Wind River, Shoshone, also started out in the Snake country. But after acquiring horses, they began moving steadily southeast, toward more open lands. At one time, the Comanche are believed to have been part of the eastern Shoshone, but they continued into Texas, while the main body settled on the Wyoming plains in about 1750.

The Shoshone engaged in constant raids and counterraids with neighboring tribes. On one of them, a young Bannock girl, Sacajawea, was carried off by Lakota raiders. She later married a white trapper who lived with the Mandan on the Missouri River. It was there that Sacajawea met Lewis and Clark, who wintered with the Mandan in 1803, and entered American history. She remembered the lands to the west from her childhood and offered to be their guide into this wilderness that was unknown to Europeans. The image of this slight Indian woman, carrying her infant son on her back and acting as interpreter for the exploring party as it passed into the country of her people, is one of the most enduring images in western history. In the brief list of Native American women whose names are known to the general public, hers ranks at the top with that of Pocahontas.

What happened to Sacajawea after the historic venture is not clear.

According to some accounts, she and her husband returned to Saint Louis with Lewis and Clark. But Sacajawea left her husband and moved to Comanche territory, where she married a member of that tribe. After his death, she rejoined her own people in the Wind River country and died here in 1884. Some historians dispute this account, and a few claim that she died as early as 1812. But the Shoshone regard the grave here as that of the historical Sacajawea.

Washakie lived until 1900, to the age of 102, his lifetime spanning a time when no European had ever seen these lands to the coming of the automobile. The story is told that at age 71, when impatient younger men discussed replacing him as chief, he rode out by himself and returned with the scalps of seven Sioux. That ended the discussion. He is buried in the cemetery of the U.S. military post (closed in 1909) that was named for him. The Shoshone later erected a monument in his honor at the post.

The Shoshone also operate the Living History Indian Village in Fort Washakie, meant to replicate a typical encampment of nomadic hunters, living in buffalo skin tepees. Shops in town sell the beadwork for which the tribe is best known.

LOCATION: *Fort Washakie is on U.S. 287, about 15 miles northwest of Lander. Sacajawea's grave is about 3 miles south of the nearby settlement of Wind River, in the reservation cemetery. Washakie's monument is immediately west of the middle of Fort Washakie. The Indian Village is in town on U.S. 287.*
HOURS: *The hours for the Indian Village vary; check in advance.*
TELEPHONE: *(307) 332-3532.*

Saint Stephens

MISSION HERITAGE CENTER

Among the tribes with whom the Shoshone were traditional enemies were the Arapaho. But in 1878, in an irony of fate, and of federal desperation, the two tribes were thrown together on the Wind River Reservation by emergency decree. The arrangement has lasted ever since, and the two tribes still share the 1.9-million-acre reservation.

However, in the early years, there was little mixing between the two groups, and intermarriage was regarded as a disgrace. Now the tribes run a few cooperative enterprises, most notably Singing Horse Tours, which take visitors on an itinerary that includes both parts of the reservation. It operates out of Saint Stephens, the Arapaho administrative center.

The Arapaho originally were a woodland tribe, living in agricultural villages in Minnesota. But with the great migratory upheavals of the seventeenth century, they were slowly pushed southwest, onto the Plains, where they adapted to a hunting culture. They were closely allied with the Cheyenne and joined that tribe in its military campaigns against the federal government during the 1860s. But when the Arapaho agreed to cede their claims in Wyoming, the reservation lands offered to them were unsatisfactory. They would have been dominated by the Sioux in the Dakotas, and if they rejoined the southern portion of their own tribe in Oklahoma, the hot southern summers would not have suited their way of life. So they encamped at the headwaters of the North Platte River and refused to move until better arrangements were made. With winter approaching and fears of mass starvation looming, the government prevailed on Washakie, leader of the Shoshone (*see* Shoshone Reservation Headquarter, Fort Washakie, Wyoming), to temporarily permit the Arapaho on his lands. As compensation, in 1937, the Shoshone were finally awarded four million dollars by Congress.

The Arapaho were enthusiastic supporters of the Ghost Dance movement of the 1890s, and their Sun Dance ceremonies, held each July (call for exact dates), are among the most solemn and impressive in the country. The Saint Stephens Mission, built by public subscription in Catholic parishes in the East in 1884, now houses a small museum of Arapaho artifacts. Another such exhibit is located in St. Michael's Mission, in the other major Arapaho settlement, Ethete.

LOCATION: *Saint Stephens is located in the southeastern corner of the Wind River Reservation, just south of Riverton, on Wyoming 789. Ethete, which also is the site of the Sun Dance, is much closer to the Shoshone towns, just 5 miles east of that tribe's administrative center of Fort Washakie.*
TELEPHONE: *(307) 332-6120.*

Sheridan

FETTERMAN MASSACRE

Ten years before General George Custer and his entire command were wiped out at the Little Big Horn (*see* Little Big Horn National Battlefield, Montana), a rehearsal for this engagement took place a bit farther south along the Bozeman Trail. The 1866 opening of this shortcut between the North Platte River and the new mining fields of Montana infuriated the northern Plains tribes. They had been guaranteed that these lands would be kept open as permanent hunting grounds. Now wagon trains were moving along the trail and hard experience taught the Plains tribes that permanent settlers would not be far behind.

Two Sioux leaders, Red Cloud and Man Afraid of His Horses, could not be coerced into signing a treaty consenting to the new road. They subsequently closed the road with a series of attacks on wagon trains. The government responded by opening a string of forts, undermanned and led by inexperienced officers who had been given battlefield commissions in the Civil War. One of them was Lieutenant Colonel William J. Fetterman, stationed at Fort Phil Kearny. The outpost was under constant attack by Red Cloud's forces. During the fort's construction, wagons sent out to bring in timber from nearby mountains were raided on an almost daily basis.

On December 21, 1866, Fetterman and a column of eighty-one soldiers rode out on assignment to relieve one such wood train. Contemptuous of his opponents, Fetterman disregarded orders not to pursue them beyond a nearby ridge. Laying the same trap that would later be set for Custer, Red Cloud decoyed Fetterman's party into the main body of his own forces—an alliance of Cheyenne, Arapaho, Oglala, and Sioux—and then cut them to pieces. By the time a rescue party arrived, the soldiers had been killed to the last man.

An investigative committee made the fort's commander, General Henry B. Carrington, the scapegoat of the incident, and he was discharged in 1869. But the government, satisfied that the tribes had been diverted from the new Union Pacific Railroad in southern Wyoming, agreed to a treaty that again guaranteed the tribes rights to the hunting lands. In another few years, though, these rights would be violated again by miners in the Black Hills. Custer would then demonstrate that since Fetterman's miscalculation of his opponent, nothing had been learned about respecting Indians as fighters.

LOCATION: *The site of the Fetterman engagement is 17 miles south of Sheridan along U.S. 14. A memorial marks the spot.*

Thermopolis

GIFT OF THE WATERS PAGEANT

The healing properties of the Big Horn Hot Springs were known well before the days of European settlement. The waters were a favorite resort of Chief Washakie, of the Shoshone, who bathed and drank here frequently. That he lived to the age of 102 seems an excellent testimonial. The spring releases four million gallons of water at 135 degrees Fahrenheit into the Big Horn River. A state park protects the land around it.

The spring was part of the original Wind River Reservation grant. In 1896, Washakie released the area around the spring to the federal government, which turned it over to the state. His only proviso was that Indians from Wind River would always be given free access to the spring.

In commemoration of this bequest, a pageant is given in the park annually on the first Sunday in August. Gift of the Waters features many members of the Shoshone and Arapaho tribes and also includes traditional dances.

LOCATION: *Hot Springs State Park is just north of Thermopolis on U.S. 20.*
HOURS: *Vary; check in advance.*
ADMISSION: *Free.*
TELEPHONE: *(307) 864-2176.*

GREAT PLAINS—SOUTH

Iowa
Kansas
Missouri
Nebraska
Oklahoma
Texas

Great Plains
— South

IOWA
1 Council Monument, *Council Bluffs*
2 Chief Keokuk Monument, *Keokuk*
3 Effigy Mounds National Monument, *Marquette*
4 War Eagle Monument, *Sioux City*
5 Mesquakie Pow Wow, *Tama*

KANSAS
6 Council Oak and Kaw Mission, *Council Grove*
7 Pawnee Village Museum, *Courtland*
8 Iowa, Sac and Fox Mission, *Highland*
9 Huron Cemetery, *Kansas City*
10 Shawnee Mission, *Kansas City*
11 Haskell Indian Junior College, *Lawrence*
12 Peace Treaty Park, *Medicine Lodge*
13 Potawatomi Pay Station, *Saint Marys*
14 El Cuartelejo Ruins, *Scott*
15 Mid-America All-Indian Center
   and Museum, *Wichita*

MISSOURI
16 Trail of Tears State Park, *Cape Girardeau*
17 Van Meter State Park, *Marshall*
18 Osage Village Historic Site, *Nevada*

NEBRASKA
19 Susette LaFlesche Grave and John Neihardt
   Center, *Bancroft*
20 Fort Robinson State Park, *Crawford*
21 Omaha Powwow, *Macy*

OKLAHOMA
22 Chickasaw Cultural Center, *Ada*
23 Delaware Tribal Museum, *Anadarko*
24 Indian City–USA, *Anadarko*
25 Kiowa Murals, *Anadarko*
26 National Hall of Fame for Famous Indian
   Americans, *Anadarko*
27 Southern Plains Indians Museum, *Anadarko*
28 Quanah Parker Starr House, *Cache*
29 Kiowa Tribal Museum, *Carnegie*
30 Washita Battleground, *Cheyenne*
31 Cherokee Courthouse, *Gore*
32 Peter Conser Home, *Heavener*
33 Fort Sill Cemetery, *Lawton*
34 Wheelock Mission Church, *Millerton*
35 Ataloa Lodge, *Muskogee*
36 Five Civilized Tribes Museum, *Muskogee*
37 Creek Council House, *Okmulgee*

38 Osage Museum, *Pawhuska*
39 Home of Sequoyah, *Sallisaw*
40 Spiro Mounds Archeological Park, *Spiro*
41 Cherokee Heritage Center, *Tahlequah*
42 Cherokee National Capitol, *Tahlequah*
43 Murrell House, *Tahlequah*
44 Chickasaw Council House, *Tishomingo*
45 Tonkawa Tribal Museum, *Tonkawa*
46 Choctaw National Museum, *Tuskahoma*
47 Seminole Nation Museum, *Wewoka*
48 Jim Thorpe Home, *Yale*

TEXAS
49 Alabama–Coushatta Museum, *Livingston*
50 Tigua Museum and Reservation, *Ysleta*

50
El Paso

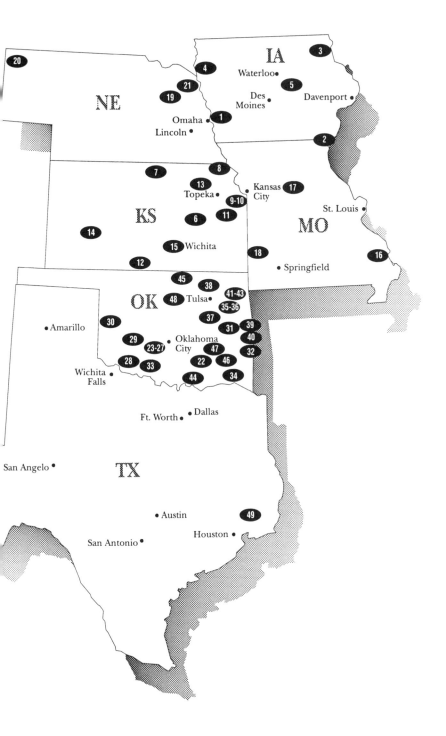

IA

Waterloo •

20

4

3

NE

21

19

5

Des
Moines •

Davenport •

Omaha •

1

Lincoln •

2

7

8

Kansas
City

17

13

KS

Topeka •

9-10

St. Louis •

6

11

MO

14

15 Wichita

18

12

Springfield •

16

45

38

OK

48 Tulsa •

41-43

35-36

30

37

• Amarillo

31

39

29

23-27

Oklahoma
City

47

40

28

33

22

46

32

Wichita
Falls •

44

34

Ft. Worth •

• Dallas

San Angelo •

TX

• Austin

49

Houston •

San Antonio •

IOWA

COUNCIL MONUMENT

The bluffs along the Missouri River just north of the mouth of the Platte were a place for meetings and trade for generations. This is where the Oto tribe met with French fur traders, the first Europeans to venture up the Missouri. But their most famous conference came in 1804, when the Lewis and Clark expedition camped and parleyed here.

According to tradition, the Oto and the Missouri had lived around Green Bay, Wisconsin, as neighbors of the Winnebago. They began migrating west together in the seventeenth century, until they had a falling out over the seduction of a Missouri chief's daughter. That incident gave the Oto a new identity, from a word meaning "lecher" in the Siouan language. The Oto arrived at the junction of the Platte and Missouri in 1717 and stayed on until losing their lands by treaty in 1854. Eventually, they reunited with the Missouri, and both tribes were awarded one million dollars by the U.S. Supreme Court in 1955 for illegal land purchases by which they gave up this territory and moved to an Oklahoma reservation. The Oto-Missouri today are regarded as one tribe.

The place at which they met with Lewis and Clark was known as Hart's Bluff. The name Council Bluffs had been given to the whole line of hills on the east bank of the river, and, in 1852, the newly formed town on this site chose that name for itself.

LOCATION: *The monument depicting the historic conference between Lewis and Clark and the Oto chiefs is north of the city center, along the bluffs, on Rainbow Drive. It is easily accessible from 8th Street.*

CHIEF KEOKUK MONUMENT

T he Sauk and Fox retained separate tribal identities but were so closely
linked in culture and in their migrations that they are virtually considered
as one by historians. But even within the Sauk, there were strong divisions. The
outrage over the fraudulent Sauk and Fox Treaty of 1804, by which the tribe
had surrendered its land claims in Illinois, was shared by all the Sauk leaders.
Black Hawk decided to resist. But Keokuk, knowing the fight was hopelessly
unequal, withdrew to the western side of the Mississippi River and stayed out of
the Black Hawk War of 1832.

He was then recognized as principal chief of the tribe by the federal
government, but the withdrawal bought him only a little more time. Within
ten years he had joined his people on the forced migration west to Kansas and
died there at age 68 in 1848. Even before the Black Hawk War, however, this
city at the junction of the Mississippi and Des Moines rivers, at Iowa's southeastern tip, had been given its present name by local settlers wanting to stay on
Keokuk's good side. A ten-foot-high statue of Keokuk in Rand Park, erected
in 1883, rests on a twenty-foot-high brownstone pedestal, under which are his
remains, brought back from Kansas. Only in death could he return from
expulsion to the city that was named for him.

LOCATION: *The park and statue are in the northern part of town, with the main
entrance at 15th Street and Grand Avenue.*

EFFIGY MOUNDS NATIONAL MONUMENT

O n a bluff above the Mississippi River, in the hilliest part of Iowa, a long-
departed people endeavored to shape the earth into animal forms. The
dozens of effigy mounds they left here are the most extensive such grouping in
the Midwest, running almost six miles along the bluffs and divided into two
separate sections by the Yellow River. One of the largest bear effigies ever
found is here, measuring 70 feet across at the shoulders and 137 feet long. It is
part of the Fire Point Mound group. Other effigies are in the shape of wolves,
serpents, and birds. The structures range from five hundred to more than two
thousand years in age. Footpaths lead from the visitor center to the effigy
groups and to scenic overlooks atop the bluffs into neighboring Wisconsin.

LOCATION: *The Effigy Mounds are off Iowa 76, just north of the town of Marquette, in the northeastern corner of the state.*
HOURS: *Daily, 8–5.*
ADMISSION: *Free.*
TELEPHONE: *(319) 873-2356.*

Sioux City

WAR EAGLE MONUMENT

I n 1849, a French trader named Theophile Bruguier moved into the area along the junction of the Missouri and Big Sioux rivers. He said that he had seen this place in a dream. Such foreknowledge was helpful, but even more to the advantage of the new settlement was Bruguier's father-in-law, War Eagle, a chief of the Yankton branch of the Sioux, known as the Dakota. He had already expressed a willingness to accommodate white expansion and had been decorated by President Martin Van Buren. The Yankton were then the dominant tribe in the area, ranging into Minnesota and South Dakota. Settlers in nearby parts of Iowa experienced severe conflicts with the Sioux, especially around Spirit Lake in 1857, when treaty violations brought settlers onto their lands. Sioux City, however, was protected by War Eagle until his death in 1851. In gratitude, the city erected a monument to him on the bluffs overlooking the Missouri. He was buried at this spot, a favorite viewpoint of his, and the monument was built there in 1922.

LOCATION: *The War Eagle grave is west of downtown, out West 4th Street.*

Tama

MESQUAKIE POW WOW

W hen the Sauk and Fox ceded their Iowa lands in 1842, the two allied tribes agreed to move to reservations in Kansas. But, individually, tribal members began drifting back to their former lands. The process accelerated in the late 1850s when many members of the Fox decided to separate from the Sauk. The two were very similar in culture and had migrated together from Wisconsin after disease and wars with the Ojibwa had decimated the Fox. By

1856 there was a sizable Fox presence again in Iowa, and the state legislature passed a law allowing them to remain. Calling themselves by an older tribal name, Mesquakie, or "people of the red earth," the Indians purchased land along the Cedar River. The nearby town came to be known as Tama, in honor of one of their chiefs during the earlier stay in Iowa.

This is not a reservation. The three thousand acres the tribe controls here is known officially as the Mesquakie Indian Settlement. On the second weekend of August each year, they hold a traditional celebration. The dances here are regarded as the best and most authentic in the Midwest, and prizes are awarded for the most adept dancers. There are tours of the settlement, and a Fox encampment as it would have looked in the nineteenth century is reconstructed each year. There are also craft booths with the floral-design beadwork for which the tribe is noted.

LOCATION: *The Mesquakie Settlement is just south of U.S. 30, about 50 miles west of Cedar Rapids.*
TELEPHONE: *(515) 484-4678.*

KANSAS

Council Grove

COUNCIL OAK AND KAW MISSION

This well-shaded town at the ford of the Neosho River once was the jumping-off point for the American dream. It was the last outfitting center on the Santa Fe Trail, and for a generation the forces that fed expansion into the Southwest funneled through it. Council Grove claims, in fact, to be the birthplace of the celebrated trail because it was under a massive oak here in 1825 that American commissioners signed a treaty with leaders of the Kaw (who were also known as the Kansa) and the Osage to guarantee a right-of-way through the lands they controlled. (Once out of that territory, travelers were on their own. The preferred route of the trail shifted constantly, depending on relations with the Comanche at its western end.) The oak under which the treaty was approved is preserved near downtown.

The Kansa and Osage were closely related. They were both Siouan tribes and, according to their traditions, had migrated west together through the Ohio Valley. The Osage had settled in Missouri but ceded their lands in 1808 and moved to Kansas, where they were rejoined by the Kaw. This tribe had originally settled near the location of present-day Kansas City, but they gradually drifted southwest to the vicinity of Council Grove. A reservation was established for them here in 1847.

Four years later, the Methodist Episcopal Church sent a missionary, Thomas S. Huffaker, to convert the Kaw. The Kaw were not terribly interested. A similar mission had been sent to the Osage a few years earlier, and when the minister read the story of Jonah and the Whale, the tribal members walked out in disbelief and refused to attend any more services. The Kaw were similarly skeptical. The mission was soon closed as an Indian school, only to reopen in 1854 as the first public school for whites in Kansas. Huffaker did remain in Council Grove and was a conciliatory influence in the deteriorating relations between the town and its Native American neighbors. Finally, the Kaw moved to Oklahoma in 1873. The tribe was dissolved as a legal entity in 1902, but in recent years it has reorganized and formed a tribal council in Kaw City, Oklahoma.

LOCATION: *The Council Oak is two blocks east of the Neosho Bridge, on Main Street. The Kaw Mission is just north of the business district at 500 N. Mission.*
HOURS: *The mission is open Tuesday through Saturday, 10–5; Sunday, 1–5.*
ADMISSION: *Donation.*
TELEPHONE: *(316) 767-5410.*

Courtland

PAWNEE INDIAN VILLAGE MUSEUM

The earth lodge excavated here preserves the site of a Pawnee residence just as it was in the first years of the nineteenth century. This tribe lived along the Platte and Loup valleys of Nebraska and northern Kansas. They were a Caddoan people who migrated into the area from the Southwest by the sixteenth century. Because they lived off the main, traveled trade routes, they were among the last of the western tribes to come into direct contact with Europeans. But their skill as horsemen established trade relations with the French.

The Pawnee were known for their distinctive hairstyle, with thickly greased locks that stood up from the scalp and gave the appearance of horns. The tribal name has been translated as meaning "horn." It also became a generic term for "slave" among other tribes because so many of their people were carried off by raiders and sold to the Spanish in the Southwest and the French in the Northeast. In attempting to defend themselves from these raids, the Pawnee were continuously at war with the Apache, Dakota, and Osage.

By the time the residence preserved here was built, the tribe was already in decline. War and disease had severely reduced its population, and starting in 1833 they began ceding their lands to the U.S. government in return for a small reservation on the Loup in Nebraska. Many of them served with the U.S. Army as scouts during the Indian Wars on the Plains. By 1876, they had been removed completely to new lands in Oklahoma.

A museum has been constructed directly over the floor of the earth lodge here, on the banks of the Republican River, and items recovered from the dwelling were replaced exactly where they were found. Other exhibits depict the life of the Pawnee.

▲ *The Iowa, Sac, and Fox Mission building, dating from 1843, is now a museum of that era, with many artifacts of the tribes for whose good it was ostensibly built.*

LOCATION: *The Pawnee Village is east of Courtland on U.S. 36, then north on Kansas 266.*
HOURS: *Tuesday through Saturday, 10–5; Sunday, 1–5.*
ADMISSION: *Donations.*
TELEPHONE: *(913) 361-2255.*

Highland

IOWA, SAC AND FOX MISSION

M any of the oldest towns in Kansas got their start as religious missions to the tribes that had been expelled from Iowa and Missouri. The very success of the mission community, however, doomed the native presence in the area. That was the story of Highland's beginnings. When the Iowa, a Siouan people, ceded their lands in the state of Iowa in 1836, they were placed on a reservation near the junction of the Missouri and Great Nemaha Rivers, in the northeastern corner of Kansas. Two other tribes, the Sac (Sauk) and Fox, joined them there shortly afterward. They were Algonquian people who really had little in common with the Iowa, aside from the fact that they, too, had been removed from Iowa after ceding land rights. A Presbyterian mission was established there in 1837 for purposes of education and religious instruction. But within seventeen years, the reservation lands were whittled away because so many white settlers were drawn to the area by the mission. Highland was then opened completely to white settlement. While most of the Indians were given new lands in Oklahoma by 1883, many Fox chose to return to Iowa. Only a twelve-hundred-acre sliver of the Kansas reservation remains today, with a few hundred Iowa continuing to make their home there. The mission building dates from 1843 and replaces the one-room log structure that housed the original church. It is now a museum of that era, with many artifacts of the tribes for whose good it was ostensibly built.

LOCATION: *The mission is on U.S. 36, just east of town.*
HOURS: *Tuesday through Saturday, 10–5; Sunday, 1–5.*
ADMISSION: *Donation.*
TELEPHONE: *(913) 442-3304.*

Kansas City

HURON CEMETERY

For a short time, there was not a more controversial piece of urban real estate in the country than this cemetery plot in downtown Kansas City. This is the area to which the Huron, also known as the Wyandots, finally came in 1842, almost two hundred years after they had been driven from their traditional homeland on Canada's Georgian Bay by the Iroquois. They had traveled all around the Great Lakes, settled for a time in northern Ohio, and finally ceded those lands to come to Kansas. But little more than a decade later, as settlers poured into Kansas, they were forced to move again, to the Indian lands in Oklahoma. In the treaty that extinguished their claims in the Kansas City area, it was stipulated that their burial ground here would be preserved.

In 1906, when everything was up-to-date in Kansas City and business was booming, a group of urban developers pushed a bill through Congress that permitted the site to be sold. The approximately four hundred bodies buried there were to be moved to a new cemetery. The case reached the U.S. Supreme Court four years later, and the court upheld the bill. But the public outcry against it was so great that Congress repealed the bill in 1913 and created a city park around the burial ground instead. The cemetery today is in the heart of the business district, part of a central downtown plaza.

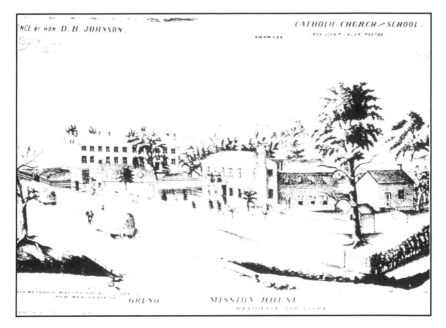

▲ *An 1874 view of the Shawnee Mission.*

LOCATION: *The cemetery is on Center City Plaza, between 6th and 7th Streets.*
HOURS: *Daily, dawn to dusk.*
ADMISSION: *Free.*

SHAWNEE MISSION

As the federal government became committed to a policy of transporting native people from the East to the unsettled lands west of Missouri, the question become where to put them. The answer, eventually, was Oklahoma, which was known for many years as Indian Territory. But prior to that decision, which was made in the 1830s, it was thought that Kansas was the best solution. For seventeen years, from 1825 to 1842, the Kansas Territory was the preferred resettlement site and twenty-eight tribes signed treaties that granted them new lands there. Kansas, however, became a political prize in the sectional differences that led to the Civil War. As both pro- and antislavery forces vied for political control of the territory, white settlers on both sides of the issue were encouraged to move there and establish a presence for their faction. In 1854, the entire territory was opened to white settlement and the Native American position became impossible. Another removal resulted, this time to the final destination of Oklahoma.

But in the early years of Kansas history, the Indian settlements and the missions sent out to educate and convert their inhabitants became the focus of growth. Shawnee Mission was the first and the most important. In 1838, the Missouri Conference of the Methodist Episcopal Church sent out Rev. Thomas Johnson to minister to the Shawnee, the first of the eastern tribes to settle in Kansas. This was the tribe that had fought expansion of the white frontier for a century, throughout Ohio and Indiana. By 1825, their greatest leader, Tecumseh, was dead, the tribe was exhausted, and they accepted relocation.

When Johnson opened his school there, the enrollment was seventy-two children. The boys were taught farming techniques, and the girls home economics. Students were housed in dormitories. The first orchard in Kansas was planted on the grounds, and eventually the student body was expanded to include a number of black slaves owned by Johnson.

The mission thrived for a time, actually being enlarged with new dormitories in 1845. But as the slavery question started to override all other considerations, Shawnee Mission was swept up in it. Andrew Reeder, the first elected territorial governor, moved his offices here from Fort Leavenworth in 1854. The school was closed and the government took over the grounds. Uncomfortable with the area's proslavery sentiment, Reeder transferred the capital, but in 1855, when the Free-Soilers lost their majority in the legislature, it was moved back. While meeting at Shawnee Mission, the legislature passed the laws that legalized slavery in Kansas, touching off a round of violence that swept the state and was a bitter prelude to Civil War. By the time the capital left Shawnee Mission for good, so had the Shawnee, as well as most of the other tribes. Disturbed by the growing circle of violence in a quarrel that did not involve them, many individuals sold their lands here and moved to Oklahoma of their own volition. Johnson, however, remained and, although a slaveholder, he pledged his loyalty to the Union. He was gunned down by Confederate raiders in 1865 and is buried nearby in the Shawnee Cemetery.

Three mission buildings remain on the site. The school, dormitory, and superintendent's house have been restored and contain many historical items relating to both the native people who attended classes here and the political strife that shut the mission down.

LOCATION: *The mission is just south of Kansas City, on Mission Road at West 53rd Street. From downtown take U.S. 169 south to Johnson Drive, then west to Mission Road.*
HOURS: *Tuesday through Saturday, 10-5; Sunday, 1-5.*
ADMISSION: *Free.*
TELEPHONE: *(913) 262-0867.*

Lawrence

HASKELL INDIAN JUNIOR COLLEGE

M any of the educational facilities established for native people in the late nineteenth century were designed expressly to separate students from tribal tradition. Reformers were convinced that only by wiping out the old ways and imbuing youngsters with white values could the students hope to become "useful citizens" of the United States. Those who opposed such plans were scorned as "blanket Indians." Eventually, however, a recognition grew that something of value was being lost, and most of these Indian schools went out of business. An exception is Haskell Indian Junior College, which still fulfills the mission for which it was created in 1884 by the federal government. The school was named for the congressman who was instrumental in getting it placed in Kansas. By the 1930s, educational theories had changed and funding was cut off for schools not located on reservations. While the other Indian schools adhered to their original rigid formats, Haskell had developed a greater sensitivity to Indian educational needs. The outcry over its closing was so great that Congress reversed itself in 1934 and Haskell was permitted to continue. Haskell's enrollment of one thousand students now comes from more than one hundred tribes in thirty-five states.

The entire campus is a National Historic Landmark, with several buildings dating from the nineteenth century. It also houses the American Indian Athletic Hall of Fame. While never attaining the national ranking of Carlisle (*see* Indian School, Carlisle, Pennsylvania), Haskell was a regional football power in the 1920s and competed successfully against schools in the Big Eight Conference. One season it defeated Kansas, Nebraska, and Missouri. Pete Hauser and John Levi were Haskell All-American selections.

LOCATION: *The college is located in central Lawrence, at 23rd and Barker Streets.*
HOURS: *The campus is open daily. The Hall of Fame is open 9–5, Monday through Friday.*
ADMISSION: *Free.*
TELEPHONE: *(913) 749-8450.*

Medicine Lodge

PEACE TREATY PARK

P eace Treaty Park commemorates one of the most remarkable gatherings in the history of the relations between native peoples and white settlers. In the fall of 1867, war on the western Plains had been raging for three years and both sides were seeking an honorable peace. The government wanted to secure a right-of-way for railroads, and the tribes were exhausted and could not carry on the fight through another winter. This place in southern Kansas was chosen as a conference site. It was well within the Indian lands and had been recognized as neutral ground among the Plains tribes for generations. The river waters were believed to have healing powers, and many of the tribes came here to rest and bathe wounds. The Kiowa, Arapaho, Comanche, Apache, and Cheyenne sent delegations to the conference, and about fifteen thousand native people showed up to meet with six hundred representatives from Washington.

A full list of Indian grievances was discussed, with Little Raven, an Arapaho, making an address so moving that almost half a century later white participants in the conference could quote from it. The leaders met in a large tent on the river, facing each other on stools. After two weeks of negotiations, the southern border of Kansas was fixed and the lands to the south given to the Indians as their territory "for all time." The agreement opened western Kansas to settlement and also secured the Smoky Hill Trail to Colorado, which quickly resulted in that territory being populated.

Congress refused to ratify several parts of the treaty, and within a year warfare had broken out again. But the gathering still went down as the largest of its kind in American history. Every three years, the treaty signing is reenacted at the original spot. In 1994 there is a ceremony scheduled in the first weekend of October. Subsequently, Medicine Lodge won even greater fame as the home of the hatchet-wielding temperance advocate, Carrie Nation.

LOCATION: *Peace Treaty Park is on the northern end of Main Street. Medicine Lodge is located on U.S. 160 about 85 miles southwest of Wichita. A memorial depicting members of the treaty delegation clasping hands in friendship was erected in 1929.*

▲ *The Potawatomi Pay Station (1857) houses a small museum on the history of Saint Marys.*

Saint Marys

POTAWATOMI PAY STATION

S aint Marys is another of the Kansas towns that had its origin in a mission to the local reservation. These lands had been given to the Potawatomi, a tribe that formerly lived in the southern Great Lakes, ranging across Michigan and northern Indiana. They were transported here in the 1830s, and a mission was established by Jesuits in 1848. A feature of many treaties in this era called for tribal members to receive monthly pay allotments from the reservation agent, a policy that turned native people into dependents of Washington. The pay station here was part of the Catholic mission and has been restored to its original appearance. A portion of the reduced Potawatomi Reservation is still in existence north of here and displays a buffalo herd near the tribal offices. Built by the government in 1857, the building is listed on the National Register of Historic Places.

LOCATION: *The pay station is in central Saint Marys, at 1st and Mission Streets.*
HOURS: *Tuesday through Sunday 1-4, May through September.*
ADMISSION: *Donation.*
TELEPHONE: *(913) 437-2391 or (913) 437-6600.*

▲ *El Cuartelejo: These adobe ruins, reconstructed in 1971, are presumed to have been a Picuris settlement.*

Scott City

EL CUARTELEJO RUINS

W hen the Spanish imposed their rule over the pueblos of New Mexico, many native people chafed under the harshness of the regime. There was a massive revolt in 1680 during which the invaders were driven out of the country. But in a few years they returned in force and the cycle of repression began again. According to a semilegendary account, one of the Pueblo peoples, the Picuris, decided to run away during this period and make their home in the unknown lands to the northeast, on the Plains. El Cuartelejo adobe ruins are presumed to be the settlement they established. The timing fits. The ruins have been dated to the late seventeenth century, about when the Picuris would have broken away. This northernmost extension of the Pueblo culture lasted about fifty years. Spanish soldiers eventually located the Picuris in 1720 and persuaded them to return. The ruins remained deserted, although they were once a familiar landmark to the Comanche who lived in the area, many of whom even made temporary camp among them. The site is now a state park.

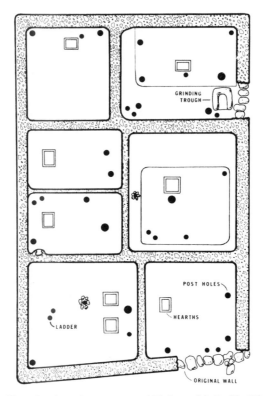

GRINDING
TROUGH—

POST HOLES

HEARTHS

LADDER

ORIGINAL WALL

▲ *Floor plan from the reconstructed El Cuartelejo Pueblo. When the site was excavated in 1970, all that remained were portions of the stone hearths, two sections of the outer wall, and several post holes.*

LOCATION: *The pueblo is 12 miles north of Scott City by way of U.S. 83 and Kansas 95.*
HOURS: *Daily, dawn to dusk.*
ADMISSION: *$2.50 a car.*
TELEPHONE: *(316) 872-2061.*

Wichita

MID-AMERICA ALL-INDIAN CENTER AND MUSEUM

K eeper of the Plains, the statue in front of the Mid-America All-Indian Center and Museum, has become a local landmark and is said to be the most photographed site in the state. The museum is devoted to the arts and culture, past and present, of the Plains tribes. Operated by Native Americans, the Center reflects the Indian viewpoint in its exhibits, educational programs, and collection policy. The museum is housed in an arrowhead-shaped building, the center of which–a 10,000 square foot open area with a 30-foot ceiling–is a kiva, or ceremonial area.

Exhibits of artifacts, tools, crafts, and contemporary Native American artwork rotate every 6 to 10 weeks. From time to time, the museum exhibits Hopi baskets, pottery, painting, and beadwork, in addition to Southwest and Plains Indian art. Based on the premise that the art of the Native American is social, the Center encourages "art in motion," emphasizing live demonstrations and participation. On Tuesdays, Native American food is served. The gift shop carries only works of Native American artists.

LOCATION: *The museum is situated in a park at the junction of the Arkansas and Little Arkansas rivers, just west of the business district, at 650 North Seneca.*
HOURS: *Monday through Saturday, 10–5; Sunday, 1–5, May through September. Closed Monday, rest of year.*
ADMISSION: *$1.75.*
TELEPHONE: *(316) 262-5221.*

▲ *The statue* Keeper of the Plains *at Mid-America All-Indian Center and Museum is said to be the most photographed site in the state.*

MISSOURI

TRAIL OF TEARS STATE PARK

The Trail of Tears blufflands mark the place at which a large portion of the Cherokee Nation crossed the Mississippi River on its terrible march to Oklahoma from the Southeast in the 1830s. The park is used mostly for recreational purposes, but a museum at the visitor center relates the history of the Trail of Tears and the Cherokee crossing of Missouri.

Opened in 1988, the museum features a diorama of a typical Cherokee family on the forced march, various media presentations concerning the history of the Cherokee nation, and occasional native craft demonstrations. A small library holds resources on Cherokee subjects and genealogy, and contemporary Cherokee art work complements the displays.

LOCATION: *The park is about 10 miles north of Cape Girardeau by way of Missouri 177.*
HOURS: *The visitor center is open daily, 9–5, May through September. Call for other times.*
ADMISSION: *Free.*
TELEPHONE: *(314) 334-1711.*

VAN METER STATE PARK

When the earthwork at Van Meter was built, the rise on which it was located stood on the south bank of the Missouri River. But over the centuries, the river shifted its course and the old fort now sits alone on a high plateau. The 2,700-foot-long enclosure was probably a fortification, since it was built to close off access from the river. It is very similar in plan and execution to the Fort Ancient works in Ohio (*see* Fort Ancient State Memorial, Lebanon, Ohio). Two ridges on its northern end, called The Pinnacles, mark the location of the Missouri. About half a mile east of the fort are the remains of a Native American village, which has been excavated in recent years by teams from the University of Missouri. The village is estimated to date back as far as 10,000 B.C.

LOCATION: *The park is northwest of Marshall by way of northbound Missouri 41 and westbound Missouri 122.*
HOURS: *Daily, dawn to dusk.*
ADMISSION: *Free.*
TELEPHONE: *(816) 886-7537.*

Nevada

OSAGE VILLAGE HISTORIC SITE

The Osage were the dominant native people in Missouri when the Europeans arrived. A Siouan group, they probably migrated west through the Ohio Valley, reaching this area in the seventeenth century. Their communities were built along rivers, mainly the Missouri, Osage, and in later years, the Arkansas. After 1720, the Missouri River group became known as the Little Osage, and the segment living on the Osage were called the Great Osage. The life they established here was nearly idyllic, a mixture of farming in the fertile riverlands and buffalo hunting on the adjacent prairies. They had a well-established charitable system, with hunters always securing extra provisions for those families without adult males. Formidable warriors, they had few local enemies to fear and raided west among the Pawnee and Ponca to resupply shortages in livestock.

They established friendly relations with the French and, according to tribal traditions, traveled great distances to assist them in their wars with England. Their trade association with the wealthy Chouteau family of Saint Louis led to a segment of the tribe's moving south to Arkansas to maintain the mutually enriching arrangement. Inevitably, the onrush of white settlement overwhelmed them. The Osage ceded most of their lands in western Missouri and northern Arkansas in 1808. By 1836, they had all been transported west of the state line to reservations in Kansas, and by 1870, to Oklahoma. The good fortune of this tribe prevailed; their new holdings in Oklahoma sat on top of oil reserves, and by the 1920s they were among the wealthiest of native groups. The site here preserves a Great Osage village that was active until 1777.

Markers outline where various parts of the community were located and also relate a brief history of the Osage.

> LOCATION: *From Nevada, the Osage village is east on U.S. 54, then north on Vernon County Road C. Watch for markers to a westbound gravel road in about 11 miles.*
> HOURS: *Daily, dawn to dusk.*
> ADMISSION: *Free.*

NEBRASKA

SUSETTE LAFLESCHE GRAVE AND
JOHN NEIHARDT CENTER

Bancroft is a little town situated just outside the boundaries of the Omaha Reservation. The life of the town and that of the reservation are closely tied.

Susette LaFlesche belonged to a family who had assumed leadership roles among the Omaha for many years. Her father, Joseph, was of French and Ponca descent and was adopted as a son by the Omaha chief Big Elk. Big Elk urged his people early in the nineteenth century to accommodate themselves to the coming of the whites. He deliberately sought out a successor who would carry on his policies; Joseph LaFlesche, also called Iron Eye, was that person. LaFlesche was an energetic leader who led temperance crusades and tried to enforce a policy of abstinence on the reservation.

His son, Francis, became a pioneer in the field of tribal psychology and the symbolism of Indian language. He wrote a history of the Omaha and worked for the Bureau of American Ethnology in Washington. But it was Susette LaFlesche who became the most visible member of the family. With her husband, Thomas H. Tibbles, she toured the country in the late nineteenth century, under the name Bright Eyes, to lecture and campaign for Indian rights and recognition of land claims. Her long and arduous crusade finally was rewarded with federal legislation defining those rights. She returned to the reservation, where she was raised, shortly before her death in 1903 and is buried in the cemetery here.

John Neihardt's series of epic poems about Nebraska, many of them incorporating legends he had gathered on the Omaha and nearby Sioux reservations, earned him the title of poet laureate. His home in Bancroft was made into a museum after his death in 1973. It contains many items of Indian origin and also a Sioux prayer garden.

LOCATION: *Bancroft is about 75 miles northwest of Omaha. The cemetery is just outside of town on Nebraska 16. The Neihardt Center is at the corner of Washington and Elm Streets.*
HOURS: *The cemetery is open daily, dawn to dusk. The Neihardt Center is open Monday through Saturday, 8-12, and 1:30-5, April to mid-November. Open afternoons only on weekends, rest of year.*
ADMISSION: *The center is $2.*
TELEPHONE: *(402) 648-3388.*

Crawford

FORT ROBINSON STATE PARK

C rawford was an outpost established by the U.S. Army as a cavalry base in 1874. It survived until after World War II, one of the last such military bases in the country. In its early years, however, it developed a sinister reputation among Native Americans. Two leaders, both of whom surrendered voluntarily, were killed at the fort under circumstances that are hard to describe as anything other than homicide.

The first victim was Crazy Horse, the Oglala Sioux chief who is credited for being the top strategist in the Little Big Horn campaign. After being pursued and harassed by federal troops all through the following winter, with his people near starvation, he arrived at the fort in May 1877 to turn himself in. Four months later, he was dead, killed by repeated bayonet wounds. The official version was that he was stabbed while attempting to escape, but there is evidence to suggest that military authorities wanted him dead to remove a dangerous rallying point among the still restive Plains tribes.

The following year, the scenario was repeated. Dull Knife was the leader of a group of Cheyenne who had broken away from a reservation in Oklahoma, to which they had been arbitrarily assigned with the southern branch of the tribe. They wanted to return to familiar surroundings on the northern Plains and fought a running battle with pursuing army forces in trying to get there. Dull Knife finally surrendered, was imprisoned at Fort Robinson, and was killed in an episode that was described as an attempted escape.

Fort Robinson is now a state park, situated among the hills of the Pine Ridge country. The museum here contains displays on its history as a military base, and there is a memorial at the place of Crazy Horse's death nearby.

LOCATION: *The fort is 3 miles west of Crawford on U.S. 20.*
HOURS: *The visitor center is open daily, 8–5, Memorial Day through Labor Day. The museum is open Monday through Saturday, 8–5, and Sunday, 9–5, Memorial Day through Labor Day. Sunday hours, 1:30–5, April through late May and early September to mid-November. Closed weekends, rest of year.*
ADMISSION: *State park fee is $3. Admission to museum is $1.*
TELEPHONE: *(308) 665-2660.*

Macy

OMAHA POWWOW

W hen Lewis and Clark passed the Omaha villages on their voyage up the Missouri River in 1803, they witnessed the tribe's dance of thanksgiving. The ceremony has been held ever since without a break and is regarded as the oldest such Native American observance in the country, the father of all powwows.

The Omaha were closely related to the Osage, Quapaw, and Ponca. They all originated in southwestern Indiana and began a two hundred-year migration along the Ohio, Mississippi, and Missouri rivers. According to tradition, when the group came to the Mississippi, the Quapaw chose to go downstream and the others went upstream. So the latter were called Maha, which means "upstream" in the Siouan language.

Eventually, the main body of Omaha settled in northeastern Nebraska and became involved in the fur trade. They were consistently friendly toward white settlers. Nonetheless, in 1854 they were forced to cede most of their lands and were settled on a reservation. Even so, eleven years later when the Winnebago were expelled from Minnesota in the aftermath of the Sioux uprising there, the Omaha lopped off the northern half of their lands and, in a gesture of fraternal concern, gave them to this homeless people. The Winnebago still occupy those lands.

LOCATION: *The administrative center of the reservation is in Macy, on U.S. 75 about 60 miles north of Omaha.*
HOURS: *The Powwow is always held during the first full moon of August.*
ADMISSION: *Free.*
TELEPHONE: *(402) 837-5391.*

OKLAHOMA

CHICKASAW CULTURAL CENTER

The old Chickasaw Nation occupied the southwestern corner of the territory allotted to the Five Civilized Tribes, between the Canadian and Red rivers. They purchased the tract from their former neighbors in Mississippi, the Choctaw, who had preceded them to the Indian Territory. In historic times, the Chickasaw had ranged from northern Mississippi all the way into western Kentucky, on the east bank of the Mississippi River. They allied themselves with the British in the colonial wars and were regarded as formidable foes by the French. The ongoing struggle took a heavy toll on the tribe, both in numbers and material goods. After American control was extended over the area, the Chickasaw settled down to become farmers, many of them owning large cotton plantations employing black slaves. But by 1832, they were forced to cede their lands and join the trek to Oklahoma, where one census counted five thousand members of the Chickasaw nation and one thousand slaves when they arrived.

The Chickasaw thrived in Oklahoma, and by the time of the Civil War their capital of Tishomingo (*see* Chickasaw Council House, Tishomingo, Oklahoma) was one of the territory's most prosperous towns. Like most of the other Civilized Tribes, they supported the Confederacy and with the peace were forced to cede some of their westernmost lands by the federal government. Since 1906, when their nation was dissolved, the Chickasaw have been assimilated into the general population. About seven thousand people still identify themselves by their tribal affiliation. Tribal headquarters are in Ada, and the Chickasaw also operate a trading post here and an outlet for their woodworking enterprise. The cultural center displays craft items.

LOCATION: *The center is at 520 East Arlington Street, in downtown Ada.*
HOURS: *Monday through Friday, 8–5; Saturday, 10–4.*
ADMISSION: *Free.*
TELEPHONE: *(405) 436-2603.*

Anadarko

DELAWARE TRIBAL MUSEUM

E ven though the Delaware were known as the "Friendly Indians" because of their support of peace in treaty negotiations, they were nevertheless continually pushed westward by the unfriendly tide of immigration. Members of the Algonquian linguistic stock, they called themselves the Lenni-Lenape, and were known to other tribes as "the Grandfathers"; by the time of European contact in the 17th century, the Delaware had resided in the eastern United States for some 76 generations. It was the Delaware who signed the famous treaty with William Penn, and it was they who signed the first Indian treaty with the United States in 1778.

Toward the end of the 18th century, the main body of the tribe resided along the White River in what is now Indiana. A smaller group crossed the Mississippi River into Spanish Missouri, where they received a land grant in 1793, near Cape Girardeau. This segment of the tribe came to be known as the "Absentee Delaware," and they entered Spanish Texas in the early part of the 19th century, where they again received a land grant. The Delaware continued to be persecuted, however, and part of the tribe was forced across the Red River while others were removed to Indian Territory.

Until 1960, the Delaware—who by now had changed their name from the Absentee Delaware to the Delaware Tribe of Western Oklahoma—had no tribal lands, even though they once controlled much of the land in the eastern United States. The Delaware tribe now has a tribal facility situated on land that they own jointly with the Wichita and Cadilo tribes. The tribal headquarters, located 2 miles north of Anadarko, includes a small museum, archive, and a library. Items of interest in the museum include replicas of prayer sticks, tools, a hunting bag and wampum belt, and a 1778 buckskin jacket. There are photographs of scouts, leaders, chiefs, and their descendants, as well as maps and charts explaining the history of the Lenni-Lenape people.

LOCATION: *The Delaware Museum is 2 miles north of town on U.S. 281.*
HOURS: *Monday through Friday, 8-5.*
ADMISSION: *Free.*
TELEPHONE: *(405) 247-2448.*

INDIAN CITY—USA

Seven southwestern tribes are represented at Indian City, an outdoor museum with authentic reproductions of typical communities the tribes would have inhabited in the past. For four groups of southern Plains people— the Wichita, Kiowa, Apache, and Comanche—the physical setting is accurate, too, since this is the actual territory they ranged across. The Caddo come from a bit farther south, in Texas. As for the Navajo and Pueblo villages, while accurate in other detail, the site is rather far removed from the true homes of those people, New Mexico and Arizona. Nonetheless, this is a good cultural sampling, and the displays are especially adept at delineating distinctions between tribes that seem almost alike to outsiders.

The villages incorporate tools, cradles, cooking utensils, weapons, musical instruments, games, and toys in the dwellings of the different tribes. Artifacts are used to tell a tribe's story: displays include buffalo skins stretched to dry outside a Comanche traveling home (tipi); a family altar inside a Pawnee dwelling; an adobe Pueblo home with retractable ladders and no ground-floor entry; a Navajo outdoor bread baking oven; and a "wickiup" steam lodge, an Apache version of a steam bath. A herd of buffalo roam on the 140 adjoining acres, and Native American dancing and pow-wows are scheduled throughout the year.

LOCATION: *South of town on Oklahoma 8.*
HOURS: *Summer: Daily, 9-6. Winter: Daily 9-5.*
ADMISSION: *$6.50.*
TELEPHONE: *(405) 247-5661.*

KIOWA MURALS

The American Indian Exposition is held in Anadarko during the third week of every August, and the momentum generated by that celebration has turned Anadarko into Oklahoma's biggest Native American tourist center. It bills itself, in fact, as "The Indian Capital of the Nation." The title grew out of the town's history as a political and business center for Native Americans. Anadarko occupies land first set aside for the Wichita tribe in 1867. Most of the Wichita were Union sympathizers during the Civil War. That struggle had turned into a bitter intertribal battle in Oklahoma as supporters for both sides raided the lands of the others. The Wichita fled north to pro-Union Kansas, around the city that bears their name, and then returned to this area after the war. Nine years later they were joined on this land parcel, west of the 98th meridian and between the Canadian and Red rivers, by several southern Plains tribes. The Kiowa, Comanche, and Apache were brought here as part of the

▲ *A mother and daughter from the Comanche tribe at the American Indian Exposition at Indian City—USA.*

federal policy of finding homes in Oklahoma for the unsettled tribes in the region.

An office of the Bureau of Indian Affairs, responsible for all the Indian communities of western Oklahoma and Kansas, was then established here. The bureau's placement ensured that Anadarko was to grow up as a major center for Native American concerns. Bureau offices remain downtown, and the federal building is decorated with murals depicting Native American life and people. They were painted by Mopope, a Kiowa artist whose tribe remains the leading Indian population group in the area.

LOCATION: *The Federal Building is at 120 South First Street and the murals are in the main lobby.*
HOURS: *Monday through Friday, 9–5.*

NATIONAL HALL OF FAME FOR FAMOUS INDIAN AMERICANS

T he National Hall of Fame for Famous Indian Americans is an outdoor museum in which bronze busts of individuals of Native American extraction are displayed in a garden setting. For those not familiar with Indian history, it is a good introduction to the people who figured in some of its most significant events. Visitors may opt to take a self-guided tour of the Hall of Fame, which includes biographies and background information about the subjects' tribes. A recirculating fountain—built from stones from the gypsum Slick Hills, used by Plains tribes as medicine hills—was added in 1992.

LOCATION: *East edge of Anadarko on U.S. 62.*
HOURS: *Monday through Saturday, 9–5; Sunday, 1–5.*
ADMISSION: *Free.*
TELEPHONE: *(405) 247-5555.*

SOUTHERN PLAINS INDIANS MUSEUM

S outhern Plains Indiana Museum is operated by the Indian Arts and Crafts Board of the U.S. Department of the Interior, and the exhibits reflect its high standards. The historical sections that exhibit featherwork, hide painting, and skin sewing are especially fascinating. The permanent exhibit gallery contains items created by the tribal people of western Oklahoma, including a display of the traditional costumes of southern Plains men, women, and children. Other displays relate various art forms to the social and ceremonial aspects of the tribal cultures. Four dioramas and a mural illustrate cultural subjects, and the museum's changing exhibition gallery presents art and craft works of contemporary Native Americans. During the summer season, there's a display of full-scale painted tipis on the grounds. This is an outstanding, well-run museum, and its lucidly labeled exhibits (not always the case in smaller museums) are an excellent way of learning about the culture of these people.

LOCATION: *East edge of Anadarko on U.S. 62.*
HOURS: *Monday through Saturday, 9–5; Sunday, 1–5, June through September. Closed Monday, rest of year.*
ADMISSION: *Free.*
TELEPHONE: *(405) 247-6221.*

Cache

QUANAH PARKER STARR HOUSE

The Quanah Parker Starr House was the residence of the last chief of the non-reservation Comanche, and his story may strike a familiar chord with fans of John Ford movies. Ford adapted elements of the story in his classic film *The Searchers*. The Comanche were a nomadic people who moved to the southern Plains from the Wyoming Rockies late in the seventeenth century. Shortly afterward, they acquired horses and became the most esteemed riders and raiders in the region. They warred with many other tribes and, in the years after Texas won its independence from Mexico, fought a bloody battle with the government of the republic, which was determined to drive them from its borders. Atrocities on both sides were horrendous and left scars that did not heal for a century. On one raid into Texas in 1836, a Comanche band carried off nine-year-old Cynthia Parker; the rest of her family was killed. Relatives and Texas Rangers searched for her for years. She married Peta Nokoni, a Comanche chief and, when finally located, she refused to return to white settlements, identifying herself as a Comanche. This was not an unusual situation. The Comanche regularly adopted captives into the tribe to replace their numbers lost through continual warfare. The Rangers forcibly took her back, but one of her sons, Quanah, stayed on to lead the Quahadi band.

While other members of the tribe agreed to resettlement in Oklahoma, Quanah fought on against buffalo hunters and federal troops. Finally, seeing that further battle was hopeless, he rode in to Fort Sill at the head of his band in 1875 and accepted resettlement. He built this home fifteen years later and spent the rest of his life there. In his later years he became something of a national celebrity and even developed a friendship with Theodore Roosevelt. Polygamy was still practiced by the Comanche, a normal cultural trait among people who struggle to replenish their population. Roosevelt supposedly urged him to give up all his wives but one, to which Quanah quickly replied, "You tell the others." He died here in 1911. The house now contains mementos of his life and of that era in Oklahoma history.

LOCATION: *The house is in the center of town, on U.S. 62 and Oklahoma 115, about 12 miles west of Lawton.*
HOURS: *Call for appointment.*
ADMISSION: *Free.*
TELEPHONE: *(405) 429-3238.*

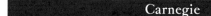

Carnegie

KIOWA TRIBAL MUSEUM

Like the Comanche, with whom they were allied for many years, the Kiowa migrated to the southern Plains from traditional homes in the northern Rockies. According to tribal tradition, they came from the country near the headwaters of the Missouri River, in Montana. The Kiowa language has puzzled experts for years, since it seems related to no other. The tribe reached the Arkansas River in Oklahoma in the late eighteenth century, made peace with the Comanche, and subsequently joined them in ongoing raids into Mexico for horses. The two tribes were regarded as the most skillful horsemen of the Plains. The Kiowa resisted the movement of white settlers through their lands, but after the Civil War, when the federal government was able to free up large numbers of troops against them, they were forced to accept assignment to a reservation in this area. The tribe has a long artistic tradition, and over the years many talented muralists have come from the Kiowa (*see* Kiowa Murals, Anadarko, Oklahoma). The Tribal Museum displays many of these works, depicting the history of the Kiowa people. Other exhibits show cultural items of the tribe and explain their significance.

LOCATION: *The Kiowa Museum is west of Carnegie on Oklahoma 9. Carnegie is about 25 miles west of Anadarko.*
HOURS: *Monday through Friday, 8–4:30.*
ADMISSION: *Free.*
TELEPHONE: *(405) 654-2300.*

Cheyenne

WASHITA BATTLEGROUND

G eneral George Custer first won the enmity of the Plains tribes for his actions here in 1868, at what has been called the Battle of the Washita. In a dawn assault on a Cheyenne encampment, members of Custer's Seventh Cavalry killed more than two hundred unsuspecting members of Black Kettle's band. The attack came almost four years to the day after the Sand Creek massacre (see Sand Creek Massacre, Chivington, Colorado), from which Black Kettle had managed to escape. This time, Black Kettle was killed in the first assault. The Cheyenne managed to put together some resistance this time as well, and the raid turned into an all-day battle as reinforcements arrived from nearby villages along the Washita River. Custer finally ordered the place burned and withdrew to his base. He also abandoned twenty men who had ridden off in pursuit of the retreating Indians and never returned. Their bodies were found several weeks later.

Major E. W. Wynkoop, the former commandant at Fort Lyons, Colorado, insisted the entire campaign against Black Kettle was a mistake because the Cheyenne leader had accepted the army's peace terms in 1864 and offered no resistance before Sand Creek. Wynkoop continued to be ignored, though, while Custer's reputation as an Indian fighter was enhanced. It would last another eight years, until tested far to the north, at the Little Big Horn (see Little Big Horn National Battlefield, Montana).

LOCATION: *The battlefield is just west of Cheyenne, on Oklahoma 47A, about 25 miles north of Interstate 40 from the Sayre exit. The Black Kettle Museum, which displays artifacts from the battle, is located in town, at the junction of U.S. 283 and Oklahoma 47.*

HOURS: *The museum is open Tuesday through Saturday, 9-5, and Sunday, 1-5. The battlefield site is open daily, dawn to dusk.*

ADMISSION: *Both are free.*

TELEPHONE: *Both can be reached at (405) 497-3929.*

▲ *Replicas of the Cherokee Council House and Court House at Tahlonteeskee, which was once the center of the Cherokee Nation West.*

Gore

CHEROKEE COURTHOUSE

The displacement of the Cherokee from their traditional homes in Georgia, North Carolina, and Tennessee took place in two distinct stages. It was the second episode, the infamous Trail of Tears, that resonates in history. But during the 1820s, a sizable contingent of the Cherokee accepted federal terms for movement west under less onerous conditions. They established themselves in the northeastern section of the Indian Territory and made their capital at Gore, on the Arkansas River. It was called Tahlonteeskee, after the founder of the western Cherokee. This group formed a separate nation for about a decade, until the main body of the tribe joined them and gained control of the government. The restored courthouse here was their administrative center until 1843, when the capital was moved to Tahlequah (*see* Cherokee National Capitol, Tahlequah, Oklahoma).

Sam Houston, a resident of the town in those years, had moved west from Tennessee after serving as governor of that state. He married a Cherokee woman and was formally adopted into the tribe by a special act of the council there. He then moved on to his rendezvous with destiny in Texas. Years later, however, his association with the Cherokee resulted in the deliverance of the Alabama tribe in Texas. When the Cherokee were threatened with expulsion from their lands, Houston came vigorously to their defense (*see* Alabama-Coushatta Museum, Livingston, Texas) and protected their grant, which they hold to this day. The courthouse contains exhibits on the building's role in the history of the western Cherokee.

LOCATION: *East of Gore on U.S. 64, just north of Exit 291 of Interstate 40.*
HOURS: *Tuesday through Saturday, 9–5; Sunday, 1–5, May through October. Open Wednesday through Sunday, rest of year.*
ADMISSION: *Free.*
TELEPHONE: *(918) 489-5663.*

Heavener

PETER CONSER HOME

The Oklahoma Territory was a wild and lawless place when the first arrivals of the Five Civilized Tribes reached it. It was a refuge for outlaws fleeing beyond the reach of the court in Fort Smith, Arkansas. The Cherokee refugees from the Southeast, having lived among whites for generations, often were victimized by raiders from the southern Plains tribes, on their immediate west. One of the best-known law enforcement groups formed to keep order in those days was the Choctaw Lighthorse. Peter Conser, one of the leaders of the Choctaw Nation and also a wealthy trader, headed up this unit, which was the law in southeastern Oklahoma. Conser's restored home is now a museum of his life and of that era among his people.

LOCATION: *Southwest of Heavener by way of U.S. 59 and an unnumbered county road. Heavener is on the northern edge of Ouachita National Forest.*
HOURS: *Tuesday through Friday, 9–5; weekends, 2–5.*
ADMISSION: *Free.*
TELEPHONE: *(918) 653-2493.*

Lawton

FORT SILL CEMETERY

F ort Sill, a military installation, is now the headquarters of the U.S. Field Artillery. The fort began as an outpost in the last campaign against the tribes of the southern Plains, and it remains haunted by the spirit of its most famous prisoner, the Apache chief Geronimo.

Fort Sill was established in 1869 by General Philip Sheridan, who named it after a West Point classmate and fellow officer in the Civil War. This was the primary base from which U.S. Army units tried to control the defiant holdout bands of the Comanche and Kiowa. In the early 1870s, they raided frequently into northern Texas and even into Mexico, led by resourceful chiefs like Quanah Parker and Santana. The tribes used the Plains like an ocean, moving quickly and silently, always just eluding capture.

In 1874, frustrated by the long and inconclusive struggle, the military began arresting recognized tribal leaders on sight and sending them to prison in Florida. They were, in effect, held there in return for the good behavior of their followers. The strategy was effective, and Parker rode in with his last band of Comanche the following year.

Afterward, the fort switched its military role, being more concerned with protecting the subdued Indians from the hordes of unscrupulous traders who moved into the area in anticipation of its being opened to white settlement. These were the last of the lands that had been guaranteed to the Indians, a promise that survived only until 1901, when the final Oklahoma land rush took place here.

Geronimo came to Fort Sill in 1894, after eight years of imprisonment in Florida and Alabama. He had surrendered in Arizona in 1886, probably the most famous Native American in the country at the time. His five-year campaign against the military in southeastern Arizona was trumpeted by the eastern press as the "last Indian war," and its lurid coverage turned the Chiricahua leader into a national figure. The number of combatants involved was actually quite small, and there was already too large a white presence in Arizona for Geronimo to have had any chance of success. For the last years of his life he toured the country as a celebrity guest at countless Wild West shows, while curious crowds shuddered. Geronimo lived out his years in what amounted to house arrest at Fort Sill. He was not confined and was free to wander the military base, but could not leave the post unless under special guard. He died here in 1909 and is buried in the Apache Cemetery, in the Old Post section of the base. His few remaining followers were then returned home to reservations in Arizona. Other native people who died in captivity are buried on Chiefs Knoll, in the Old Post Cemetery.

LOCATION: *Fort Sill is 5 miles north of Lawton by way of Interstate 44, the Key Gate exit. Follow posted directions to the Old Post area, the original fort built by Sheridan. The guardhouse here was a place of imprisonment for many Indian leaders, and it now contains displays relating to the history of the campaigns against the southern Plains tribes and Geronimo.*
HOURS: *The Old Post area is open daily, dawn to dusk. The guardhouse and other museums are open daily, 9–4:30.*
ADMISSION: *Free.*
TELEPHONE: *(405) 351-5123.*

Millerton

WHEELOCK MISSION CHURCH

Millerton was one of the first settlements of the Choctaw Nation upon their arrival in Oklahoma. A girl's academy was built here in 1832 and named for Eleazer Wheelock, the founder of Dartmouth University. That Ivy League institution in New Hampshire was opened as a school for Native Americans in 1769. But when enrollment remained low, it was converted into a general college. Wheelock's name, however, remained strongly associated with Indian causes in the Presbyterian Church. So the academy here was named for him, and so was the mission church, built in 1842. The mission still stands and is now the oldest religious structure in Oklahoma.

LOCATION: *Millerton is located just off U.S. 70, in the southeastern corner of the state.*
HOURS: *Phone in advance.*
ADMISSION: *Donation.*
TELEPHONE: *(405) 286-2321.*

Muskogee

ATALOA LODGE

Bacone College is famous for its School of Indian Arts. The Ataloa Lodge on its campus in Muskogee was designed to show off works produced and contributed by graduates, students, and benefactors. Among its collections of traditional and contemporary Native American art, the lodge houses one of the largest collections of Maria Martinez's San Indefonso pottery anywhere in the Southwest. An 88-piece Kachina doll collection was recently added; the hand-carved pueblo dolls are given to children to help them identify dancers during tribal ceremonials. Ataloa also houses a large collection of Native American baskets from all parts of the North American continent.

LOCATION: *North edge of Muscogee at the intersection of U.S. 62 and Oklahoma 16.*
HOURS: *Monday through Friday, 10–4.*
ADMISSION: *Free.*
TELEPHONE: *(918) 683-4581.*

FIVE CIVILIZED TRIBES MUSEUM

The location of Muskogee, on the Arkansas River near the border of the former Creek and Cherokee Nations, made it a logical base for adminis-tration of the Five Civilized Tribes. These five entities, which also included the Choctaw, Chickasaw, and Seminole Nations, had been transported here from the southeastern states by 1840 and guaranteed title to the Indian Territory forever. Many of the tribes held slaves and were deeply influenced by years of residence among white southerners. Once established in Oklahoma they pros-pered, although never forgetting the bitterness that accompanied their forced move on the Trail of Tears. Each tribe was given the status of a nation, but their sovereignty was, in reality, controlled by the U.S. Congress. Accordingly, the Union Indian Agency was established here in 1875. By that time, pressure for abolition of the Indian claims was growing irresistibly. Too many powerful interests supported the opening of the lands to white settlement.

The tribes had agreed among themselves to form an Indian-run confed-eration in 1871, but Congress refused to act on the plan. Instead, railroads were given rights-of-way across the Indian lands, and settlers began edging over the borders, staking out claims without any title to them in defiance of federal law. Lands unassigned to any of the tribes, but lying within the Indian territory, were thrown open to settlement in the great Land Rush of 1889, and the Cherokee Strip, on the Kansas border, was opened four years later.

With this sort of pressure growing all around them, the Five Civilized Tribes did what they could to maintain their independence. The concept of the All-Indian Fair was born in meetings at Muskogee's Union Agency in 1879 as a way of asserting tribal identity. But the Five Tribes were so assimilated into white culture by that time that the idea had no relevance to their lives. The All-Indian Fair concept was instead used by the Indian Bureau as the foundation for many of the Native American cultural observances, which continue to this day in the western states.

In 1893, the Dawes Commission was formed and located in Muskogee.

By that time, Oklahoma Territory had been formed on the western borders of the Five Tribes. The commission's charter was to negotiate for the rest of their lands. The leaders of the tribes flatly refused to negotiate, but the lands were surveyed anyhow and plans made to allot them individually, rather than on a national basis. When the Five Tribes realized what was happening, they called an assembly here in 1905 and drew up a constitution for a new state. It was to be formed out of the remaining Indian lands and called Sequoyah, for the great Cherokee leader. The measure was put to a popular vote and passed overwhelmingly, but Congress refused to approve it. Instead, Congress combined their lands with the Oklahoma Territory and formed a new state on that basis. The area entered the Union in 1907 as Oklahoma. Ironically, this is a Choctaw word meaning "red people," and it had been suggested as the name for the proposed Indian confederation.

Displays from all the Five Tribes, as well as historical exhibits relating to these dramatic events, are shown at this hillside museum, housed in the original Union Agency building.

LOCATION: *The museum is in the northwestern part of town, on Agency Hill in Honor Heights Park.*
HOURS: *Monday through Saturday, 10–5; Sunday, 1–5.*
ADMISSION: *$2.*
TELEPHONE: *(918) 683-1701.*

Okmulgee

CREEK COUNCIL HOUSE

The Creek occupied the central portion of the lands given to the Five Civilized Tribes, and because of that position, they played a key role in the attempt to form a confederation of the separate nations. A confederacy was a familiar system to them because it was how the tribe was organized in its former home in Alabama and Georgia. Most Creek sided with Great Britain during the War of 1812 and, consequently, were among the first to have their lands taken from them. Many fled south to join the Seminole, but most were among the first Native American arrivals in the Indian Territory. The Creek prospered for a time, but they suffered grave losses from pro-Union raiders during the Civil War and chose to relocate their capital to this relatively undamaged community in 1868. It was then given the name of the traditional capital in Georgia, Okmulgee.

This area was a hotbed of sentiment for Indian self-rule. At the old Creek Council House, leaders of the Five Tribes met to plan policy that pertained to all. When they started inviting representatives of all the tribes in Oklahoma, the federal government became alarmed. By 1875, there were twenty-nine tribes represented here at council sessions. Washington then refused to finance its meetings and informed its leaders that any legislation it passed would be subject to a congressional veto. That ended the dream of confederation.

The Council House that stands today was built in 1878 and served as the Creek capitol for the last twenty-eight years of nationhood. It was here that the final issues of self-rule versus land concessions to the federal government were debated, often painfully, as the realization dawned that Washington was going to get what it wanted anyhow. After statehood, the building served as a courthouse until 1916. It is now a museum of the Creek Nation, containing priceless early documents of the tribe as well as other cultural and historical items and displays relating to the events that occurred in this building.

LOCATION: *The Council House sits in a square near the center of Okmulgee, at 112 West 6th Street.*
HOURS: *Tuesday through Saturday, 9–5.*
ADMISSION: *Free.*
TELEPHONE: *(918) 756-2324.*

Pawhuska

OSAGE MUSEUM

Pawhuska is one of the most picturesque old towns in Oklahoma, with eighty-nine buildings on the National Register of Historic Sites. It is the seat of Osage County, whose boundaries are coterminous with those of the Osage Nation. The territory was purchased from the Cherokee, the neighbors on the east, when the Osage moved here from Kansas after the Civil War, having been driven from earlier homes in Missouri and Arkansas by white settlement. The factional divisions caused by that war, in which members of the Osage fought on both sides, gradually healed and the tribe did well in its new home. After 1916, however, it did exceptionally well. Osage lands were among the first on which oil was discovered in Oklahoma. The leases from those wells turned the tribe into the wealthiest in the country at the time. On of the first projects the Tribal Council approved was the foundation of the Osage Museum to preserve the language and traditions of the people. It was the first museum of its kind in the country. Its current home was built in 1938 and exhibits a fine collection of documents, artifacts, and exhibits on the history of the tribe, which figured prominently in American history. Because the character of Pawhuska is so thoroughly entwined with that of the Osage, this is a great place for strolling and soaking up the local color. Pick up a walking map at the Chamber of Commerce, at 114 West Main.

LOCATION: *The museum is on Grandview Street, on a hill overlooking the business district. Pawhuska itself is about 50 miles northwest of Tulsa by way of Oklahoma 11.*
HOURS: *Monday through Friday, 8–4:30.*
ADMISSION: *Free.*
TELEPHONE: *(918) 287-2495.*

Sallisaw

HOME OF SEQUOYAH

B orn George Gist, Sequoyah was the inventor of the Cherokee written language, and one of the tribe's first arrivals in Oklahoma. He moved west in 1818, partially to gain the solitude he required to get on with the obsessive task he had set for himself. Born in Tennessee, Sequoyah was the son of a British father and Cherokee mother. He was convinced that the well-being of his people depended on mastery of an alphabet. Through trial and error, he reduced the tribal alphabet to eighty-five. Some pieces were borrowed from English; others he made up. But they were so logically devised and so simple that he claimed anyone could master the alphabet in three days.

Sequoyah returned East in 1821 to demonstrate the ease with which his invention could be used. Within a few years, the Cherokee had become the first fully literate Native American people, with their own newspaper and a means of communication between the eastern and western branches of the tribe. That was a critical factor in easing the reunification process when the eastern remnant was forced onto the Trail of Tears in 1838. By that time, the Cherokee were already operating the first schools in Oklahoma, and shortly thereafter, in 1843, a newspaper was reestablished there as well.

Sequoyah built his log home upon his return to the West in 1829, when he already was acknowledged as a hero of the Cherokee Nation. It is maintained as a shrine to him and contains personal artifacts as well as exhibits on the invention of his alphabet.

LOCATION: *The home is 11 miles northeast of town by way of U.S. 59 and Oklahoma 101.*
HOURS: *Tuesday through Friday, 9–5; weekends, 2–5.*
ADMISSION: *Free.*
TELEPHONE: *(918) 775-2413.*

Spiro

SPIRO MOUNDS ARCHEOLOGICAL PARK

This is one of the great archeological detective stories in North America. The people who lived at Spiro seemed to belong to the Temple Mound culture of the lower Mississippi Valley. Many of the items found here resemble statues and tools recovered at Moundville, Alabama, and Etowah, Georgia, and all of them show influences from Mexican cultures. Until their discovery, there had been no evidence of prehistoric mounds this far west, however, and when a local farmer uncovered them in his fields, there was no immediate safeguard. With a group of friends, he dynamited the largest of the nine mounds and carted off the artifacts to sell. Only in 1935 did scientists from the University of Oklahoma obtain title to the site and start to salvage what was left.

While the archaeologists worked at Spiro, a group of tireless amateurs set out to trace, from sales receipts, the people who had purchased the items taken from the mounds. They spent sixteen years tracking them down and studying them. In the end, it was through their efforts that the picture of the Spiro community became clear. It was much older than first thought. It is now agreed that Spiro reached its peak between A.D. 800 and 1100 and that its influence spread eastward, rather than the other way around. That occasioned a significant revision in the way historians view the development of the Temple Mound culture. There is an interpretive center on the site and a reproduction of a dwelling from the Spiro community.

LOCATION: *The mounds are about 7 miles northeast of town by way of Oklahoma 9 and a county road. From Interstate 40, take the southbound U.S. 59 exit at Sallisaw and then go east on Oklahoma 9.*
HOURS: *Tuesday through Saturday, 9–5; Sunday, 11–5.*
ADMISSION: *Free.*
TELEPHONE: *(918) 962-2062.*

▲ *At Tsa-La-Gi, the Ho-Chee-Nee Trail of Tears Memorial Prayer Chapel offers visitors a place for private meditation and spiritual renewal; its seven roof beams represent the seven clans of the Ancient Cherokee Nation.*

Tahlequah

CHEROKEE HERITAGE CENTER

The Cherokee Heritage Center is an outstanding cultural facility with both indoor and outdoor exhibits relating to Cherokee history. It encompasses the Tsa-La-Gi outdoor theatre, a reconstructed Ancient Village at Tsa-La-Gi, Adams Corner Rural Village, the Ho-Chee-Nee Trail of Tears Memorial Prayer Chapel, and the Cherokee National Museum and Archives.

The Ancient Village at Tsa-La-Gi recreates the lifestyle of the Cherokees during the 16th century, prior to European contact. During the summer months, guided tours are available in the village, where thirty inhabitants create an authentic feel. Visitors hear narratives about Cherokee history and customs, and witness villagers going about their daily rituals, such as preparing food; making arrowheads and weapons; playing stickball; working with clay pottery and beads; shaping baskets; and sometimes performing stomp dances. During the summer months, "Trail of Tears," a historic pageant staged by a cast of professional actors, is presented nightly in the Tsa-La-Gi outdoor

▲ *The Cherokee National Museum develops special educational programs, including "Sequoyah Speaks," a dramatic presentation created to familiarize youngsters with Sequoyah's contributions to the nation's history.*

amphitheater; the drama begins with the removal of the Cherokees from their ancestral homes in 1838, and continues through their struggle to reach Indian territory.

Adams Corner, representative of a rural community during 1875–1890, showcases a typical crossroads community within the Cherokee Nation. It includes a one-room school, log cabin, smokehouse, general store, church, and other typical constructions. During the summer months, staff wearing period costumes carry on the business activities of the village for visitors to observe.

The Cherokee National Museum and Archives preserves and exhibits historic documents and items relating to the entire sweep of tribal experience. The museum's collections include approximately 4,000 artifacts related to Cherokee history and culture, as well as valuable art objects. The archives—a 24,000 square foot building housing the official archives of the Cherokee Nation—contains more than 4,000 volumes related to Cherokee history and culture, including special collections of out-of-print Bibles, books in the Cherokee language, and photographs related to Indian Territory. Approximately 55 hours of oral history tapes are also preserved here. Special events include the annual Trail of Tears Art Show. The center sponsors educational programs, including the popular "Sequoyah Speaks," a dramatic presentation that familiarizes youngsters with Sequoyah's contributions to Cherokee history.

LOCATION: *The center is south of Tahlequah on U.S. 62, then east on Willis Road.* HOURS: *Tsa-La-Gi is open Monday through Saturday, 10–5, and Sunday, 1–5, early May to late August. Adams Corner and the National Museum are open Monday through Saturday, 10–8, and Sunday, 1–5, mid-June to late August. Closed Monday and closes at 5 P.M. on other days, rest of year. "Trail of Tears" is performed Tuesday through Saturday, at 8:30, early June to late August.* ADMISSION: *Tsa-La-Gi Village: Adults $4, Children $2. Museum and Adams Corner, $2.75. Trail of Tears package tickets including both other attractions: Adults $13, Children $6; individual tickets: Adults $9, Children $4.50.* TELEPHONE: *(918) 456-6007.*

CHEROKEE NATIONAL CAPITOL

At the end of the Trail of Tears, leaders of the eastern and western Cherokee came together at the tiny settlement of Tahlequah, and on July 12, 1839, named it the capital of the newly unified nation. It remains the center of the Cherokee Nation of Oklahoma and one of the most historic Native American communities in the country. The exterior walls of the Supreme Court Building, erected in 1844, and later the home of the first newspaper in Oklahoma, the *Cherokee Advocate*, still stand in the central square. The national prison dates from the same year. Nearby is the Cherokee National Capitol, built in 1867 as the tribe repaired the damage from heavy fighting around the town in the Civil War. The first commercial telephone line in Oklahoma was also set up in Tahlequah in 1885, and there is a monument to that in the court house square, too. A walking tour guide to the historic sites in this charming old town can be picked up in the capitol, which still houses the administrative offices of the Cherokee.

LOCATION: *The capitol adjoins Court House Square, at 101 South Muskogee.* HOURS: *Monday through Friday, 8–5; Saturday, 9–4, Memorial Day through Labor Day; closed weekends, rest of year.* ADMISSION: *Free.* TELEPHONE: *(918) 456-3742.*

MURRELL HOUSE

G eorge Murrell prospered as a merchant after moving west from Georgia with the John Ross branch of the Cherokees on the Trail of Tears. For the stately home he built in 1845, the furnishings were imported by steamboat up the Mississippi and Arkansas rivers from New Orleans. The home was regarded as the showplace of the Cherokee Nation. With the surrounding country devastated during the Civil War, and his close friend Ross an ardent Union supporter, it was something of a miracle that Murrell's home escaped destruction. But it passed through the conflict undamaged. After Murrell's death, it went through a succession of owners, was made into a school, and was finally used as a refuge for tenant farmers. Restoration has turned it into the jewel it was when the Murrells occupied it, and much of the interior is original.

LOCATION: *The Murrell House is south of Tahlequah on Oklahoma 82, then east on Murrell Road.*
HOURS: *Tuesday to Saturday, 9–5; Sunday, 1–5.*
ADMISSION: *Free.*
TELEPHONE: *(918) 456-2751.*

Tishomingo

CHICKASAW COUNCIL HOUSE

T ishomingo was the capital of the Chickasaw Nation through its entire Oklahoma existence (*see* Chickasaw Center, Ada, Oklahoma). When the main body of this people arrived in the Indian Territory from Mississippi and Tennessee, they lived on the western portion of the Choctaw lands. They separated to form their own government in 1855 and built this council house, a log structure, as the seat of government. It was replaced by a brick capitol, which burned. But the first log building survived and now serves as a museum of Chickasaw history, relating the experiences of the people on their westward migration. Adjacent to the council house is the restored Chickasaw Bank, built in 1902.

LOCATION: *The Council House is on Court House Square. Tishomingo is about 30 miles east of Interstate 35, at the Ardmore exit, by way of Oklahoma Highways, 199, 1, and 78.*
HOURS: *Tuesday through Friday, 9–5; weekends, 2–5.*
ADMISSION: *Free.*
TELEPHONE: *(405) 371-3351.*

Tonkawa

TONKAWA TRIBAL MUSEUM

The Tonkawa Museum is a tribute to a small tribe that seemed on the verge of extermination several times in their history. They were a nomadic people, speaking a language related to no others and called by a name that means "they all stay together." They were driven from their Texas homes when the state voted to expel all native people, and became wanderers through the Indian Territory, with no fixed place of residence. While camped near Anadarko in 1862, they were attacked by tribes of that region who suspected that the Tonkawa were cannibals.

Finally, tiny slivers were carved from the westernmost Cherokee lands after the Civil War and allotted to several small tribes, among them the Tonkawa. In the early 1940s, the tribal census listed only eighteen persons surviving, but since then the Tonkawa have tried to reaffirm an identity. Among the measures taken to accomplish that was this museum, which shows off the artifacts of a people returning from the edge of oblivion. Tonkawa is also the place where Chief Joseph and several of his Nez Perce followers were imprisoned following their surrender in 1879.

LOCATION: *The museum is east of town on Oklahoma 156, then south on Allen Drive. Tonkawa lies just east of Interstate 35, at the U.S. 60 exit.*
HOURS: *Monday through Friday, 8:30–4:30.*
ADMISSION: *Free.*
TELEPHONE: *(405) 628-5301.*

CHOCTAW NATIONAL MUSEUM

W hen the Choctaw gave up title to their Mississippi lands through the 1830 Treaty of Dancing Rabbit Creek, one of the provisions made was that a council house would be built for them near the center of their new lands. The place selected was called Tuskahoma, the second half of the word coming from the same Choctaw root that gave name to the entire state, meaning "red." This is beautiful, hilly country, on the edge of the Kiamichi Mountains, and a natural mound is situated nearby. That was important to the Choctaw because in their former home the capital was situated near Nanih Waiya (*see* Preston, Mississippi), a mound from which the tribe had sprung, according to tradition. The Oklahoma mound was given the same name, and the new council house was built in 1838, starting the new Choctaw Nation on a solid foundation. The original council house was replaced by a brick structure in 1883, and that served as the seat of government until the Indian nations were absorbed by the rest of the Oklahoma Territory in 1906. On the centennial of the first council house, in 1938, the structure was dedicated as the Choctaw National Museum, the historical repository of the people. Nearby is the old burying ground, with graves of many prominent leaders of the Choctaw Nation.

The physical structure of the council building is impressive, and reflects the old Choctaw governmental structure: the large rooms with 18 foot-ceilings housed the Senate, the House of Representatives, and the Supreme Court. A room above a walk-in vault provided an observation point for armed guards; the attic, which included a cistern, was sometimes used as a jail. Collections include spoons made of bone, vintage clothing, old documents, Choctaw pottery, and items moved over the Trail of Tears.

LOCATION: *The museum is north of U.S. 271 on a marked county road. Tuskahoma is about 30 miles east of the Indian Nation Turnpike by way of Oklahoma 43 and U.S. 271.*
HOURS: *Monday through Friday, 8–4:30.*
ADMISSION: *Free.*
TELEPHONE: *(918) 569-4465.*

Wewoka

SEMINOLE NATION MUSEUM

The Seminole were the last of the Five Civilized Tribes to be transported west. Their arrival caused a great deal of friction with their closest neighbors and former allies, the Creek, over the issue of black slaves. The two people nearly went to war over the issue. A good portion of the Seminole were Native American and black refugees from British and American rule. They had escaped south into Spanish-held Florida for generations. Many southern Creeks joined this movement after siding with Britain in the War of 1812 in order to flee revenge-minded Americans. Escaped slaves had found a refuge among the Seminole for generations, ever since the Spanish had encouraged their coming as a way of disrupting the southern British colonies. They fought together at many engagements of the Seminole Wars, and when the main body of the tribe was expelled to the west in 1845, blacks made the trip with them. The relationship was a complicated one, but the blacks were able to hold title to land and were regarded as employees rather than involuntary servants.

The Creek, onto whose lands the Seminole moved, were scandalized by this arrangement. This tribe was deeply influenced by the slave society it had lived among in Alabama and Georgia and regarded the presence of free blacks on its lands as a threat to its own slaveholders. In 1849, a party of Creek and white sympathizers marched on the Seminole lands, demanding that they turn over blacks from Florida as escaped slaves. Federal troops from Fort Smith had to intervene. As a result of these tensions, the Seminole were given their own lands in 1856 and joined the other Five Tribes as a separate nation. Wewoka was made the capital, but because of an earlier surveying error, the boundary line with the Creek ran right through the middle of town. Many of the Seminole Nation landmarks are on South Wewoka Avenue and so the museum is dedicated to its history. The museum also contains exhibits about the oil boom of the 1920s, which turned these lands into some of the richest in Oklahoma.

LOCATION: *The Seminole Museum is at 524 South Wewoka Avenue. The town is 17 miles south of Interstate 40 at the southbound Oklahoma 56 exit.*
HOURS: *Tuesday through Sunday, 1–5.*
ADMISSION: *Free.*
TELEPHONE: *(405) 257-5580.*

Yale

JIM THORPE HOME

J im Thorpe, the great Sauk and Fox athlete (*see* Jim Thorpe Memorial, Jim
Thorpe, Pennsylvania) was born near the town of Prague, about fifty miles
south of here, on tribal lands. It was from there that he left for athletic glory at
Haskell Institute of Kansas and then Carlisle Indian School. He returned to
Oklahoma in 1937 and lived near this community for several years. After his
death in 1953, original plans called for a permanent memorial to be erected to
him in this area. But when fund-raising hit a snag, his widow had the body
removed to Pennsylvania after two towns voted to combine and rename the
new town in his honor. His home here exhibits many personal items.

LOCATION: *The house is at 706 East Boston. Yale is 20 miles east of Stillwater on Oklahoma 51.*
HOURS: *Tuesday through Friday, 9–5; weekends, 2–5.*
ADMISSION: *Free.*
TELEPHONE: *(918) 387-2815.*

TEXAS

ALABAMA-COUSHATTA MUSEUM

The history of the Alabama and the Coushatta, two closely related tribes that were originally members of the Creek Confederacy, is an unfortunate illustration of white settlers at their most rapacious. The tribes were found by the first Spanish explorer of the region, Hernando De Soto, living in central Mississippi in 1541. Eventually the tribes became so well established along the southern Alabama River that the tribal name was applied to both the river and the future state. By the time statehood arrived, however, the Alabama had been pushed out of their traditional homes. Slowly moving westward under the pressure of the expanding white frontier, they entered Texas in 1807 and settled along the Neches River in the Big Thicket country.

Early Texans were earnestly devoted to driving native people completely out of their republic. The Caddo, the most populous native people in the area at the time of white settlement, were expelled to Oklahoma. But the Texans made an exception for the Alabama, who fought with the colonists during the War for Independence against Mexico, and set aside land for them in 1840. The designated land was claimed by whites almost immediately and the Indians driven out. Texas hero Sam Houston came to their defense, and in 1854 the claims were reinstated. The property was bought back from the whites who had illegally seized it, and the Alabama resettled on it, along with the Coushatta.

After the Civil War, however, the state agent who looked after their welfare was withdrawn and the tribes were at the mercy of local whites, who destroyed their crops and stole their stock. Assisted by a handful of sympathetic whites, the Alabama and Coushatta managed to persevere, however, and in 1918 the federal government finally intervened. Their land claims were expanded and funds allotted for schools and farming instruction.

Given this respite, the tribes have prospered and in recent years have taken advantage of their unique position as the only Native American culture in this heavily populated area. They have set up a reconstructed traditional village and a museum at which tribal history and crafts are displayed. In addition, a train ride through the neighboring portion of the Big Thicket has been set up. Tribal dances are held on weekends, and a restaurant on the property serves traditional dishes.

LOCATION: *The museum and reservation are about 15 miles east of Livingston on U.S. 190.*
HOURS: *Monday through Saturday, 10–6, and Sunday, 12:30–6, June through August. Closed Monday and Tuesday, March through May. Open Friday through Sunday only, September through November.*
ADMISSION: *$8.*
TELEPHONE: *(409) 563-4391.*

Ysleta

TIGUA MUSEUM AND RESERVATION

N ot all of the New Mexico pueblo communities rose up against the Spanish during the Rebellion of 1680, which drove Europeans out of the area for twelve years. A few Native American groups stayed loyal to Spain and accompanied the soldiers on their retreat to the south. One such group moved to the area just east of present day El Paso and became virtually a Lost Pueblo (scattered village). The community and mission they founded here in 1682 is regarded as the oldest continuously inhabited place in Texas, strictly because the Rio Grande shifted its course a few years later. Otherwise, Ysleta would still be a part of Mexico. The people here became known as the Tigua, a form of Tiwa, the language group to which they belonged. This is the language spoken today in several New Mexico pueblos, including Taos.

The mission of Nuestra Señora del Carmen, built in 1682, stands at the center of Ysleta. Next to it is the pueblo itself, part of which incorporates material used in the original structure. The Tigua were forgotten by the other Pueblo communities for centuries, and even now there is a reluctance to include them among the related New Mexico settlements. But the Tigua have developed a strong cultural identity of their own. They run a museum, crafts center, and restaurant, at which visitors can observe traditional bread ovens in operation. Dances are held on the plaza throughout the year.

LOCATION: *Ysleta is about 14 miles east of El Paso, by way of Interstate 10, southbound Zaragosa Road (Exit 32) and then east on Alameda. The pueblo is located on Old Pueblo Road.*
HOURS: *Daily, 9–6. Dances are held Wednesday through Sunday, June through August; weekends only, rest of year.*
ADMISSION: *$2.50 during dances; free at other times.*
TELEPHONE: *(915) 859-3916.*

SOUTHWEST AND GREAT BASIN

Arizona
Colorado
Idaho
Nevada
New Mexico
Utah

SOUTHWEST AND GREAT BASIN

ARIZONA

1 Yavapai-Apache Visitor Center, *Camp Verde*
2 Cliff Dwellings, *Canyon de Chelly National Monument*
3 Hohokam Ruins, *Casa Grande Ruins National Monument*
4 Amerind Foundation, *Dragoon*
5 Museum of Northern Arizona, *Flagstaff*
6 Apache Culture Center Museum, *Fort Apache*
7 Hubbell Trading Post, *Ganado*
8 Besh-ba-Gowah Ruins, *Globe*
9 Tusayan Museum, *Grand Canyon National Park*
10 Walpi, *Keams Canyon*
11 Cliff Dwelling, *Montezuma Castle National Monument*
12 Navajo Reservation, *Monument Valley Tribal Park*
13 Anasazi Cliff Dwellings, *Navajo National Monument*
14 Old Oraibi, *Oraibi*
15 Colorado River Tribes Museum, *Parker*
16 Cochise Stronghold, *Pearce*
17 Heard Museum, *Phoenix*
18 Pueblo Grande Museum, *Phoenix*
19 Gila Basin Indian Center, *Sacaton*
20 Hopi Cultural Center, *Second Mesa*
21 Havasupai Reservation, *Supai*
22 Cliff Dwellings, *Tonto National Monument*
23 Arizona State Museum, *Tucson*
24 Mission San Xavier del Bac, *Tucson*
25 Cliff Dwellings, *Tuzigoot National Monument*
26 Cliff Dwellings, *Walnut Canyon National Monument*
27 Navajo Tribal Headquarters and Museum, *Window Rock*
28 Pueblo Community, *Wupatki National Monument*

COLORADO

29 Archeological Area, *Chimney Rock*
30 Sand Creek Massacre, *Chivington*
31 University of Colorado Center, *Cortez*
32 Anasazi Heritage Center, *Dolores*
33 Sky Ute Center, *Ignacio*
34 Bent's Old Fort, *La Junta*
35 Cliff Palace, Other Dwellings, and Chapin Mesa Museum, *Mesa Verde National Park*
36 Ute Indian Museum, *Montrose*
37 Lowry Ruins, *Pleasant View*

IDAHO

39 Fort Hall Reservation, *Fort Hall*
40 Old Mission State Park, *Kellogg*
41 Appaloosa Museum, *Moscow*
42 Heart of the Monster, *Nez Perce National Historical Park*
43 Lapwai Tribal Headquarters, *Nez Perce National Historical Park*
44 Lapwai Mission, *Nez Perce National Historical Park*
45 Weippe Prairie, *Nez Perce National Historical Park*

NEVADA

46 Hickison Summit Petroglyphs, *Austin*
47 Stewart Indian Museum, *Carson City*
48 Lost City Museum, *Overton*
49 Valley of Fire State Park, *Overton*
50 Paiute Reservation, *Pyramid Lake*

NEW MEXICO

51 Acoma Pueblo, *Acoma*
52 Indian Pueblo Cultural Center, *Albuquerque*
53 Maxwell Museum of Anthropology, *Albuquerqu*
54 Aztec Ruins National Monument, *Aztec*
55 Coronado State Monument, *Bernalillo*
56 Pueblo Bonito, *Chaco Culture National Historical Park*
57 Cochiti Pueblo, *Cochiti*
58 Jicarilla Apache Center, *Dulce*
59 Red Rock State Park, *Gallup*
60 Navajo Code Talkers Exhibit, *Gallup*
61 Mogollon Ruins, *Gila Cliff Dwellings National Monument*
62 Laguna Pueblo, *Laguna*
63 Bandelier National Monument, *Los Alamos*
64 Apache Cultural Center, *Mescalero*
65 Pecos National Monument, *Pecos*
66 Picuris Pueblo, *Picuris*
67 Quarai, Abo, and Gran Quivira, *Salinas Pueblos National Monument*
68 San Ildefonso Pueblo, *San Ildefonso*
69 Santa Clara Pueblo, *Santa Clara*
70 Museum of Indian Arts and Culture, *Santa Fe*

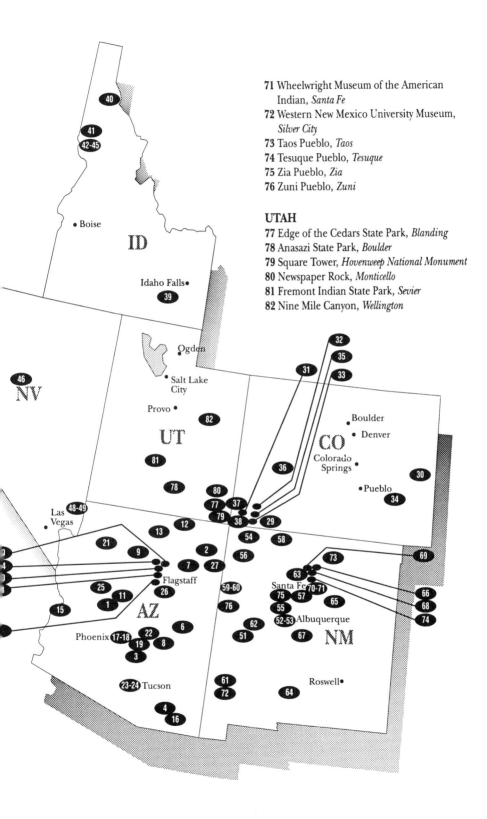

71 Wheelwright Museum of the American Indian, *Santa Fe*
72 Western New Mexico University Museum, *Silver City*
73 Taos Pueblo, *Taos*
74 Tesuque Pueblo, *Tesuque*
75 Zia Pueblo, *Zia*
76 Zuni Pueblo, *Zuni*

UTAH
77 Edge of the Cedars State Park, *Blanding*
78 Anasazi State Park, *Boulder*
79 Square Tower, *Hovenweep National Monument*
80 Newspaper Rock, *Monticello*
81 Fremont Indian State Park, *Sevier*
82 Nine Mile Canyon, *Wellington*

ARIZONA

YAVAPAI-APACHE VISITOR CENTER

The Yavapai are closely related to the tribes of the Grand Canyon area and Colorado River Valley. They spoke a similar language and lived in loosely associated bands in which the head man relied on his powers of persuasion rather than demanding submission to lead his group. The southeastern branch of the Yavapai, however, came into close contact with the westernmost bands of Apache, and that altered the way they lived. Over time, they became known as Mojave Apache, occupying a cultural niche between these two groups.

The Yavapai adopted many Apache rituals and taboos, such as masked dances, and matrilineal clans in which a man was forbidden to speak to or even look at his mother-in-law. The Yavapai became adept warriors and allied themselves with the Apache in raids and battle. They were placed on the San Carlos reservation with the Apache in 1875, but over the years most of the Yavapai tribe drifted back to the northwest and their ancestral lands. Most of these Yavapai settled outside Prescott; a smaller body moved near the site of Camp Verde, which had opened in 1868 to protect white settlers. In 1905 a tuberculosis epidemic decimated the tribe. By the 1930s, only fifty surviving Yavapai were known. Most of the remaining members in the Camp Verde area are so mixed with Apache that the hyphenated form of the two tribal names, Yavapai-Apache, has come into use to identify them.

The visitor center contains information on the history and culture of the tribe. Other Native American attractions in this area are also spotlighted.

LOCATION: *The Yavapai-Apache Center is at the Arizona 279 exit of Interstate 17, about 50 miles south of Flagstaff.*
HOURS: *Daily, 8-5.*
ADMISSION: *Free.*
TELEPHONE: *(602) 567-5276.*

CLIFF DWELLINGS

The Basket Makers came to Canyon de Chelly first, as long ago as 350 A.D. They built their homes within sunken circles carved out of the canyon floor. They left their mummified dead in caves. Then they passed on, to be replaced by the Pueblo Builders.

These people constructed towering apartment-like structures atop the sheer red cliffs. Some of them loom above the canyon like European castles. Some of them are tucked into almost inaccessible corners where the sun penetrates only four hours a day and an eerie stillness prevails in the half-light. These people, too, passed on and were replaced by the Hopi.

The Hopi moved into the abandoned pueblos of their ancestors in the fourteenth century and stayed for about three hundred years. They eventually left the area to join the main body of their people in new communities to the west.

Finally, the Navajo arrived, making their way slowly down from the northwest. Canyon de Chelly is in the middle of their reservation and is regarded with reverence as a central part of the tribe's history. It was a refuge for centuries, a place for people to seek shelter when danger threatened. It was regarded as impenetrable, and enemies of the Navajo did not dare pursue them into its recesses for fear of ambush.

In the early 1860s, however, when Arizona passed under American control, it became federal policy to move the Navajo to new reservation lands in New Mexico. The start of the Civil War made Washington edgy about its relations with all the tribes in the Southwest, since this area was known to be a target of a Confederate invasion from Texas. So Kit Carson was dispatched to direct the roundup of the Navajo and move them east to where they could be more easily supervised. This forced march of 1864 was a horrendous episode, matching the tragedy of the Cherokee Trail of Tears of the 1830s. Carson burned the Navajo crops, deliberately using starvation as a weapon to force acceptance of the move. His troops then sealed off the entrance to Canyon de Chelly and systematically routed out those who had fled there in an attempt to escape transportment. More than one-quarter of the eight thousand Navajo sent on the brutal march either died on the way or in the months immediately following.

Once at Bosque Redondo, outside of Fort Sumner, New Mexico, the Navajo could not adapt to the new climate and land. They were preyed upon by Kiowa and Comanche raiders. Finally, in 1868, they refused to plant any crops and used Carson's own starvation measure as a tactic against the government. With the Civil War over, the federal government decided it had made a mistake, and permitted the Navajo to return home to the newly established reservation to rejoin the few members of the tribe who had escaped the roundup.

The canyon is remarkable for its almost unbroken history of habitation, its spectacular ruins, and the sheer majesty of the setting. Its floor has been used as grazing land for centuries and can be entered by outsiders only when accompanied by a Navajo guide. There are drives along the canyon rim, however, that lead to the major overlooks and the White House ruin, one of the largest and best preserved in the canyon. Other places may only be visited with a National Park ranger or a Navajo guide.

LOCATION: *Canyon de Chelly is in northeastern Arizona, off U.S. 191 near the town of Chinle, on the Navajo Reservation. Guide service can be arranged at the Thunderbird Lodge in Chinle.*
HOURS: *Daily, 8–5. (In summer months, the reservation observes Daylight Savings Time and is one hour ahead of the rest of the state.)*
ADMISSION: *Free.*
TELEPHONE: *(602) 674-5436.*

Casa Grande Ruins National Monument

HOHOKAM RUINS

W hen Father Eusebio Kino arrived in Arizona in 1694, he was taken to see the ruins of a four-story building towering like a prehistoric skyscraper above the desert floor. When he asked the Pima who took him there about the builders of this vast structure, he was told it was the work of the Hohokam, "those who have gone." According to contemporary dating techniques, they had gone about 250 years before Father Kino arrived. While there is reason to suspect the Pima are descendants of this ancient people, much as the Hopi are descended from the pueblo-building Anasazi of the north, no hard evidence proves the linkage. Kino stayed long enough to give the place its name, "big house" in Spanish, and moved on, leaving the ruins virtually forgotten by Europeans until the coming of the colonists.

The Hohokam were the first to figure out how to make the hot, arid deserts of southern Arizona habitable. They grew beans, corn, and squash, and raised cotton. The outlines of their irrigation systems can still be seen at Casa Grande and other places across Arizona's now blooming deserts. However, the balance of nature is extremely tenuous here, and the fragile soil turned alkaline after years of uninterrupted cultivation.

Casa Grande was built in about 1350, at a time of large-scale migrations of other people into this area. There is some evidence that the top story of the building was a watchtower, although there is no evidence of battle in the area. Remains of a village clustered around the walls of this imposing building have also been uncovered. It is the only one of its type found in the southern part of the state. The ruins are now shielded from further damage by a protective roof, and a museum on the site explains the significance of Casa Grande and the Hohokam role in Arizona history.

LOCATION: *Casa Grande Ruins is on Arizona 87 just north of the town of Coolidge, about 55 miles southeast of Phoenix by way of Interstate 10 and Arizona 387.*
HOURS: *Daily, 7–6.*
ADMISSION: *$1.*
TELEPHONE: *(602) 723-3172.*

Dragoon

AMERIND FOUNDATION

William Fulton ventured to Texas Canyon, near Dragoon, in the 1930s, attracted by the wealth of relatively undisturbed native ruins in the area. An anthropologist by training, Fulton was convinced that a fuller understanding of contemporary Indian culture could be obtained only by broadening our comprehension of the culture of their ancestors. He had roamed Arizona gathering artifacts, finally settling here in 1937 and opening the Amerind Foundation for research on what he had found. The foundation was expanded in 1959 and now includes material from several North American Indian cultures, although its principal focus remains the Southwest. Exhibits include examples of Plains beadwork and costumes, ritual masks, shields and weapons, children's toys and clothing, nineteenth-century Navajo weavings, and Cree snowshoe-making tools. There is also a section of artwork by white portraitists who had a chance to observe and record Native American life before it was overwhelmed by white culture.

LOCATION: *The Amerind Foundation is off Interstate 10 at the Dragoon exit (318), about 60 miles east of Tucson, in Texas Canyon.*
HOURS: *Daily, 10–4, September through May. Call in advance for summer hours.*
ADMISSION: *$3.*
TELEPHONE: *(602) 586-3666.*

▲ *The Amerind Foundation is headquartered on what was originally William Shirley Fulton's home, the FF Ranch.*

Flagstaff

MUSEUM OF NORTHERN ARIZONA

Founded in 1926 by the son of a Philadelphia banker who was fascinated by the culture of Arizona's native peoples, the Museum of Northern Arizona is a tribute to the energy and purpose of Harold Colton. He was the first white man to visit many of the most significant prehistoric sites in the state. His interest also extended to the culture of the contemporary inhabitants of the area. During his thirty-two-year tenure as director of this museum, he turned it into a showcase for the work of the Navajo and Hopi people. The annual Craftsman Exhibitions of these two tribes are numbered among the most significant shows of their kind in the Southwest. The Hopi show is held on the first weekend of July, followed by the Navajo exhibition during the final week and last two weekends of the month.

LOCATION: *The museum is north of central Flagstaff on U.S. 180, Fort Valley Road.*
HOURS: *Daily, 9–5.*
ADMISSION: *$3.*
TELEPHONE: *(602) 774-5211.*

Fort Apache

APACHE CULTURE CENTER MUSEUM

The name Fort Apache has become an echo of all the Indian stereotypes that pervade American popular culture. So instantly identifiable is it as the symbol of a white outpost surrounded by hostile country that, more than a century after the actual fort was built, the name was used to describe a beleaguered New York City police precinct station in the Bronx. The name was all that was needed to get the situation across.

Of all the native people who warred with the United States at one time or another, it is the Apache who most symbolized the supposed cruelty and treachery of the Indians. There are several reasons for that. The situation in Arizona was, in fact, cruel and treacherous on both sides. What the Apache did was provoked by the savage treatment they had received at white hands.

The battles with the Apache were also among the last large-scale Indian operations in the country and came at a time when newspapers were already a strong force in shaping opinion in the East. Large newspapers sent correspondents to cover the campaigns, and they embellished freely on what they saw. Big cities that had not seen a native inhabitant for more than a century were vicariously thrilled by the struggle against Geronimo, Nana, and other Apache leaders. Their names became as well known as the heroes of pulp fiction. The military campaigns of the 1880s influenced an entire generation of white Americans who grew up to write books and make movies that perpetuated the images for another one hundred years.

Another reason the vivid image of the Apache has survived for so long is that Apaches were very good at making war. Several of their leaders, in command of bands that rarely were larger than a few dozen men, were able to elude and defeat all the troops thrown against them. One army officer describing one such campaign wrote, "Thirty-five men and eight half-grown boys, encumbered with the care and sustenance of 101 women and children, with no base of supplies and no means of waging war or obtaining food or transportation other than what they could take from their enemies, maintained themselves for 18 months against 5,000 troops, 500 Indian auxiliaries and an unknown number of civilians."

Fort Apache was established in 1870 to supervise the newly created White Mountain Reservation. This was at a critical time of racial tension in Arizona. There were still only a few thousand whites in the territory. But the cruelty with which they treated the Apache they found there, and the ferocity with which the Apache responded, had turned it into a vast killing ground. White parties almost routinely raided any Indian village they found and murdered the inhabitants, and Cochise, in turn, wreaked vengeance on anything that moved overland in southeastern Arizona. The remote White Mountains were chosen as an Indian reserve because they were well removed from areas of

white settlement and transportation and because they contained decent grazing land for the Apache herders. Cochise refused to settle there, but eventually
most of the western Apache leaders did. For the next decade, though, broken
promises by corrupt federal agents and attempts to lop off portions of the
reservation caused almost unrelieved tensions between the army and the
Apache. Even the fort itself came under attack in 1881 when inexperienced
troops interrupted a religious ritual on the reservation.

Since 1897, the huge tract has been divided into the Fort Apache and
San Carlos reservations for administrative purposes. The fort was demilitarized
in 1924 and many of its buildings converted into a school. The Apache Culture
Center is situated on the site. It contains exhibits on the history of the Apache
people and the way they live now on the White Mountain reserve. The puberty
rites for girls, among the most solemn and important in the Apache culture, are
held almost every weekend in summer. It is best to check in advance for the
schedule.

LOCATION: *Fort Apache is located on Arizona 73, the loop road through the
reservation. It is 21 miles southeast of U.S. 60 from the town of Carrizo.*
HOURS: *Monday through Friday, 8–5.*
ADMISSION: *Donation.*
TELEPHONE: *(602) 338-4625.*

Ganado

HUBBELL TRADING POST

The institution of the trading post is as old as the initial meeting of white
and native cultures in North America. The Pilgrims set up the first one at
Aptuxcet (*see* Bourne, Massachusetts) within a few years after landing at
Plymouth to facilitate trade among the Indians of southern New England and
the Dutch colony at Manhattan. The trading post was the economic engine of
the European westward movement, part of the fur trade and situated on the
overland wagon trails. The exchange of manufactured goods for the natural
riches of the land transformed the economy of the continent.

In most places, the Indian trader and his post are part of a vanished
America. But on the Navajo Reservation, the post established by John Lorenzo
Hubbell in 1878 is still doing business at the same stand, pretty much as it
always has. Hubbell died in 1940 after a long career as a politician and business
leader. The Hubbell Trading Post, however, still has a place in Navajo life and
is designated as a National Historic Site.

Hubbell was one of the first men to recognize the artistic importance of

Navajo silversmiths and rug makers. In the late nineteenth century, the sense of cultural inferiority to Europe was giving way to a new pride in American heritage. Indian art, seen as barbaric and unworthy of serious study by earlier generations, was now valued as part of an ancient tradition, part of the developing definition of what it meant to be an American. Hubbell knew there was a market for Navaho art, and he encouraged his clients to adhere to the highest standards. In return, he gave them access to a national market.

His post and home became a landmark of the Southwest. He welcomed white artists to stay with him, and in return all they had to leave was a painting. From visiting politicians, he asked support for Navajo causes in Washington. In this way, he both assembled one of the most valuable collections of Western art in Arizona and earned the trust of the Navajo. At its peak, the trade empire encompassed twenty-four posts while Hubbell himself was a state senator.

The post that stands today was built in 1883, and the National Park Service attempts to run it just as it would have operated in those days. A separate building has been set aside for weavers so that visitors can watch them at their craft. Many of them are women from distant parts of the reservation. They speak no English, or choose not to in the presence of outsiders. Another building houses a museum that explores the role of the trader in the economy of the old Southwest.

LOCATION: *The post is in Ganado, in the southeastern part of the reservation, on U.S. 191. It is 38 miles north of the Chambers exit of Interstate 40.*
HOURS: *Daily, 8–5. (In summer months, the Navajo reservation observes Daylight Savings Time, which is one hour ahead of the rest of the state.)*
ADMISSION: *Free.*
TELEPHONE: *(602) 755-3254.*

Globe

BESH-BA-GOWAH RUINS

G lobe became one of the great copper camps in the West when the Old Dominion Mine opened in the 1880s, but half a millenium before that, Native Americans knew of the ore and settled here to use it for trade goods and for paint pigment. The name of these ruins in the Apache language means "camp for metal." Jars filled with copper ore were uncovered at the two-hundred-room complex, which was built by the Salado culture in the thirteenth century; Salado is the name used to designate those invaders from the north who replaced the even older Hohokam culture in this part of Arizona.

Many of the items found at Besh-ba-Gowah are displayed in Globe at the Gila County Historical Museum.

LOCATION: *The ruins are just south of central Globe, by way of South Broad Street and Ice Box Canyon Road. The museum is north of town on U.S. 60.*
HOURS: *The ruins are open daily, dawn to dusk. The museum is open Monday through Saturday, 9–5.*
ADMISSION: *Both are free.*
TELEPHONE: *There is none at the ruins. The musuem is (602) 425-0320.*

Grand Canyon National Park

TUSAYAN MUSEUM

Anasazi ruins are a familiar feature of the Southwestern landscape. This ancient people inhabited many of the most scenic corners of this country. However, none of their habitations was quite as spectacularly situated as Tusayan, on the southern rim of the Grand Canyon. Archeologists estimate this pueblo was built near the start of the thirteenth century and abandoned about one hundred years later. In later years, the Havasupai (*see* Havasupai Reservation, Supai, Arizona) inhabited sections of the canyon floor. The first European known to have climbed down to the level of the Colorado River was Father Francisco Tomas Garces, who made the descent in 1776 in an effort to minister to this tribe. He also is credited with giving the river its name; when he saw the Colorado it was colored (*colorado*) bright red with mud.

Visitors may tour Tusayan Ruin by following a 0.1-mile paved path located directly east of the museum. The loop provides a glimpse into the daily lives of an Anasazi community around A.D. 1185. Exhibits along the path explain features of the ruin, and a connecting gravel trail overlooks the field where these prehistoric farmers grew their food crops. The museum was established to interpret the partially-excavated ruin. Through artifacts discovered at the site, archaeologists have deduced much about the Anasazi, but much remains to be learned about this culture, whose name comes from a Navajo word meaning "Ancient Peoples."

LOCATION: *The Tusayan ruins and museum are on the East Rim Drive, about 20 miles east of Grand Canyon Village.*
HOURS: *Daily, 9–5.*
ADMISSION: *Free.*
TELEPHONE: *(602) 638-2305.*

▲ *The 5-story Montezuma Castle is one of the best-preserved cliff dwellings in the Southwest.*

Keams Canyon

WALPI

W alpi is the most eastern of the Hopi mesa-top communities, and in many ways the most visually striking. Its closely packed structures cling tightly to the contours of the mesa, and from a distance the sight is reminiscent of a Middle Eastern hilltop town. The use of stone rather than adobe, the usual southwestern building material, heightens this sense. It is about five hundred years younger than the oldest Hopi village, Old Oraibi, but it has the appearance of almost unimaginable age. It is certainly one of the most haunting images in all of Native America, one that photographers return to again and again for the shifting light on the old stones. Nearby communities are inhabited by members of the Tewa and Hano tribes, longtime allies and cultural partners of the Hopi.

LOCATION: *Walpi is on First Mesa, along Arizona 264, about 8 miles east of the Hopi Cultural Center at Second Mesa.*

Montezuma Castle National Monument

CLIFF DWELLING

M ontezuma Castle, of course, has nothing whatsoever to do with the ruler of the Aztecs. It was already abandoned by 1450, more than half a century before Montezuma assumed power. But the European settlers of the Southwest, familiar with Oliver Prescott's nineteenth-century best-seller, *History of the Conquest of Mexico*, were ready to ascribe any impressive ruin to the one Indian leader whose name they knew. The adobe castle is tucked majestically into an opening in the sheer rock wall of a 145-foot-high cliff, inaccessible except by ladders. It soars five stories above its foundation ledge and contains two hundred rooms. It is one of the best-preserved cliff dwellings in the Southwest but can only be viewed, not entered.

LOCATION: *Montezuma Castle is just off Interstate 17, about 50 miles south of Flagstaff.*
HOURS: *Daily, 8–5.*
ADMISSION: *$1.*
TELEPHONE: *(602) 567-3322.*

Monument Valley Tribal Park

NAVAJO RESERVATION

A nyone who has ever seen a Western movie knows this landscape. The fantastically shaped red rocks and mesas towering over the desert floor have become a signature of the Southwest ever since director John Ford first shot on location here in the 1930s. "Monument Valley is to the Western movie what Yankee Stadium is to baseball," wrote one film commentator. In his later films, Ford was sensitive to the issue of fairness in the depiction of Native Americans, but in many of the films shot here, the Indian is the evil figure of menace.

Monument Valley is located in the midst of the Navajo Reservation, partially extending across the state line into Utah. The tribal park, administered by the Navajo Agency, takes in some of its most haunting terrain. In Mystery Valley, especially, the red buttes rise sheer from the desert floor to a height of more than one thousand feet. It is here that you can most feel what Ford did, that the scenery is almost a silent commentary on how trivial the human affairs being dramatized in the film really are. Make an attempt to visit

▲ *Keet Seel Ruin at Navajo National Monument is part of a cluster that forms the largest Anasazi ruins in Arizona; the park is situated within the Navajo Reservation, at an altitude of 7300 feet.*

the area either at sunrise or sunset, when the colors are at their most intense. There is a visitor center four miles southeast of the park entrance from U.S. 163, in Utah. Horseback and four-wheel-drive tours of the valley can be arranged at the Monument Valley Lodge, in Goulding's Utah. (Although the lodge is in Utah, most of the tribal park is situated in Arizona.)

LOCATION: *Off U.S. 163, between Kayenta, Arizona, and Mexican Hat, Utah.*
HOURS: *Daily, 7–8, mid-March through September; daily, 8–5, rest of year.*
ADMISSION: *$1.*
TELEPHONE: *(801) 727-3287.*

Navajo National Monument

ANASAZI CLIFF DWELLINGS

T hese are the largest Anasazi ruins in Arizona, and also the ones that take the most time and effort to see. The walk to the Betatakin ruin, the main cliff dwelling in the park, takes three to four hours round trip over rough terrain and is not recommended for those who are not in good physical condition. The guided hike is limited to twenty-four people, on a first-come, first-served basis. For most visitors, the better strategy would be to take the one-half mile walk to the Betatakin overlook, which is a splendid view of the ruins across the canyon. They are built in a red sandstone cliff, and the striations on the rocks, made by running water, shift colors in the changing light. In addition, the trail to the overlook is lined with plants the Anasazi utilized in their daily lives. Each one is labeled, and a short description on the many uses to which they were put is placed alongside. The park is situated within the Navajo Reservation, at an altitude of seventy-three hundred feet— another reason the shorter walk may be preferable. There is a small museum and crafts shop at the park headquarters.

LOCATION: *North from U.S. 160 by way of Arizona 564, about 20 miles southwest of Kayenta.*
HOURS: *Daily, 8–5.*
ADMISSION: *Free.*
TELEPHONE: *(602) 672-2366.*

Oraibi

OLD ORAIBI

W hen Moscow was a collection of huts and Berlin a wide spot on the Prussian plain, the Hopi lived in Oraibi. There is evidence of a residential presence here dating back to 1150, making it the oldest continuously inhabited place in North America. It dates from the time when the Anasazi, "the ancient ones" who left the ruins of their cliff dwellings all across the Southwest, arrived at this mesa-land in northern Arizona, and settled down permanently to become what are now called the Hopi. Whatever the process was that drove them from one place to another—drought, hostile neighbors, cultural evolvement—it ended here. Except for a brief period spent under

Spanish rule in the seventeenth century, the Hopi were left to themselves and developed one of the most stable, tradition-rich societies in the world.

Old Oraibi was built on the westernmost mesa of Hopi land, which is now entirely surrounded by the Navajo Reservation. Its claim of uninterrupted habitation is hanging by a thread, though. The pueblo now is mostly in ruins. Beginning in the 1870s, farmers from Oraibi moved farther west to more promising soil around Moenkopi, which lies outside the Hopi lands. In 1890, another group moved to the base of the mesa and established Lower, or New, Oraibi. But the real crisis came in 1906, when a religious dispute arose within the community. The more conservative portion of Oraibi became unhappy at modernizing tendencies that were being adopted at the pueblo, especially the issue of educating children in government schools. The dispute was settled by means of a communal tug-of-war. The conservatives were pulled over the line and promptly packed up and left, to settle the new town of Hotevilla six miles northwest. Much like a core city that has been deserted by suburbanites, Old Oraibi has declined ever since. A handful of residents still occupy its ancient lanes, however.

Regulations on visiting the pueblo change from year to year, and it is best to check in advance with the tribal offices at Kykotsmovi, immediately west of Old Oraibi.

LOCATION: *Old Oraibi occupies the top of Third Mesa, on the western part of the Hopi tribal lands, along Arizona 264.*
TELEPHONE: *(602) 734-2445.*

Parker

COLORADO RIVER TRIBES MUSEUM

The Parker Dam was one of the most controversial water projects in the history of the Southwest. The states of Arizona and California fought for decades over the formula for the allocation of its water, a dispute that finally was decided by the U.S. Supreme Court. In California the dam also flooded traditional lands of the Chemehuevi people, a small offshoot of the southern Paiute who lived along the Colorado River. The Chemehuevi were given a $1 million settlement for the loss by the federal courts in 1951. Some of that money was used to develop recreational marine facilities along the waterway the dam created. So there was a certain rough justice to it, after all.

Most of the Chemehuevi moved onto the Colorado River Reservation. A segment of the tribe had lived here since 1865 with the Mojave, who had always been the dominant Native American group in the region. Although the two tribes had developed amiable relations, Mojave culture had come to dominate that of their smaller neighbors, which was why many Chemehuevi had preferred living on their own lands, speaking their own language. The Mojave were a far more aggressive people, conducting almost constant warfare with the southern Arizona tribes, whom they raided for females. They were adept at using the annual Colorado floods in cultivating their fields, subsisting on these crops and fish. They were also great traders, acting as middlemen between the Hopi and the Pacific Coast tribes. Seashells were highly prized as decorations in their own crafts.

The surrounding area has become one of the top water recreation areas in the parched Southwest, the "Arizona coastline," and Parker, the main town on the reservation, has developed into a boating center. The museum is located at tribal headquarters and displays the traditional crafts of the two tribes as well as historical exhibits on Native Americans along the Colorado. The collection of baskets is outstanding. The Mojave also had a richly developed song cycle for major rituals, and portions of them may be heard. Small segments of the Navajo and Hopi also make their homes here, but the museum is concerned primarily with the tribes that were historical occupants of these lands.

LOCATION: *The museum is south of downtown by way of Arizona 95, at Mohave and 2nd Streets.*
HOURS: *Monday through Friday, 8–5.*
ADMISSION: *Donations.*
TELEPHONE: *(602) 669-9211.*

Pearce

COCHISE STRONGHOLD

As you drive south along U.S. 666, through the farmlands of the Sulphur Springs Valley, the Dragoon Mountains rise in a solid, purple mass to the west, sealing off the sunset. It was from these dark canyons that one of the greatest Apache warriors kept all the forces the federal government could send against him at bay. It is still known as the Cochise Stronghold, and today it holds his tomb.

Cochise was a leader of the Chiricahua band of Apache, and had concluded it was pointless to oppose the movement of stagecoach traffic west along the Overland Trail. He was given a free hand to raid for what he required in Mexico and maintained generally friendly relations with the Butterfield Stage Line personnel. He was a frequent visitor at the station nearest his home, at Apache Pass, supplying it with firewood.

Late in 1860, however, a group of Pinal raided the area and carried off an eleven-year-old white child. A young officer sent to the area to recover the youngster somehow became convinced that the Chiricahua were at fault, although stage line employees tried to explain that he was mistaken. Cochise was summoned to appear before him. Arriving under a flag of truce, Cochise was accused of the crime, told he was lying when he denied it, and arrested. He pulled out a knife, slashed a hole in the tent where he was being interrogated, and escaped into the brush. Six of his men were held prisoner, however, three of them close relatives of Cochise. All of them were hanged.

Within sixty days, it was reported that 150 travelers on the Overland Trail had been killed. And for the next eleven years, this section of southeastern Arizona became the most dangerous corner of the country as Cochise defeated or eluded every force sent against him. For portions of that period, the settlement at Tucson, the largest in the territory, was completely isolated as nothing could move through Apache Pass.

Finally, both sides wearied of the long struggle. The government sent out General O. O. Howard, former head of the Freedmen's Bureau, the agency responsible for freed black slaves, and the man for whom Howard University is named. He found an ally in Tom Jeffords, the owner of a small stage line and the only white in the area with access to Cochise. Some said that was because he supplied the Apache with weapons, others because Cochise found him an honorable man. For whatever reason, Howard and Jeffords managed to conclude a peace treaty in 1872, with the proviso that Jeffords be named Indian agent.

In his early fifties by this time, Cochise had been at war for twelve uninterrupted years. Within two more years he was dead. His body was brought to the stronghold. After burial, the Chiricahua rode their horses back and forth across the site so no evidence of its location would remain. It was said that Jeffords knew, but he never revealed it. The site of the stronghold is now a part of Coronado National Forest.

LOCATION: *Cochise Stronghold is 10 miles west by dirt road from U.S. 666 at Sunsites. There is now a picnic area at the canyon mouth and hiking trails through the area.* TELEPHONE: *(602) 826-3535 at the Pearce Chamber of Commerce.*

▲ *The Heard Museum's exhibits sometimes include Native American house types that visitors can step inside, such as this tepee.*

Phoenix

HEARD MUSEUM

The Heard Museum is an internationally acclaimed institution celebrated for its vast collection of material relating to Native Americans of the Southwest. The museum was founded in 1929 by a prominent Phoenix couple, Dwight B. and Maie Bartlett Heard, who were avid collectors of native artifacts and art, especially of the Southwest. Heard established the *Arizona Republic*, the state's largest daily newspaper.

The museum's displays include some of the oldest Navajo blankets known to exist, in addition to contemporary examples of Pueblo weaving and embroidery. The kachina doll collection, which showcases dolls from the collections of Senator Barry M. Goldwater and businessman Fred Harvey, is unmatched. The dolls play an important role in Pueblo tribal religion: during annual dances, they are distributed to children of the pueblos by masked dancers who represent the spirit forms of great natural forces.

The Heard Museum's jewelry collection represents the traditions of the

▲ *Collections at the Heard Museum are a starting point for learning about the people who used the artifacts and created the art displayed here.*

Navajo, Zuni, and Hopi cultures, and contains examples of the turquoise and shell jewelry from the Rio Grande Pueblos of New Mexico. Turquoise is a distinctive feature of southwestern jewelry, and the gem's importance extended into native religious beliefs. The ceramic collection—including more than 3500 examples of southwestern ceramics from prehistory to the present—illustrates the differences in pottery designs among the various pueblos. There are several hundred examples of beadwork and quillwork, used to ornament clothing, home furnishings, pouches and other containers. One fine example of the museum's collection is a Kiowa girl's dress of buckskin, ornamented with glass seed beads, elk teeth, shells, and ribbon; it is painted with green pigment made from algae and yellow made from bison gall stones.

A family exhibit, "Old Ways, New Ways," features hands-on activities geared toward children: visitors may play alongside a Kiowa drum group through video technology, or they may design their own Navajo rug with the help of a user-friendly computer terminal. Every day, Native American artists demonstrate beadworking, weaving, sculpting, or carving, and on weekends, performers demonstrate native music and dance.

LOCATION: *The museum is at 22 East Monte Vista Road, just off Central Avenue, immediately north of downtown.*
HOURS: *Monday through Saturday, 10–5; Sunday, 12–5.*
ADMISSION: *$5 Adult; $4 Seniors and Students; $3 Youth (13-18); $2 Children (4-12). Free on Wednesday, 5–9.*
TELEPHONE: *(602) 252-8840.*

PUEBLO GRANDE MUSEUM

This is the place that gave the sprawling, modern metropolis of Phoenix its name. When the earliest white settlers arrived here in the 1860s, they were drawn to the ruins of the great Hohokam community that had existed here more than one thousand years before. It was hoped that a new city would rise on the site of the old one. From Greek mythology they recalled the story of the phoenix, the bird that was consumed by fire but arose from its own ashes.

The complex system of irrigation canals used by the Hohokam totaled more than 125 miles. It also was an inspiration for the European pioneers who tapped the Salt River and watered their fields in the same way. Until the construction of the great southwestern dams began in 1910, however, the Hohokam were only imitated, not surpassed. The museum here preserves the mound under which the pueblo was excavated. It is estimated that the settlement was abandoned in about 1450. An Indian market, featuring the crafts of most southwestern tribes, is held here annually on the first weekend in December.

LOCATION: *Pueblo Grande is in eastern Phoenix, at 4619 East Washington Street, just south of U.S. 60, 89 (Van Buren Street).*
HOURS: *Monday through Saturday, 9–4:45; Sunday, 1–4:45.*
ADMISSION: *50 cents.*
TELEPHONE: *(602) 495-0900.*

▲ *Pueblo Grande's museum complex preserves the mound where excavations revealed the ruins of the great Hohokam community that had existed here more than 1100 years ago.*

Sacaton

GILA BASIN INDIAN CENTER

The water that flowed through the Gila River may have been a thin stream, but it was enough to divide the cultures of the Pima and their close relatives, the Papago. The Pima lived along the river and became an agricultural people. In their irrigated fields they grew corn and squash and later developed wheat. They lived in permanent houses. The Papago, although sharing a language and most of their culture with the Pima, did not have access to the river. So they became nomadic hunters and gatherers, "desert people." The two tribes still occupy separate reservations, divided by a thin strip of land near the town of Casa Grande.

Gila Basin Indian Center is devoted primarily to the Pima and another river people who became their allies, the Maricopa. This group had first lived near the Yuma tribe, to which it was closely related, along the Colorado River. Sometime around 1800 they started drifting east along the Gila and became friendly with the Pima. This antagonized their former neighbors, since the Yuma and Pima were traditional enemies. The Yuma and their allies, the Mojave, were very aggressive people. For the next half-century, they continually conducted raids on the Maricopa and Pima, who also had to contend with Apache raids on their eastern flank. They managed to win themselves a measure of peace in 1857 by defeating a large Yuma war party sent into their lands. By that time the white presence in Arizona was already becoming dominant. Within thirteen years, this reserve on the Gila was set aside for the Pima and Maricopa.

The striking museum here displays the crafts of the two tribes, especially their basketry and pottery. An adjacent outdoor exhibit consists of reconstructed villages of these two cultures as well as the Hohokam, the prehistoric inhabitants of this area, and the Apache, whose westernmost bands once ranged through here, too.

LOCATION: *The museum is at the Sacaton exit of Interstate 10, at Casa Blanca Road, about 40 miles south of Phoenix.*
HOURS: *Daily, 9–5.*
ADMISSION: *Free.*
TELEPHONE: *(602) 963-3981.*

Second Mesa

HOPI CULTURAL CENTER

Second Mesa is the heartland of the Hopi reserve (*see* Old Oraibi and Walpi, Arizona, for other important sights), the middle of the three mesas on which the Hopi have made their homes for hundreds of years. The stability of the culture has produced some of the most richly expressed artwork and complex ceremonial life of any native people. The Hopi are famous for their weaving, their work with silver, and their finely wrought kachina dolls. Exquisite examples of this work are on display here, as well as exhibits that relate the history of this unique people. There is also a full calendar of traditional dances and other observances held at the cultural center. The dates vary from year to year and frequently are not scheduled until a few weeks in advance, so it is best to check by phone for the calendar.

LOCATION: *Second Mesa lies along Arizona 264, the road that traverses the Hopi Reservation. It is also on Arizona 87, which runs 63 miles north from Interstate 40 to this site.*
HOURS: *Monday through Friday, 8–5, and weekends, 10–4, June through September. Closed Sunday, rest of year.*
ADMISSION: *Donations.*
TELEPHONE: *(602) 734-6650.*

▲ *The Havasupai Reservation is situated on the floor of the Grand Canyon.*

Supai

HAVASUPAI RESERVATION

This may be the most spectacularly situated native community in America, since it is on the floor of the Grand Canyon. The Havasupai were a small group, never numbering more than a few hundred people. They roamed the canyon country, planting crops of peaches and vegetables in summer, and then climbed to the rim in October to spend the winter. They apparently came to the area in the fourteenth century seeking a sanctuary from more powerful neighbors. Six hundred years later, anthropologists declared them the Native American group whose culture was least affected by white contact in the United States. They were, however, influenced by the Hopi, many of whom sought refuge with them during drought times. The only white known to have lived among them was John D. Lee, a Mormon fugitive from justice. Lee, ironically, was being sought for his role in the Mountain Meadow Massacre, an incident in which he and other whites had slaughtered the passengers on a California-bound wagon train and blamed the crime on Indians. While living with the Havasupai, he taught them ways to improve their peach cultivation, and the crop still plays an important part in tribal life. The Peach Dance is held in August. Call in advance for times. The reservation's surroundings are gorgeous, and the tribal offices give tours to many little-known scenic places within the canyon.

LOCATION: *As you can imagine, this is not an easy place to reach. A road from the neighboring Hualapai reservation leaves Arizona 66 just east of Peach Springs and runs 62 miles to Hualapai Hilltop, at the canyon rim. From there you can either hike 8 miles to the floor or call for mules to help you in the descent. Lodging and food also must be arranged in advance.*
TELEPHONE: *(602) 448-2121.*

Tonto National Monument

CLIFF DWELLINGS

Tonto National Monument preserves the most accessible cliff dwelling ruins in southern Arizona. Like the ruins at Casa Grande, they are regarded to be the work of the Salado people, invaders from the north who gradually supplanted the Hohokam in this part of the state. The two great adobe pueblos here date from the first part of the fourteenth century and are tucked into a natural cave. There is a museum and visitor center. Much of the attraction here is the drive across the famous Apache Trail. This highway, built in 1906 during the construction of the nearby Roosevelt Dam, actually follows the route of several old mountain trails used by the Apache. Many Apaches contributed to the construction of the road.

LOCATION: *The Apache Trail, Arizona 88, forms a loop, connecting with U.S. 60 at either end. From the west, at Apache Junction, it is 46 miles here, and from the east, at Claypool, it is 29 miles. The drive is far more scenic on its western leg.*
HOURS: *Daily, 8-5.*
ADMISSION: *$3 a car.*
TELEPHONE: *(602) 467-2241.*

ARIZONA STATE MUSEUM

T he Arizona State Museum houses the definitive collection of materials relating to the culture of Arizona's native peoples, from prehistoric times to contemporary cultures. Displays demonstrate the use of everyday things in ancient communities and how they evolved into the tools and crafts used by Arizona residents today. The emphasis is on the continuity of cultural life in this area.

Prehistoric materials include Hohokam and Mogollon decorated ceramic bowls, human figurines of clay and stone, 12,000-year-old stone points, carved shell jewelry, and turquoise beads. Historic tools, clothing, and other utensils give insight into native lifestyles that often went unrecorded. Collections of objects from contemporary Indian cultures include Tohono O'odham baskets, Navajo rugs, and Hopi pottery. The museum's 3,000-volume library specializes in materials related to anthropology and the Southwest, and other collections include photographs, letters, documents, and oral histories. Temporary exhibits have included snapshots of reservation life from 1900 to 1980, and a display of a modern revival of traditional Navajo pottery.

LOCATION: *The museum is part of the University of Arizona campus, at the University Boulevard entrance.*
HOURS: *South Building: Monday through Saturday, 9–5; Sunday, 2–5. North Building: Monday through Friday, 8–5.*
ADMISSION: *Free.*
TELEPHONE: *(602) 621-6302.*

MISSION SAN XAVIER DEL BAC

L ocated on the Papago Indian Reservation, just south of the city, Mission San Xavier del Bac is the last Spanish mission surviving in Arizona. It is nationally famous as the Jewel of the Desert, an outstanding example of Spanish colonial architecture. The Spanish concept of mission life, however, usually resulted in peonage for native peoples unfortunate enough to be chosen for salvation. They were forced to work the fields for no pay and punished if they tried to escape. San Xavier has become an important part of Papago life in this community. Since 1911, when it was restored, it has been a beneficial force in both religion and education.

Father Eusebio Kino came to this area around 1700 to preach to the Papago. This tribe is very closely related to the Pima, but lived as hunters and gatherers in the desert environment. This did not fit in with the mission way of life. They were forced to become farmers, a situation that had become so intolerable by 1751 that Luis Oacpicagigua was able to lead a revolt to drive the Jesuits out. They returned three years later, only to be expelled by the civil authorities in 1767. The Franciscans attempted to take over the mission, but they were immediately attacked by the Apache and other local tribes, who had no wish for the onerous system to be reestablished. The Franciscans persevered though, and by 1797 had completed the church that exists today. Within thirty years, however, the Franciscans were, in turn, expelled by the Mexican government, and for almost a century afterward San Xavier was allowed to slowly crumble away.

Since its restoration, however, the church has played a central role in the religious life of the Papago. The dances here on the Friday following Easter Sunday are memorable, and there are also Indian celebrations at the mission on the feast days of October 3 and December 2.

LOCATION: *The mission is reached from central Tucson by way of southbound Interstate 19 to San Xavier Road.*
HOURS: *Daily, 9–5.*
ADMISSION: *Free.*
TELEPHONE: *(602) 294-2624.*

Tuzigoot National Monument

CLIFF DWELLINGS

The importance of the cliff dwellings at Tuzigoot is in the high degree of culture of the occupants, evident from the trade goods and articles of daily life that were left behind. The people were called the Sinagua, and they carried on a large-scale trade with tribes on the California coast. Many of their belongings were found in various rooms of the pueblo, as if their owners had just put them down and stepped out for a moment. The Sinagua give Tuzigoot (Apache for "crooked water," in reference to a nearby lake) a unique niche among the Arizona ruins. Many of these items are exhibited in the adjacent museum, positioned just as they were found in the pueblo. Tuzigoot was occupied for about two hundred years and was abandoned in the fifteenth century. When Spanish soldiers reached the place a century later, Yavapai were living among the ruins.

▲ *Trade goods and articles of daily life were preserved in the Tuzigoot cliff dwellings and are now exhibited in the museum.*

LOCATION: *Tuzigoot is off U.S. 89A just east of Clarkdale.*
HOURS: *Daily, 8–5.*
ADMISSION: *$1.*
TELEPHONE: *(602) 634-5564.*

Walnut Canyon National Monument

CLIFF DWELLINGS

S inagua was a name made up by Harold S. Colton, the founder and longtime director of the Museum of Northern Arizona (*see* Museum of Northern Arizona, Flagstaff). It is Spanish for "without water," and Colton used it to describe the difficult conditions under which the occupants of the north central Arizona cliff dwellings lived. Walnut Canyon, on the eastern outskirts of Flagstaff, was one of their major settlements. Unlike most of the surviving ruins of this period, Walnut Canyon was made up of about three hundred individual pueblos, almost like a suburban subdivision, as opposed to an urban apartment house. The protective limestone shelf in which they were built has preserved them well. About twenty-five of them may be visited easily

on a trail along the canyon rim. The Sinagua lived here from about A.D.
1150–1250.

LOCATION: *Walnut Canyon is reached most easily from Interstate 40, about 15 miles*
east of central Flagstaff.
HOURS: *Daily, 8–5. Snow may close the area for brief periods in winter.*
ADMISSION: *$3 a car.*
TELEPHONE: *(602) 526-3367.*

Window Rock

Navajo Tribal Headquarters and Museum

The Navajo are one of the great success stories among Native Americans.
After the terrible Long Walk to Bosque Redondo in 1864 (*see* Canyon de
Chelly National Monument, Arizona), the tribe had dwindled to about 8,000
people, living in poverty in one of the most isolated corners of the United
States. Then some of its best grazing land was taken away for railroad right-of-
way. Yet the Navajo nation today numbers over 200,000, the largest Native
American group in the country. Its reservation is a major tourism center, with
some of the most visited scenic, recreational, and cultural attractions in the
Southwest. (Descriptions of many of these places are contained under their
own headings in this chapter and the one on New Mexico.) The tribe found
itself sitting on rich energy reserves, and since the 1920s it has prospered
through the oil and natural gas leases it granted to exploit them. The Navajo
also formed an effective tribal government at that time, which has managed to
balance the needs of a modern community with adherence to traditional
beliefs. A measure of its success is the great number of younger people who
choose to live on the reservation. About 60 percent of its population is under
age 25, according to tribal statistics.

The Navajo arrived in this area early in the thirteenth century, at the
end of a long migration from western Canada in concert with the Apache.
Once established here, they lived in close proximity to the Hopi, and their
culture was heavily influenced by them. The use of masked dances, especially,
was borrowed from the Pueblo tribes whom the Navajo found in this area.
They also were transformed from hunters to an agricultural and stock-raising
people. Rug-making techniques were learned from the Pueblo and silversmith-
ing from Mexican workers who lived among them, but the Navajo took both
crafts to higher levels and stamped them with their own identity.

The reservation stretches across twenty-five thousand square miles and
four state lines. The Four Corners Monument, the only place in the country at

▲ *Window Rock, a community named for this sandstone formation which was formed by wind erosion at its crest, is the Navajo tribal headquarters and administrative center.*

which four states meet, is within its borders. The reservation is about the same size as the state of West Virginia. Window Rock, a community named for a sandstone formation with a circular hole formed by wind erosion at its crest, is the tribal headquarters and administrative center. The Tribal Council, with an elected president and delegates representing the 109 local government bodies within the reservation, meet here at least four times a year. It is, in effect, the second state capital of Arizona and New Mexico.

The Tribal Museum, opened here in 1961, is a massive compilation of the history and culture of the Navajo Nation, an invaluable reference center as well as a showcase for the arts. It also includes important material on the Anasazi, the cliff dwellers who inhabited these lands before the Navajo. Changing exhibitions are scheduled here throughout the year.

The octagonal, red sandstone Navajo Council Chambers, seat of tribal government, may be visited during the week. Also in Window Rock is a Navajo Tribal Zoo, exhibiting animals important to life on the reservation and to the culture of the tribe. Tse Bonito Park memorializes the place at which the Navajo camped at the start of the infamous Long Walk of 1864. There is a central Arts and Crafts Enterprise, with some of the finest examples of Navajo work at guaranteed quality. The Navajo Fair is held here during the week after Labor Day and is one of the most colorful Native American observances in the country.

At St. Michael's Mission, just west of Window Rock, is a small museum housed in a church built in 1898; the museum relates the ongoing importance of Catholicism among the Navajo and describes the work of the Franciscans in this area.

LOCATION: *Window Rock is located just across the state line from New Mexico on Arizona 264, the main east-west route across the reservation. It can be reached by Reservation Road 12 from Interstate 40, about 25 miles north of the Lupton exit.*
HOURS: *The museum, council chambers, and arts and crafts center are open Monday through Friday, 9–4. Zoo hours are daily, 8–5. St. Michael's Mission is open Monday through Saturday, 9–5, and Sunday, 10–6, Memorial Day through Labor Day.*
ADMISSION: *Donations at the museum and mission.*
TELEPHONE: *The museum is (602) 871-6673. The mission is (602) 871-4171. Navajo Tourism Office has information on other places in the area at (602) 871-6436.*

Wupatki National Monument

PUEBLO COMMUNITY

A natural disaster in the eleventh century turned this area into one of the most densely populated communities in the Southwest. Sunset Crater, located just to the south, began erupting with devastating force at that time and continued to erupt for the next two hundred years. The ash that scattered across the area from these eruptions enriched the soil here and created exceptionally rich cropland. Within a generation, a Pueblo community sprang up on the site. By 1300, when the soil was depleted, the site was abandoned. More than any other place in the area, Wupatki enables the visitor to see the structure of an entire community. The one-hundred-room Tall House is the most impressive, but there is also a citadel, an amphitheater (which first was thought to be a kiva but contains no other religious features), ball courts, and a great variety of smaller residential pueblos. A self-guiding trail winds through the area.

LOCATION: *Wupatki is off U.S. 89 about 30 miles north of Flagstaff.*
HOURS: *Daily, 8–6.*
ADMISSION: *$3 a car.*
TELEPHONE: *(602) 527-7040.*

COLORADO

ARCHEOLOGICAL AREA

T he Anasazi, the "ancient ones" of the Southwest, established themselves
throughout the canyon and mesa country of this region. Chimney Rock is
the only instance, however, in which their ruins have been found in the high
country. The habitations here also define the limit of their northeastern
expansion. A chamber measuring two hundred by eighty feet has been uncovered here, but it is the setting that makes Chimney Rock a significant historic
area. It is located within the San Juan National Forest, and rangers conduct
tours of the ruins.

LOCATION: *South of U.S. 160 at the town of Chimney Rock, about halfway between
Durango and Pagosa Springs.*
HOURS: *Daily, dawn to dusk, mid-May to mid-September.*
ADMISSION: *Free.*
TELEPHONE: *(303) 264-2268.*

SAND CREEK MASSACRE

D uring the summer of 1864, raids on wagon trains along the Santa Fe
Trail grew so numerous that at times the route was shut down completely. The territorial governor was incensed. A treaty had been signed with the
Arapaho and Cheyenne ceding those lands in return for five $450,000 pay-
ments. That the terms of the treaty had not been met and several tribal groups
were going hungry seemed beside the point in Denver. The Cheyenne leader,
Black Kettle, also pointed out that only a handful from his tribe had joined the
raiders. They were mostly Comanche and Sioux. This argument, too, was

brushed aside. Black Kettle was told that he would be attacked unless he reported to the nearest garrison and "laid down his arms."

The Cheyenne leader followed instructions. He reported to Fort Lyons, on the Santa Fe Trail, and expressed his willingness to remain at peace under those terms. The commandant, Indian agent, and post interpreter all attested to that in later investigations. Black Kettle was told, however, that there was not enough food at the fort to feed his band and to return to their winter encampment on Sand Creek, thirty-five miles to the north.

While this was going on, a volunteer militia regiment was being formed in Denver under the leadership of Major John Chivington. He was a Methodist elder, a frustrated politician, and an ambitious soldier who fully supported the policy of attacking the Indians until they surrendered unconditionally. Fearing that the enlistment terms of his troops were about to expire without a resolution of the issue, he marched them secretly through a snowstorm to Fort Lyons in November. A new commandant at the fort told him that the camp at Sand Creek was made up of hostile Arapaho. So on the evening of November 28, he marched his force, with the addition of regular troops from Fort Lyons, to the village. He attacked without warning at dawn. The surprise was complete, and Chivington gave orders to take no prisoners. There are disputes about how many were killed, and of that total how many were women and children. The best estimate seems to be 650 Indian dead, of whom 450 were noncombatants. A few of Chivington's soldiers later testified that they saw "fresh white scalps" in the camp, but if they ever existed they were burned when the camp was torched in the evening.

Even in the midst of the bloodbath of the Civil War, the episode sparked an outrage in the East. An investigatory commission was formed two months later and Chivington was threatened with court martial. But he was never tried. He testified later that he believed he was attacking a hostile camp and to his knowledge women and children had all escaped. A regular army lieutenant said, however, that "the slaughter was continuous; no Indian, old or young, male or female was spared."

Sand Creek led directly to three years of almost continuous warfare between the army and the tribes of the western Plains. It was also an incident that would be surpassed in cruelty only a generation later at Wounded Knee.

LOCATION: *A dirt road runs from the eastern edge of Chivington, on Colorado 96, about 8 miles north to the massacre site. There is a historic marker.*

University of Colorado Center

This town in the southwestern corner of the state is situated among one of the greatest concentrations of Native American ruins in the country. It also adjoins the Ute Mountain Reservation. Taking advantage of the location, the University of Colorado has set up a unique program here. It is a clearing-house of archeological information. It is also an opportunity for Indian residents of the area to tell stories about their culture and history to visitors. There are crafts displays and discussions of Native American religions and the significance of the dances that the area tribes perform. Programs are held throughout the summer months, and it is best to call in advance for the latest information on events.

LOCATION: *The center is in downtown Cortez at the junction of U.S. 160 and U.S. 666.*
HOURS: *Daily, 9-5.*
ADMISSION: *Free.*
TELEPHONE: *(303) 565-1151.*

Anasazi Heritage Center

This unique museum is dedicated entirely to the Anasazi, the remarkable people who left their dwellings and religious structures throughout this part of the country. The native people referred to as the "Anasazi" began to develop their culture in the Four Corners region some time around A.D. 1. While the early inhabitants hunted game and gathered wild plant foods, agriculture became the mainstay of the Anasazi economy. They developed architectural skills and produced baskets, pottery, ornaments, woven goods, and tools, which they exchanged with other communities.

The Heritage Center's 2 million artifacts, samples, and documents illustrate the Anasazi way of life, their crafts, how they planted and prepared food, their trade connections—everything that anthropologists and archeologists have been able to piece together about them. An introductory movie summarizes the prehistoric cultural development in southwest Colorado, and gives an overview of the McPhee Reservoir Project, the Dolores Archaeological Project, and the creation of the Anasazi Heritage Center. There are a number of hands-on and interactive displays to make the story connect for

▲ *At summer programs sponsored by the University of Colorado Center, Native American residents of the area share the significance of their dances and tell stories about their culture and history.*

children. Four interactive computer games cover Anasazi life, the last pictograph, archaeological sites, and public lands, and a new exhibit, "Our Fragile Legacy," which explains why keepsakes fall apart and what we can do about it. Hands-on exhibits allow visitors to grind corn into meal with a mano and metate; to weave on a pueblo-style loom; to handle real Anasazi implements such as bone drills, stone points, and pottery; and to use microscopes to identify seeds and to understand the importance of microanalysis and organic evidence in archaeology. There is also a partial reconstruction of a typical Anasazi dwelling from around A.D. 880. A test trench reconstruction of an actual excavation on record shows the first stage of excavation, soil changes that reveal occupation levels, artifacts exposed, trench mapping, and recording.

If you plan to visit any of the Anasazi ruins in this area, this stop is absolutely essential to putting what you will see in proper historical perspective. The facility, built by the Bureau of Reclamation, is run by the U.S. Bureau of Land Management.

▲ *Sky Ute Center houses a museum of Ute history and a gallery of contemporary artists.*

LOCATION: *Just west of town on Colorado 184, or 10 miles north of Cortez by way of Colorado 145.*
HOURS: *Daily, 9–5, April 15 through October 31. Rest of year: open weekends, closed 2 days per week. Call for days and hours of operation.*
ADMISSION: *Free.*
TELEPHONE: *(303) 882-4811.*

Ignacio

SKY UTE CENTER

A ll of western Colorado was the Ute domain in the days before white settlement. They were a hunting people, ranging freely through the game-rich valleys on the Rockies' western slope and through the "parks," the bountiful green areas lying between the towering Front Range and the peaks to the west. The approach to South Park was known for generations as Ute Pass. The tribe jealously guarded access to their lands at this narrow pass against the Arapaho and other Plains tribes. Only the Comanche on their southern border challenged their dominance.

Following the Medicine Lodge Treaty of 1867 (*see* Peace Treaty Park,

Kansas), however, the most direct overland trails opened to Colorado, and the Ute were pushed steadily westward by the expanding white population. In 1868, they agreed to move to the far side of the Continental Divide, which would be made into a reserve for them. But when gold was discovered in the San Juan Mountains five years later, the treaty was abrogated and they were once more forced to cede their lands. In 1877, a new reservation was set up along the southernmost strip of Colorado, on land that was desirable neither to miners or ranchers. Other parcels were made available to them in Utah. The Ute had formed into seven separate bands, and two of them, the Mouache and Capote, combined as the southern Ute and settled on the eastern portion of the Colorado lands. This turned out to be a good choice. This was high country, and when the tribe started collecting lease payments on oil and natural gas holdings, it invested much of the money in building a recreational industry. Sky Ute Lodge was put up as a base for excursions into the surrounding mountains. It also houses a museum of Ute history and a gallery of contemporary artists. Tribal members are regarded as outstanding leatherworkers, and their crafts are on sale here. A youth group from the tribe also puts on traditional dances during the summer months.

LOCATION: *Ignacio is south from U.S. 160 by way of Colorado 172, about 25 miles southeast of Durango.*
HOURS: *Daily, 9–5.*
ADMISSION: *Free.*
TELEPHONE: *(303) 563-4531.*

La Junta

BENT'S OLD FORT

In the 1830s, as trade began to move across the Santa Fe Trail, three businessmen from Saint Louis headed west to seize a chance at making their fortunes. They came to a place known as La Junta, on the Arkansas River in southeastern Colorado. It was here that the most heavily traveled route of the Santa Fe Trail turned south toward Raton Pass. This was also where it met the Navajo Trail from the west, which is why it was called "The Junction" in Spanish. The Bent Brothers, Charles and William, and their associate, Ceran St. Vrain, had experience dealing with the northern tribes in the fur trade. They felt that if they could bring the Arapaho and Cheyenne to their depot at La Junta, they could establish the most important trading outlet on the way to Santa Fe.

According to western historian Bernard de Voto, the methods they

▲ *Artworks featured at the Sky Ute Center include this doll made by Orian Box.*

employed were revolutionary. Rather than attempting to cheat the Indians they dealt with, they instead "maintained an unheard standard of honor in dealing with them." As a result, Bent's Fort became the trade hub of the Southwest, with native people coming in with pelts and buffalo hides to exchange for the manufactured goods of the East. For two decades, it was an island of amity, with trappers and travelers and natives pursuing their ends and getting along without trouble. But American political ambitions cut it down. By 1846, it became apparent that the United States was preparing to go to war with Mexico over the southwestern territories. Bent's Fort became a military staging area for the impending invasion of New Mexico. The tribes became alarmed and then angered at the arrival of so many soldiers in their lands, especially when they seized all the good foraging land in the area. The truce was broken and the tribes became actively hostile, avoiding the fort altogether. In 1849, a bitter and broken Charles Bent set fire to the place and left.

But in 1976 the National Park Service took over the desolate ruin and Bent's Old Fort rose again. Its fifteen-foot-high adobe walls, looking like a fortress in the surrounding plains, now house a living museum. It is always 1845 in this place, and all the people who came to the fort then—traders and trappers and native people—are represented now. Each of them reenacts what he would have been doing then in various activities held throughout the year. This is the best chance to see what a frontier outpost was like in the nineteenth-century West and what role native people played in it.

LOCATION: *Bent's Old Fort is 8 miles east of La Junta, on the north bank of the Arkansas, by way of Colorado 194.*
HOURS: *Daily, 8–4:30.*
ADMISSION: *$3 a carload or $1 a person.*
TELEPHONE: *(719) 384-2596.*

Mesa Verde National Park

Cliff Palace, Dwellings, and Chapin Mesa Museum

In the entire federal system, this is the only national park dedicated to the history of Native Americans. Several of the archeological sites in the Southwest and elsewhere are national monuments. But being a national park is the five-star insignia of American tourist attractions. Usually, it is reserved for the most magnificent natural wonders of the continent. But Mesa Verde evokes such a sense of awe in all who see it that there was general agreement in 1906, when the federal Antiquities Act was signed to protect such places from scavengers, that it merited inclusion for special care as a national park.

The Cliff Palace here is one of the country's most recognizable sights, a visual signature for all the Indian ruins of the Southwest. Its evocative setting has become a symbol of the mystery and romance of this entire region of the country. It is a place where people speak in whispers. The ancient stone cities crowded into the crannies and cliffs of this long, green tableland have excited the popular imagination ever since they were first discovered by whites in 1859. Seventeen years later, photographs and clay models of Mesa Verde were exhibited at the Centennial Exposition in Philadelphia and caused a sensation. The wonder of it has not faded.

Who built these hanging cities in the cliffs, and why, and what happened to them? The historical evidence shows that nomadic people in the process of becoming farmers began moving onto the mesa top in the sixth century, seeking an assured source of water, shelter, and good soil. Over the years, they advanced from underground pit houses to pueblos, and their culture became increasingly complex. They built kivas and made elaborate pottery and decorated cloth. Around 1200, they started constructing the astonishing cliff dwellings that are the best known part of the park. Curiously enough, by the end of that century Mesa Verde was entirely abandoned. Research indicates

▲ *Prehistoric ruins at Mesa Verde National Park. The dwellings are thought to have been built by a nomadic people around A.D. 1200.*

that the most elaborate building activity was going on after the population already had started to leave. It was as if the occupants were determined to put up ever more splendid facades for a culture that already was leaving out the back door. By 1300, everyone was gone.

There was drought, a twenty-four-year period of low rainfall. But there had been much more severe droughts before that, and they had been survived. There was also an increase in hostile raids at this time, which probably explains why the cliff houses were built for enhanced security. Apparently, the combination was too much to overcome and the Mesa Verde culture suffered something close to a nervous breakdown. The Hopi of Arizona believe that they are descended from the Anasazi who once lived here.

The place was visited by Spanish explorers in the eighteenth century, but not until the 1880s did anyone really comprehend the richness of what was here. The land was owned by the Wetherhill family, who grazed sheep in the area. They were familiar, of course, with the earlier investigations of the mesa that had been displayed in Philadelphia, and they had seen many of the ruins themselves. But Richard Wetherhill was convinced that far more had not yet been found. His conviction was borne out in 1888, when on one of his exploratory rambles across the mesa, he came upon Cliff Palace. The find caused a sensation in the scientific community, and a few years later Wetherhill invited Swedish archeologist Gustavus Nordenskiold to make the first systematic probe of the ruins.

Much of the mesa was situated on Ute reservation lands, however, and the ruins began to be plundered by outsiders. The tribe did not have the resources to protect the sites, and the state was powerless to extend its authority onto the reservation. So in 1891 Colorado began to petition for federal protection, a move opposed for many years by those with mining interests, who suspected the mesa also contained valuable mineral resources. When the Antiquities Act was passed in 1906 and Mesa Verde was made a national park, it was belatedly discovered that the most significant historical features had been placed outside the park boundaries. The Utes held out for seven years before giving up this property in return for extension of their reservation lands. As new finds have been discovered on the mesa, the boundaries have been extended three other times, the last as recently as 1963.

Cliff Palace, the best known of the Mesa Verde ruins, is closed during the winter months and may be visited only with a ranger guide in spring and fall. Another of the most impressive ruins, Balcony House, which can be reached only by climbing a thirty-two-foot ladder, is also accessible only with a ranger and is closed in winter. The Spruce Tree Ruin, near the Far View Visitor Center, is open all year, however. The center, sixteen miles south of the park entrance, should be the first stop for all visitors to get a general orientation of the park's attractions. There are also two excellent multimedia shows projected on nine screens here. "Anasazi" tells the story of the Mesa's history, and a second program describes the lives of Native Americans in the region today. The Far View ruins in this area preserve some of the pueblo homes that preceded the cliff dwellings. Four miles farther south is the Chapin Mesa Museum, with exhibits on the arts and daily lives of the people who lived here. Loop drives to other points of interest in the park begin at either the visitor center or museum, and maps can be obtained at both places.

LOCATION: *Mesa Verde lies just south of U.S. 160, about 10 miles east of Cortez.*
HOURS: *The Chapin Mesa Museum is open daily, 8–5, while the visitor center is open the same hours, Memorial Day through Labor Day. Several ruins are closed during the winter months, and others may be temporarily inaccessible because of snow. The multimedia shows at the visitor center are usually scheduled on the half hour, daily, from 6:30 P.M. to 9:30 P.M.*
ADMISSION: *$5 a carload. The multimedia shows cost $2.50.*
TELEPHONE: *(303) 529-4465.*

UTE INDIAN MUSEUM

T he museum sits on property once owned by Ouray, the great leader of the Utes. His strategy was to retreat with dignity before the unstoppable tide of white settlement, always trying to bargain for the best possible deal with every land concession. Every deal he made, however, was eventually over-turned. Miners took away Ute claims in the San Juan Mountains when gold was discovered there. When settlers reached the fertile Uncompahgre Valley, in this area, Ouray was forced from his own farm and his tribe shoved into the barren southwestern corner of the state. For a time, Colorado tried to expel the entire Ute tribe into Utah, which was only a territory at the time and had less clout in Washington. The tribe finally was granted secure land rights in 1878, but Ouray died a deeply embittered man. Before his death in 1881 he made his wife, Chipeta, swear that she would never reveal his burial place; so profound was his distrust of whites. She finally broke her vow shortly before her own death in 1924 and Ouray was reinterred near Ignacio (*see* Sky Ute Center, Ignacio, Colorado) on the Southern Ute Reservation. There is also a memorial to him here, near the grave of Chipeta. This is the only museum in Colorado dedicated to the history, and culture of a single tribe. Dioramas depict many of the pivotal events in Ute history, and there are also displays of their artifacts and crafts.

LOCATION: *The museum is just south of Montrose, on U.S. 550, the road that becomes the famous Million Dollar Highway.*
HOURS: *Monday through Saturday, 10–5, and Sunday, 1–5, Mid-May through mid-October.*
ADMISSION: *$2.*
TELEPHONE: *(303) 249-3098.*

LOWRY RUINS

T he Lowry Ruins mark an outlying settlement of the same people who inhabited the community at Hovenweep National Monument (*see* Utah) and are more accessible than that park. The great painted kiva here is the most significant find. There were ten kivas in all, indicating that the place had special religious meaning to the Hovenweep people. There is also an eleventh

▲ *The ten kivas at Lowry Ruins held special religious meaning for the Hovenweep people who built and inhabited them.*

century pueblo, built atop the ruins of a residence constructed three hundred years earlier.

LOCATION: *West of town by dirt road, off U.S. 666. Pleasant View is about 20 miles north of Cortez.*
HOURS: *Daily, dawn to dusk.*
ADMISSION: *Free.*
TELEPHONE: *(303) 882-4811.*

Towaoc

UTE MOUNTAIN TRIBAL PARK

When the Ute reservation was divided in 1877, the westernmost lands were taken by the Weminuche band. With their settlement on the slopes of 9,977-foot-high Ute Peak, this branch of the tribe began referring to its land as the Ute Mountain Reservation. The initial division was made because the Weminuche were sheepherders and their land was held in common, while the other Utes were farmers and owned land individually. In recent years, the Ute Mountain group has built up a tourist industry and opened the Tribal Park at Towaoc. A pottery here produces ceramics using traditional patterns and methods. Visitors can observe the process. There are also guided trips to Anasazi ruins on the reservation lands. These are especially well preserved because visits to them are strictly controlled.

LOCATION: *Towaoc is west of U.S. 160, 666, about 12 miles south of Cortez.*
HOURS: *Daily, 9–6, June through September.*
ADMISSION: *Admission to the pottery is free. There is a fee for tours of the ruins.*
TELEPHONE: *(303) 565-8548.*

IDAHO

RESERVATION

A clerical error made when Fort Hall Reservation was being formed resulted in another of the brief, costly wars between native peoples and the army in the Northwest. The mistake came when the Bannock, a branch of the Shoshone that ranged along the Snake River, agreed to settle here. They were a seminomadic people, depending on salmon from the Snake and buffalo hunted on the Montana plains. During the summer, they gathered camas roots on the Idaho prairies.

This blue flower bloomed from April to July, growing wild across vast meadowlands. Its bulbs are edible, and the Idaho tribes would dig them up and steam them for twenty-four hours in a cooker of heated stones. Possession of camas meadows was a major source of conflict among the tribes in the state. When the Bannock moved to Fort Hall in 1877, during the Nez Perce revolt under Chief Joseph (*see* Nez Perce National Historic Park, Spalding, Idaho), they thought the treaty guaranteed them access to camas. But when the document was transcribed by a clerk unfamiliar with the word, the clause came out "Kansas meadows." Since this made no sense, it was dropped from the final draft.

The reservation lands were not fertile, and in the spring of 1878 several members of the Bannock left to dig for camas. When they reached the meadows, however, they found them occupied by white herdsmen. A confrontation developed and two settlers were shot. The Bannock then retreated west, in the opposite direction of the Nez Perce trek of the previous year. They gathered several bands of Paiute with them and made their way into Oregon. Over a campaign that lasted four weeks, the Bannock and their allies were overtaken and defeated by the First Cavalry in a series of battles that inflicted a heavy toll on Indian noncombatants.

The reservation itself was built around the site of Fort Hall, a landmark of the Oregon Trail when it was occupied by the British Hudson's Bay Company. It was demolished by a flood in 1863, eight years after being abandoned. Fort Hall Days, held on the second weekend in August, is the largest Native American gathering in the Northwest. This is a major observance, with danc-

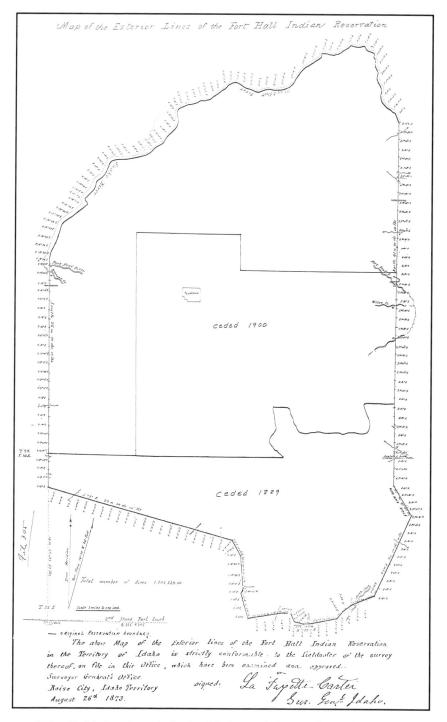

▲ *Fort Hall Indian Agency is the site of the largest Native American gathering in the Northwest.*

ing, rodeo competition, crafts, and traditional foods. There are also stores open year-round in Fort Hall selling crafts and artwork.

LOCATION: *Fort Hall is located just off Interstate 15, about 7 miles north of Pocatello.*
TELEPHONE: *(208) 238-3700.*

Kellogg

OLD MISSION STATE PARK

T he church at Mission State Park is a restoration of the oldest building in Idaho. It was erected by members of the Coeur d'Alene tribe working with the Jesuit Father Antonio Ravalli. The Mission of the Sacred Heart was built in 1848 of logs drawn here by hand-pulled carts and was decorated with Native American depictions of heaven and hell. The Coeur d'Alene are a Salishan people who originated on the Pacific coast of British Columbia and gradually became hunters after acquiring horses. They were defeated by the U.S. Army in 1858 after a brief uprising in protest of accelerating white settlement. They were forced to cede these lands in 1887 when they were moved to a smaller reservation southwest of here and the mission fell into ruin. It was restored, however, in 1930, and care was taken to preserve the elements of Native American design.

LOCATION: *The mission is off Interstate 90, about 10 miles west of Kellogg.*
HOURS: *Daily, 8–6, June through August; daily, 9–5, rest of the year, except December through February, when it's closed.*
ADMISSION: *$2.50 per vehicle.*
TELEPHONE: *(208) 682-3814.*

Moscow

APPALOOSA MUSEUM

T he Nez Perce are credited with developing this breed, famous for its durability and size. It turned the Nez Perce into the Northwest's most accomplished horsemen and made their settlements a special target for raids by other tribes, who prized the animals. The roan horses marked with spotted

▲ *The church at Old Mission was constructed in the mid-1800s by members of the Coeur d'Alene tribe and Catholic missionaries.*

rumps have remained very popular over the years, and this museum celebrates the lore that has grown up around them.

Exhibits trace the Appaloosa back to their origin with the Nez Perce. The museum's collections are broken down into materials devoted to Native American Horse Cultures, the Pioneering Northwest, the Development of the Appaloosa Horse Club, and contemporary issues of the breed today. Strongest emphasis is placed on how the horse culture was reflected in the Nez Perce way of life through arts, crafts, tools, clothing and utensils. Among the many fine examples of early Nez Perce horse tack are a woman's saddle dated to 1877, a rare beaded bridle and apishmore, and several unique horse blankets. A paddock in the back holds a number of Appaloosas for visitors to view.

LOCATION: *The museum is in the western part of town, on Idaho 8, the Moscow-Pullman Highway.*
HOURS: *Monday through Friday, 8–5. Also open Saturday 9-3, June through September.*
ADMISSION: *Free.*
TELEPHONE: *(208) 882-5578.*

Nez Perce National Historical Park

The Nez Perce National Historical Park is one of the most interesting concepts the National Park Service has developed. The park links twenty-four different sites across twelve thousand square miles in the vicinity of the Nez Perce Reservation, near the base of Idaho's northern panhandle. Each place is meant to illustrate a different aspect of the history and culture of this people.

The Nez Perce are best remembered for their epic running battle with the U.S. Army in 1877. Under Chief Joseph, they eluded pursuing forces from their home in the Wallowa Valley of Oregon all the way to Bears Paw Battlefield in northern Montana (*see* Bears Paw State Monument, Chinook, Montana). The Nez Perce reservation, at Lapwai, was established in 1855, then severely reduced when gold was discovered nearby. It was the refusal to leave their lands in Oregon and move there that resulted in Chief Joseph's trek. The course of that campaign passed right through the middle of this area before crossing the Lolo Trail into Montana. Descendants of his band now live in the Colville Reservation in Washington, not Lapwai.

Any visit to the park should begin at the visitor center, near the town of Spalding. A complete list of sites in the park is available there, along with displays on Nez Perce culture.

LOCATION: *The visitor center is on U.S. 95 near the town of Spalding, about 12 miles southeast of Lewiston.*
EXHIBITS: *Displays relate to Nez Perce life and the Lewis and Clark Expedition. There is an audiovisual show and maps of the various park units in the area.*
HOURS: *Daily, 8–6, June through Labor Day; 8–4:30, rest of year.*
ADMISSION: *Free.*
TELEPHONE: *(208) 843-2261.*

CAMAS PRAIRIE AND WHITE BIRD BATTLEFIELD

A marker on the road to White Bird Summit explains the role that camas roots played in Nez Perce diet and culture. The blue flowers once grew in profusion in this valley, which is now a major wheat-producing center. The view over this beautiful, bountiful valley from the 4,245-foot-high summit of White Bird Hill is well worth a stop. White Bird Battlefield, sixteen miles south of Grangeville, was the site of the first major battle of Chief Joseph's War. A cavalry detail was sent out from Fort Lapwai to pursue his band when it refused to enter the reservation. The troopers were attacked in this canyon on June 17, 1877, and routed, with thirty-four killed. The battle was the first indication for the army that this campaign was going to be long and difficult.

LOCATION: *South of Grangeville by way of U.S. 95.*
HOURS: *Dawn to dusk.*
ADMISSION: *Free.*

HEART OF THE MONSTER

According to Nez Perce legends, the Heart of the Monster, a volcanic rock formation along the Clearwater River, was the birthplace of the tribe.

LOCATION: *South of Kamiah on U.S. 12.*
HOURS: *Mid-June through Labor Day.*
ADMISSION: *Free.*

LAPWAI MISSION

The Lapwai Mission was the first permanent European settlement in Idaho, established in 1836 by Rev. Henry Spalding and his wife, Eliza. These missionaries established a firm rapport with the Nez Perce. Besides religious teaching, they offered valuable instruction on agricultural techniques. The Nez Perce returned their friendship, but it could not survive the onrush of white settlement in the following generation. The Spaldings are buried in an adjacent Indian burial ground.

LOCATION: *Adjacent to the park's visitor center, in Spalding, southeast of Lewiston on U.S. 95.*
HOURS: *Daily, 8-6, June through Labor Day; 8-4:30, rest of year.*
ADMISSION: *Free.*
TELEPHONE: *(208) 843-2261.*

LAPWAI TRIBAL HEADQUARTERS

Buildings that were originally a part of Fort Lapwai, the U.S. Army base put here in 1862 to supervise the reservation, are still used by tribal administrators. The Tribal Community Building has information on gatherings and crafts. The Warriors Memorial Pow Wow, held here on the third weekend of June, honors Chief Joseph and his band.

LOCATION: *Southeast of Lewiston on U.S. 95.*
HOURS: *Monday through Thursday, 8–12 and 12:30–4:30.*
ADMISSION: *Free.*
TELEPHONE: *(208) 843-2253.*

WEIPPE PRAIRIE

T he Weippe high prairie, which extends east to the base of the Bitterroot Range and the Continental Divide, was another source of camas roots for the Nez Perce. The Weippe area was also the starting point for Chief Joseph's crossing of the mountains on the Lolo Trail. Portions of the actual trail are still open but should only be attempted with four-wheel-drive vehicles. U.S. 12 closely parallels the trail in many places. Markers in the Weippe area relate the story of the trail, which also was used by Lewis and Clark.

LOCATION: *East of Weippe from U.S. 12, on Idaho 11, about 32 miles northeast of Kamiah.*

NEVADA

HICKISON SUMMIT PETROGLYPHS

U.S. 50 has been called The Loneliest Road in America because for 260 miles on its run through central Nevada it never goes through a community of more than one thousand souls. Hickison Summit, at about the midway point of this journey, is as lonely as it gets. Near the northern slopes of Antelope Peak, with views of barren country extending for miles in every direction, an unknown native people left messages in the rocks. Important because of its strategic location at a mountain pass, the site contains drawings dated as far back as 1000 B.C. that are among the most important in Nevada.

LOCATION: *Hickison Summit is 24 miles east of Austin on U.S. 50.*
HOURS: *Daily, dawn to dusk.*
ADMISSION: *Free.*

STEWART INDIAN MUSEUM

The Washoe were a fairly secluded people living along Lake Tahoe, into the Sierra Nevada and the well-watered valleys of Nevada to the east. This was land that most settlers passed through on their way to California, and the tribe was pretty much left in peace. They lived in very small family settlements, relying on fishing and gathering for their sustenance. But with the discovery of the Comstock Lode in 1858, settlers came pouring into their territory, displacing them from traditional habitations and ways of life. In addition, their enemies, the Paiute, defeated them at about the same time. With no lands of their own, the Washoe were reduced to working at odd jobs on the fringe of white settlements.

Among those who worked on their behalf was U.S. Senator William M. Stewart. He helped establish the Carson Indian Agency in 1890 to give them education and medical care. Two years later, the first of the tiny reserves, consistent with the small size of the traditional Washoe communities, was set aside for them in the Carson City area. There are now four such colonies along the Nevada-California boundary area.

The Stewart Museum, located on the site of the former Indian school, displays the high level of Washoe achievement in basketry. Other exhibits are concerned with the history of the Great Basin tribes and examples of jewelry and contemporary art. There is an annual crafts show and powwow held here on the third weekend in June.

LOCATION: *The museum is 5 miles south of Carson City off U.S. 395.*
HOURS: *Daily, 9–4.*
ADMISSION: *Free.*
TELEPHONE: *(702) 882-1808.*

Overton

LOST CITY MUSEUM

L ake Mead, the catch basin for the Colorado River behind Hoover Dam, transformed southern Nevada from empty desert to a water recreation land. Among its casualties, however, was the site of the state's oldest pueblo community. Pueblo Grande de Nevada flourished after 600 A.D. and at its peak may have extended for thirty miles along both banks of the Muddy River. But the cycle of drought eventually led to its abandonment after three hundred years. Its inhabitants are believed to be ancestors of the Hopi of Arizona.

Most of this village, the Lost City, was flooded by the lake, but not before an extensive sampling of ancient tools, pottery and baskets was rescued from the site. The museum here was built to house them in the 1930s. The facility itself rests on what was once part of the village, and adjacent pueblo dwellings have been rebuilt on their ancient foundations.

LOCATION: *The museum is just south of town, on Nevada 169, about 13 miles south of Interstate 15.*
HOURS: *Daily, 8:30–4:30.*
ADMISSION: *$1.*
TELEPHONE: *(702) 397-2193.*

▲ *Restored Anasazi Pueblo dwellings on the grounds of Lost City Museum.*

VALLEY OF FIRE STATE PARK

There may not be a more vivid and dramatic setting in the country for petroglyphs made by prehistoric native peoples. This twisted forest of sandstone was sculpted by the wind into incredible shapes and colored a vibrant red. The Valley of Fire was probably occupied from 300 B.C. to A.D. 1150, and prehistoric users included the Basket Maker people, and later, the Ansazi Pueblo farmers from the nearby Moapa Valley. Although the scarcity of water probably limited the length of their stay, the visits of these people probably involved hunting, food gathering, and religious ceremonies.

Several sites within the park contain examples of rock art left by these people. Shapes of circles and squares, lizards and sheep, men, and deer are all drawn on this fiery-looking surface. The petroglyphs are probably related to the nearby Pueblo Grande de Nevada settlement, which would date them between the 7th and 10th centuries, A.D. Atlatl Rock is of particular interest, and is named for its depiction of the atlatl, a notched stick that added speed and distance to a thrown spear, and was a predecessor to the bow and arrow.

Valley of Fire is Nevada's oldest state park, and it contains an interesting assortment of flora and fauna. The area's plant community is dominated by widely spaced creosote bush, burro bush, and brittle bush, and several varieties of cactus are common. There are many species of lizards and snakes in the park, as well as the coyote, kit fox, black tailed jackrabbit, and antelope ground squirrel. Interpretive centers with trailside displays are located at the most impressive sites, and a map can be obtained at the park visitor center.

LOCATION: *The visitor center is located near the park's eastern boundary, about 15 miles southwest of Overton and 25 miles from Interstate 15.*
HOURS: *Daily. The park is open from dawn to dusk; the visitor center, 8:30–4:30.*
ADMISSION: *$3 per car.*
TELEPHONE: *(702) 397-2088.*

Pyramid Lake

PAIUTE RESERVATION

This mysterious body of water, rimmed by painted hills and studded with fantastically shaped rock formations, has been home to the northern Paiute since the beginning of tribal memory. They zealously guarded this territory, even after the Comstock Lode brought whites pouring into the area. Game was depleted and the piñon trees, a primary source of food, were cut down for fuel and supports for mine tunnels.

In 1860, with the Paiute already enraged by these actions, two Indian women were kidnapped by settlers. Their rescuers killed five whites in a raid on a trading post near Carson City. A punitive expedition was organized and dispatched to Pyramid Lake, along the Truckee River trail. But almost within sight of the lake's southern shore, the Paiute attacked and inflicted tremendous losses on the militia. Almost half were killed, and when the rest straggled back to safety, their reports raised a furor throughout the Pacific Slope. Troops were summoned from as far away as San Francisco. With a clear superiority in numbers and weaponry, they managed to defeat the Indians three weeks later in a three-hour battle near the site of the first engagement. The Paiute retreated into the desert and for the next several years established themselves as the most feared obstacle along the Humboldt Trail to California. In 1874, the government finally concluded a treaty, which established their rights to Pyramid Lake and the surrounding country.

The Tribal Council has turned the lake into prime recreational grounds. Its trout fishing is famous in the West, and its scenery is among the most evocative in the high desert country. Visitor centers at the trout hatchery in Sutcliffe and south of agency headquarters in Nixon supply information on the major scenic points and necessary fishing licenses. You can still see the pyramids, formed of porous rock, or tufa, which led John C. Fremont to give the lake its name during his exploration of 1844. The largest of them stands almost five hundred feet above the lake surface. Others resemble sharp needles rising from the water and a woman covered by an overturned basket. An island near the southeastern shore is a sanctuary for white pelicans. The lake is all that remains of prehistoric Lake Lahontan, which once covered most of the Great Basin in northern Nevada and Utah. Irrigation projects have severely restricted the flow of water into its southern end along the Truckee River, and the lake is slowly shrinking.

LOCATION: *The lake and reservation are about 35 miles north of Reno by way of Nevada 445, or 16 miles north of the Wadsworth exit of Interstate 80 by way of Nevada 447. The western shore drive, Nevada 446, leads to the best viewpoints.*
HOURS: *Visitor centers are open daily, 9–5.*
ADMISSION: *Free.*
TELEPHONE: *(702) 574-0140.*

NEW MEXICO

ACOMA PUEBLO

New Mexico's license plate motto reads "Land of Enchantment." If there were ever any doubts about truth in advertising, they are dispelled here. Acoma, the sky city, is truly a place of enchantment. Even the people who live on this mesa-top pueblo refer to the adjacent mesa as Enchanted. According to Pueblo tradition, that was originally their home, until a great storm washed away the only access to its top, but that was a long time ago. Acoma now contends with the Hopi town of Old Oraibi (*see* Oraibi, Arizona) as the oldest continuously inhabited community in the United States. Scientists have dated logs used in construction here to the middle of the twelfth century, approximately the same time period as the founding of Oraibi. But an Acoma tradition extends the period of residence back another one thousand years. Like Oraibi, however, only a handful of people still live here permanently. Most have moved to communities at ground level, where modern amenities such as electricity and running water are possible, and only return to the pueblo for feast days.

Acoma's rock rises from the desert floor to a height of 367 feet. It was a thriving farming community when Coronado's exploration party visited in 1540. Residents would descend to the ground to work the fields by day and then climb back to the pueblo at night by a finger-and-toe ladder trail cut into the sheer rock. A graded trail is available to visitors today, which is moderately strenuous but not difficult for those in reasonably good shape. A shuttle bus also makes the trip from the visitor center at the base.

Acoma was able to resist Spanish demands for submission for several years, until a three-day siege and assault finally captured it in 1599. The Spanish then were thrown out during the Pueblo Rebellion of 1680 and had to wait another twelve years before they could reassert their authority here. The Spanish grant by which Acoma's land claims were recognized in 1659 was continued by the United States more than two hundred years later when New Mexico passed under American control.

Besides the three-story pueblo buildings, the most remarkable structure on the mesa is the mission church, San Esteban del Rey. Parts of it date to the original church on the site, built under the supervision of Father Juan Ramirez

▲ *Acoma Pueblo is one of the oldest continuously inhabited communities in the United States.*

in 1629. Acoma legends tell of the priest walking alone from Santa Fe carrying only a cross and then climbing the mesa through a storm of arrows and missiles. When he revived a young girl who had fallen from the mesa top during the excitement, he was accepted into Acoma and allowed to found his mission. This is one of the largest of the pueblo churches, and every piece of it had to be carried up to the mesa by human labor. The church was restored in 1923 and most of the rich interior ornamentation in the chancel brought back to its original colors.

All visitors to the pueblo must register at the visitor center at Acoma's base. Access to the mesa top is only through guided tours. A small historical museum and a shop selling some of the distinctively patterned pottery made here, as well as a restaurant serving local specialties, are also at the visitor center. There are several celebrations during the year, the largest and most important being St. Esteban (St. Stephan) Day on September 2.

LOCATION: *Acoma is 13 miles south of Interstate 40 by way of New Mexico 23.*
HOURS: *Daily, 8-6, March through September; 8-4:30, rest of year. Closed for religious observances July 10-13 and the first weekend of October. The last tour leaves the visitor center one hour before closing time.*
ADMISSION: *$5, plus additional fees for photography and sketching.*
TELEPHONE: *(505) 252-1139.*

Albuquerque

INDIAN PUEBLO CULTURAL CENTER

The Indian Pueblo Cultural Center is a centralized facility owned and operated by all the state's nineteen pueblo communities and gives visitors a sampling of the history and culture of each. There are craft demonstrations, art galleries, a crafts shop, traditional dances on weekends, and a restaurant serving typical pueblo-style dishes. A yearly calendar of Indian dances and events includes celebrations of feast days, puberty rites, harvest dances, rooster pulls, rain dances, and more. For those who do not have the time to see more than one or two of the pueblos, the center gives a sample of what you are missing. It is also a handy guide to finding which pueblos suit your particular interests.

The Pueblo House Children's Museum is a "hands-on" facility for children to learn about the history of the Pueblos. Children may handle tools, stone weapon points, a fire drill, and a mano and metate (used to grind corn). There are also language tapes, drums, and materials for firing pottery.

LOCATION: *The center is at 2401 12th Street, NW, just west of downtown, off the 12th Street exit of Interstate 40.*
HOURS: *Daily, 9-5:30. Closed Christmas, Thanksgiving, and New Years Day. Children's Museum open Tuesday, Wednesday, and Friday, 9-4, and by appointment.*
ADMISSION: *$2.50.*
TELEPHONE: *(505) 843-7270.*

MAXWELL MUSEUM OF ANTHROPOLOGY

Part of the University of New Mexico, the Maxwell Museum has one of the finest collections of material relating to early native communities in the state. The museum holds major collections of Native American Southwest arts, including Hopi kachina dolls, Navajo weaving and sandpainting, historic and

▲ *Traditional dances are held at Indian Pueblo Cultural Center.*

prehistoric Pueblo pottery, and Apache, Pima, Pago, and other tribal baskets. Its Photographic Archive contains over 250,000 images, including many of the earliest photographs of Pueblo and Navajo subjects taken in the late 19th century.

Maxwell has sponsored numerous archaeological excavations; the museum's holdings include the materials excavated in the Chaco Canyon area since the early 1920s, the largest and most comprehensive archaeological research collection of Anasazi materials in existence. Maxwell's collections use recent research projects to illustrate anthropological goals and methods. A recent exhibition recreated portions of an archaeological dig that had been conducted in Tijeras Canyon, using the context of the project to depict how archaeologists uncover and analyze the past.

LOCATION: *The museum is near the northwestern corner of the campus, on Roma Avenue, NE, and University Avenue. The area is east of downtown by way of Lomas Boulevard.*

HOURS: *Monday through Saturday, 9–4.*

ADMISSION: *Free.*

TELEPHONE: *(505) 277-4404.*

▲ *The community of pueblos at Aztec Ruins was built about A.D.1100 —not by the Aztec, as European settlers presumed, but by the Anasazi.*

Aztec °

AZTEC RUINS NATIONAL MONUMENT

The appelation Aztec Ruins is yet another of those spurious references to the Mexican Empire in which the Southwest abounds. The first white settlers were quick to attribute any impressive ruins they came upon to the mighty Aztecs. However, the Aztecs lived centuries after the rise and decline of this Anasazo town. Although these ruins were known to Spanish explorers by the eighteenth century, systematic excavation did not begin until 1923. A massive quadrangle containing five hundred rooms was uncovered within its stone walls, with most of it built around A.D. 1100. But the most significant find was the great kiva. This underground ceremonial chamber, measuring forty-eight feet in diameter, is the most impressive ever found in the United States. There are larger ones, but none in such good condition. The restoration was done with fine sensitivity, enhancing the sense of religious awe the pueblo residents must have felt when they entered it. As one commentator put it "The kiva is not a primitive hole in the ground; it is architecture." The great kiva is the centerpiece of this monument and sets it apart as a memorable place. There is also a small museum on the site, displaying articles found in the excavation.

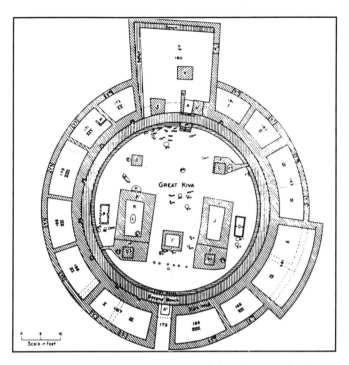

▲ *The great kiva at Aztec Ruins is a marvel of prehistoric engineering. It was excavated in 1921 and rebuilt in 1934.*

LOCATION: Aztec Ruins is in the northwest corner of the state, off U.S. 550, north of the town of Aztec.
HOURS: *Daily, 8–5.*
ADMISSION: *$1 a person or $3 a carload.*
TELEPHONE: *(505) 334-6174.*

Bernalillo

CORONADO STATE MONUMENT

C oronado State Monument is named for the Spanish invader who ransacked New Mexico in his misguided search for the Seven Golden Cities of Cibola. It is, however, the ruin of the Tiwa village of Kuaua, at which Coronado spent the winter of 1540–41. The Tiwa ranged through this area, and the language group survives today in the nearby pueblos of Sandia and Isleta, as well as the better-known Taos pueblo, to the north. Kuaua was settled in about 1300, but when the Spanish returned to the area to complete their conquest, in 1598, they found it already deserted. The murals uncovered in the great kiva here are extremely rare multicolored depictions of humans, animals, and ceremonial activities. The kiva has been restored, and the original murals are displayed in the visitor center. The museum here explains the cultural changes that swept over the Pueblo culture as a result of the Spanish invasion.

LOCATION: *The monument is just across the Rio Grande from the New Mexico 44 exit of Interstate 25.*
HOURS: *Daily, 9–5.*
ADMISSION: *$2.*
TELEPHONE: *(505) 867-5351.*

Chaco Culture National Historical Park

PUEBLO BONITO

P ueblo Bonito can be reached only by dirt road. By that measure, there has not been much in the way of technological advance in this part of the country for the last milennium or so. The people who lived in the massive pueblos here were road builders, too. They constructed straight-line, twenty-to-thirty-foot-wide thoroughfares from this settlement to outlying communities near Aztec Ruins National Monument (*see* Aztec Ruins National Monument, Albuquerque, New Mexico) and satellite settlements in other directions. Moreover, the builders possessed neither horses nor wheels. The thoroughfares are the only known example of roads built north of Central America before the Spanish conquest and a fair example of the advanced level at which the Chaco people lived.

The Chaco were a subgroup of the Anasazi. Nomads at first, they adapted to an agricultural society and by the tenth century had occupied Bonito Canyon. The four-story pueblo built here, with more than six hundred rooms and kivas, was one of the largest dwellings in the Southwest. It held a population of more than fifteeen hundred, larger than most communities in the area today. Judging from the variety of trade goods, especially the finely worked turquoise, found in the area, the Chaco were wealthy people. They mastered the mechanics of irrigation, diverting storm runoffs into their fields.

But years of drought finally reduced the water levels in the canyon to a point that could not sustain life. The Chaco people scattered in the thirteenth century and were probably absorbed by the other populations in the area. Their culture is still being studied intensely, as one of the most brilliant flowerings of Anasazi life. The park preserves thirteen separate ruins in this area, each of them attesting to the level of achievement the Chaco had reached. Some of their pueblos are easily the size of a contemporary city block, and all exhibit a high degree of workmanship. A visitor center near the park's south entrance puts the Chaco culture in historical perspective. A series of trails leading to the various parts of the park also originates here.

LOCATION: *The park is fairly difficult to reach because of the absence of paved roads. The best route is to take New Mexico 57 north from Interstate 40 at the Thoreau exit and follow it north for 63 miles, of which the last 20 are dirt.*
HOURS: *Daily, 8-5.*
ADMISSION: *$1, or $3 a carload.*
TELEPHONE: *(505) 988-6727.*

Cochiti

COCHITI PUEBLO

C ochiti is one of the Keresan-language pueblos, related to several others in the Rio Grande Valley between Santa Fe and Albuquerque. The Church of San Bueneventura, portions of which date from 1628, is a great example of Spanish-Indian mission architecture. The drums made here of aspen and cottonwood are famous for their tone and quality. They are heard to best advantage during the annual feast day, July 14, on which the traditional Corn Dance ritual is blended into the Catholic celebration. Cochiti tradition teaches that their people originated in Frijoles Canyon (*see* Bandelier National Monument, Albuquerque, New Mexico). They occupied several sites in this valley but have been situated here at least since the sixteenth century, when they were first visited by the Spanish. The pueblo was abandoned for nine years, from 1683 to 1692, in the turmoil following the rebellion against Spanish rule. The population took up a fortified position in a nearby canyon, but were persuaded to return to their homes. The greatest part of the mission church dates from their return.

LOCATION: *The pueblo is best reached from the Domingo exit of Interstate 25 on New Mexico 22, then north to the Rio Grande bridge. The pueblo is on the far side.*
HOURS: *Daily, dawn to dusk.*
ADMISSION: *Free. No cameras.*
TELEPHONE: *(505) 465-2244.*

Dulce

JICARILLA APACHE CENTER

J icarilla means "little baskets," and this branch of the Apache was given the name by the Spanish because of their proficiency in making small drinking vessels. This is the most northern of all the Apache groups, and also the highest, with part of the reservation lands situated on the Continental Divide. The Jicarilla originally lived farther east in New Mexico and were an agricultural people, heavily influenced by the Pueblo cultures they lived among. But they were driven from their homes by Comanche in the early eighteenth century and moved to the high country. They formed an alliance with the Ute against their old enemies but were defeated again. Demoralized, they took to raiding the Santa Fe Trail, which brought them into conflict with federal troops. After making peace in 1854, they were moved to several reservations until these lands, originally claimed by their Ute allies, were opened up for them in 1887. The Jicarilla have developed a prosperous recreational industry, licensing hunting and fishing on their lands and also running a cross-country ski operation. The Jicarilla Center in Dulce, the tribal headquarters, has many examples of the basketry that gave the tribe its name. Visitors may also watch artisans at work.

LOCATION: *Dulce is on U.S. 64, just south of the Colorado line.*
HOURS: *Monday through Saturday, 9–5.*
ADMISSION: *Free.*
TELEPHONE: *(505) 759-3515.*

Gallup

RED ROCK STATE PARK

L ocated athwart the Santa Fe Railroad main line and Route 66, the "mother road" of the early automotive era, the mining town of Gallup became closely associated with native culture. Situated just south of the huge Navajo reservation and immediately north of the Zuni lands, it is the place where most travelers from the East first encountered real Indians. Enterprising native craftsmen would meet the trains at the station here to sell their goods. So Gallup developed an image as the place where the Southwest of the romantic adventure stories really began. In 1922, a group of local businessmen decided to capitalize on this reputation. They met with representatives of several nearby native groups and together they drew up plans for a huge intertribal celebration. It was to be an annual observance that highlighted the culture, tradition, and crafts of all the Southwestern tribes. From that beginning, the Inter-Tribal Ceremonial has grown into the best-known event of its kind in North America, almost a signature of native culture. More than fifty tribes from all over the continent now participate.

The celebration quickly expanded far beyond the capacity of the county fairgrounds, where it was first held. Red Rock State Park, a natural amphitheater just east of Gallup, was then developed for the ceremonial, which is held in mid-August. Originally the date was the last week in August, but according to local lore, that was the same date on which the Hopi, to the west, held their Snake Dances, and the rains they brought kept washing out the events in Gallup. So in 1939, the date was moved up a week and it now begins on the second Thursday of the month.

The rodeo arena at Red Rock seats sixty-eight hundred and is used in the ceremonial. There are also tribal dances, crafts booths, and traditional games and foods. The ceremonial lasts for four days. But even at other times, Red Rock keeps the spirit alive. Dances are held on every evening during the summer, and the museum here has permanent exhibits of the art of Navajo, Zuni, and Hopi.

LOCATION: *Red Rock is 8 miles east of Gallup, off Interstate 40.*
HOURS: *Daily, 8 A.M. –9 P.M. , Memorial Day through Labor Day; Monday through Friday, 8-4:30, rest of year. Traditional dances are held daily, at 7:30 P.M. , Memorial Day through Labor Day.*
ADMISSION: *Donations. $3 to dances.*
TELEPHONE: *(505) 722-3839.*

NAVAJO CODE TALKERS EXHIBIT

The Navajo Code Talkers Exhibit tells the story of one of the more unusual episodes of World War II. In an effort to draw up a code that would defy Japanese cryptologists, the U.S. Marines turned to the Navajo language. Philip Johnston, an intelligence officer who grew up on the reservation as the son of a missionary, knew that the Navajo language depended strongly on vocal inflection and believed that any code based on it would be impossible for an outsider to break. So four hundred tribe members were enlisted as code talkers, communicating by spoken radio transmissions. According to marine histories, their efforts were invaluable in securely relaying advance plans for the landing on Iwo Jima. A room has been set aside in the Chamber of Commerce building to salute their service to the country.

LOCATION: *The Gallup-McKinley County Chamber of Commerce is in the center of town, at 103 West 66th Avenue (old U.S. 66).*
HOURS: *Monday through Friday, 9–5.*
ADMISSION: *Free.*
TELEPHONE: *(505) 722-2228.*

Gila Cliff Dwellings National Monument

MOGOLLON RUINS

The Gila Cliff Dwellers are spectacularly situated ruins carved out of the face of a cliff in a canyon on the Gila River, in spectacularly rugged country. They are worth visiting for the scenery as well as the history. The dwellings were inhabited by Mogollon culture, which thrived here in the early fourteenth century. About forty rooms have been excavated. Although the area seems tremendously isolated, the people who lived here conducted a lively trade with neighboring communities. But after an occupation that lasted only half a century, the area was abandoned. A self-guiding trail leads to the dwellings, and there is also a museum at the visitor center.

LOCATION: *The 44-mile drive north from Silver City, by way of New Mexico 15, leads through the center of the Gila Primitive Area. It is a magnificent mountain excursion, not recommended for camper vehicles.*
HOURS: *Daily, 8–6, Memorial Day through Labor Day; 9–4, rest of year.*
ADMISSION: *Free.*
TELEPHONE: *(505) 536-9461.*

Laguna

LAGUNA PUEBLO

The lake for which Laguna Pueblo was named dried up long ago. But the village established here in the early fourteenth century survives, although occupied primarily now only during ceremonials. Most of the population is scattered around several satellite farming settlements. The pueblo was settled by Keresan people, whose tradition tells of an earlier home in what was possibly Mesa Verde (*see* Mesa Verde National Park, Colorado.) When drought made

▲ *About forty rooms have been excavated at the Gila Cliff Dwellings, which were inhabited by Mogollon culture in the fourteenth century.*

that area uninhabitable, the Keresan migrated into this part of New Mexico. Right along the route that was later chosen for the Santa Fe Railroad and U.S. 66, Laguna was in constant contact with most of the tribes in this state. It absorbed emigrants from Acoma and Zuni, but also was raided by Apache, Ute, and Navajo. Its position also led to a high degree of acculturation, and religious tensions developed within the community. Much like the case of the Hopi town of Old Oraibi (*see* Oraibi, Arizona), the more conservative factions left, and soon Laguna had shrunk to a sliver of its former size.

Modernity paid off for Laguna, though, in the years after World War II. Uranium was discovered on Laguna lands, and for a while the mines provided a major source of income, used as seed money for several tribal enterprises and providing a source of steady employment. The mines are now closed and the sites are being reclaimed. The pueblo mission, built in 1699, is worth a visit to see its brightly decorated interior. The feast day on September 19 honors Saint Joseph and draws celebrants from all the Laguna villages.

LOCATION: *Old Laguna is just off Interstate 40, about 45 miles west of Albuquerque.*
HOURS: *Daily, dawn to dusk.*
ADMISSION: *Free. Camera regulations vary according to activities at the pueblo. It is best to check in advance.*
TELEPHONE: *(505) 552-6654.*

Los Alamos

BANDELIER NATIONAL MONUMENT

Adolph Bandelier was the first European to explain the historical importance and the unique culture of the Pueblo peoples to a general audience. The Swiss-born ethnologist wrote extensively on his scientific studies of the area. But it was his novel *The Delight Makers*, published in 1890, that first made the Pueblo religion and traditions accessible to the average reader. Frijoles Canyon was the setting he gave to the novel, an imaginative reconstruction of how these societies functioned before the European incursion. So the cliff dwellings in the canyon were named in his honor. The community built on the rocks and slopes of Frijoles Canyon thrived from about 1200 to 1400 and is noteworthy for a circular dwelling on the canyon floor. A trail leads to the more accessible ruins of the farming village, and there is a museum in the visitor center. The site is a 32,000 acre park.

LOCATION: *Bandelier is located off New Mexico 4, about 10 miles west of Los Alamos.*
HOURS: *Daily, 8–4:30.*
ADMISSION: *$5 a car.*
TELEPHONE: *(505) 672-3861.*

Mescalero

APACHE CULTURAL CENTER

To the Apache who lived in the deserts of southern New Mexico, mescal was truly the staff of life. In the words of one chronicler, this desert plant gave them, "a quasi-bread, two intoxicants, thread, clothing and countless minor staples." It was a nutritious food when roasted and was found almost everywhere on the Apache range. So important was this plant in the life of the desert Apache that the Spanish simply referred to the Apache as *Mescalero*. Their way of life enabled them to be an especially fast-moving group of people, a fact that confounded the white forces who sought to control them. They lived on both sides of the Rio Grande and, for a time, were allied with the Spanish authorities in Mexico. Their ability to disappear over the border, where federal troops could not follow, and then reappear on American soil many miles away was a source of endless frustration to the authorities. They were not defeated until the army developed a strategy of staking out the water holes they used and waiting in ambush.

The Mescalero were placed on the Fort Sumner reservation, used as a catch-all for the tribes the federal government regarded as hostile, in the 1860s. They were joined by the Navajo, forced to move there on the Long March from Arizona. The arrangement between traditional enemies did not work out at all. The Navajo went on strike, refusing to plant crops and forcing the government to move them back to Arizona. The Mescalero simply left and for the next twenty years defied the authorities on both sides of the Mexican border. Many of them joined the Chiricahua in their campaigns of the 1880s and were among the last of the tribes to lay down their arms. As late as 1913, Mescalero were still held as prisoners of war as a result of these campaigns.

This reservation was established in 1873, and it is one of the more encouraging Native American success stories. Timber and grazing lands are excellent, and in recent years the Mescalero have developed some of the finest recreational facilities in the state. Inn of the Mountain Gods is a luxurious four-season resort, and the tribe also operates a ski resort on nearby Sierra Blanca. The ceremonials and rodeo at Mescalero, held on the first four days of July, are among the best-attended in the region. Especially interesting are the Maidens' Puberty rites. There is also a tribal museum with historical and crafts displays.

LOCATION: *Mescalero is on U.S. 70, about 30 miles northeast of Alamogordo.*
HOURS: *The museum is open Monday through Friday, 9–4.*
ADMISSION: *Donation. No cameras are allowed at the ceremonials.*
TELEPHONE: *(505) 671-4494.*

Pecos

PECOS NATIONAL MONUMENT

Pecos was one of the strongest pueblo settlements at the time of Coronado's visit. It was the easternmost of the pueblos, situated on the edge of the Plains rather than deep in the mountains. That proved to be a mixed blessing. It gave Pecos an advantage in trading with the Plains tribes, and in the fourteenth century, according to the archeological evidence, it was among the wealthiest of New Mexico's native communities. But the site was also difficult to defend. The Spanish had no problem taking it in 1590, and in the following centuries it was a constant target for raids by the Comanche. A counterattack sent into Comanche country was ambushed and annihilated in 1750. Finally, its position simply became untenable, and in 1838, when the population was reduced to seventeen survivors, they simply walked away and moved west to Jemez, on the far side of the Rio Grande. Many of their descendants can still be found in Jemez. The ruins here consist of two seventeenth-century Franciscan churches and dwellings that once housed two thousand people. There is a self-guided walking tour and a museum.

LOCATION: *Pecos is just off Interstate 25, about 25 miles southeast of Santa Fe.*
HOURS: *Daily, 8–5.*
ADMISSION: *$1 a person or $3 a carload.*
TELEPHONE: *(505) 757-6414.*

Picuris

PICURIS PUEBLO

The Picuris pueblo is a community that has always chosen to go its own way. A bit more isolated than most of the pueblos, it retains a traditional system of self-government, with a governor and a tribal council. It was one of the centers of anti-Spanish sentiment during the Pueblo Rebellion of 1680, and a Picuris man, Tupatu, eventually became the leader of the dissidents. When the pueblo was unhappy with the restored Spanish rule, a large group moved to Kansas, 350 miles away, and built the El Cuartelejo community (*see* Scott, Kansas). Early Spanish explorers reported seeing buildings six and seven stories tall on this site. But they were destroyed during the rebellion, and the present community dates from the late seventeenth century. That is also when the San Lorenzo de Picuris Church was built, although most of it dates from 1776. Picuris is famous for its mica-flecked pottery, which gives it an unusual luster. A museum displays items recovered in archeological digs near the old pueblo and examples of the local pottery. The feast day for Saint Lawrence (San Lorenzo) is held on August 9 and 10, with traditional dances and footraces.

LOCATION: *The pueblo lies between Santa Fe and Taos, on the western slope of the Sangre de Cristo range. From Santa Fe, it is best reached by U.S. 285, then north on New Mexico Highways 4 and 76. From Taos, New Mexico 3 and 75 make the connection.*
HOURS: *The pueblo and museum are open daily, 8–8.*
ADMISSION: *$2.50.*
TELEPHONE: *(505) 587-2957.*

▲ *Abo ruins at Salinas Pueblos National Monument.*

Salinas Pueblos National Monument

Quarai, Abo, and Gran Quivira

Salinas Pueblos historical park contains the ruins of three pueblos that were among the last to be permanently abandoned. Most of them were occupied well into the seventeenth century, and a church at the Quarai site was built as late as 1820. The theme developed in all three sites within the park is the interaction between the Native American and Spanish cultures, and the ruins are among the most impressive existing from the colonial era. Abo, in particular, contains the best example of a medieval European church in North America. It was built by Tompiro Indians under Spanish direction in the 1620s. The buttressed wall rising in stark isolation in the desert is one of the most dramatic sights in the state.

This area was located amid salt deposits, and its inhabitants operated as middlemen in the salt commodity, trading between pueblo communities farther west and the Plains tribes. The inhabitants were especially vulnerable to the Apache, who became increasingly hostile to the pueblos the more closely they were tied to the Spanish and their slave raids. Finally, the combination of drought, disease, and unrelenting raids by the Apache forced the abandonment of these communities.

The park visitor center is in the town of Mountainair, and a museum there gives a historical overview. The Abo unit is just to the west, and to the north is Quarai, the last of the communities to be given up, with its unexcavated pueblo ruins, a convent, and two old churches. Gran Quivira, the original segment of the national monument, preserves the population center of the Salinas people, a pueblo that once was home to more than fifteen hundred people. Other seventeenth century churches are located here. Most of those who once lived here are believed to have fled south and established new communities in the El Paso area (*see* Tigua Museum, Ysleta, Texas). There are visitor centers at all three sites where leaflets for self-guided tours may be obtained.

LOCATION: *Abo is about 7 miles west of Mountainair on U.S. 60. Quarai is about 5 miles north on New Mexico 14. Gran Quivira is 25 miles south on New Mexico 14.*
HOURS: *The sites and visitor center in Mountainair are open daily, 9-5.*
ADMISSION: *Free.*
TELEPHONE: *(505) 847-2585.*

San Ildefonso

SAN ILDEFONSO PUEBLO

San Ildefonso pueblo has been known as an arts center since the early years of this century, when the black-on-black pottery of Maria and Julian Martinez became nationally famous. The inspiration for this technique came from shards recovered from ruins on the nearby Pajarito Plateau. Not quite as well known are the many painters who came from this pueblo, including some who exhibited at the Museum of Modern Art in New York. Why such talent should be concentrated in this community is still an open question. Edgar Hewett, of the Museum of New Mexico, encouraged the Martinez family and those they trained, and the tradition seems to have perpetuated itself. The Eight Northern Pueblos Artist and Craftsman Show, held here on the third weekend of July, is the largest Indian event of its kind in the country. A museum also shows off examples of local artists. The buffalo and Comanche dances are performed here on the feast day, January 23.

LOCATION: *San Ildefonso is on New Mexico 4, just west of U.S. 84, 285, about 20 miles north of Santa Fe.*
HOURS: *Daily, dawn to dusk.*
ADMISSION: *Free. $5 fee for photography, $10 for painting or sketching.*
TELEPHONE: *(505) 455-3549.*

▲ *The Indians of the San Ildefonso Pueblo are known for their pottery, and the pueblo itself has become an arts center.*

Santa Clara

SANTA CLARA PUEBLO

M any of the New Mexico pueblos have origin legends, tales about where the tribe began and how it got to this corner of the world. Santa Clara, however, is the only pueblo that actually runs tours to its place of origin. This settlement on the west bank of the Rio Grande believes that cliff dwellings at Puye, several miles away on the Pajarito Plateau, are the place from which their ancestors came. The 740-room communal ruin was built in the middle of the fifteenth century and was at its peak just before the Coronado expedition entered New Mexico in 1540. There are also habitations carved into caves on the rock face of the mesa extending for about a mile. According to tradition, these were used as winter residences because they offered more shelter. Puye was deserted by 1580 because of drought, and the rest of the population moved to Santa Clara, which was already settled. These are among the most recently abandoned cliff dwellings in the state. Because the state of deterioration was so slight, they were able to be stabilized, and a very clear picture emerges of what life was like in one of these ancient pueblos.

Santa Clara owns this land and regulates visits to Puye. The red and black pottery made in Santa Clara also is influenced directly by shards found in

Puye. There are many stores in the pueblo that sell them. The feast day here is August 12.

LOCATION: *Santa Clara is just south of Espanola, on New Mexico 30, about 30 miles northwest of Santa Fe. Puye is west of Santa Clara on New Mexico 5.*
HOURS: *Santa Clara is open daily, dawn to dusk. Puye is open daily, 9–6.*
ADMISSION: *Santa Clara is free, with a $4 fee charged for still photography, $10 for camcorders, and $15 for painting or sketching. Puye is $4.*
TELEPHONE: *(505) 753-7326.*

Santa Fe

MUSEUM OF INDIAN ARTS AND CULTURE

The Museum of Indian Arts and Culture is a branch of the Museum of New Mexico and part of its Laboratory of Anthropology. It was organized in 1923 to preserve a core collection of pottery from this region before too much of it was destroyed or dispersed into private hands. It continues to conduct systematic research on historic items produced by native peoples of the Southwest. The collections of Pueblo and Navaho basketry, jewelry, and textiles, as well as pottery, are regarded as among the finest in existence. Most material recovered from the state's archeological sites is brought here and analyzed. The bulk of the displays were drawn from these sources. The museum also conducts Living Traditions sessions, in which artisans from the various state communities demonstrate their crafts.

LOCATION: *The museum is at 710 Camino Lejo, which branches east from the Old Pecos Trail, on the southeastern approach to the city.*
HOURS: *Daily, 10-5, March through December; closed Monday, rest of year.*
ADMISSION: *$3.50.*
TELEPHONE: *(505) 827-8941.*

WHEELWRIGHT MUSEUM OF THE AMERICAN INDIAN

The Wheelwright was originally intended to be a museum of Navaho ceremonial art. The museum building was, in fact, inspired by the religious hogans of that tribe. The collection of sand paintings here is regarded as the best in the world. Founded to house the collection of Mary Cabot Wheelwright, one of the top collectors of Navaho art of this century, the museum has since expanded its collection to include other New Mexico peoples. The crafts shop here is among the best in the state for Native American objects.

LOCATION: *The Wheelwright is a neighbor of the Museum of Indian Arts (see the preceding entry), at 704 Camino Lejo.*
HOURS: *Monday through Saturday, 10–5, and Sunday, 1–5, March through October. Closed Monday, rest of year.*
ADMISSION: *Donation.*
TELEPHONE: *(505) 982-4636.*

Silver City

WESTERN NEW MEXICO UNIVERSITY MUSEUM

T he Mimbres were a people who inhabited the river valley of the same name in southwestern New Mexico. They were related to many of the other Pueblo cultures, reached their peak at about the same time, and were victimized by the same cycle of drought that forced the abandonment of most of these ancient communities. The Mimbres left behind few great ruins, though. Instead, their legacy was a white-on-black pottery that is among the most beautiful made in the area. The highly stylized animals and geometric designs that adorn it are tremendously prized by knowledgeable collectors. The museum in this colorful old mining town has the largest Mimbres collection in the country.

LOCATION: *The campus is west of downtown and the museum is housed in Fleming Hall. Silver City is on U.S. 180, about 50 miles northwest of Interstate 10.*
HOURS: *Monday through Friday, 8–4:30; Sunday, 1–4.*
ADMISSION: *Free.*
TELEPHONE: *(505) 538-6386.*

▲ *The five- and six-story dwellings of Taos Pueblo, which is believed to have been settled by the Chaco people in the fourteenth century.*

Taos

TAOS PUEBLO

Taos is the most visited of all the New Mexico pueblos, the stuff of the picture postcard Southwest. Its five- and six-story-high apartments are the skyscrapers of native New Mexico. They face each other across a broad plaza, with Taos Creek running through the center of it. The slopes of the Sangre de Cristo rise on the near horizon. Many travelers who may never see another pueblo are haunted by the beauty of this one and return repeatedly. The entire place is a National Historic Site. The surroundings are so unforgettable that the neighboring Anglo community of Taos developed into a major art center, with painters and writers drawing inspiration from the magnificent landscape and the mixing of three cultural strains.

The beauty of the place masks an often violent history. Taos is believed to have been settled by Chaco people (*see* Chaco Culture National Historical Park), who wandered east in the fourteenth century in search of water and fertile land. They found it here and built the most northern of the permanent pueblos. Taos was heavily influenced by the Plains tribes, with whom it carried on a lively trade. Many of the pueblo men adopted the leggings worn by the Comanche and Apache with whom they dealt and by whom they suffered frequent raids. A Taos resident, Pope took the leading role in the Pueblo

Rebellion of 1680, which drove the Spanish out of the area. A century and a half later, in another revolt against Mexican rule, it was a Taos man who was governor of the rebel state. Lying on one of the primary routes of the Santa Fe Trail, Taos came into early and frequent contact with Americans. When the Americans arrived in force to replace Mexican rule in 1847, it was Taos that led the insurrection against them and killed the new governor, Charles Bent. One hundred and fifty members of the community were killed in the ensuing military campaign, and fifteen more were executed.

Taos is a very traditional, religiously observant place. The pueblo is sometimes closed to outsiders with no advance warning for a religious rite. The September 29–30 celebrations honoring San Geronimo are famous for their dancing and greased pole climb.

LOCATION: *Taos is on U.S. 64, 2 miles north of the town of Taos and 80 miles northeast of Santa Fe.*
HOURS: *The pueblo is open daily, 9–4:30, with extended hours during the summer months.*
ADMISSION: *Parking charge of $5. Still photography fee of $5, and video camera fee of $10.*
TELEPHONE: *(505) 758-4604.*

Tesuque

TESUQUE PUEBLO

Tesuque is the southernmost of the Tewa-speaking pueblos, just a few miles from the bustle of Santa Fe. But like many of the New Mexico pueblo communities, the closer to outside influences they are, the more conservative they seem to become, as if in self-protection. There are two pueblos here, the older one dating to 1250, being one of the most ancient habitations in the state, and the newer one, dating to the Spanish restoration in 1692. Tesuque was the site of furious fighting during the Pueblo Rebellion, and most of the older structures were heavily damaged then. The entire pueblo has been designated a historic site by the state. The feast day honoring San Diego is held November 12.

LOCATION: *Tesuque is just north of the Santa Fe city limits on U.S. 285.*
HOURS: *Daily, dawn to dusk.*
ADMISSION: *Free. $5 permit for photography.*
TELEPHONE: *(505) 983-2667.*

Zia

ZIA PUEBLO

A lthough Zia is a tiny pueblo, it produced the symbol that occupies the center of New Mexico's state flag. The official state emblem, the orange sunburst, was adapted from Zia symbolism. This is a Keresan people. The orange-on-white pottery produced here is highly regarded and on sale in several shops locally. The mission church dates from 1692, the date of the Spanish restoration following the Pueblo Rebellion, in which Zia was an enthusiastic participant. The feast day is August 15.

LOCATION: *Zia is on New Mexico 44, about 20 miles northwest of Interstate 25 from the Bernalillo exit.*
HOURS: *Daily, dawn to dusk.*
ADMISSION: *Free. No cameras allowed.*
TELEPHONE: *(505) 867-3304.*

Zuni

ZUNI PUEBLO

T he Zuni pueblo is the largest Native American community in the state, with a population of fifty-five hundred. It was also the first to bear the brunt of Spanish fury in the conquest of New Mexico and their lust for gold. One of the outlying Zuni communities, Hawikuh, was the first Pueblo community reached by the advance party of Spanish exploration, making its way north through the mountains of eastern Arizona in 1539. Estavenico, a black adventurer, had left the rest of the party, headed by Father Marcos de Niza, several days behind. Against his orders, he entered the village alone and tried to convince its leaders that he was the emisssary of supernatural forces. He failed. When Father Marcos heard the news of Estavenico's death, he decided to turn back. But what he had seen of the pueblo from a distance convinced him that he had found one of the legendary Seven Cities of Cibola. The myth of these golden cities "to the north" had inflamed imaginations in Mexico ever since a party of shipwrecked Spanish seamen, including Estavenico, had turned up in Mexico City, repeating the tales they had heard from the Apache. Father Marcos's report clinched the case. Gold fever rose to a frenzy. The following year, the Coronado expedition was on its way back to the Zuni lands.

The Zuni, a unique people both in language and many elements of their culture, had lived in this area since the eleventh century. Immigrants from the drought-stricken Chaco culture steadily enhanced their numbers. They were prepared to resist the invasion, but were no match for the advanced weaponry brought into the fight. They were defeated at Hawikuh and then retreated to the top of nearby mesas for safety. The Spanish, eager to claim their prize, found only abandoned adobe farming villages. Cursing the name of Father Marcos, they proceeded ever farther to the northeast, searching for a treasure that did not exist.

For the next century and a half, the Zuni chafed under the religion being imposed upon them by Spanish missionaries. Occasionally, there would be an uprising, a priest would be killed, and they would retreat to the mesas again to avoid reprisals. They eagerly joined the great rebellion of 1680 but abandoned the old village for good in search of safety when the Spanish returned. Most of the Zuni pueblo that exists today was built after 1699, when they moved to this site.

Zuni is a bustling place, with modern neighborhoods to the north of the highway and stores lining the road through town. The older part of the pueblo lies within the twisting streets south of the road. This is where the Seowtewa family had been engaged in the restoration of the old Francisan mission church since 1972. The church, built at the beginning of the eighteenth century, had been abandoned for many years. But exterior renovations were begun there in 1966, and six years later it was rededicated as a church. Alex Seowtewa, a bus driver for the new church school, came from a family with an artistic background. According to legend, there had been murals all around the walls of the old church, and he asked to be allowed to restore them. Drawing from traditional Zuni beliefs and Catholic teachings, Seowtewa, assisted by his son, has depicted the passage of the religious year, with all the appropriate ceremonies and masked kachina dancers. A family member is always on hand at the church to explain and interpret the work to vistors. The project received a grant from the National Endowment for the Arts in 1989.

The Zuni are famed for their skill as jewelers, and there are many examples of silver and turquoise work in the shops throughout the community. The Shalako dances held here in late fall, usually early December, are among the most colorful ceremonies in the Southwest. Since 1990, however, they have been closed to outsiders because of violations of the photography ban. They may be reopened, though, and it is advisable to check in advance for exact dates and rules.

LOCATION: *Zuni is on New Mexico 53, about 40 miles southwest of Gallup.*
HOURS: *Daily, dawn to dusk. The church is open Monday through Friday, 8-12 and 1-4:30.*
ADMISSION: *Free. Donation asked at church.*
TELEPHONE: *(505) 782-5581.*

UTAH

EDGE OF THE CEDARS STATE PARK

The contemporary town of Blanding is the largest community in one of the most lightly populated corners of the continental United States. Its three thousand people make it a metropolis in the San Juan country of southeastern Utah. It was also a population center about one thousand years ago when it was the site of a major Anasazi community. The ruins of this residential complex, situated on a ridge on the northern edge of Blanding, are impressive. But the state-run museum, with its fine collection of pottery from that era, is what makes the visit particularly worthwhile. There are exhibits on the history of settlements in the area as well as an audiovisual presentation on the development of the Pueblo culture.

LOCATION: *Edge of the Cedars is off U.S. 191, on West 400 North Street. A loop drive, Trail of Ancients, begins here and leads to many of the Anasazi sites in the area. The route follows U.S. 191 south to Mexican Hat, north on Utah 261, and then east on Utah 95. Total distance is 108 miles.*
HOURS: *Daily, 9–5.*
ADMISSION: *$1.*
TELEPHONE: *(801) 678-2238.*

ANASAZI STATE PARK

This is another of Utah's more remote communities. The first automobile road here was not opened until 1935, and according to local lore the first vehicle used for errands in the area was brought in disassembled on packhorses, and then put together once it arrived. Mail was still being delivered by mule until 1942. This was also the site of an Anasazi village, occupied from about A.D. 750 to 1200. It was the largest such community in the state west of the Colorado River. A six-room portion of the pueblo has been reconstructed to give visitors a feel for how daily life was carried on here. A museum displays artifacts from the site.

LOCATION: *The park is on Utah 12 just south of Boulder and about 75 miles northeast of the entrance to Bryce Canyon National Park.*
HOURS: *Daily, 9–5.*
ADMISSION: *$1.*
TELEPHONE: *(801) 335-7308.*

Hovenweep National Monument

SQUARE TOWER

A s you approach the Square Tower, you might get the feeling that you somehow have been transported across the Atlantic and are about to visit one of the turreted medieval fortresses of Europe. The bulk and shape of these pueblo towers have the same look—and were even built at about the same time. The Hovenweep community once supported a population larger than that of San Juan County today. They were skilled farmers who constructed irrigation systems and stored surplus production in bins. It has been suggested that storage, in fact, may have been one of the uses for these great towers. They also were employed as lookouts, for ceremonial purposes, and as celestial observatories. But the cycle of drought that intensified through the thirteenth century forced the residents to abandon these massive pueblos and move farther south. There are other groups of ruins in the park, which is partially in Colorado. But Square Tower is by far the most impressive. It is also where the park information station is located.

LOCATION: *Hovenweep is about 30 miles east of U.S. 191, by way of Utah 262 and county roads, the last 15 miles of which are unpaved.*
HOURS: *Daily, dawn to dusk.*
ADMISSION: *Free.*
TELEPHONE: *(303) 562-4248.*

Monticello

NEWSPAPER ROCK

O ne of the great pictograph collections in Utah, Newspaper Rock looks, to all the world, like a page of newsprint laid out on a rock at the base of the Abajo Mountains. The inscriptions were made by members of the Anasazi communities that once dotted the nearby canyonlands.

LOCATION: *The rock is 12 miles west of U.S. 191 on Utah 211, the main entry road from the east into Canyonlands National Park.*
HOURS: *Daily, dawn to dusk.*
ADMISSION: *Free.*
TELEPHONE: *None.*

Sevier

FREMONT INDIAN STATE PARK

F reemont State Park marks the site of another of Utah's Anasazi villages; this one was located at nearby Five Fingers Hill. It was a bit removed from the other major centers of that period, which were clustered in the Four Corners area. But this community followed the same cycle: agricultural progress, followed by years of severe drought, and then abandonment around A.D. 1300. An interpretive center explains the culture, and a trail leads to a reconstructed home and granary. There are also pictographs.

LOCATION: *The park is just west of U.S. 89 at the Interstate 70 exit for Sevier, on Clear Creek Canyon Road.*
HOURS: *Daily, 9–5.*
ADMISSION: *$1.*
TELEPHONE: *(801) 527-4631.*

NINE MILE CANYON

N ine Mile Canyon is a bit out of the way, but it is home to one of the most dramatic concentrations of ancient pictographs in the West. The drawings fill virtually every space in the canyon wall and are the most northern evidence of Anasazi habitation in Utah. Research on these drawings and on the unique pueblo remains, which were built atop pinnacles, was done here by Harvard University archeologists in the 1930s. They established its peak years of occupancy as the tenth century A.D.

LOCATION: *The Carbon County road leading here branches north from U.S. 6, 191, about 3 miles east of Wellington. It is 37 miles to the canyon, about the last third being unpaved.*
HOURS: *Daily, dawn to dusk. Winter travel into the area can be hazardous.*
ADMISSION: *Free.*
TELEPHONE: *None.*

PACIFIC COAST AND ARCTIC

Alaska
British Columbia
California
Oregon
Washington

Pacific Coast and Arctic

ALASKA

1 Museum of History and Art, *Anchorage*
2 Duncan Cottage Museum, *Annette Island*
3 Alaska Indian Arts and Chilkat Dances, *Haines*
4 Totem Heritage Center, Saxman Totem Park, and Totem Bight Historical Site, *Ketchikan*
5 Tongass Historical Society Museum, *Ketchikan*
6 Sheldon Jackson Museum, *Sitka*
7 Sitka National Historical Park, *Sitka*

BRITISH COLUMBIA

8 Mungo Martin Memorial and U'Mista Cultural Center, *Alert Bay*
9 Ksan Indian Village, *New Hazleton*
10 Kwakiutl Museum, *Quadra Island*
11 University of British Columbia Museum of Anthropology, *Vancouver*

CALIFORNIA

12 Malki Museum of the Morongo Reservation, *Banning*
13 Owens Valley Paiute-Shoshone Indian Culture Center, *Bishop*
14 Tribal Museum, *Hoopa*
15 Southwest Museum, *Los Angeles*
16 Sierra Mono Indian Museum, *North Fork*

17 Miwok Tribal Museum, *Novato*
18 Cherokee Ghost Town, *Oroville*
19 Indian Grinding Rock State Historic Park, *Volcano*
20 Fort Yuma Quechan Museum, *Winterhaven*

OREGON

21 Old Chief Joseph Monument, *Joseph*
22 Pendleton Roundup, *Pendleton*

WASHINGTON

23 Lummi Stommish and Reserve, *Bellingham*
24 St. Anne's Church and Tulalip Reserve, *Marysville*
25 Makah Cultural and Research Center, *Neah Bay*
26 St. Mary's Mission and Boarding School, *Omak*
27 Sacajawea State Park, *Pasco*
28 Thomas Burke Memorial Washington State Museum, *Seattle*
29 Museum and Grave of Chief Seattle, *Suquamish*
30 Yakima Nation Cultural Center, *Toppenish*
31 Whitman Mission Historical Site, *Walla Walla*

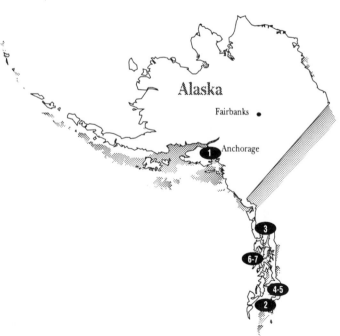

Alaska

Fairbanks

Anchorage

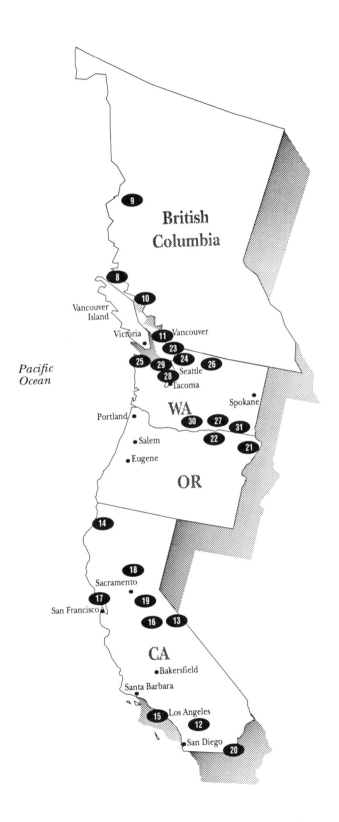

British
Columbia

Vancouver
Island

Victoria

Vancouver

Seattle

Tacoma

Spokane

Portland

WA

Salem

Eugene

OR

Pacific
Ocean

Sacramento

San Francisco

CA

Bakersfield

Santa Barbara

Los Angeles

San Diego

ALASKA

Anchorage

MUSEUM OF HISTORY AND ART

The Anchorage Museum of History and Art houses the most complete collection of crafts and artifacts from native cultures in Alaska. It is worth a visit as an orientation course on the great variety of tribes associated with this state, many of them unfamiliar to the casual student of North American Indian history.

The Alaska Gallery displays more than one thousand objects to portray the history of Alaska. The cultures of the Athapaskan, Aleut, Tlingit, Haida, and Eskimo people are described in dioramas and models. The Russian period, American whaling, the gold rush, World War II, and contemporary life are illustrated with documents, artifacts, photographs, dioramas, and models. Items include three-thousand-year-old spear points, contemporary paintings, Russian icons, and Eskimo ivory carvings.

LOCATION: *The museum is downtown at 121 West Seventh Avenue.*
HOURS: *May 15 to September 15, daily 9-6; September 16 to May 14, Tuesday through Saturday, 10–6; Sunday, 1–5; closed Monday.*
ADMISSION: *Adults $4; Seniors (over 65) $3.50; Juniors (under 18) Free.*
TELEPHONE: *(907) 343-4326.*

Annette Island

DUNCAN COTTAGE MUSEUM

William Duncan was a lay preacher sent from London by the Church of England in 1857 as a missionary to the Tsimshian tribe. The tribe, who had lived along the Skeena and Nass rivers of western British Columbia, moved north of Prince Rupert on the Metlakatla Peninsula in order to take advantage of trade opportunities when the Hudson Bay Company built Fort Simpson. Duncan took his assignment to heart. He learned the tribe's language and left the security of the fort to live among the Tsimshian. He helped them establish a new community at Metlakatla and assisted them in setting up a sawmill.

After twenty years, however, a dispute developed between the church and its far-flung pastor. Duncan was replaced by Bishop Ridley, who made no effort to adjust to the Tsimshian culture. Hostility grew between Ridley and the Tsimshian, and the bishop eventually had to send for a man-of-war to rescue him. Duncan, meanwhile, had won congressional support in the States to establish a reserve for the tribe on Annette Island, Alaska, just to the northwest of Metlakatla. In 1887, about four hundred Indians moved with Duncan to the island, and it was officially established as a reserve four years later. By the time of Duncan's death in 1918, New Metlakatla had a solid economy, thanks to its sawmill and salmon cannery. Duncan's home is now a museum and that displays artifacts of the Tsimshian culture.

LOCATION: *Annette Island is accessible from Ketchikan by regularly scheduled motor launch. The one-way trip takes about 90 minutes.*
HOURS: *Monday through Friday, 9–5.*
ADMISSION: *Free.*
PHONE: *(907) 886-4868.*

Haines

ALASKA INDIAN ARTS AND CHILKAT DANCES

Fort William Seward, named for the man who arranged the Alaskan Purchase from Russia, was once the most northerly U.S. Army base. It was shut down after World War II and every building was converted to private use as residences, shops, and bed and breakfasts. The former post hospital houses Alaska Indian Arts, where visitors have the rare opportunity to observe Native American craftsmen at work in a unique historic setting: there are weavers, silversmiths, and makers of ceremonial masks. The world's largest totem pole, exhibited at the Osaka World's Fair of 1970, was carved here.

Traditional Tlingit dances are performed at the Chilkat Center for the Arts, a former cannery that was moved to the base in 1919 as a recreation hall. The dance troupe has toured the world, and its members are famed for their dexterity; their fringed and vividly colored shawls are made by local native people. The fort's parade ground has been turned into a typical Indian village of the nineteenth century, with a replica of a tribal house and several totem poles.

LOCATION: *The fort is right on the harbor. Haines can also be reached overland from the Alaska Highway by way of Haines Junction, Yukon.*
HOURS: *The fort and Indian Arts are open Monday through Friday, 9–12 and 1–5, April through October. The Chilkat Dancers perform Monday, Wednesday, and Saturday at 8:30 P.M., mid–June through Labor Day.*
ADMISSION: *The fort is free. Tickets to The Chilkat Dancers are $6.50.*
TELEPHONE: *(907) 766-2202.*

Ketchikan

TOTEM HERITAGE CENTER, SAXMAN TOTEM PARK, AND TOTEM BIGHT HISTORICAL SITE

The totem pole is probably the single most recognizable symbol of Alaska. These painted red cedar poles played a prominent role in the culture of the Haida and Tlingit, the native peoples who dominated the coastlines of British Columbia and southeastern Alaska. The poles were not objects of worship, nor did they tell a continuous story; rather, they were usually carved to commemorate a special event, and were commissioned by a village or clan. They were used to mark the graves of prominent individuals, to observe the building of a new house, and to mark the ceremonial exchange of gifts.

The figures on the pole represent the clan to which its patron belonged. These peoples had no written language, and thsee poles were visible records of great events in their past. Once erected, they remained in place, even when the community was abandoned. Since the 1930s, there has been an ongoing program in Alaska to rescue poles from remote locations either to restore or to remake the most significant poles.

Ketchikan can be considered the totem pole capital of the world. Three of the greatest collections of poles in existence are clustered around this town, the southernmost major settlement in the state. The Totem Heritage Center, right in Ketchikan, displays unrestored totems from deserted Tlingit and Haida villages. Five of the tallest totems are strikingly displayed in the central gallery. Surrounding cases show off carving tools and other artifacts. Since this is a working crafts center, visitors may observe native people working on beading, basketry, and engraving.

South of town is Saxman Totem Park, named for a Tlingit village formed here in 1886. The name itself honors a teacher who died during the search for a new village site. The poles here were brought from deserted communities, and many have been restored. The symbol of the raven occurs often in Tlingit mythology: the raven is believed to be a trickster hero who gave

▲ *The Totem Heritage Center in Ketchikan displays unrestored totems from nearby deserted Tlingit and Haida villages.*

the tribe the sun, water, and fish. Sun and Raven Totem stands at the entrance to the park and is the best-known of the poles here.

Totem Bight, at the northern end of the island, is best known for its spectacular setting, on a cove overlooking Tongass Narrows. It contains a reproduction of a community longhouse.

LOCATION: *Totem Heritage Center is at 601 Deermount Street, which runs north from Tongass Highway, east of the ferry docks. Saxman is 3 miles south on Tongass Highway, and Totem Bight is 10 miles north, also on Tongass Highway.*

HOURS: *Totem Center is open daily, 8:30–5:30, mid-May through September; Tuesday through Friday, 10–5, rest of year. Saxman and Totem Bight are open daily, dawn to dusk.*

ADMISSION: *$1.50 to Totem Center during the peak season; free on Sunday and rest of year. Saxman and Totem Bight are free.*

TELEPHONE: *Totem Center is (907) 225-5900. No telephones at Saxman and Totem Bight.*

▲ *Young carvers at Saxman Totem Park have brought about a revival of the art.*

TONGASS HISTORICAL SOCIETY MUSEUM

T his downtown facility, built right over rushing Ketchikan Creek, features good displays on the historic crafts of native peoples. Prominently featured are bentwood boxes, made of a single piece of cedar bent three or four times to form a container. There are also brilliantly colored, intricately patterned Chilkat blankets and several examples of wood carving. The museum emphasizes the changing culture of the local peoples.

LOCATION: *The museum is at 629 Dock Street, downtown.*
HOURS: *Daily, 8:30–5:30, June through August; Wednesday through Saturday, 1–5, rest of year.*
ADMISSION: *$1.*
TELEPHONE: *(907) 225-5600.*

Sitka

SHELDON JACKSON MUSEUM

B efore Alaska's economy was transformed by the discovery of gold in the Klondike, Sitkar, an old town founded by the Russians, was territorial capital. The town still retains traces of its ethnic heritage, and is one of the most spectacularly scenic places in the country. When political power departed for Juneau and points west, the influence of Sheldon Jackson—one of the remarkable men who came to Alaska as missionaries to help lay the foundation for statehood—came to an end.

Jackson is credited with establishing Alaska's public education system, and he introduced the state's reindeer herd, in an effort to rebuild the Eskimo peoples' shattered economy when whaling died out. He arrived here in the 1870s as an agent of the Presbyterian church. Within the next twenty-five years, he became the general agent for education and a powerful political force. Like his fellow missionary, William Duncan of Meklatakla, he was an advocate on behalf of native peoples in Washington. He repeatedly appeared before Congress to plead for programs to assist them. In the America of the 1890s, Jackson was probably the best-known symbol of the mysterious wilderness that was Alaska.

Jackson traveled the Alaskan wilderness extensively, making frequent trips beyond the Arctic Circle to visit native peoples to assess their needs. During those trips he assembled the finest collection of Eskimo and Aleut artifacts in existence. Many of them are of enormous historical importance:

they are irreplaceable vestiges of cultures that have been isolated for centuries and are just now beginning to experience change. The museum housing these articles is the oldest in Alaska, having opened here in 1895. The masks, clothing, tools, and carvings on display cannot be duplicated anywhere in the world. Jackson was removed from office in 1906 when the last territorial agencies went to Juneau. But his legacy lives on in this museum, located on the campus of Sheldon Jackson College.

LOCATION: *The museum and campus are immediately east of the harbor, off Lincoln Street.*
HOURS: *Daily, 8–5, mid-May to mid-September. Hours vary rest of year.*
ADMISSION: *$1.50.*
PHONE: *(907) 747-5940.*

SITKA NATIONAL HISTORICAL PARK

T he Russians arrived at Sitka in 1799, intent on making this harbor the center of their ambitious attempt to place colonies on the Pacific Coast of North America. Alexander Baranof, manager of the Russian-American Company, wanted to move its headquarters from Kodiak Island, on the far side of the Gulf of Alaska. He brought with him a company of about thirty Russians and several dozen Aleut hunters.

The harbor at Sitka acquired a reputation in 1741, when Captain Alexei Chirikof anchored here, led an exploring party ashore, and was never seen again. Chirikof's successors searched for him for the next eighty years. By the time Baranof arrived, Sitka was established as a port of call for New Englanders engaged in the China trade. The leaders of the nearby Tlingit community—which prospered through barter with the traders—were not happy at the prospect of having Baranof settle in. Nonetheless, he bargained for a site to build a fort, six miles north of town. Things did not go well. Russian policies toward the Tlingit were brutal, the climate did not agree with the newcomers, and hostilities between the local Indians and the Aleuts sharpened. In June 1802, the Tlingit attacked the fort while the Aleuts were on a hunting trip, killing the Russians.

Two years later, the Russians returned in force, this time with heavy guns mounted on Baranof's ships. The Tlingit made a stand at their fort, which stood at the mouth of the Indian River. Although the Russians could not land, but the Tlingit could not stand up against the shelling. After several days of negotiations and intermittent cannonades, the Tlingit secretly retreated to Chicagof Island and the Russians came ashore to found the present-day city of Sitka. This conflict was the last sustained Indian resistance to European

▲ *Totem pole at Sitka National Historical Park.*

settlement in Alaska, and the battle site is now preserved in the Sitka National Historical Park.

The Tlingit returned to Sitka in 1821 and became a strong presence in the community once again. Many exhibits in the park are dedicated to their culture, including replicas of several totem poles that were first displayed at the Saint Louis World's Fair of 1904. One of them, Raven Crest, is original. The Southeast Alaska Indian Cultural Center, located in the visitor center, has native craftsmen working on projects with their traditional tools. There is also an audiovisual presentation on the native history of Sitka.

LOCATION: *The site is 1 mile east of downtown Sitka, at the end of Lincoln Street.*
HOURS: *The historical site is open daily, dawn to dusk. The Cultural Center is open daily, 8–5, June through September; closed Sunday, rest of year.*
ADMISSION: *Free.*
TELEPHONE: *(907) 747-6281.*

BRITISH COLUMBIA

MUNGO MARTIN MEMORIAL AND U'MISTA CULTURAL CENTER

Mungo Martin was born into the Kwakiutl tribe, carvers of some of the most exceptional totem poles in the Pacific Northwest. He was trained in the artistic tradition as a young man, instilled with the symbolism and techniques that go into the making of the pole. But he grew up as the old traditions were dying out, and when he reached adulthood there was not enough work to sustain him. So he became a fisherman. By 1949, when Martin was seventy years old, a renewed appreciation for these works had developed. He was chosen by the government to head the restoration efforts for British Columbia's totem poles, wherever they could be found. He also continued to work himself, and some of the finest modern poles in the province, including a 127-foot-high masterpiece in Victoria's Beacon Hill Park, were carved by him. While his work in his final years kept him in the cities of Victoria and Vancouver, his heart remained on the islands he knew as a fisherman. When he drowned on a fishing trip in 1962, at eighty-three years of age, he was buried here, near the water he knew well, at his request. A memorial pole to him stands near the center of the village.

Alert Bay is on Cormorant Island, which is inhabited almost entirely by Kwakiutl fishermen. Their rows of houses facing the waters of Queen Charlotte Strait are striking. The important works of Kwakiutl culture—carved masks, copper items, traditional potlatch gifts—are displayed at the U'Mista Cultural Center a few blocks from the ferry dock.

LOCATION: *Port Alert can be reached by ferryboat from Port McNeill, on the northeastern corner of Vancouver Island.*
HOURS: *The cultural center is open Monday through Friday, 9–5, and Saturday, 1–5, May through September; open Monday through Friday only, rest of year.*
ADMISSION: *$3.*
TELEPHONE: *(604) 974-5403.*

New Hazleton

KSAN INDIAN VILLAGE

K san is a museum village built by the Gitksan people to illustrate the way they lived through different periods of their history. Seven tribal longhouses on the site are living museums of the various crafts and cultural functions of this people. One of the houses also functions as a museum of the upper Skeena River region. Many of them have interior totem poles, and all are richly decorated with traditional carvings and bright paintings. Visitors can watch craftsmen at work in several of the houses.

LOCATION: *The village is just north of New Hazelton on the Yellowhead Highway, the overland route that connects the coastal town of Prince Rupert with the rest of the province. It is about 170 miles east of Prince Rupert.*
HOURS: *Daily, 9–6, May to mid-October; closed weekends, rest of year.*
ADMISSION: *$4.50.*
TELEPHONE: *(604) 842-5544.*

Quadra Island

KWAKIUTL MUSEUM

T he Kwakiutl Museum is slightly more accessible than the museum at Alert Bay (*see* Mungo Martin Memorial and U'Mista Cultural Center, Alert Bay, British Columbia) and contains many of the same sorts of poles, masks, and copper work exhibited there. In addition, the strait between this island and Campbell River, on Vancouver Island, is prime whale-watching territory and has been made an ecological reserve. A ferry runs between Campbell River and Cape Mudge on Quadra. There are also many freestanding totem poles on the island that may be seen on walks from the ferry dock.

LOCATION: *The museum is 2 miles south of the ferry terminal on Green Road.*
HOURS: *Daily, 10–4:30, mid-May to mid-September; Tuesday through Saturday, 12–4:30, rest of year.*
ADMISSION: *$2.50.*
TELEPHONE: *(604) 285-3733.*

UNIVERSITY OF BRITISH COLUMBIA
MUSEUM OF ANTHROPOLOGY

T he finest Canadian collection of material relating to the arts and culture of native peoples of the Pacific Northwest is housed in the striking University of British Columbia Museum of Anthropology, a glass and concrete structure on cliffs above the ocean. The Great Hall, with its enormous totem poles and dugout canoes, is a dramatic entryway into the museum. There are also exceptionally fine carved masks and jewelry of argillite, a black stone found in this region. The museum includes displays of other Pacific cultures, but the native section is the centerpiece.

LOCATION: *The university campus is on Point Grey, overlooking the Strait of Georgia, west of downtown. The museum is located at 6393 Northwest Marine Drive.*
HOURS: *Tuesday to Sunday, 11–5.*
ADMISSION: *$4; free on Tuesday.*
TELEPHONE: *(604) 228-3825.*

CALIFORNIA

MALKI MUSEUM OF THE MORONGO RESERVATION

The Spanish missions that link the California coastal cities along the El Camino Real are the state's top historical attraction. Many of them are architectural masterpieces that capture the nostalgic glow of a lost California. For Native Americans, however, the missions represented disaster. The Franciscan priests who arrived in 1769 from Mexico were zealous in their eagerness to convert the California Indians. Backed by the military, they rounded up Native Americans and brought them to the missions as new Christians. Torn away from traditional ways of life, they were reduced to a semifeudal condition, with forced prayer and rigid rounds of hard, unpaid labor. Attempted escapes were met with whippings and sometimes executions.

The Mission Tribes revolted frequently, sometimes coordinating their efforts to rise up as one. None were successful. Finally, the Mexican government broke up the mission holdings with its secularization decree of 1833. The tribes who had lived under the system for three generations found freedom was difficult: traditions had been forgotten, the native people had no way of making a living, and the population was demoralized. Although a few members of these tribes managed to reach wilderness areas to reestablish themselves in their former homes, by the time California became a state in 1850, the state's Indian population was barely one-third of what it had been before the missions were founded.

The Morongo Reservation was set up for two of the tribes most victimized by the mission system, the Cahuilla and Serrano. In recent years, the Malki Museum was organized as a way to retain elements of tribal heritage and to display traditional crafts and clothing. On Memorial Day weekend, a fiesta is held here, with games, dances, and songs performed by various southern California tribal groups.

LOCATION: *Malki Museum is north of Interstate 10 from the Fields Road exit.*
HOURS: *Monday through Friday, 9–5; weekends, 10–4.*
ADMISSION: *Donation.*
TELEPHONE: *(714) 849-4697.*

Bishop

OWENS VALLEY PAIUTE-SHOSHONE INDIAN CULTURE CENTER

The Owens is known as the deepest valley in America because it lies between two of the country's highest mountain ranges, with the Sierra Nevada on the west, and the White Mountains on the east. It is a magnificently scenic place and, by California standards, well watered. In fact, in the early twentieth century, Los Angeles collected water from here for its aqueduct system, which enabled the parched metropolis to grow into the country's second largest city.

The Owens Valley was also home to the northern Paiute, who were closely related to the Shoshone. The Paiute had one of the most basic structures of any tribe in America: the family was its fundamental unit and gathering food was its main activity. Although they did not practice cultivation, they did master rudimentary techniques of dam-building and irrigation. Some of the hostilities of the Paiute War from the 1860s spilled over into this valley from Nevada, but for the most part, the Paiute moved onto small reservations in the area with little resistance. The Paiute-Shoshone Indian Culture Center in Bishop, the largest town in the Owens Valley, displays clothing, tools, and basketry. There are also exhibits explaining how the Paiute obtained food.

LOCATION: *West of U.S. 395 and the city center, at 2300 West Line Street.*
HOURS: *Monday through Friday, 9–5; weekends, 10–4.*
ADMISSION: *Donation.*
TELEPHONE: *(619) 873-4478.*

Hoopa

TRIBAL MUSEUM

E arly California was a patchwork of small tribes, who live independently in family-sized units and usually demonstrated no aggression toward their neighbors. In fact, they did not have much to do with each other at all. *A Concise Dictionary of Indian Tribes of North America* claims that a native person living in California would have had to travel only fifty miles or so to encounter another group whose language he could not understand.

The Hoopa, who lived along the Trinity and Klamath rivers in the state's northwestern corner, are fairly typical of native California peoples. Part of the Athabasacan language family, they were related to tribes living further north on the Pacific coast. The Hoopa remained isolated from white settlement until gold strikes on the Trinity brought a rush of miners into their area in 1853. Some of them remained, and for twelve years the Hoopa conducted sporadic raids on the mining communities. Fort Gaston was established in the area to protect the whites, and Ulysses S. Grant was once stationed there. In 1864, a reservation was set aside for the Hoopa along the rivers on which their traditional villages had been situated. An oddly shaped reserve, it has one regularly delineated chunk of land, with a thin arm extending northwest along the Klamath to its outlet at the sea. The most populous reserve in the state, it has few more than one thousand residents.

The tribe takes pride in its traditions, so do not let the museum's location in a shopping mall put you off. A redwood canoe, used for salmon fishing, is displayed, along with basketry, ceremonial clothing, and jewelry.

LOCATION: *The museum is on California 96 in the Hoopa Shopping Mall. Trips to the ruins of Fort Gaston and villages elsewhere on the reservation may be arranged here.*
HOURS: *Monday through Friday, 9–5; weekends, 10–4; May through September.*
ADMISSION: *Donation.*
TELEPHONE: *(916) 625-4110.*

Los Angeles

SOUTHWEST MUSEUM

The museum's collections represent Native American cultures from Alaska to South America; nearly every Western tribe is featured. The facility's main strength, however, is its regional exhibit, which is one of the best collections in the country of arts and crafts associated with the tribes of the desert Southwest. Holdings include important collections of Mesoamerican and South American Precolumbian pottery and textiles, and Hispanic folk and decorative arts; the museum's basketry collection is among the largest such collections in the United States. The four main exhibit halls focus on the native people of the Southwest, California, the Great Plains, and the Northwest Coast. Changing shows highlight the culture of various native groups.

Designed by the firm of Sumner Hunt and Silas Burns, the Southwest Museum building opened its doors to the public in 1914; the oldest museum in Los Angeles, it is an historic landmark.

LOCATION: *The museum is at 234 Museum Drive, immediately east of downtown by way of the Pasadena Freeway. Watch for exit markers.*
HOURS: *Tuesday through Sunday, 11–5. Closed major holidays.*
ADMISSION: *Adults $5; Seniors and Students $3; Youths (7-18) $2; Children (6 and under) Free.*
TELEPHONE: *(213) 221-2163.*

North Fork

SIERRA MONO INDIAN MUSEUM

The Sierra Mono tribe is related by language to the Shoshone of the Great Basin states, and to the Paiute of the neighboring Owens Valley, on the far side of the Sierra Nevada. Because their homes were so remote and secluded in the foothills of the Sierra Nevada's western slope, the Mono (or Monache, as they are sometimes called) managed to avoid contact with whites until much later than most California tribes. They were hunters and gatherers, and basketry occupied a position of great importance in their culture. The varieties of twined and coiled work they used in basketry was limited only by imagination. Even boats were made of baskets, as were hats and cradles. Their small settlements, known as *rancherias*, are scattered throughout the central California counties on the western slope. There is a celebration on the first weekend of August.

LOCATION: *The museum is in the middle of town, which is about 65 miles northeast of Fresno by way of California 41 and county roads from Oakhurst.*
HOURS: *Monday through Saturday, 9–4.*
ADMISSION: *$1.50.*
TELEPHONE: *(209) 877-2115.*

Novato

MIWOK TRIBAL MUSEUM

The Miwok once stretched across a band of central California territory from the Pacific to the western slope of the Sierra Nevada. They were, in fact, indirectly responsible for turning Yosemite Valley into a tourist attraction. While pursuing a band of Miwok who had resisted the entry of miners into their lands in 1851, a volunteer brigade under Major James D. Savage accidentally found themselves at Inspiration Point, with its picture postcard view of the valley. They never found the Miwok but returned to the coast with tales of the wonders they had seen. It was the beginning of Yosemite's progression from paradise to parking lot.

Most of the Miwok rancherias are located in the Sierra Nevada foothills. The tribal museum, however, is situated near the coastal branch of the Miwok, in Olema. This facility concentrates on the native cultures of Marin County, and hosts a celebration on the first week in June with traditional dancing, crafts, and food. There is also a garden of native plants on the property.

LOCATION: *The museum is in Miwok Park, at 2200 Novato Boulevard, off U.S. 101.*
HOURS: *Tuesday through Saturday, 10–4; Sunday, 12–4.*
ADMISSION: *Donation.*
TELEPHONE: *(415) 897-4064.*

CHEROKEE GHOST TOWN

N ot only Europeans were bitten by the gold bug, joining the forty-niners in the rush to California. News of the riches to be found here made its way to the Cherokee reservation in Oklahoma. A generation after the Cherokee had been expelled from the Southeast, a restlessness gripped many younger men who felt no special attachment to the home to which they were forcibly moved. Ironically, while the discovery of gold in Georgia had doomed their attempts to hold on to their ancestral homes, a group of Cherokees moved to California in the early 1850s to try their luck with the metal. Although they found an estimated five million dollars worth of gold here, the tribe was much more excited when they struck diamonds. The Cherokee Diamond Mine opened in 1873, but the stones were of industrial quality and the mine quickly expired. In a few years, the town was abandoned, and today it may well be the only Native American mining ghost town in the West.

LOCATION: *Cherokee is 10 miles north of Oroville, off California 70.*
HOURS: *Daily, dawn to dusk.*
ADMISSION: *Free.*

INDIAN GRINDING ROCK STATE HISTORIC PARK

J ust outside Volcano, a gold rush ghost town, is a group of limestone rocks. Miwok Indians once came here to obtain the material for mortar cups, in which they pulverized food and seed. California has constructed a Native American cultural facility around these ancient grinding rocks. There is a restoration of a Miwok village, a ceremonial roundhouse, and a museum that includes exhibits on all the tribes that made their home in the California Sierra Nevada. The Chaw'Se Celebration, held here during the last weekend of September, has developed into a major observance among the California tribes, with representatives from most of them participating in the dances and crafts booths. There is, by the way, no volcano in the vicinity. The name was given to the settlement by pioneers who thought its position, surrounded by steep hills, made it look like the crater of a volcano.

LOCATION: *The park is off California 88, just outside Volcano, which is about 10 miles east of Jackson and California 49.*
HOURS: *Park is open daily, 8–5. Museum is open daily, 10–5, Memorial Day through Labor Day; Monday through Friday, 11–3, and weekends, 10–4, rest of year.*
ADMISSION: *$5 per vehicle.*
TELEPHONE: *(209) 296-7488.*

Winterhaven

FORT YUMA QUECHAN MUSEUM

The Quechan Museum sits on a hill overlooking the city of Yuma, across the Colorado River in Arizona. Settlement at this critical river crossing was clustered around the military post, which was erected in 1850. Four years later, when a group of settlers decided the ferryboat rates were exorbitant, a community was established on the opposite bank.

The Yuma were a powerful people, adept at warfare. Martial status was important in their culture: even when horses were introduced to these people, they refused to use them in battle, regarding mounted battle as unworthy of a warrior. The Yuma did not take kindly to intruders in their land, as Father Francisco Tomas Garces learned in 1781 when the mission he founded on this spot was destroyed and its occupants killed. The Yuma, outraged by their treatment at the hands of arrogant Spanish soldiers, retaliated against their antagonists, and were virtually left alone for the next seventy years.

The rush to southern California along the Overland Trail—a route roughly followed today by Interstate 8—suddenly brought thousands of intruders pouring across their territory at Yuma Crossing. In the winter of 1850–51, approximately sixty thousand people came to California by this route. The Yuma rebelled, but the federal government rushed troops to the area, and by 1852 the final resistance had ended. The Fort Yuma reservation was established here in 1883.

The museum contains exhibits on the history of this people, the significance of the Yuma Crossing, and the crafts of other native groups of the Colorado River. Also on the grounds are mission buildings associated with Indian schools.

LOCATION: *The museum is directly across the bridge from downtown Yuma.*
HOURS: *Monday through Friday, 8–12 and 1–5.*
ADMISSION: *50 cents.*
TELEPHONE: *(619) 572-0661.*

OREGON

Joseph

OLD CHIEF JOSEPH MONUMENT

The Nez Perce could not bear to give up the Wallowa Valley in the northeastern corner of Oregon. Their refusal to move from here to the Lapwai reservation in Idaho precipitated Chief Joseph's masterful campaign against the U.S. Army in 1877, which ended fifteen hundred miles away in Montana. The grave of his father, Old Chief Joseph, on a knoll near the northern shore of Wallowa Lake, is the final remnant of the Nez Perce in the land they loved so well.

LOCATION: *Joseph is one of the more remote locations in Oregon, tucked in between the Hells Canyon and Wallowa National Forest wilderness areas. It is about 70 miles east of Interstate 84 at the La Grande exit by way of Oregon 82. The monument is just south of town on the lakeshore.*

Pendleton

PENDLETON ROUNDUP

The Umatilla reservation lies just to the east of this northeastern Oregon city, and Native Americans have actively participated in this town's famous western celebration since its inception in 1910. One of the first winners of the all-around cowboy award was Jackson Sundown, a nephew of Chief Joseph, whose wife was a member of the Umatilla tribe. Native people play a prominent role in the parades, and there is usually a traditional tepee encampment near the stadium. The event attracts Native Americans from all across the northwestern states. The Umatilla have worked to turn their reservation into a prime recreational attraction, with good fishing, hunting, and camping opportunities in the foothills of the Blue Mountains. The Emigrant

Hill overlook, located on Interstate 84 in the reservation, is a famous view-point, with vistas over vast wheatlands to the distant Cascades. On clear days, the snowy cone of Mount Hood, one hundred miles to the west, is visible.

LOCATION: *The Roundup is held at Pendleton Stadium, at the western edge of this city. Reservation headquarters are located at Mission, about 5 miles east by way of Interstate 84.*

HOURS: *The Roundup is held during the second weekend of September. Reservation headquarters, open Monday through Friday, 9–5.*

TELEPHONE: *Roundup information is available at (800) 524-2984. Tribal offices are at (503) 276-3165.*

WASHINGTON

LUMMI STOMMISH AND RESERVE

Lummi Stommish is perhaps the most spectacularly situated Native American reserve in the United States. It occupies a peninsula jutting into Bellingham Bay, with the Strait of Georgia on the west. South across the waters rise the snowy peaks of the Olympic Peninsula. To the west are the San Juan Islands, and on the east, the busy port of Bellingham, backed by the Cascades. Taking full advantage of the setting, the Lummi operate a restaurant, Fisherman's Cove, at the southern tip of their peninsula, with magnificent views any way you look. Specialty of the house is the fresh seafood that has been the tribe's livelihood throughout its history.

The Lummi are a branch of the Salishan people. At their peak they ranged across this part of Washington, into the San Juans, and as far north as the Fraser River of British Columbia. But by 1849, disease and ongoing warfare with their neighbors had reduced their numbers so severely that they were forced to enter this reservation. Through retention of fishing rights, however, the Lummi have managed to assemble the largest commercial fleet in the Pacific Northwest, the backbone of the tribal economy. They are experts at preparing the barbecued salmon that is a staple at so many restaurants in the Pacific Northwest.

The annual Stommish Festival, with its war canoe races and traditional music, games, and dances, is one of the most unusual and colorful in the country. It is based on the traditional potlatches of the Northwest, gatherings at which tribes met for a communal feast and exchange of gifts. The festival is usually held on the third weekend of June, but schedule shifts are possible and it is best to call in advance. The Lummi operate a charter boat, manned by tribal members, for cruises through the local waters. A gift shop next to the restaurant carries wool sweaters, baskets, and carvings, characteristic Lummi crafts.

LOCATION: *The reservation is reached from Bellingham by way of northbound Interstate 5 to the Marietta exit, then west on county roads.*
TELEPHONE: *(206) 734-8180.*

Marysville

ST. ANNE'S CHURCH AND TULALIP RESERVE

Tulalip Reserve occupies a lovely Puget Sound location, across the inlet from the bustling port of Everett. Remnants of various small tribes, mostly Dwamish and Snohomish, were gathered here around 1900 from other reserves deficient in fishing sources; like most tribes of the area, they draw their livelihood from the sea. Historically a site of native settlements, the area was visited by Father E. C. Chirouse, who in 1858 established the first Catholic mission here, on what is still known as Priest Point. Nearby is Mission Beach Cemetery, which contains the graves of several Indian leaders. Most prominent is that of Patkanim, a signer of the Mukilteo Treaty, which ceded the coastal lands of northwest Washington. St. Anne's Church, about one mile beyond the cemetery, was built in 1904, and the bell from the old mission is in its belfry. Also in town is an Indian Shaker Church and the historic Superintendent's Office, dating from 1907.

LOCATION: *The reserve is directly west of Marysville, across Interstate 5 by way of Washington 506.*
TELEPHONE: *(206) 653-4585.*

Neah Bay

MAKAH CULTURAL AND RESEARCH CENTER

Neah Bay is located at the extreme northwestern corner of the continental United States. Across the Strait of Juan de Fuca is Vancouver Island, Canada; and to the west is the open Pacific. A Greek navigator, Apostolos Valerianos, sailing in the service of Spain, claimed to have reached a broad inlet at about this latitude in 1592, although no other verification was ever made. Nonetheless, his account was published in England and served as a guide to Captain James Cook when he explored the area in 1778. Cook called the headland here Cape Flattery, because, he wrote, "it flattered us with hopes of finding a harbor." The hopes were, however, unrealized. A subsequent British expedition mapped the strait, then in 1791 a Mexican party tried to set up a colony here. It was abandoned after just five months, and for the next sixty years the area was all but forgotten by outsiders.

On this legend-shrouded coast lived the Makah, a people more closely related to Alaskan-based tribes than any other in Washington. They lived in several coastal villages around the cape, gathering food during the summer months and inhabiting longhouses large enough to accommodate up to forty people in winter. The Makah were also accomplished whalers, hunting the huge mammals in oceangoing cedar canoes with eight-man crews. Their weapons included a harpoon on a twenty-foot rope, attached to a float made of seal bladder. The float prevented the animal from diving, and when it surfaced another harpoon was thrown. The meat and skin of sea mammals was the basis of the Makah economy and also their most valuable trade good. Eventually, however, they became exclusively seal hunters, and when that practice was outlawed in 1890, Makah traditional culture was unable to continue.

The Makah Center at Neah Bay, however, preserves artifacts from their settlements. One of them was buried by a mudslide in the fifteenth century, and when it was uncovered, like a Native American Pompeii, it yielded an incredibly complete picture of what daily life was like. The museum here was built to house these finds. Dioramas of Makah history join replicas of tradition-al longhouses and whaling canoes. The Makah Days Celebration, held on the third weekend of August, is well attended and is especially memorable on this dramatic site.

LOCATION: *Neah Bay is on Washington 112, a great scenic drive, about 80 miles west of Port Angeles. Just west of the town is Koitlah Point, with magnificent views across the Strait of Juan de Fuca to British Columbia, and at the road's end a foottrail leads to Cape Flattery itself.*

HOURS: *Daily, 10–5, June to mid-September; Wednesday through Sunday only, rest of year.*

ADMISSION: *$2.50.*

TELEPHONE: *(206) 645-2711.*

Omak

ST. MARY'S MISSION AND BOARDING SCHOOL

The first church at St. Mary's Mission was founded by Father Etienne de Rouge, a French Jesuit who sought to minister to the tribes of the Colville Reservation. This reserve was initially set up in 1872 for several tribes who had fought briefly with the U.S. Army during the Yakima Wars of the 1850s. The original tract stretched south from the Canadian border between the Columbia and Okanogan rivers. But when gold was discovered on its northern portion in the 1890s, that area was simply lopped off the reserve. The Colville Reservation is also where Chief Joseph and his Nez Perce followers (*see* Nez Perce Historical Park, Spalding, Idaho, and Big Hole National Battlefield, Montana) were taken after their surrender at Bears Paw in 1878. Their descendants still make their homes here, but a total of ten different tribes now live in Colville. The so-called Colville, a Salish band, make up about 30 percent of the reservation population.

Father de Rouge arrived on the reservation in 1886 and endeared himself by delivering sermons in local native dialects mixed with Latin. Among those who participated at his masses was Chief Joseph. The original church burned in 1938 and was replaced on the same site. Next to it is the Paschal Sherman Indian School, the only Native American boarding school in the state.

LOCATION: *The mission and school are just east of Omak on Washington 155.*
HOURS: *Daily, dawn to dusk.*
ADMISSION: *Free, but visitors are asked to register at the school office.*
TELEPHONE: *(509) 826-2097.*

Pasco

SACAJAWEA STATE PARK

Sacajawea State Park marks the spot at which the Lewis and Clark expedition first saw the Columbia River, the final passageway on their voyage from Saint Louis, Missouri, to the sea. This is where the Columbia meets its longest tributary, the Snake River. Sacajawea, the Shoshone woman who had joined them in North Dakota, had grown up along the Snake River and remembered tales from childhood about the great ocean that lay at its end. She was instrumental in guiding them here. The park is dedicated to her role on the expedition and to the culture of the native people they encountered in this area. A small museum displays local artifacts.

LOCATION: *The park is southeast of Pasco by way of U.S. 12.*
HOURS: *The museum is open Wednesday through Sunday, 10–6, mid-April to mid-September.*
ADMISSION: *Free.*
TELEPHONE: *(509) 545-2361.*

Seattle

THOMAS BURKE MEMORIAL WASHINGTON STATE MUSEUM

This facility, on the University of Washington campus, is thought to have the most extensive collection of material relating to the native peoples of the Pacific Northwest.

The only major natural history museum in the Pacific Northwest, the Burke Museum was founded more than a century ago by the Young Naturalists' Society. It houses nationally ranked collections totaling over 3 million specimens, and is divided into three scientific divisions—anthropological, geological, and zoological. The museum aims to encourage understanding of the cultural history of Washington State, the Pacific Northwest, and the Pacific Rim, and collections include ethnological and archaeological materials from Pacific Rim cultures. The totem poles and canoes alone are worth the visit.

LOCATION: *The museum is closest to the 17th Avenue, NE, or western campus, entrance. Take Interstate 5 north from downtown, then east on Washington 520 to the university exit.*
HOURS: *Daily 10–5 and Thursday until 8.*
ADMISSION: *(Suggested) General $3; Seniors and Students $2; Youths 6-18 $1.50; Children 5 and under Free.*
TELEPHONE: *(206) 543-5590.*

Museum and Grave of Chief Seattle

The Suquamish were part of a confederacy of native peoples who occupied the land around Puget Sound and Lake Washington. The confederacy's leader when the first American settlers arrived in the area was Seattle. A practical man whose primary policy was securing the well-being of his people, he consistently offered friendship toward whites; initially because he saw them as a bulwark against the Cowichan, a powerful confederation who lived on Vancouver Island and periodically conducted slaving raids against their weaker neighbors. Later, however, Seattle realized that there was no end to the number of white settlers and decided that any course but accommodation was futile. He was the first to sign the Port Elliott Treaty of 1855, which ceded lands in return for reserves with firm borders. But even as he signed, Seattle, who was then about sixty-five years of age, knew that no borders could remain firm in the face of what was to come.

As was the custom on many parts of the frontier, white settlers named their new town in honor of the displaced chief, hoping it would preserve a spirit of amity with the Indians. Seattle charged them a tax to use his name, however, citing a tribal belief that to speak a dead man's name disturbs his spirit. A widely circulated speech attributed to Seattle poetically summarizes the passing of his time and people from the land. Unfortunately, it has been shown to be a later invention. Nonetheless, its vision of an Indian presence remaining on the land is a haunting evocation of vanished glory: "At night, when the streets of your cities and villages are silent and you think them deserted, they will throng with the returning hosts that once loved this land." If Seattle did not actually say that, maybe he should have.

His descendants live on the Port Madison Reservation, directly across the Puget Sound from Seattle. The Suquamish Museum is an outstanding facility that illustrates the way of life of native people in this area. Its presentations on the life of Seattle and the customs and beliefs of his people have won international acclaim in traveling exhibitions. The museum is built on a beach along the western shore of the sound. A restaurant and gift shop are also located on the premises. On a hillside nearby is Chief Seattle's grave. The Boy Scouts of America hold a service here each year to honor his memory.

Also in the area is the site of Old-Man House. This was the birthplace of Chief Seattle and was one of the most distinctive structures in the Northwest. A cedar longhouse, it was the residence of the chiefs of the Dwamish Confederacy; from the archeological evidence it was 520 feet long, covering an area of one-and-a-quarter acres. The cross-beams supporting the roof were 65 feet long and up to 22 inches in diameter. The house was built on the beach, and its shape followed the contours of the shore. It fell apart more than a century ago, but its outline and some of its stakes are still visible.

LOCATION: *Suquamish is best reached by the ferry to Winslow from downtown Seattle, and then north on Washington 305.*
HOURS: *Daily, 10–5, April through September; 11–4, closed Monday, rest of year.*
ADMISSION: *$3.*
TELEPHONE: *(206) 598-3311.*

Toppenish

YAKIMA NATION CULTURAL CENTER

Quite literally, before the ink was dry on the Port Elliott Treaty of 1855, the tribes with whom it had been made saw its shortcomings and repudiated it. Relegating native populations to inferior lands, the document was designed to open up the most fertile portions of eastern Washington to white settlement. But Looking Glass of the Nez Perce and Kamiakin of the Yakima vigorously opposed its provisions and the pressures put on the signers, and only the intervention of the aptly named Lawyer, of the Nez Perce, kept the dissidents at the council table. Immediately after the treaty signing, though, Kamiakin took the lead in a concerted effort aimed at driving settlers out of the territory. Even the white settlement of Seattle came under assault, with heavy guns from a sloop on Elliott Bay finally repelling the attackers.

The so-called Yakima War dragged on for three years, settling down to a series of raids and reprisals. The U.S. army's position seemed to be that if the situation could be ignored long enough, it would go away. Not until a group of 150 soldiers was overwhelmed by more than 1,000 native forces near the town of Rosalia was the army stirred to concerted action. Armed with howitzers and the latest-issue rifles, the army defeated the allied tribes in two engagements outside Spokane. Peace terms were harsh, and twenty-four leaders accused of instigating the rebellion were hanged. The Yakima and their allies were confined to this reservation, on the west bank of the Yakima River, in 1865. Among the tribes that joined in the war, only the Palouse held out, refusing to move from their villages along the Snake. But they, too, were forced to give in and were moved to the Colville Reservation (*see* St. Mary's Mission and Boarding School, Omak, Washington) in 1872.

After years of litigation, in 1972 about twenty-two thousand acres of land were restored to the Yakima Reserve, extending up to the base of the tribe's sacred mountain, Mount Adams, on the western edge. That land-claim settlement seemed to spark a renewal of interest in Yakima tribal traditions. The Cultural Center, which holds classes in the Yakima language for residents of the reservation and also promotes the observance of rituals, is a major result of that renewal. The facility is housed in a structure meant to resemble a winter lodge, with a central seventy-six-foot-high beamed hall. The tribe's history and crafts are chronicled in the displays.

LOCATION: *The center is just south of Toppenish on U.S. 97 and can be reached from Interstate 82 by way of the Washington 22 exit.*
HOURS: *Daily, 9–6, March through October; 10–6, rest of year.*
ADMISSION: *$3.*
TELEPHONE: *(509) 865-2800.*

Walla Walla

WHITMAN MISSION HISTORICAL SITE

The Cayuse were a relatively small but influential tribe because of the military superiority they gained through their horsemanship. They were so respected as riders that the term for an Indian pony used throughout the West was *cayuse*. They were feared as adversaries even by tribes that far outnumbered them and were proud of their accomplishments in war. Shamans held a position of great respect among the Cayuse and were responsible for treating illness according to their understanding of disease cause-and-effect. These factors led to the tragic events that have become known as the Whitman Massacre.

Narcissa Whitman was one of the first white women to make the trip west along the Oregon Trail. She and her husband, Marcus, arrived in 1836 to open a mission along the Walla Walla River, at Waiilatpu. The mission's central structure was built of adobe and surrounded by gardens. The Whitmans were honestly concerned with the culture of the native peoples around them and were successful in gaining trust and winning converts. But a series of dry years in the 1840s severely worsened living conditions among the nearby tribes. Famine was followed by pestilence as an outbreak of measles spread death among the Cayuse. The shamans were convinced that only the presence of the mission could explain such catastrophes, which never before had befallen their people. In November 1847, the mission was attacked and all thirteen of its occupants slain. Two years later, the Cayuse surrendered the five tribesmen regarded as responsible for the massacre, and they were hanged.

The National Park Service administers the site and fairly describes the desperation and the great cultural gap that resulted in this tragedy. Displays of typical daily activities at the mission include the Indian crafts that were carried on there, such as weaving, mat assembly, and cooking.

LOCATION: *The mission is west of Walla Walla by way of U.S. 12.*
HOURS: *Daily, 8–4:30.*
ADMISSION: *Free.*
TELEPHONE: *(509) 522-6360.*

GLOSSARY

Agency. The administrative office on a reservation.

Atlatl. A notched stick for throwing a spear or dart; predecessor to the bow (and arrow).

Calumet. A pipe bearing symbolic or religious significance. It was believed that its use gave access to the spirit world.

Camas. A plant, native to the northwestern United States, it is sometimes called the wild hyacinth. Its bulbs were steamed and eaten by native peoples in the region, and access to camas fields became a major source of conflict between tribes and white settlers.

Cayuse. An Indian pony, given its name because the Cayuse tribe of the Pacific Northwest was famous for horse-raising and trading.

Chickee. Grass huts elevated on wooden stilts, used by the Seminoles.

Confederation. An alliance of two or more tribes.

Earth lodge. A circular building—sometimes used for ceremonies.

Ghost Dance. A blend of Christianity and tribal religion, the spiritual dance was associated with the coming of a messiah. To the Plains tribes, the Ghost Dance was a message of hope, a way of regaining their lost freedom.

Hogan. A Navajo dwelling, built of logs and boughs and covered with earth.

Hominy. Hulled corn, usually boiled and served as a soup by Algonquian tribes.

Kachina. Ancestral spirits whose masked images visit the living in ceremonies of many Pueblo tribes.

Kiva. An underground ceremonial chamber used for secret rituals by many Pueblo peoples.

Maize. A Spanish word given to the native grasses domesticated by native peoples and grown for food. In the United States, the word "corn" has come to refer specifically to this grain, but in the British Isles, corn can also mean wheat or oats.

Mescal. A liquor made from the leaves, stalk, and roots of certain species of the agave cactus, found in the Southwest. The Mescalero Apache were famed for their use of this material.

Petroglyph. From the Greek words *petros* (rock) and *glyphe* (carving).

Potlatch. A ritual practiced by many Northwestern tribes, involving the distribution of gifts to enhance the status of leaders.

Powwow. An Algonquian word that has come to mean any gathering for peaceful reasons.

Pueblo. The Spanish word for "town" or "village." Used in the Southwest to refer to stone or adobe villages built by Indians.

Rancherias. The small settlements of the Sierra Mono tribe.

Reservation. A tract of land set aside for an Indian community.

Sachem. Name given to the leader of several Algonquian tribes of the Northeast.

Tepee. A conical tent, usually made of skins; used by tribes on the Great Plains. The word is Siouan.

Travois. A horse-drawn sledge used by Plains tribes; consists of two trailing poles bearing a platform or net for the load to be carried.

Tribe. A social group comprising families, clans, or generations. People who are bound together by common characteristics, including religion, government, and language.

Wickiup. A shelter made of reeds and grasses covering a rough, wood frame. Used by nomadic tribes of the Southwestern deserts.

Wigwam. An arched shelter, using a framework of poles overlaid by bark, rush mats, or hides. The word comes from the Abnaki language of northern New England.

FURTHER READING

Brown, Dee A. *Bury My Heart at Wounded Knee.* New York: Henry Holt, 1992.

Ceram, C. W. *The First American.* New York: Harcourt Brace Jovanovich, 1971.

Champagne, Duane, ed. *The North American Indian Almanac.* Detroit: Gale Research, 1993.

Chapman, Carl H. *Origin of the Osage Indian Tribe.* New York: Garland Publishers, 1974.

Cushman, Horatio Bardwell. *History of the Choctaw, Chickasaw and Natchez Indians.* New York: Russell and Russell, 1972.

Deloria, Vine. *Behind the Trail of Broken Treaties.* New York: Delacorte Press, 1974.

Dooling, D. M., ed. *The Sons of the Wind: The Sacred Stories of the Lakota.* New York: Parabola Books, 1984.

Dooling, D. M., and Paul Jordan-Smith. *I Become Part of It: Sacred Dimensions in Native American Life.* New York: Parabola Books, 1989.

Dozier, Edward P. *Pueblo Indians of North America.* New York: Holt, Rinehart and Winston, 1976.

Driver, Harold E. *Indians of North America.* Chicago: University of Chicago Press, 1969.

Fairbanks, Charles H. *The Florida Seminole People.* Phoenix: Indian Tribal Series, 1973.

Forbes, Jack D. *Warriors of the Colorado.* Norman: University of Oklahoma Press, 1965.

Gibson, Arrell M. *The Chickasaws.* Norman: University of Oklahoma Press, 1971.

Green, Donald F. *The Creek People.* Phoenix: Indian Tribal Series, 1973.

Gunnerson, Dolores A. *The Jicarilla Apaches.* DeKalb: Northern Illinois University Press, 1974.

Gussow, Zachary. *Sac, Fox and Iowa Indians.* New York: Garland Publishers, 1974.

Hirst, Stephen. *Life in a Narrow Place.* New York: David McKay, 1976.

Howard, Harold P. *Sacajawea.* Norman: University of Oklahoma Press, 1971.

Jennings, Jesse D. *Prehistory of North America.* Mountain View, Calif.: Mayfield Publishing, 1989.

Josephy, Alvin M. *The Patriot Chiefs.* New York: Viking Press, 1961.

———. *Red Power.* New York: American Heritage Press, 1971.

Kluckhorn, Clyde and Dorothea Leighton. *The Navajo.* Cambridge: Harvard University Press, 1946.

Krause, Aurel. *The Tlingit Indians.* Seattle: University of Washington Press, 1956.

Leitch, Barbara A., ed. *A Concise Dictionary of the Indian Tribes of North America.* Algonac, Mich.: Reference Publications, 1979.

McClintock, Walter. *The Old North Trial: Lifes, Legends & Religion of the Blackfeet Indians.* Lincoln: University of Nebraska Press, 1992.

Mails, Thomas F. *The People Called Apache.* Englewood Cliffs, N.J.: Prentice Hall, 1974.

Marriott, Alice. *Kiowa Years.* New York: Macmillan, 1968.

Matthiessen, Peter. *In the Spirit of Crazy Horse.* New York: Viking Press, 1983.

Meyer, Roy W. *History of the Santee Sioux.* Lincoln: University of Nebraska Press, 1967.

Minge, Ward Alan. *Acoma, Pueblo in the Sky.* Albuquerque: University of New Mexico Press, 1976.

Mooney, James. *Historical Sketch of the Cherokee.* Washington: Smithsonian Institution Press, 1975.

Nabokov, Peter. *Native American Testimony: A Chronicle of Indian-White Relations from Prophecy to the Present, 1492-1992.* New York: Viking, 1991.

Peale, Arthur L. *Uncas and the Mohegan-Pequot.* Boston: Meador Publishing, 1939.

Peckham, Howard H. *Pontiac and the Indian Uprising.* Princeton: Princeton University Press, 1947.

Ruby, Robert H. and John A. Brown. *The Cayuse Indians.* Norman: University of Oklahoma Press, 1972.

Silverberg, Robert. *The Mound Builders.* New York: New York Graphic Society, Ltd., 1970.

Sonnichsen, C.L. *The Mescalero Apaches.* Norman: University of Oklahoma Press, 1973.

Spencer, Robert F., and Jesse D. Jennings, et. al. *The Native Americans: Ethnology and Backgrounds of the North American Indians.* New York: Harper & Row, 1977.

Taylor, Colin F., ed. *The Native Americans: The Indigenous People of North America.* New York: Smithmark Publishers, 1992.

Terrell, John Upton. *Apache Chronicle.* New York: World Publishing, 1972.

———. Land Grab. New York: Dial Press, 1972.

Trenholm, Virginia C. *The Arapahoes, Our People.* Norman: University of Oklahoma Press, 1970.

Turner, Geoffrey. *Indians of North America.* New York: Sterling Publishing, 1992.

Unrau, William E. *The Kaw People.* Phoenix: Indian Tribal Series, 1973.

Wallace, Anthony and Sheila C. Stein. *Death and Rebirth of the Seneca.* New York: Alfred A. Knopf, 1969.

Wallace, Ernest and E. Adamson Hoebel. *The Comanches: Lords of the Southern Plains.* Norman: University of Oklahoma Press, 1952.

Weatherford, Jack. *Native Roots: How the Indians Enriched America.* New York: Fawcett Columbine, 1991.

Wellman, Paul I. *The Indian Wars of the West.* New York: Doubleday & Co., 1947.

Weslager, C.A. *The Delaware Indians.* New Brunswick, N.J.: Rutgers University Press, 1972.

Wilson, Edmund. *Apologies to the Iroquois.* New York: Farrar, Straus, Cudahy. 1960.

D

T

U

V

W

TRAVEL NOTES

TRAVEL NOTES

TRAVEL NOTES